$5.00
#43

25

D0090507

GUIDEPOSTS

A Match Made in
HEAVEN

*A Collection of Inspirational
Love Stories*

SUSAN WALES & ANN PLATZ

Guideposts®

CARMEL, NEW YORK 10512

www.guidepostsbooks.com

This Guideposts edition is published by special arrangement with
Multnomah Publishers, Inc.

Some of the stories in this book are true, and others, while based on true stories,
have had certain names and details changed in order to protect the privacy of the
individuals.

A MATCH MADE IN HEAVEN
published by Multnomah Publishers, Inc.

© 1999 by Susan Huey-Wales and Ann Williams-Platz
International Standard Book Number: 1-57673-393-9

Cover photograph by Joel Larson/Tony Stone Images
Cover design by Kirk DouPonce

Scripture quotations are from
The Holy Bible, New International Version
© 1973, 1984 by International Bible Society,
used by permission of Zondervan Publishing House

Multnomah is a trademark of Multnomah Publishers, Inc.,
and is registered in the U.S. Patent and Trademark Office.

Printed in the United States of America

Stories included in this book were collected over a period of eight years.
Reasonable care has been taken to trace original ownership and, when necessary,
to obtain permission to reprint. If the authors have overlooked giving proper credit
to anyone, please contact the publisher at the address below, and corrections will
be made prior to the next printing.

For information:
MULTNOMAH PUBLISHERS, INC.•POST OFFICE BOX 1720•SISTERS, OREGON 97759

Library of Congress Cataloging-in-Publication Data
Match made in heaven / [compiled] by Ann Platz and Susan Wales.
     p. cm.   ISBN 1-57673-393-9 (alk. paper)
   1. Love—Religious aspects—Christianity. 2. Love—Anecdotes.
   3. Marriage—Religious aspects—Christianity. 4. Marriage—Anecdotes.
   I. Platz, Ann. II. Wales, Susan.
BV4639.M334   1999   98–46112
242'.644—dc21   CIP

This book is dedicated to the glory of God
and His special gift to us,
our devoted and loving husbands,

KEN WALES & JOHN PLATZ,

with deep gratitude and appreciation for your patience,
guidance, encouragement, advice, and support
throughout this project.

The minute I heard my first love story

I started looking for you,

not knowing how blind that was.

Lovers don't finally meet somewhere.

They're in each other all along.

RUMI

CONTENTS

Divine Appointment

The Moment We Met

Will You Marry Me?

CONTENTS

With This Ring

I Thee Wed

To Have and to Hold

From This Day Forward

CONTENTS

To Love, Honor, and Cherish

For Better, for Worse

For Richer, for Poorer

CONTENTS

In Sickness and in Health

As Long As We Both Shall Live

ACKNOWLEDGMENTS

For a rich heritage of storytelling, family, and faith, a loving thanks to our parents, Mr. and Mrs. Arthur J. Huey Jr. and Mrs. Margaret Williams, and to the memory of the late Senator Marshall Williams. Love to our darling daughters, Meg Chrane, Courtney Norton, and Margo Cloer, plus a reminder that "God gives His best to those who leave the choice to Him."

A tribute to our enduring friendship and a special thanks to all our dear friends who shared their hearts and their love stories; our wonderful publisher, Multnomah, and everyone involved in the project: Matt Jacobson, Alice Gray, Larry Libby, Heather Kopp, David Kopp, Jennifer Curley, Steve Curley, Kirk DouPonce, Ken Ruettgers, and Cliff Boersma; and Kerri Loesche, our computer pro, for her dedication and encouragement.

To our readers: May you be blessed with love and the desires of your heart!

Delight yourself in the LORD *and he will give you
the desires of your heart.*
PSALM 37:4

Dearest Readers,

My earliest recollections of childhood are the story hours—hours spent with my parents telling my sister, Vickie, and me Bible stories, fairy tales, yarns, and classics. Few things have influenced my life as much, and I have loved to read and tell stories ever since!

As a single woman, I was blessed to have dear friends like Ann Platz. The stories of Ann and others not only encouraged me but provided me with an inspirational repertoire to share with lonely friends or sometimes strangers with broken hearts who were disappointed in love and marriage. When I saw how much these stories encouraged them, I approached Ann with my idea for a book, and we began.

That was over eight years ago—thanks to welcome interruptions, including my exciting marriage to Ken, moving to California, and the fulfillment of Ken's lifelong dream of making Catherine Marshall's book, Christy, into a television series. As I traveled throughout the country on speaking engagements with my husband, I received great response when I shared the story of how we met. When our daughter, Meg, left for college, I knew the timing was now perfect to complete this book.

So, eight years later, Ann and I are blessed to present to you A Match Made in Heaven. It is my hope that you will be encouraged, inspired, and entertained as you enjoy these inspiring stories shared by special people. Dare to dream yourself, and send us your love story!

—Susan Wales

Dear Ones,

Often I am asked to speak to groups about my profession of interior design. I do so gladly to encourage my audience to bring beauty and order into their homes, as well as love and graciousness into their lives. I usually include a love story or two to add the flavor of romance, and the audience always loves it. They remember these stories, frequently repeating them back to me years later.

As a consequence, I collect stories and will stop on a dime to hear a good one. When I have told my story of how I went halfway around the world to meet and fall in love with my husband, John, the response has been, "You have to write a book!" So my dear friend Susan Wales and I started on this journey eight years ago, combining our stories and searching for more. We both love people and the challenge of pulling the story out of the story giver, especially a wonderful love story!

With this book, our dream has become a reality. I invite you to come along with us through the pages of A Match Made in Heaven and laugh, cry, smile, dream, hope, and most of all be blessed and encouraged by these love stories. Enjoy them, and tell a friend.

—ANN PLATZ

Divine Appointment

IN THE BEGINNING, GOD BROUGHT THE WOMAN TO THE MAN. THEY WERE ALONE IN A WIDE AND STRANGE NEW WORLD. THEY HAD THE FRIENDSHIP OF THEIR CREATOR, THEY HAD AN ENEMY THEY KNEW NOTHING ABOUT, AND THEY HAD EACH OTHER. GOD IS STILL IN THE BUSINESS OF BRINGING THE WOMAN TO THE MAN, AND THE MAN TO THE WOMAN. IN HIS GREAT GRACE AND KINDNESS AND WISDOM, HE GIVES US TO ONE ANOTHER.

MY WILD ITALIAN ROSE

Gather ye rosebuds while ye may
Old time is still a flying.

ROBERT HERRICK

As she was growing up, the last thing on Angela Corelli's mind was marriage. While other little girls giggled over boys and assigned future husbands to each other, Angela daydreamed about diagnosing mysterious diseases. Since the second grade, she had known she wanted to be a doctor.

When she announced her plan to her parents, her Italian mother, Maria, reacted with alarm. "How will you grow up to have a husband and many babies, as God intended, if you are a doctor, Angela?"

Maria tried to persuade herself that her daughter's plan was just a passing whim. But instead of dating in high school, Angela spent her leisure time changing bedpans at the hospital. And no one was surprised when after college Angela enrolled in medical school and then graduated with honors.

Now even Maria had to accept that her daughter was going to practice medicine, but she wasn't about to concede that her daughter might remain single. "These are the nineties!" she reminded Angela, using a favorite phrase of her daughter's. "Women can have it all. At least they can if they will go out on dates or try to meet eligible young men!" But Angela's work was truly her first love, and it left little time for socializing.

Not to be dissuaded, Maria cried, cajoled, pleaded, and begged—all to no avail.

Weary from her mother's constant nagging, Angela finally sat her down for a heart-to-heart talk. After two hours of conversation, tears, screams, and hugs, the two women agreed to a truce. Maria gave her word never again to mention marriage in regard to her daughter. In return, Angela promised she would take more time to "stop and smell the roses," as her mother put it.

To everyone's great surprise, Maria managed to hold up her end of the bargain. Angela was so appreciative that she also made an effort to do as she'd promised.

Then one day in the early spring, on her way to the hospital, Angela spotted some beautiful red roses entwined on an iron fence that enclosed an old brownstone. She smiled, recalling her mother's recent good behavior, and deliberately paused to lean in and smell the roses. When she pulled away, she discovered her skirt was caught on the thorns.

As she struggled to free herself without tearing her dress, two little girls, nine and ten, watched her from a window of the brownstone. "Daddy!" they called in unison. "You've got to help that lady!"

When their father rushed outside to free the pretty prisoner, the two girls giggled and immediately began to scheme. Since their mother's death a few years before, the two had become almost as notorious as Maria Corelli at playing matchmaker.

But as it turned out, their father needed no encouragement. The minute he laid eyes on the pretty doctor, he was enchanted. Soon he'd fallen head over heels in love with Angela, and she with him.

When they were married a year later, Angela and her two young bridesmaids carried pink roses from the garden. Following the ceremony, Maria Corelli beamed with joy. Repeatedly she thanked heaven for its wisdom. "See!" she declared. "God has had mercy on Angela and given her a head start with two half-grown daughters!"

"Yes, Mama," agreed Angela. "And maybe, if we're lucky, they'll grow up to be doctors!"

LOVE FROM THE SKY

~

Oh promise me that some day you and I,
Will take our love together to some sky
Where we can be alone and faith renew,
And find the hollows where those flowers grew.

CLEMENT WILLIAM SCOTT

While I was growing up, my mother worked as a nurse for a doctor in New Zealand. The two grew to be very close friends and remained so even after "Doc" relocated to America. When I, too, moved from New Zealand to California as a young woman, Doc became a surrogate father to me.

I adored Doc and often looked to him for advice and guidance. But when I reached my late thirties, he began to fret and cluck like a mother hen about the fact that I wasn't married yet. I was secretly relieved that his opportunities for matchmaking had been sharply curtailed by my move to New York a few years earlier. Doc, however, didn't let the distance stop him from mentoring me through his frequent phone calls.

One afternoon Doc's assistant, Marilyn, who was also single and nearing forty, was in the middle of explaining to Doc that, yes, we'd both love to get married, but no, it wasn't that easy to find a husband. He just shook his head in disbelief and said, "You girls must not be trying very hard!"

Exasperated, Marilyn replied, "Do you think God is just going to drop a man out of the sky for each of us to—"

Before Marilyn could complete her sentence, they heard a commotion outside. Looking out the window, they saw three hang glider pilots fall from the sky and land in the field facing Doc's office, just below Mount

Whitney in the High Sierras. Incredulous, Marilyn and Doc rushed out to greet them.

As Doc and Marilyn chatted with the glider pilots, Doc was thrilled to discover they were from New Zealand. When Doc learned that the handsome trio was touring the U.S., he began telling them all the exciting places they should visit. "And you certainly should go to New York City!"

Bill, one of the pilots, asked, "Why? There's no hang gliding there!"

"That's true," Doc replied, "but New York is one of the most exciting cities in the world. You can't visit our country without seeing it." The pilots grew intrigued as Doc gave them a vivid description of New York. "We have a friend from New Zealand who lives there, and I know she'd be happy to show you around the town," Doc told them. Before the pilots had a chance to decline, Doc called me on the phone. Soon I was chatting amicably with one of the pilots, and the next thing I knew, all three men were visiting me in New York.

I was quite taken with the pilot named Bill, who was a textile engineer in New Zealand. Bill and I struck up a friendship, which quickly blossomed into romance. We got together whenever he visited America on his way to Europe to compete in hang gliding events, and we would laugh about the fact that he had to travel ten thousand miles to see the "girl next door."

Eventually we decided that home for each of us was wherever the other was. Doc, our very much delighted matchmaker, gave me away when Bill and I were married in Doc's ocean-side home.

Today, whenever I run into a single woman who's still waiting and praying for a husband, I encourage her not to lose hope. "You just never know," I say with a grin, "when God might drop a wonderful husband right out of the sky!"

MICHELE FISHER

THE PRAYER

⁂

He prayeth best who loveth best
All things both great and small.

s a single woman, I was always the person my friends called on
when they needed a baby-sitter, a ride to the airport, or a shoulder to cry on. Someone would always suggest, "Call Susan. She's not married. She can do it."

Many of my friends would admonish me to set boundaries. "You have
to earn a living," they'd tell me. Still, my parents had taught me to help
others, so if I was available, I'd give a helping hand or a listening ear.

One particularly hectic morning my office phone rang. It was Ann
Perdue, a good friend, calling from California, where she was on a business trip. She sounded troubled. I was immediately concerned, but as I
glanced nervously at my watch, my friends' advice echoed: *You have to earn
a living; tell her you'll call back.* I argued with myself, *I'll run behind with my
appointments for the rest of the day.* Finally I stifled a heavy sigh, pushed
back a stack of papers, and asked Ann what the problem was.

Ann said a business acquaintance of hers had just been rushed into
emergency surgery. Doctors had found a tumor in his neck that appeared
to be malignant. "The surgeon told him there's a risk his vocal cords will
be severed in surgery," she explained. "This man is a dynamic speaker who
addresses thousands of young people each year about his faith, and he may
never speak again!"

"I'm so sorry, Ann," I said. "Is there anything I can do?"

"Would you pray for him with me, Susan? I don't know a soul in California, and I knew I could call you."

I nervously glanced at my appointment book. It was crammed. People were backed up in the lobby waiting for me. But how could I tell Ann no?

"Sure," I said. "Let's pray right now."

As Ann and I prayed over the phone, we sensed God's power at work. By the time we hung up, I felt confident this man's surgery would be a success. Then it suddenly occurred to me I didn't even know his name.

Years passed. Spring found me busy as always—this time getting ready for my own wedding. Ann called to congratulate me, and out of the blue she asked, "Do you remember the man we prayed for on the phone several years ago? The one who needed throat surgery?"

"Sure," I replied. "I always wondered what happened to him. How is he?"

Ann giggled. "Why don't you tell me? You're marrying him!"

For a moment I couldn't speak. I had no idea my fiancé was the man Ann and I had prayed for that morning. Even though Ken had told me about his throat surgery and the miraculous recovery, I had never made the connection.

"Ann!" I finally blurted. "Isn't it amazing? God allowed me to pray for my future husband—and answered my prayer—when Ken was a total stranger to me!"

That day I realized the real business of life is people. What you give away to others—time, prayer, a listening ear—will come back to you somehow. And it just might be as love.

SUSAN WALES

THE LIST

&

I've sent my best, so wait upon Me.
Grow strong in the wisdom of who I am.
Let your expectancy soar to heaven
where real romance began.

DAVID HARBUCK

When I was thirty-two, I was invited to go to Greece and Israel with my mother and a friend. "Absolutely no," I told my mother. "I've got more work than ever." I continued to resist because of my pressing business, but everyone kept insisting I go. Against my better judgment—knowing I would have to work night and day to catch up when I returned—I eventually said yes.

On the day of departure we arrived at the airport, and my mother went ahead to secure seats with our tour group. When I joined her about fifteen minutes later, she was already talking with a nice-looking couple named John and Ellen.

I couldn't help noticing how attractive he was, and I especially liked the way he expressed affection so naturally for his wife. He kept looking at her as he talked, and occasionally he would give her a hug. *Ah*, I thought, *if I could only find a man like John.*

In fact, I realized John reminded me of a list I'd recently made, a list of the qualities I was praying for in a husband, like a man who would love me, a man of integrity and character, a man who is a committed Christian. And now, as I watched John, I mentally added to the list, *a man who is affectionate and attentive to me in public.*

Just then a loudspeaker announced that our plane was ready to board. As we all stood up, John's wife smiled and said to me, "I'm so glad you're able to go on this trip with us. We're both so excited about it. My brother's wife died a year and a half ago, and this trip will be so good for him."

My mouth all but dropped open. John was her brother! Then John himself walked over to me. With a big smile he said, "Well, I look forward to seeing you in Greece, Ann."

"Y-yes, me too," I sputtered, my heart suddenly racing. I couldn't think of anything else to say—I was speechless!

As soon as John was out of earshot, my friend Pat announced, "I think you are going to marry that man."

"What?" I gasped.

With hardly a hesitation, my mother chimed in. "You know, I had that same feeling when I introduced him to you."

"That's ridiculous," I snapped. "I don't even know him."

On board the huge 747, I adjusted my seat and silently continued to argue with myself. I had to admit the idea of John and me was intriguing. But people don't just meet and immediately know they will get married. Love at first sight is for fools and TV shows. Besides, I reasoned, Mother had mentioned that John was from Boston. I was from Atlanta. We lived and worked hundreds of miles apart. Of course, now we were only nine rows apart.

As you've probably guessed, John and I became very close on that trip. Imagine my amazement when he told me that he'd made a list of traits he wanted in a new wife and had prayed over them. He had completed his list the same week I'd written mine. And yes, our lists seemed to describe one another perfectly!

John and I have been married for almost twenty years. But sometimes I'm still surprised when I remember how God took us halfway around the world to fall in love. I still don't put much stock in love at first sight. But I *do* believe in prayer—and that some matches really are made in heaven.

Ann Platz

23

GRANDMOTHER'S QUILT

❧

Love comforteth like sunshine after rain.

WILLIAM SHAKESPEARE

As a young girl growing up in Cleveland, Ohio, I was especially enchanted by Grandmother Barkin's most cherished possession, a quilt she had made with swatches from the wedding gowns of generations of brides in our family.

When company would come for tea, Grandmother would spread out the quilt, enthralling her guests and especially me with her tales of each delicate piece and the bride who wore it. The well-to-do brides in our family left behind swatches of silk, satin, brocade, and velvet, while the pioneer brides of lesser means contributed their soft muslin and calico. A piece from Grandmother's own wedding gown was proudly displayed in the center of the quilt, where she had embroidered "Love One Another" atop the fading blue satin.

To my delight, Grandmother would often smile sweetly and say, "This wedding quilt will be yours one day, dear Mary." Since Grandmother had only sons and no daughter and I was the eldest granddaughter, the quilt would be passed down to me if I married first.

Although I was approaching twenty-five, I was more concerned with the kind of man I wanted to marry than getting married just for the sake of getting married. I sincerely doubted I would ever own the quilt until my childhood friend Leonard Wynn and I began to take the same path to work each day.

As Leonard and I would wind our way through the narrow streets leading to town, he would amuse me with his stories. However, one crisp fall day in 1861 any hope of our romance developing was dashed when he informed me he had enlisted in the Union army. When the day came to see him off at the train station, I felt as though my heart would break.

The enthusiasm and patriotic spirit of the women of Cleveland reached a zenith during the Civil War. And Grandmother Barkin and I were no exception. Freely and abundantly Grandmother sent supplies from her stores. But her crowning sacrifice was yet to be made.

Early one bright winter morning a carriage rolled up to Grandmother's door, and out of it stepped two eager young ladies who took Grandmother aside and said in whispered tones, "So you see, Mrs. Barkin, we are desperate for quilts for our soldiers." Slowly rising from her chair, the elderly lady stood and then proceeded to her wardrobe. Out came her treasured quilt, wrapped in white and fragrant with lavender. Calling to me, she said, "Mary, they need quilts at the hospital. I have no other ready-made ones. Are you willing to give this one up?"

I hesitated for only a moment, realizing that every gift added one more chance of comfort for my Leonard.

So Grandmother's quilt adorned one of the cots in the hospital and gave warmth and pleasure to many a poor sufferer, serving a purpose far greater than its maker had intended.

Grandmother and I joined the tireless group at the Cleveland hospital. One Christmas as I was passing from cot to cot distributing grapes and oranges, I watched the eager looks of the poor fellows. Having emptied my basket, I went to assist in feeding those who were unable to help themselves.

Taking a plate of jelly in my hand, I stepped to the side of one of the cots, noticing as I did that Grandmother's quilt lay upon the bed! The sight of it brought a rush of tender memories, filling my eyes with tears so that for a moment I didn't see the face upon the pillow.

Then, with a start, I saw Leonard Wynn. As I dried my eyes, I got a closer look at the white face with sunken eyes revealing the depth of his pain. "No, it can't be," I assured myself.

But the familiar voice erased all doubt. "Ah, Mary, I've been watching and waiting for you!"

Overjoyed I asked, "Why didn't you send for me?"

"I knew you would come sometime. The sight of this," he said, touching the quilt, "made me sure of it."

During the next few weeks, we rediscovered the joys of our companionship. That happiness was quickly extinguished, however, when I arrived at the hospital early one morning to find Leonard's bed occupied by another wounded soldier. A nurse informed me that Leonard had returned to his regiment. Along with Leonard, Grandmother's quilt had also vanished. And so, the Christmas of 1862 came and went, bringing with it joyous surprise only to snatch it and Grandmother's quilt away.

Another long year passed. I was as busy as ever, assisting the cause by trying to impart the Christmas spirit to the soldiers in the hospital. One evening at the close of the day's proceedings, I wearily laid my head down on a table. It was quickly growing dark, and I closed my eyes to snatch, if possible, a brief interval of much needed rest.

Suddenly I was startled. How long had I been asleep, and what was this lying under my head? One glance revealed Grandmother's quilt. How did it get there? I squealed with delight as I heard a familiar voice—Leonard's. "I've come for my Christmas gift, sweet Mary," he said as he drew the quilt to his chest and pointed to the inscription, "Love one another." "I wanted to ask you a year ago but decided that I would not ask you to take a maimed, sick soldier. I kept the quilt in memory of you. See, I fixed it so it would come back to you if anything happened to me." He showed me the label fastened securely to the quilt: "To be sent to Miss Mary Barkin, Cleveland, Ohio."

Then he told me how on one cold winter's day the quilt had saved his life. While sitting close to the fire to warm himself and to cook some potatoes, a stray ball from the enemy's batteries came whistling through the air, taking a straight course toward him. Luckily he was wrapped in the quilt. The ball struck him but, because of the thickness of the quilt, got no further than his coat.

That night Grandmother's quilt went back to its original owner, and my right to it as a wedding gift was firmly established by Leonard's proposal.

RETOLD FROM A STORY BY ANNIE F. S. BEARD

Story originally appeared in *The Soldier's Journal*; the Library of Congress has no record of the date. Later the story was reprinted in *Pictorial War Record: Battles of the Late Civil War,* a four-volume work published by Stearnes & Co., New York, 1881–1884.

MOTHER KNOWS BEST

All things come round to him
Who will but wait.

HENRY WADSWORTH LONGFELLOW

Marilyn cherished her time alone on the plane to read. Having given up her assigned seat to allow some newlyweds to sit together, she hardly looked up when her new seatmate arrived. But when the young woman leaned over and introduced herself as Trish, flashing a friendly smile, Marilyn instantly liked her. She laid her book aside.

Upon learning that Trish lived in Hawaii but frequently traveled to Seattle on business, Marilyn's ears perked up. "My son goes to Seattle on business. The two of you should meet," she suggested.

Without any objection, Trish handed her a business card.

It wasn't unusual for a family member to play matchmaker for Bill. He was certainly capable of meeting girls himself—he'd had dates with plenty of young women. He simply insisted on waiting for— Well, no one could figure out what he was waiting for!

Bill was more than a little skeptical when his mother gave him Trish's business card. "The next time you're in Seattle, why don't you see if the two of you can rendezvous?" she suggested.

"We'll see, Mom," he answered. He stuffed the card in his pocket, having already decided to toss it into the trash. *Who wants to meet a girl that your mother met on an airplane? And what kind of girl would give her business card to a stranger?*

A few days later as Bill was doing his laundry, he emptied his pockets and tossed the card into a dresser drawer. A couple days after that, when he was feeling a bit lonely, he ran across the card again, pulled it out, and stared at it. He picked up the phone and then put it down again. This was crazy! He promptly tossed the card into the trash—only to retrieve it in a few hours.

The next week Bill received a call about a business meeting in Seattle. *Why not?* he asked himself. He pulled the card from the drawer again. This time he dialed the woman's number in Hawaii and found her at home.

To his surprise, as soon as he began explaining who he was, she remembered his mother. She laughed good-naturedly and said, "I never thought you'd call. Most men, if their mother had given them a card…"

Bill groaned inwardly. *She must think I'm some kind of idiot—or worse, a mama's boy!*

There was nothing to do now but plunge ahead. As it turned out, Trish planned to be in Seattle at the same time as Bill, and she accepted his invitation for dinner. They agreed to meet at a popular restaurant located in the hotel where she was staying.

"Tell me what you look like," Bill said.

"Like everyone else," she answered. "I'll just leave my name with the maître d'."

Aha! She must be terribly unattractive, Bill mused. *But that's okay,* he told himself. He'd met plenty of lovely women whose beauty took more than a glance to discover. And he'd met many beauties who, upon further acquaintance, grew less and less attractive.

For convenience' sake, Bill reserved a room in the same hotel where he and Trish were to have dinner. He returned from his business meeting about three o'clock in the afternoon, leaving him four hours to kill before his rendezvous with his mystery lady.

Nervous and restless, he decided to get some coffee. As he stepped off the elevator into the hotel lobby, he stopped short. An absolutely gorgeous woman was seated on a nearby sofa. She had long, flowing red hair that framed a porcelain face. Her green eyes danced and sparkled. Her lips looked as though they had been painted by an artist.

He drew closer, scanning the immediate area for the lucky guy she was with. He saw no one. As he studied further the woman's face and expression, he felt certain he would like her. In fact, as crazy as it sounded even to him, he felt as if he already knew her.

Deciding that he absolutely had to meet this woman, he approached her. "Excuse me, miss," he said. "You look so familiar."

"I was just thinking the same thing about you," she replied with a smile.

"Would you like to join me in the restaurant for a cappuccino and find out how we know each another?" Even as Bill uttered these words he was shocked by their boldness.

"You're so kind, but I'm waiting for someone," she replied.

"It figures," Bill mumbled under his breath. Impulsively he stuck out his hand. "Hello, I'm Bill Chambers from Idaho."

The young woman just sat there with a blank look. Then suddenly she broke into a big grin. "Bill?" she said. "Bill, I'm Trish."

"Trish?" he asked, perplexed.

She smiled. "You know, the girl from Hawaii that your mother met on the plane."

"But—but you—what are you doing here?"

"Bill, this is where we're supposed to meet. Remember?"

"But you weren't supposed to arrive for another four hours."

"My flight was canceled, so I had to take an earlier flight. Because my room's not ready yet, they asked me to wait here."

Bill reissued his invitation for the cappuccino. Trish accepted, and the two spent the next several hours trading stories, smiles, and laughter. Bill's first impressions had been correct—he really liked this woman!

Soon Trish and Bill had launched on a glorious romance that would last—forever. It wasn't long before friends and family joined the two for a wedding by a lake under the light of a full moon. As part of the ceremony, Bill sang to his bride, and Trish performed a traditional Hawaiian dance for her groom.

Bill's family was thrilled to see him taking marriage vows, but no one was more thrilled than his mother. Yes, her son had been right that some things are worth waiting for. But she'd been right, as well. *Sometimes Mother really does know best!*

TOLD BY ELIZABETH CHAMBERS

ALL THINGS ARE POSSIBLE

Nothing in the world is single,
All things be a law divine
In one spirit meet and mingle.

PERRY BYSSHE SHELLEY

elp me, Lord! Please, God, lead me to the woman who will be the right wife for my whole life."

I prayed this prayer with a passion while I was finishing my twenty-year educational program to prepare me for my life's work.

I was calling out a self-centered prayer to the living, leading Lord I chose to believe and trust. "Help me!"

The God who was slowly but surely answering my first childhood prayer, "Lord, make me a preacher when I grow up," would give me guidance in life's three basic decisions. First: What do I want to do and be? That decision was made. Second: Who and what do I choose to believe? I had made the irrevocable commitment to believe in the God of Scripture. I would be a follower of Jesus Christ. He was the world's leading expert on spiritual truth. He was and is the Truth!

Now I needed His help with the third basic human decision: Whom will I marry? Or will I remain single?

The insight I needed began in the hallway outside my psychology class. The instructor, Dr. Lars Grandberg, wisely advised me, "When you get ready to be serious about marriage, start with your head and your heart will follow." To press the point he added strongly, "Never start with your heart. Lead with your head."

God was speaking to me loudly and clearly. I did not fully understand, but my young critical mind accepted that counsel without an ounce of reservation.

"Help, Lord! Tell me the kind of woman I should marry who could help me to become a good preacher," I prayed with a passion.

God answered by providing the criteria. First, she should share my faith. It would also prove helpful if she came from a background in family and religious training as close to mine as possible. Second, she should enjoy the "ministry," and she should be called and motivated to be a generous and good helpmate to me in my life's work. Third, she should be attractive to my heart and stimulating to my mind and eye. She should stimulate the desires of both my body and soul. Fourth, she should be a best friend, someone with whom I could share, talk, visit, and relate. Talking between us should be free, honest, easy, challenging, encouraging, entertaining, enlightening, comforting—and fun.

Now my head was in charge!

At the time I was steadily dating a classmate who was intelligent and attractive. But she came from a culture, family, and community quite unlike my own. My heart felt strongly for her. But suddenly my head did not agree.

Only two weeks later the school year ended. As a seminary student I was assigned a summer job to preach in a vacant Presbyterian church in Preston, Minnesota. I would stop at my home in Iowa on the way to my assignment. No sooner did I reach home than I received a telephone call from an elder at the church in Minnesota.

"Mr. Schuller, you're coming out this week?"

"Yes, sir."

"Well, we're asking you to wait one week. We're not quite ready for you. Okay?"

"No problem," I said, wondering what I would do from this Thursday until the next Thursday.

The telephone rang again. It was a call from a leader in my little country church. "Bob, we remember that wonderful prayer you prayed after the tornado. We were wondering if you could preach this coming Sunday in our church."

I was surprised and honored. "I'd love it," I answered. It would help fill my empty days with study, prayer, and preparation.

Sunday morning arrived. The elder met me at the church and led me to a little room where he introduced me to an attractive, eighteen-year-old organist. She struck me with a stunning, sparkling force I had never before felt.

We discussed the service. She would play the hymns I had chosen. That morning I forgot that I was "going steady." I thanked her for her wonderful work at the keyboard and heard myself say, "What are you doing this week? Would you like to go out with me tomorrow night?" After a slight pause she accepted my invitation.

We had our first date. She was from my kind of faith, family, community, and church. We talked. We laughed. I believe we held hands as I walked her to the door of her country home—a house as simple as my own.

I drove home, feeling sure she would make a good wife for me. I went to bed, and when I woke up the next morning, I immediately rushed for pen and paper and wrote a letter to my close friend, Bill Miedema. "Dear Bill, I've met the girl I'm going to marry. Her name is Arvella DeHaan. She is eighteen years old."

There wasn't a hint of doubt or questioning or indecision in my head—or my heart. I was consumed, not by a person, but by divine destiny. I've looked back on that moment a thousand or more times. There had to be a God in charge of my life, for truly I could not have "loved her" when I wrote those words. I simply knew that I was to marry her. And it would be right.

Four days later I said good-bye and left for my summer job.

The miles separated Arvella and me. I kept in touch throughout the summer. Then Arvella came to Hope College, which was next door to Western Seminary, where I was a student. Our relationship grew and matured. We planned our marriage for the week after I would graduate from seminary.

She would be the person God chose to help make me the preacher I had prayed all my life to become.

Our wedding took place in the middle of the century (1950), in the middle of the year (June), in the middle of the month (the fifteenth).

"Do you take this woman to be your wedded wife?" the officiating minister asked. "If so, answer 'I do.'"

"I do," I answered without hesitation or doubt.

"Will you love her?" I heard this phrase like I had never heard it before. "Will you love her?" It was future tense. Not present tense. Without any hesitation or doubt, I answered firmly and optimistically, "I will."

Never would a more self-centered prayer be answered by a supreme God more beautifully than my prayer for the right wife. First, a professor's unsolicited advice in a hallway. Next, a church calling me to interrupt my summer work schedule, keeping me home a week. Then, my home church calling to invite me to "preach this Sunday." God answered my prayer! It was a major play in His answering of an earlier prayer, "Lord, make me a preacher when I grow up!"

No one, no one, has done more to shape this "preacher" more wisely and wonderfully than Arvella. I have listened and learned from her and am always lifted by her.

DR. ROBERT SCHULLER

From *My Soul's Adventure with God, A Spiritual Autobiography* (Nashville, Tennessee: Thomas Nelson, Inc., 1995). Used by permission of the publisher.

The Moment We Met

SOMETIMES IT IS AN INSTANT RECOGNITION. "I KNEW THE MINUTE I SAW HER..."

SOMETIMES IT CREEPS UP QUIETLY, LIKE THE GENTLEST WHISPER. "WE'D KNOWN EACH OTHER FOR YEARS, BUT SUDDENLY, ONE DAY HE SEEMED DIFFERENT..."

IS IT THE WAY SHE TALKS, OR HOW HE SMILES, OR SOME PARTICULAR TALENT SHE HAS? IT MAY BE ALL OF THOSE THINGS OR NONE OF THEM, OR A COMBINATION OF A NUMBER OF QUALITIES MIXED WITH SOMETHING MYSTERIOUS AND INEXPLICABLY WONDERFUL.

AND WHETHER OR NOT THAT FIRST MEETING WAS MEMORABLE, WHETHER THE CIRCUMSTANCES THAT BROUGHT THEM TOGETHER SEEM MUNDANE OR DIVINELY ENGINEERED, THEY WILL LOOK BACK AND KNOW THAT, FROM THE MOMENT THEY MET, THEIR LIVES WERE CHANGED FOREVER.

OFF-KEY, IN TUNE

§

There is delight in singing though none hear
Beside the singer.

WALTER SAVAGE LANDOR

had just transferred from windy Chicago to sunny Los Angeles, where I had a corporate position with United Airlines. I'd found a great apartment in Marina del Rey with wonderful ocean views and all the amenities and could hardly wait for a day off to enjoy my new California lifestyle!

When that day arrived, I slept late and then headed for the pool, armed with books, magazines, water, sunscreen, my tape player, and headphones. Being a weekday, no one was around. I was determined nothing would interrupt my special day.

And what a great day it was to lie by the pool. The sun was shining, and I felt wonderful. When my very favorite Frank Sinatra song came blaring through the headphones, I shut my eyes and began singing at the top of my lungs. The fact that I have probably the worst singing voice in the world didn't stop me for a second. I was having the time of my life.

Just as the song ended, I sensed someone nearby. Suddenly I was stricken with horror. What if that person had heard me singing? I mustered up the courage to open my eyes, take off the headphones, and look around. Much to my dismay, there stood a very attractive man—laughing.

I wanted to climb under my lounge chair. When he approached, I began apologizing profusely for my voice and for not realizing I wasn't alone.

But he introduced himself and seemed to want to talk. In fact, he was so personable that I began to feel a little less embarrassed. He asked what kind of work I did, and I told him. Then I politely asked him the same question.

"You don't want to know," he assured me with a grin.

"Of course I want to know!"

I couldn't imagine why he was so embarrassed until he answered shyly, "I compose music for television and films."

"You're what? You do what?" I asked with a shaky voice.

He chuckled and nodded yes.

"And you let me sing for you? How dare you!"

That's when he asked me out to dinner. And I accepted.

That dinner was followed by another and yet another until finally we decided to marry and have dinner together forever.

Who would have dreamed it? That I would have my voice to thank for falling in love? I may sing off-key, but my husband and I plan to make beautiful music together for the rest of our lives.

CONNIE SOBEL

BUS STOP

Oh tender yearning, sweet hoping!
The golden time of first love!
The eye sees the open heaven,
The heart is intoxicated with bliss;
Oh that the beautiful time of young love
Could remain green forever.

AUTHOR UNKNOWN

As a young man, I loved to travel. So in 1971, when I was offered a job in Switzerland's village of St. Moritz, I didn't hesitate. There's hardly a prettier place on earth.

While there, I was helping to shoot a documentary film. Some days the project required me to go to the nearby city of Zurich. Generally, I drove a car when I wanted to get from St. Moritz into the city. But one particular day, I took the tram, an electric trolley that is a popular means of transportation in Switzerland.

As the tram rolled down a boulevard in Zurich, I noticed a lovely young lady hurrying down the street. When the tram stopped, she entered my car and sat down in front of me. She seemed to radiate grace and charm—and I thought she was stunning. How could I meet this interesting stranger? In only a few more blocks, she would disappear forever…

Too bad I wasn't the kind of guy who boldly approached women who interested me, I mused.

But when my stop came, suddenly I couldn't imagine getting off the tram. What kind of foolishness was this? As we rolled on through Zurich, I decided I would try to think up some way to get this young lady's attention.

I didn't speak any of Switzerland's three official languages. And behaving like an idiot had never appealed to me. Surely she would be getting off the tram soon, and I would have wasted my time. I began to berate my impulsiveness. Then I noticed her remove a book from her handbag. Peering over her shoulder, I saw that it was written in English.

Breathing a sigh of relief, I began rehearsing potential romantic lines. What would impress a sophisticated woman who obviously likes to read? Perhaps Shakespeare's "Love is not love which alters when it alteration finds."

No, that was probably a little premature. Perhaps Whittier? "We come back laden from our quest / to find that all the sages said / are in the Book our mothers read."

Then again, it was probably better not to bring Mother into this.

And then finally, I decided to attempt the contemporary American blockhead approach. I tapped the young lady on the shoulder and blurted out, "Hello, is that a book you're reading?"

She looked at me quizzically, said, "Ja," and turned back to her reading. I felt incredibly stupid, but not stupid enough not to ask yet another question. "I notice that you're reading in English. Are you from England?"

"No."

"Scotland?"

"No."

How many noes would it take? I couldn't believe my own ears as I continued to list off every English-speaking country I could think of. All she said was, "No."

Finally I asked, "So where do you come from?"

"Switzerland," she responded, and turned back to her reading.

Now, most people would have been thoroughly humiliated into silence at this point. And normally, on any other day, I would have too. But incredibly, I tapped the young lady on the shoulder again and asked, "Would you like to go out for a cup of tea?"

She looked back at me with a little curiosity and a lot of pity in her beautiful eyes. "No, thank you," she said calmly. "I have a previous engagement."

I gave up. For the next few blocks I tried intently to recover my usual dignity and common sense. When her stop finally arrived and she got up to leave the tram, it seemed that I was halfway around the world from where I had originally intended to get off.

But I hesitated for only a second before following her out of the tram. I figured I'd just catch the tram again when it looped back this way, and then take my lonely return trip to central Zurich. But also, even as my last shred of dignity was wildly objecting, I realized I had decided to try again. "Are you sure you wouldn't like to go out for a cup of tea for ten minutes?" I called out. "Could your appointment wait for ten minutes?"

She turned and looked at me steadily. Was she irritated? Or just amazed? Perhaps she hadn't seen an American blockhead close up before. Suddenly I wanted to make a dash for the tram. Or start telling her who I really was when I wasn't like this...

And then she said, "All right."

We went across the street to a tearoom and introduced ourselves to each other. Her name was Carol. She had grown up in Switzerland for most of her life and had learned English because her mother, who was Czech, and her father, who was Swiss, had met in an English class in London. They had decided to use English as the common language of the home.

As she described her work as a court reporter, and her desire to continue her studies at night, I made a delightful discovery. Carol was not only beautiful to look at—she had an inner radiance and grace unlike anything I'd ever encountered.

When it came my turn to speak, I decided that in light of my recent behavior, greatly impressing her with my wit or charm probably wasn't an option. But maybe, if I wasn't terribly obnoxious, she would accept another invitation to tea.

And she did. Two hours later, we said good-bye, promising to meet again soon. In the next few months, I saw Carol at every opportunity until it was time for me to return to America. And then, feeling as vulnerable and silly as I had on the tram that first day, I asked her to be my bride and move to New England with me.

When she said yes, I knew at that moment that I would have ridden a tram around the world for her.

We were married in Switzerland in January 1974. In the twenty-five years since, I have often shuddered to think what I would have missed had I not followed my "foreign" impulses that day. Sure, I ended up traveling a little further than I'd planned. Sure, I looked ridiculous and I took some painful risks. But if marriage has taught me one thing, it's this: *that's what love is for.*

DR. STEVEN BERRY

Her sweet "I will" has made ye one.

ALFRED, LORD TENNYSON

Used by permission of the author.

LOVE LESSONS

Love to faults is always blind
And breaks all chains from every mind.

WILLIAM BLAKE

I'd tried them all—every clever idea for meeting a nice guy. But nothing seemed to work.

There was my "Helpless in Hardware" approach, for example. I went to Home Depot in the early morning hours, where all the "real men" hang out. I asked dumb questions about what size nail to use to hang my picture on the wall, and "Can you show me how to hold the hammer straight please?"

All I got from those silly flirtations were straight pictures on my walls.

Next I tried "Meet the Chef." I went grocery shopping at 6:00 P.M., when all the single men were supposed to be cruising the aisles. I targeted the frozen food section, since I have a degree in microwave cooking—and I figured most single men do, too. But this strategy didn't deliver much either. Later, someone told me the men were all roaming the fresh produce aisles because they'd been told that's where women who can cook a real meal would be!

Right about when I decided the game of love was just not for me, a friend talked me into signing up to play in a golf tournament with a male partner I didn't know. To make matters worse, I liked him on sight—and suddenly I wished I knew something about golf.

Clearly, another fiasco was in the making. That feeling was confirmed when we got into the golf cart and he asked me, "What is your handicap?"

I replied, "Well, I have a little bitsy bladder."

He said, "You've never played golf before."

It was going to be a long, embarrassing day.

My partner's name was Mickey, and as we headed out to tee off, I wondered if he was a pro. Considering he had a woman for a partner who didn't know a club from a racquet, he was being pretty patient. So far anyway (I hadn't swung at the ball yet).

Mickey tried to help by offering a few simple lessons. He said, "Keep your head down and don't ever take your eye off the ball. Just remember the ball never moves. Don't lock your knees. Bend your left arm, and loosen your grip."

Simple, right?

I tried. Honestly, I tried. I placed that silly white ball on its tiny wooden tee (it kept falling off the tee) and took my stance (whatever that was) and aimed toward a tiny black hole in the ground somewhere out toward the horizon. Then I swung the club as hard as I could—and watched that tiny white ball dribble into the grass just a few feet in front of us.

Mickey was sweet about it. "Quit trying so hard! Relax. Have fun!" he said. That advice seemed like the best golf lesson of all, but the hardest to actually accomplish.

Making matters worse, that day turned out to be one of the hottest, most humid days of the entire summer in Atlanta. I heard somewhere that Southern girls don't perspire (we just glisten), but I was a hair-dripping, sweaty mess by the second hole. Needless to say, I was convinced that Mickey would never find me attractive.

Midway through the tournament, I decided to give up any hope of impressing this guy. After that, we began to chat amiably, and we had a lot of fun.

You can imagine how shocked I was—and how excellent Mickey is at golf—when I tell you that we actually won the tournament that day. We received lots of prizes and many accolades from the competition. But for me, the ultimate prize came when Mickey handed me the trophy and asked if I'd be his partner again the following weekend.

I happily accepted his invitation, which led to many more. Several months later, he asked me to be his partner for life. And I accepted!

I still can't hit that silly little ball into that tiny black hole. But as it turns out, my future husband's advice for my golf game was the greatest lesson on love I ever received: "Quit trying so hard! Loosen your grip! Relax and have fun!"

It works.

BARBARA BILLINGSLY MCALEXANDER

THE SINGLE DAD

He who works for sweetness and light united,
Works to make reason and the will of God prevail.

MATTHEW ARNOLD

By the time I was forty, I'd been through two broken engagements and had finally accepted the fact that I'd probably
be single forever. Fortunately I had a marvelous job at a TV station in
Canada, and I found a great deal of fulfillment in my work.

One of my duties was booking guests for a talk show. Usually I scheduled guests up to a year in advance, making changes as current events
required. This particular day I was working on a Father's Day special for
the following June. Someone had given me the name of Bill Webster, a
minister and a single father who was raising his two sons. The boys had
been only seven and nine when their mother had died of a heart attack.
According to my source, this father had done an admirable job raising his
sons alone and would be an excellent guest.

When I called the number I'd been given, a pleasant male voice
answered. I explained my reason for calling and was delighted when he
said he'd be happy to appear on the show. But then he added, "I'd also like
to talk about being a single man, as well as being a single dad."

"Mr. Webster," I replied, "if we were doing a show for singles, that
would be fine, but this is a Father's Day special, so we want you to stick
to the topic of fatherhood."

"Tell your producer I'll agree to be on the show," Bill said, "but I also would like to discuss my singles ministry."

"That won't be possible, sir," I said again firmly. "My producer wants only fatherhood discussed on this particular show."

"You and your producer are just like everyone else," he moaned. "No one seems to realize that a big part of being a single dad is coping with being a single man."

I was taken aback by his insistence, but I held my ground. "I'll have you know, sir, that I happen to care a lot about singles. I am one! It's just that we need a single *dad* for our Father's Day show."

Now that he knew I was single, he pressed his point even more. As he kept talking, I began to get a headache, and with irritation in my voice I finally said, "If you can't oblige, I'll happily call someone else."

"Oh no," he said quickly. "I'm sorry. I really do understand, and I'd be happy to come on the show."

I took his information, wondering why my source had told me that this Bill was such a nice guy. *What a bother!*

A few months later Bill Webster called me at the station. I recognized his name immediately. *That Bill guy. He's probably going to press his point about the format for the Father's Day show again.*

Instead Bill told me he was calling for a friend from London to confirm a taping the following day. I confirmed the taping, and we hung up. The next morning when I went out to greet the guest, he introduced me to the friend accompanying him. I immediately recognized Bill's name. So this was the guy who gave me a headache. At least, I decided, he was a handsome headache.

"We've already met," I said politely.

"We have?" questioned Bill.

"On the telephone," I said.

"You mean yesterday?" he asked.

"Yes, and we also talked for a while when I booked you for the Father's Day special. As I recall, you wanted to talk about singles."

Bill blushed slightly. "Oh, yes. I remember now."

While the show featuring Bill's friend was being taped, I sat in the audience as I often do. Bill sat down next to me, and we shared a whispered conversation. Much to my embarrassment, I realized later that we hadn't heard a word of his friend's segment on the program.

After Bill and his friend left, I found myself thinking it was too bad that June and the Father's Day show were still so far off.

Within a half hour, I was surprised to see Bill coming back through the studio door. "Did you forget something?" I asked.

"Yes," he said. "I forgot to ask if you would go out to dinner with me."

I hesitated for a moment. I'd pretty much given up dating, but he seemed nice enough. What could it hurt? I agreed to go.

Bill and I had an enchanted evening, and soon we began to date regularly. With every date our feelings for each other grew. I got to know Bill's boys, and I deeply admired how he fathered them.

Still, I was taken off guard when Bill proposed to me.

I hesitated. I'd been down this road twice before, and I wasn't sure I could handle a third broken engagement. And what about being a stepmom? If I married Bill, I would become a wife and a mother in one fell swoop. In the end, the enthusiasm of Bill's two beloved sons and my love for them was the very thing that convinced me we could make a family.

Six months later Andrew and Stephen lit the candles at our wedding and stood up as Bill's best men. As I gazed at their bright, happy faces, I realized Bill had been right during that first phone call. I had fallen in love with a single man *and* with a single dad. Those two roles were intricately and wonderfully linked.

And now, so were we.

JOHANNA WEBSTER

TAKE ME OUT TO THE BALL GAME

There was never any yet that wholly could escape love,
and never shall be any,
never so long as beauty shall be,
never so long as eyes can see.

LONGUS

I confess—I'm a Dodger fan. I've been one since I was eleven and moved to Southern California. Before that, as far back as I can remember, I was a Yankees fan. It never bothered me that I was a girl and not much of a ballplayer myself. I was just crazy about baseball. Of course, I like to root for a winning team, too.

When I moved to California, I discovered that not only were the Dodgers a great team, they had a radio announcer reported to have golden tonsils. Hall of Famer Vin Scully's voice was smooth and distinctive, but what I quickly came to savor were the stories he told while he was calling the game. Little did I know that someday, in the middle of a Dodger game, he'd be telling mine—play by play.

Sometimes my parents would drive the sixty miles to Dodger Stadium so I could watch my heroes, Don Drysdale and Sandy Koufax, play in person. Those were record-setting years for the Dodgers. But the game I remember most was one my dad took me to on September 15, 1971. It was the summer before I was to leave for college, and I'd been selected from a list of students with an "A" grade point average to win tickets to three ball games.

In those days, "A" student tickets didn't come with assigned seats. They were simply marked "First Base Side," as mine were, or "Third Base Side," which I wished I'd gotten. Holders of the tickets could sit anywhere in a reserved seat section on a first-come, first-served basis.

Dad and I were about to take seats on the first base side when, just before the national anthem, I decided we ought to try the third base side. Better view of the action, in my opinion. We walked halfway around the stadium, Dad thankfully not complaining. At the top of an open-seating aisle, we stood for a moment looking for a spot. Fifteen or twenty rows down, I noticed two guys who looked to be about my age seated alone in the middle of a row, no girls in the picture.

Trying to be nonchalant, I walked to their row, Dad following me, and left a discreet empty seat between the guys and me. It wasn't much of a game that night. Dodgers lost 2–1, I believe. Midway through the second inning, I stole a look at the guys to my right. To my surprise, I knew one of them. His name was Don, and I'd met him briefly at a camp where I'd been a counselor. He was as surprised to see me as I was him, and he climbed over his friend Calvin so he could sit next to me.

We quickly discovered that all three of us would be starting the same college next week. Dad moved to the far end of the row. I had my eye on Calvin, but sometime during the seventh inning, Don asked me out.

Don and Calvin became college roommates. Don and I dated, but in the end, it was Calvin who paid the most attention to me. He started by conveniently forgetting a pencil for a placement test we were required to take—so he could ask me for one and sit next to me. Then he joined the choir I sang in—that gave him a guaranteed three hours a week. He saved a seat for me at lunch, took long walks on crisp fall evenings when my heart was breaking over a relationship that didn't work out, and talked with me on the phone by the hour.

Calvin and I were both active socially, dating others, but we still hadn't officially dated each other. I liked Calvin well enough, and I knew he had his eye on me. But I guess I was too busy playing the field, and so I missed Calvin's signals.

And then, the first night of Christmas vacation, Calvin and I had our first date. He took me to the Los Angeles County Music Center to hear pianist Andre Watts.

The next week he rode his bicycle fifty miles to see me.

And then one night Calvin mentioned that he had noticed me standing at the top of the aisle at Dodger Stadium that first night, even before I found the seat in his row. He said I was wearing a short navy blue jumper with a red-, white-, and blue-striped turtleneck shirt. He remembered exactly what I looked like that night with my long, straight brown hair and blue eyes.

I think that's when the lights on the scoreboard of my heart suddenly lit up. It was like a voice somewhere inside me said, *Here comes Thomsen, rounding third. He's gonna make a run for your heart!* The voice sounded a lot like Vin Scully's. I figured I was head over heels in love.

Two and a half years later, we got married in a beautiful church in Riverside, California, with the late afternoon sun streaming through stained-glass windows that reached nearly from the ceiling to the floor.

But on the way to the wedding, there was baseball to consider. You see, I'd sent Vince Scully a short letter two days before the wedding, explaining that I had the Dodgers to thank for helping me find the love of my life. I secretly hoped—but never believed—that he'd tell our story in Dodger Stadium. And he did. As we were driving into town for the wedding, Vince Scully launched one of his stories—this time about Calvin and Marilyn and those seats above the third-base line.

Twenty-four years later, I still smile as I listen to the tape of my beloved Vinnie telling—between pitches to Cubs star Billy Williams— how Calvin and I met.

During the next ten years, the Dodgers lost every game we went to. It was an unbelievable streak of strikeouts, errors, and losses. But according to Calvin, it was a Dodger error that got us together. By mistake, the Dodgers had sent him tickets to three extra games he hadn't selected. When he called the Dodgers office about the error, they said go and enjoy the games. It was during one of those games that Calvin first laid eyes on me.

Needless to say, the team's win-loss record didn't keep us away. The

Dodgers had already worked their magic, and Calvin had won my heart in a sweep.

MARILYN THOMSEN

God knew his chosen time:
He bade me slowly ripen to my prime,
And from my boughs withheld the promised fruit,
Till storms and sun gave vigor to the root.

BAYARD TAYLOR

THE PEOPLE WITH
THE ROSES

You may break, you may shatter the vase, if you will,
but the scent of the roses will hang round it still.

THOMAS MOORE

*J*ohn Blanchard stood up from the bench, straightened his army uniform, and studied the crowd of people making their way through Grand Central Station. He looked for the girl whose heart he knew, but whose face he didn't, the girl with the rose.

His interest in her had begun thirteen months before in a Florida library. Taking a book off the shelf he found himself intrigued, not with the words of the book, but with the notes penciled in the margin. The soft handwriting reflected a thoughtful soul and insightful mind. In the front of the book, he discovered the previous owner's name, Miss Hollis Maynell.

With time and effort he located her address. She lived in New York City. He wrote her a letter introducing himself and inviting her to correspond. The next day he was shipped overseas for service in World War II. During the next year and one month the two grew to know each other through the mail. Each letter was a seed falling on a fertile heart. A romance was budding.

Blanchard requested a photograph, but she refused. She felt that if he really cared, it wouldn't matter what she looked like.

When the day finally came for him to return from Europe, they scheduled their first meeting—7:00 P.M. at the Grand Central Station in New York. "You'll recognize me," she wrote, "by the red rose I'll be wearing on my lapel."

So at seven o'clock he was in the station looking for a girl whose heart he loved, but whose face he'd never seen.

I'll let Mr. Blanchard tell you what happened.

A young woman was coming toward me, her figure long and slim. Her blonde hair lay back in curls from her delicate ears; her eyes were blue as flowers. Her lips and chin had a gentle firmness, and in her pale green suit she was like springtime come alive. I started toward her, entirely forgetting to notice that she was not wearing a rose. As I moved, a small, provocative smile curved her lips. "Going my way, sailor?" she murmured.

Almost uncontrollably I made one step closer to her, and then I saw Hollis Maynell.

She was standing almost directly behind the girl. A woman well past forty, she had graying hair tucked under a worn hat. She was more than plump, her thick-ankled feet thrust into low-heeled shoes. The girl in the green suit was walking quickly away. I felt as though I was split in two, so keen was my desire to follow her, and yet so deep was my longing for the woman whose spirit had truly companioned and upheld my own.

And there she stood. Her pale, plump face was gentle and sensible, her gray eyes had a warm and kindly twinkle. I did not hesitate. My fingers gripped the small worn blue leather copy of the book that was to identify me to her. This would not be love, but it would be something precious, something perhaps even better than love, a friendship for which I had been and must ever be grateful.

I squared my shoulders and saluted and held out the book to the woman, even though while I spoke I felt choked by the bitterness of my disappointment. "I'm Lieutenant John Blanchard, and you must be Miss Maynell. I am so glad you could meet me. May I take you to dinner?"

The woman's face broadened into a tolerant smile. "I don't know what this is about, son," she answered, "but the young lady in the green suit who just went by, she begged me to wear this rose on my coat. And she said if you were to ask me out to dinner, I should go and tell you that she is waiting for you in the big restaurant across the street. She said it was some kind of test!"

It's not difficult to understand and admire Miss Maynell's wisdom.

MAX LUCADO

As written by Max Lucado in *And the Angels Were Silent* (Portland, Oregon: Multnomah Press, 1992), original author unknown. Used by permission of the publisher.

SOMEBODY'S CALLING
MY NAME

Two souls but a single thought,
Two hearts beat as one.

FRIEDRICH HALM

When Andrew Young, former ambassador to the United Nations, graduated from Howard College in Washington, D.C., he felt a strong call to go into the ministry. But he knew that breaking the news to his family would cause quite a disturbance. It was always assumed that Andrew would become a dentist, join his father's dental practice, marry a local girl, and live down the street from his parents in New Orleans.

His family not only reacted as he feared, but they tried everything to change their son's mind. After a lot of tears and shouting, the family realized that Andrew would not be deterred. It was settled. Andrew would begin seminary in the fall.

As a peace offering, his mother arranged a ministerial summer job for her son through the bishop in their church. Andrew had planned to practice track for the Olympic tryouts in New York, but he accepted the position unenthusiastically to make amends with his family. He also later explained that it was an appointment he felt he "ought to accept." Now that he had made a decision to become a minister, he would have to discern God's will for his life without question. The bishop assigned Andrew to a small Congregational Church in Marion, Alabama, where he boarded with a local family, the Childses. Young tells the following account of meeting his beloved wife, Jean, in his biography, *An Easy Burden*.

The Childses talked to me about their five children, who were on their own or away at college. One afternoon, I began to wander around their house, since they had told me to make myself at home. While looking through one of the children's bedrooms, my attention was drawn to a senior lifesaving certificate on the wall, made out to a Jean Childs. This interested me because I didn't know many black women who could swim at all, and you had to be a very strong swimmer to qualify for a lifesaving badge. Due to segregation, there were very few pools or beaches open to blacks. The girls I knew who might have had the opportunity were usually too concerned about their hair to spend that much time in the water. I began to look at the books that were in the bookcase by the bed. Among her books there was a Revised Standard Version of the Bible, which had been published just a few years earlier by the National Council of Churches. Passages in her Bible were actually underlined, with handwritten notes in the margins.

At that very moment I figured that the Lord intended that I be in Marion, Alabama, to marry this girl whom I had never met, whose belongings I found so intriguing. It didn't hurt that her mother was a striking woman and her father resembled Clark Gable. Even her grandmother had lovely legs, which she proudly displayed by wearing high heels with her elegant Sunday dresses.

Our first meeting took place on the first day of summer, Jean's mother's birthday. I drove with Mr. and Mrs. Childs in their Chevrolet to Tuskegee to pick up Jean, who was helping her brother, Bill, and his expectant wife, Barbara, with their two active children. When we pulled up to the new, brick, ranch-style house, Jean came through the kitchen door and walked across the thick, green lawn to meet us. She was wearing a plain cotton dress, with her hair pulled back from a face that looked as if no makeup had ever dared mar its freshness. She possessed such a pure and simple beauty, it was as if she stepped out of my dreams into reality. I wanted to rush out and throw my arms around her. When we were properly introduced, I shook her hand and didn't let go. She had to tug her hand out of my grasp. When she drew away, I realized that my enthusiasm was making her uncomfortable. Although I had been dreaming about her, asking her parents every detail about her childhood, I was a stranger to her. I had to give her time to get to know me, but as I followed her into the house for cake and ice cream, I was even more convinced that she was going to be my wife.

Andrew Young was exactly right when he said that he knew why God had sent him to Marion, Alabama. Jean Childs was, without a doubt, part of God's plan for Andrew Young. He and Jean were married when she graduated from college in 1954.

Andrew Young describes their life together, saying, "Every day a challenge. Every day a blessing." So true of marriage! "Jean understood my desire through religious commitment to dedicate my life to serve; I understood and appreciated her intent to serve in the same manner through teaching, and we shared a wish to live and work in the South." It was Jean's spiritual strength and love that guided the Youngs through the exciting times of their lives—the Civil Rights movement, raising a family, and Andrew's political career.

Here were two young people who loved to serve God and wanted to make a difference in the world. God knew just the woman that Andrew

Young needed to fulfill his destiny. The Youngs were happily married for forty years until Jean lost her valiant battle with cancer.

Will You Marry Me?

MARRIAGE IS A GREAT DOOR, SHUTTING OUT AND SHUTTING IN. THE OLD NEIGHBORHOODS, THE OLD PHONE NUMBERS, THE OLD WHISPERED PROMISES, THE OLD DALLIANCES OF THE MIND, ARE BEHIND THE DOOR, OUTSIDE, AND MUST REMAIN THERE.

YET IT IS SIMPLE TRUTH THAT A DOOR THAT SHUTS OUT ONE PART OF THE HOUSE MUST ALSO GRANT ACCESS TO ANOTHER. YES, A PART OF LIFE ENDS, BUT ANOTHER PART BEGINS, AND THERE IS MUCH THAT LIES AHEAD. FORSAKING THE OLD MEANS WALKING CLEAN, UNFETTERED, AND LIGHTHEARTED INTO THE NEW. IT MEANS LEAVING THE WEATHERED BAGGAGE AT THE DOOR AND STEPPING OPENHANDED INTO AN ENDEAVOR THAT WILL REQUIRE THE BEST OF YOUR STRENGTH, THE BEST OF YOUR CHARACTER, THE BEST OF YOUR WISDOM.

AND IT WILL REQUIRE MORE THAN THAT. MORE THAN YOU HAVE TO GIVE. MORE THAN YOUR BEST. MORE THAN YOU CAN SQUEEZE FROM YOUR SOUL IN YOUR FINEST MOMENTS. IT WILL REQUIRE, IN FACT, THE VERY PRESENCE OF THE LIVING GOD WITHIN YOU.

EDWARD'S PROPOSAL

*Grownups never understand anything for themselves,
and it is tiresome for children to be always
and forever explaining things to them.*

ANTOINE DE SAINT-EXUPÉRY

*E*dward had reserved a private room at his club for the night he intended to pop that all-important question. Looking in the mirror, he straightened his tie and adjusted his collar as he practiced, "Will you *marry* me? Will *you* marry me? Will you marry *me?*" Edward thought to himself that maybe he should say, "Will *ALL of you* marry me?"

Edward gazed about the room—immaculate, starched, white table linens and flowers. Thank heaven, they'd remembered the flowers! Nosegays of violets and sweetheart roses, intertwined with a rainbow of ribbons, marked each place setting. Gleaming silverware seemed to march around the table in military precision. The chef assured him that the menu he had chosen was prepared to perfection. Never had he put so much thought and detail into the planning of any evening, but this was to be the most important evening of his life.

Edward was a prominent attorney, accustomed to tough cases. Tonight, however, might just be the toughest case he had ever argued. His palms actually felt sweaty. He had everything to gain if he won, but if he lost, he'd be lost.

Then they filed in, two small girls in pleated skirts with enormous bows atop their heads, their Mary Janes tapping along the marble hallway, announcing their arrival with the proper fanfare. A boy of six, the youngest, in gray pants and a navy blazer, brought up the rear. Edward sat each child at the table, then took his place. Three pairs of piercing blue eyes and three unsmiling faces stared back at him. Dear God, how was he to begin?

His mind flashed back. *I can't marry you, Edward, unless my children agree,* Julie had told him. *Our love is wonderful, but that's not enough. My children were so young when they lost their father, and sometimes I think they'll never lose that sad look in their eyes.* He had loved her all the more for her strong sense of responsibility to her children. *Laura will be the hardest to convince,* Julie had warned. *You'll probably have no problem with the younger ones, unless Laura sways them in another direction.*

Edward returned to the present and these three tiny faces that held his future. There were yearnings in their eyes. *They need a father,* Edward thought to himself, *and their mother needs a husband, and I need all of them! We all need each other.*

"I have a letter for each of you," Edward said, pointing.

The children picked up the envelopes with their names on them. Laura opened hers with precision while the others ripped theirs open.

"You can read the letters and give me your answer. This is very important to me," Edward added as an afterthought.

The children read their letters. Little Ted nudged his sister. "What's it say?"

"It says he wants to marry you."

Little Ted started to giggle. "Marry me?"

"Silly, it means he wants you to be his little boy."

Elizabeth, speaking for herself, then said, "I'll be your little girl."

Edward smiled, then turned to Laura, the holdout. To his dismay she frowned, hesitated, cocked her head in that familiar thinking position, then frowned again. Edward's heart plunged; the girl looked distinctly bothered. At last she spoke.

"Personally," Laura began finally, "I would be glad to marry you. And so would the children." Edward wanted to laugh but didn't let on. "But…"

"But what, sweetheart. What is it?" Edward asked.

"What about Mommy?" Laura asked. "We can't leave Mommy all by herself."

Ted chimed in, "Yeah, Mommy likes you too. I can tell."

Trying to hold back his laughter, he leaned close to the children conspiratorially and said, "Why don't we go ask her to marry us too?"

So that's how they soon married one another in an unusual joint ceremony with Edward giving silver rings to the children and a beautiful gold ring to Julie—all very legal and proper.

Many who attended the wedding grew misty eyed, but all of them agreed: This family wedding proved that one of the best things you can do for children is to really love their mother—and one of the best ways to court a mother is to really love her children.

DARLENE RUBIN

Used by permission of the author.

AN AFFAIR OF
SOME DELICACY!

Standing with reluctant feet,
Where the brook and river meet,
Womanhood and childhood fleet!

HENRY WADSWORTH LONGFELLOW

The place was India, 1924. In the heavy heat of a Bangalore afternoon, anyone who could rested under mosquito netting, waiting for the first slight breeze of evening. But in one large, two-story home, servants sat in the shaded courtyard feverishly shelling peas and sifting the rice clean.

Company was coming. The purpose of the visit was purely business—the most important business—which is falling in love, India-style. As the cook and his cohorts chopped and diced in the hot kitchen, a young girl sat on a chair upstairs and watched her mother fuss over her older sister's hair. Today the lovely thirteen-year-old Sushila was to be presented for betrothal to a boy she had never met. His name was Kolar. Sankari, younger by a year, waited, pretending not to be impressed by her sister's big day.

"Stay still, Sushila!" exclaimed their mother. "If you keep fidgeting, I will never finish." Then with a few final twists, the mother put the final touches to an elaborately coiled arrangement of her daughter's long, black tresses. Sushila gazed at the young woman in the mirror, startled by her own grown-up image.

Sankari piped up. "It's perfect! You look beautiful, Sushila."

"Yes, it will do, I think," said Mother. "Sankari, run and find out from cook how soon everything will be ready. Tell him that all must be served in an hour."

As the girl ran from the room, her mother's voice followed her, "And don't pester cook to give you a bite. You will have your chance later, once our guests have left!"

Sankari frowned. What would it matter if she had a scrumptious pakora or two? But in the kitchen, the cook was vigilant. As Sankari reached for the savory dish, he intercepted.

"I don't see what difference my having one would make," she pleaded.

"A big difference," the cook replied. "Particularly as it would never be just one."

"Huh! All this fuss, and for what?"

"You know very well what for. If this boy is secured for Sushila, it will be your turn next for all the fuss."

Sankari left the kitchen and returned to her sister's bedroom, where Sushila stood, stunning in her jewels and a flowing silk sari. "Wow!" was all the younger girl could say, her eyes round as saucers.

Their mother smiled. "Yes, 'wow!' indeed. But there is not much time left. Sankari, you must make yourself scarce now. This is your sister's moment, and you must not be seen or heard from until the visit is over. Do you understand? I am sure you can find something to do in your room for the next two hours."

Sankari knew better than to argue when her mother used that tone of voice. "I'm going. But please save some food for me. The cook's made all my favorites." As she stepped out into the hall, she added to her sister, "I hope Kolar doesn't look like a frog!"

Sankari lay sprawled on her bed reading when she heard the sound of carriage wheels turning into the courtyard. She rushed to the window hoping to steal a glimpse of the visitors, especially the young man who might someday marry her sister. As the guests were shown indoors, she caught a brief glimpse of kind dark eyes and a handsome face. This Kolar was no frog! Why was Sushila always the fortunate one?

Time moved slowly as Sankari tried to forget the boy and finish her book. But after two hours, the visitors still hadn't left. What could they be doing? *Eating all the food is what they are doing,* Sankari moaned to herself. Her mouth watered at the thought of pakoras and bajias and idlis—the finest of Indian appetizers. "This is so unfair!" she blurted. "I'm starving!"

Quietly opening her bedroom door, she peered out. Nobody was around, but she could hear the hum of conversation coming from the parlor. She crept to the head of the stairs and soundlessly padded down step by step. At the bottom she realized that the door to the parlor was open, but she was confident she could slip past without being noticed. On tiptoe she sneaked across the foyer, past the open door, and darted down the hall to the kitchen.

Spread across the counters were plates laden with pakoras and bajias and delicacies of every description. Quickly Sankari grabbed a plate and piled it with tasty morsels, then retraced her path to her bedroom. No one had seen. No one would have to know.

The next morning a messenger arrived with a note from the visitors. The father opened it with anticipation. Suddenly, he started shouting. "Sankari, Sankari! Come down at once, do you hear me?" he yelled, waving the note in the air.

"I'm coming, Appa. I'm coming." The young girl flew down the stairs to the foyer where her parents waited.

"How can this be?" her father demanded. "Weren't you in your room yesterday when the visitors came?"

"Yes, Appa, all the time."

"Then how could this be?" This time it was her mother asking, holding out the note.

"How could the young man wish to marry you, not Sushila? How could he know you are beautiful if you stayed in your room the whole time?" her father asked.

"This young man has X-ray vision to see through walls?" declared her mother.

"I—I—" stuttered Sankari.

"You sneaked down into the kitchen to eat, did you not?" Her voice was stern.

The girl's words rushed out then. "They were here so long...I was so hungry...I crept by. But nobody could have seen me!"

"Evidently you did not make yourself as invisible as you seem to think," responded her father dryly. "Well, what is done is done. But you should know, Sankari, that it would be impossible for us to agree to this while your sister Sushila remains without a marriage contract. As you well know, a younger daughter cannot be engaged when her older sister has no suitor."

Weeks passed, and no more was said. Then one day about a month later, more visitors came, and the cooks and servants were busy again. More delicacies filled the kitchen. And Sushila was begowned and bejeweled as before. But this time Sankari never once left her room.

That evening at dinner an announcement was made by the happy parents. "In time, Sushila will marry the young man who came today with his family. It is all arranged."

"Wow!" said Sankari. Sushila smiled with happiness.

"And you, Sankari," her father went on, "you will someday marry Kolar, the young man who insists that he will only marry our youngest daughter."

Sankari couldn't have been more delighted. As for Kolar, forty years of marriage never dimmed his cherished first vision of his wife as she snuck across the foyer with only pakoras and bajias and idlis on her mind.

SHALINI WARAN

Editor's note: This is the story of the author's grandmother, Sankari, which she loved to tell her grandchildren as she fried pakoras and bajias for them.

NICE GUYS

Some say the age of chivalry is past,

that the spirit of romance is dead.

The age of chivalry is never past,

so long as there is a wrong left unaddressed on the earth,

or a man or a woman left to say,

I will redress that wrong or spend my life in the attempt.

CHARLES KINGLSEY

Y met David Wilson in a class at college. My first impression was that he was handsome and nice. In fact, very nice. But soon I decided David was a little *too* nice—especially to me.

From the start, David wasn't coy about being attracted to me. No matter how often I turned down his advances, he made no secret of the fact that he was smitten with me. Every day he'd think of a new way to compliment me in class. "Look, everyone. Doesn't Rubria look nice in her new dress?" "Isn't Rubria's new haircut cool?" "Red is Rubria's color, don't you agree?"

Pretty soon, I felt like I was drowning in compliments. I dated a lot of sharp guys, some seriously, but I had never met anyone quite like David who lavished such attention on me. All the guys I dated were too cool to make such a fuss over me or any girl. I decided that David wasn't enough of a challenge for me…he was too nice.

Just the same, something about David's brand of confidence intrigued me. He was smart, and he had impeccable manners. I decided I wouldn't date David, but there was no point in being completely rude to him either.

One morning driving to classes, I looked up as I approached my exit and almost ran off the road. I couldn't believe what I was seeing, but I knew exactly who was behind it. There, stretched across the freeway over-pass, was a banner that read "Happy Birthday, Rubria!"

I was mortified. Everyone at the university would know it was me. How many Rubrias could there be? How, I wondered, did he know it was my birthday? I'd said nothing. But David had this uncanny way of know-ing everything about me.

When I walked into class, I was fuming, and I shot David an angry look. Undaunted by my glare, he hopped to his feet and announced to the class, "Today is Rubria's birthday! Won't you join me in singing 'Happy Birthday'?"

The entire class serenaded me as I churned with embarrassment and anger. When the song was over, I declared aloud, "This guy just doesn't quit!" So much for being appreciative.

For the next couple of days, I gave David the coldest shoulder possi-ble. Whenever he tried to be friendly, I responded with a cool to the point of rudeness. "I'm sorry, David, but I don't have time to talk to you," I'd say. Finally he backed off, though I noticed he didn't turn his attention toward any other girl.

And then something quite unusual happened. As the weeks passed, I began to miss David's compliments. I'd gotten so used to them I hadn't realized how they boosted my spirits. I began to notice how rare it was for a guy to care about and affirm a girl so much. Suddenly the shallow and often self-serving attention of other young men had less appeal.

Gradually I began to warm up toward David again. He responded with his typical enthusiasm, and soon I was again basking in David's ado-ration. And then finally the unthinkable—I accepted his invitation to go out.

One date led to more. But as our relationship began to take off, other obstacles loomed. Now that I was responding to David's advances, I began to worry if they'd continue. What if he'd only been intrigued by the chal-lenge of getting me to like him? Or, worse, what if David really did believe all the marvelous things he said about me? As we got to know each other better, he would discover all my faults. And then what?

But David continued to treat me like a queen, and in time I realized my fears were unfounded. We began to date one another exclusively. And by the time we graduated, I knew I'd fallen deeply in love with him. When I introduced David to my family, they were as crazy about him as he'd always been about me.

Then David pulled another one of his tricks. He kidnapped me from work, having cleared this ahead of time with my boss. After a romantic picnic on the beach, he asked me to take a walk with him in the moonlight. As we strolled along, I kept discovering roses strewn on the sand that David had put there earlier for me to find. When David dropped to his knees, I knew exactly what was coming. He proposed to me in the moonlight.

And I agreed to marry the nicest guy I'd ever met.

Today David is still as romantic, thoughtful, and full of surprises as ever. And I consider myself the luckiest woman in the world to be married to him. I know people say that nice guys always finish last. But they're wrong. If the nice guy is truly in love with you, my guess is he'll finish first.

RUBRIA PORRAS WILSON

UNDER HIS NOSE

This bud of love, by summer's ripening breath,
May prove a beauteous flower when next we meet.

WILLIAM SHAKESPEARE

*B*ob grew up admiring the small-town values of his mother, a schoolteacher, and his father, a lawyer. But like many young men, he had ambitious plans. Instead of accepting a scholarship to his state college, Bob opted for Harvard Law School. After graduation, he joined a prestigious New York firm.

Soon Bob was on the fast track to success. And as they say, behind every successful man is a woman who believes in him. In Bob's case, this woman was his secretary, Elizabeth. She was efficient, professional, and thorough. She also had come from a small town and seemed to share his "old-fashioned" values.

Bob knew how much of his professional success he owed to Elizabeth, but he didn't realize that she was attracted to him because she hid her feelings carefully. Behind her capable, professional demeanor was a woman in love.

Elizabeth had originally come to New York to pursue her dream of becoming a dancer, but she soon discovered the cruel realities of the entertainment business. She was just another pair of dancing legs, and it would take a great deal of time and effort to claw her way to the top. Meanwhile, working for Bob was a good way to pay the rent—but it was hard on her heart.

She'd known that Bob sometimes dated, and that had been painful enough. He obviously wasn't interested in her in that way. But Elizabeth was devastated when she heard that Bob was about to propose to Laura, a beautiful young lawyer and the daughter of wealthy New Yorkers. If the chatter in the coffee room was any indicator, Laura cared very little about the feelings of others. Elizabeth was convinced that despite her beauty and brains, Laura was not the girl for Bob.

The day Bob announced at the office his engagement to Laura, Elizabeth warmly congratulated him, trying hard to maintain her professional decorum. Later, Laura dropped by to show off the ring on her finger. "Isn't it the most beautiful ring you have ever seen?" she boasted to Elizabeth.

"It's very lovely," said Elizabeth politely.

"You should see the wedding band we've chosen," Laura continued. "I won't be able to lift my finger!"

For the next several days at work, Elizabeth fought back tears. How long could she pretend to be glad for Bob when she was aching inside? Finally she decided it would be too difficult to continue working for him when she wanted more—a more that would never be possible. She began looking for another position and, when she found it, turned in her resignation.

"Elizabeth, I can't accept this!" Bob exclaimed. "How can I persuade you to stay?" He pleaded with her, but her mind was made up.

Bob was both disappointed and perplexed. They'd worked so well together. After Elizabeth left, he hired another woman to fill her position. But the new secretary, though capable, just couldn't replace Elizabeth. She had understood him and anticipated his needs, always figuring out just how to help. Within weeks Bob came to an even more difficult realization—when Elizabeth had walked out of his life, he'd lost the one person who'd given him inspiration and confidence.

A few weeks later Bob lost an important trial case. When he tried to talk about it with Laura, she didn't appear interested. In fact, she seemed to want him to keep the details of his work life to himself. A warning light flashed in Bob's head. Similar incidents came to mind, and Bob wondered why he hadn't noticed this side of Laura before. If only she were more like—

Elizabeth! Suddenly he knew he had to find Elizabeth, talk to her. He dialed her number but only reached her answering machine. He canvassed the office, asking for information about where Elizabeth was now working, until finally someone gave him the address of a dance studio.

The place was near enough, and Bob didn't want to wait for a taxi. He started to run down the streets of Manhattan, dodging the bustling midday crowd. He reached the address, breathless, nervous, and with no idea of what to say. At the top of the stairs to the studio, he stopped to look through the glass door. In the room in front of him Bob saw a dozen tiny ballerinas twirling across the hardwood floor, executing their pas de deuxs under the watchful eye of their teacher—Elizabeth.

Bob gazed at her in shock. He'd never before noticed the tall, lovely artist behind the capable secretary. How tender and kind she was to her young students. When Bob entered the room, the little girls stopped midstep and turned to stare at the intruder. Elizabeth, too, turned around to see him.

"Elizabeth," he announced, as though saying her name for the very first time.

"Why, Bob!" she said. "What can I help you with?"

With everything! With my heart! With my life! he wanted to shout. But instead he invited her to lunch.

She agreed to meet him after her class. And a short time later, he was again trying to find the right words to bring her back.

"No," she said firmly. "You've got a new secretary, Bob. And besides, I've decided that dancing is the love of my life!"

Bob shook his head. "No. You don't understand." Suddenly he felt tears stinging his eyes. How could he explain? "I've decided something too," he said. "And that is that *you* are the love of my life. And...I want you to be my wife."

Once the words were out, he could hardly believe he'd said them, but he also knew he would never take them back. His thoughts raced. Yes, he was engaged to marry Laura. But that engagement could be broken, and now he doubted that it would break Laura's heart. The only thing he knew for sure—beyond all reason—was that he didn't want to lose this amazing woman again.

He watched Elizabeth from across the table, trying to read her reaction.

Her eyes had filled with tears, but a shocked smile was slowly spreading on her beautiful lips. Yes, he could see it on her face. She loved him too! Impulsively he scooped her up in his arms and kissed her—as if trying to convince her that business was the last thing on his mind.

Six months later the two were married in a beautiful ceremony. A dozen giggling ballerinas were among the happy guests. In the years since then, Elizabeth has brought grace and success to many young dancers. And even though she never went back to work in Bob's office, he would be the first to say that Elizabeth's love for him has been the reason for his success every step of the way.

AUTHOR UNKNOWN

HARK,
THE WEDDING ANGEL

For memory has painted this perfect day
With colors that never fade.

No one in my family will ever forget the Christmas I invited them to travel from the West Coast to spend the holidays in my new home on the East Coast. They assumed I simply wanted to introduce them to the man I'd fallen in love with, Larry Dimitri, as well as his family. But Larry and I had something even more special in mind!

We had a lovely dinner and Christmas party for forty of our closest friends and relatives. Everyone was having a merry time when suddenly we heard a loud knock on the front door. To the delight of our young nieces and nephews, Santa Claus appeared with a bag full of gifts.

The adults smiled as Santa called the children's names one by one and gave each a special Christmas present. My mother looked at me and whispered, "Angie, is Santa Larry?"

I shook my head no just as Larry appeared at Santa's side. Santa called out, "Angie, come up here. Santa's got a present for you!"

A delighted chorus of oohs and aahs filled the room. Obviously a lot of people expected that they were about to witness a marriage proposal. As I went forward, I heard whispers of, "It's going to be a ring!" But when I opened the package, it contained only a box of engraved stationery. "Thank you, Santa," I said, "but my name is not Angie Dimitri."

"I told you," someone squealed. "Larry's going to propose!"

But he didn't—not exactly anyway.

"Come here, Angie and Larry," Santa beckoned. "What do you want for Christmas?"

"We want to get married," Larry told him. Everyone applauded. Surely now Santa was going to pull a diamond out of his bag. Or maybe Larry was about to get down on his knee and propose.

Instead, to the utter amazement of our guests, Santa Claus—who was really a good-natured justice of the peace—pulled a Bible out of his bag of toys. "Well then, if you two are willing and everyone here is willing, let's have a wedding right now!" he chuckled.

And Santa married us on the spot. As we spoke our vows, "Hark, the Herald Angels Sing" played softly on the stereo. Children giggled, adults shed happy tears, and all the folks we loved best welcomed the new Mr. and Mrs. Larry Dimitri into the world.

We may have had the world's shortest engagement ever, but we're planning to have a long and very merry marriage!

ANGIE AND LARRY DIMITRI

THE GOVERNESS

⟨ornament⟩

The red rose whispers of passion
and the white rose breathes of love.

JOHN BOYLE O'REILLY

*I*n 1918 if a woman had not married by age thirty-two, folks considered her well past her prime. Well-meaning friends and relatives would often chide pretty, blue-eyed Alice about being an "old maid." But Alice, who had had her share of proposals, didn't let it bother her. She was waiting for true love.

Just returning from Boston where she had modeled hats and gloves for a department store, Alice arrived at her family's home in St. Louis. The first morning she was reading the classifieds in search of a job when an ad caught her eye.

> Widower seeking governess for two young children:
> One son and one daughter. Employer owns his own
> business
> Mr. John Henry Platz
> Texarkana, Arkansas

Alice cut the advertisement out of the newspaper and placed it on her dresser. Every time she walked by, it seemed to be calling to her. Although she loved children, she had never considered being a governess, nor had she planned to leave St. Louis, and yet, the ad touched her heart. *Those poor orphaned children,* she thought. *They need a lot of love.* She decided to write the gentleman in the ad.

After several letters back and forth, Mr. Platz and Alice agreed that she would take the job on a trial basis. He sent her a ticket and said he would meet her at the train station. Alice told him she would be wearing a straw hat with flowers.

When John spotted the hat, he was not prepared for the beautiful woman wearing it. Alice was stunning—sky blue eyes, a flawless complexion, and wavy brown hair. John was so taken with her beauty and charm that he could hardly speak to welcome the governess.

John took Alice to his home and introduced her to his children: Augusta, seven, and Henry, five. Alice and the children bonded immediately. Ever since his wife had died, John had tried managing his company and his family, but he knew the children needed a mother. Looking on that first evening as Alice read them a story, listened to their prayers, and kissed the children good night, he was confident he had found the right woman to raise his children.

The next morning John awoke to the aromas of coffee and fresh bread baking. He looked out his window and saw Alice in the garden, gathering flowers for the house. John was exhilarated that Alice's feminine touch was restoring order in his home.

As the weeks went by, John was deeply touched by the love Alice showered upon his children. Alice also had great respect for John from the moment she met him, but as his employee, the proper young woman never allowed herself to think of him in any other way.

Neither John nor Alice can tell you the moment they fell in love, but two years after she arrived, John picked a bouquet of his prize roses for Alice. When he presented the bouquet to her, he said, "Sweetheart roses for my sweetheart." Alice blushed and thanked John as she accepted his invitation to walk through the garden. When they returned, John told his children that Alice had accepted his proposal to become his wife.

When the couple married, Alice carried a bouquet of roses from John's garden. As they spoke their vows, the man Alice had secretly loved in her heart and the children she loved and cared for became her true family. Alice and John were happily married and had four more children (who love to tell the tale of how the governess became their mother).

Alice and John had a once-in-a-lifetime love that began with a small advertisement in a newspaper and a young woman who was willing to wait for the love of her life. You just never know where your heart might lead you if you, too, are willing to listen and wait!

TOLD BY JOHN PLATZ

SURPRISE, SURPRISE, SURPRISE!

❦

I have built a moment
more lasting than bronze.

HORACE

A young man in our home church recently pulled off a romantic surprise that's one of the best I've ever heard. It's something his wife-to-be will never forget, and it will make a great story for his grandchildren one day.

It was a beautiful, clear desert morning. The sun was still minutes away from its grand entrance, but it teased the Eastern sky with a hundred shades of gold. The mountains kept their silent sentinel in the cold, crisp dawn, the brilliant stars shining behind them like silver sequins on black velvet.

"WHHHOOOOOOOSSSHH." The sound of the hot-air balloon's burner broke the desert's quiet with resounding force. In a few heartbeats, its brilliant blue and red canopy sprang to life and lifted off the ground. It floated upward, carrying a basket with Steve, Jan, and the pilot cradled inside.

Going up in a hot-air balloon was something they'd both wanted to do for a long time, and now they were in the air! In just a few moments, they were several hundred feet up, gliding along with the wind's gentle currents.

The scene was spectacular, and while Steve and Jan were busy enjoying the moment, the pilot was making sure the flight continued to go smoothly.

All at once, the incredible quiet was broken by the distinct drone of an engine. At first, Jan thought it must be the sound of a truck on the road below them, but then she realized it was getting louder. Startled, Jan looked up to see an airplane headed right for them! She was paralyzed with fear—but if she had looked at Steve or the pilot, she'd have seen them both smiling.

The plane Steve had hired to "buzz" the hot-air balloon was right on time. When it turned close to them, a long tail appeared behind it, revealing a message that read, in larger-than-life letters, "I love you, Jan. Will you marry me?"

When the words on the banner finally hit her, she was beside herself; she jumped up and down in the confines of the balloon basket like a six-year-old on Christmas morning. "Yes, I'll marry you!" she said, laughing and crying at the same time. For this couple, a special surprise was an indication that creative romance would stay a part of their relationship.

Surprising ways to say "I love you" aren't reserved for restricted air space. They can be a note put in a lunchbox, a cassette tape with a loving greeting put in the car's tape player in secret, or a frozen yogurt that arrives with you at your husband's office on a hot, summer's afternoon. Planning can make sure that romance stays a consistent part of your relationship. But surprises can make the moment a cherished one. These actions all say, I'm thinking about you, my love for you is secure, you're important to me, we're together for life.

GARY SMALLEY

From *Love Is a Decision* (Nashville, Tennessee: Word Publishing, 1989). All rights reserved.

LOVE AND LETTERS

⚮

Never seek to tell thy love
Love that never told can be;
For the gentle wind does move
Silently, invisibly.

WILLIAM BLAKE

Skywriting? Been done. Engagement ring on the lobster claw? Boring. What Bill Gottlieb was searching for was the *perfect* way to propose to his sweetheart, Emily Mindel. And that's when Gottlieb got a clue. "Emily does the puzzle every day," says the twenty-seven-year-old New York City corporate lawyer, referring to the venerable *New York Times* crossword. "I thought that would be a romantic way to propose." So last October, Gottlieb called *Times* puzzle editor Will Shortz and asked him to play Cupid. "My reaction was, 'Wow, what a great idea!'" says Shortz, who agreed to weave a wedding proposal into the puzzle as "a onetime thing."

The puzzle ran on January 7. Gottlieb invited Mindel, a Brooklyn Law School student, to brunch. "I just said, 'Let's grab the paper,'" he recalls. "Very casual. But I was so nervous." Gottlieb feigned interest in the rest of the paper while Mindel, twenty-four and a crossword whiz, penciled in answers: 38 Across asked for a Gary Lewis and the Playboys hit ("This Diamond Ring"); 56 Across was a Paula Abdul song ("Will You Marry Me"). Other answers included "Emily," "BillG," and "Yes" (the hoped-for response to 56 Across). "I had the feeling the puzzle was saying something," says Mindel, no dummy. "My heart was racing, and I got all hot and flushed."

With only four squares undone, Mindel faced her beau and stammered, "This puzzle..." over and over.

"Her voice was all shaky," he says. "I smiled and asked, 'Will you marry me?'" Mindel's reply: an eight-letter phrase for *absolutely* ("Of course!"). Now the couple, fixed up by their families in 1995, are shopping for a ring and planning an intimate wedding (Shortz is on the guest list). When's the big day? Umm, they haven't a clue.

ALEX TRESNIOWSKI & HELENE STAPINSKI

Alex Tresniowski & Helene Stapinski/*People Weekly* © 1998.

With This Ring

IT IS THE MOST SUBTLE OF WEIGHTS ON THE THIRD LEFT FINGER, BARELY EVEN FELT UNTIL CONSCIOUSLY REMEMBERED. AND THEN...THERE IT IS, THE SLIGHTEST TOUCH OF SMOOTH METAL ON SKIN. THE SOFT, YET PERSISTENT REMINDER THAT LIFE IS FOREVER DIFFERENT. A DECISION HAS BEEN MADE. A CORNER HAS BEEN TURNED. VOWS HAVE BEEN UTTERED BEFORE THE LISTENING EARS OF HEAVEN. TWO LIVES HAVE BEEN IRREVOCABLY LINKED, FLESH TO FLESH, HEART TO HEART, SOUL TO SOUL. WITH SIMPLE ELOQUENCE, THE RING SAYS, "I AM WED. I HAVE A LIFE COMPANION. I BELONG TO SOMEONE ELSE. MY HEART, MY PASSION, THE DEEPEST RESERVOIRS OF MY AFFECTION ARE THE PROPERTY OF A DEAR PERSON WHO MEANS MORE TO ME THAN LIFE ITSELF."

CRACKER JACKS

I have been here before,
But where or how I cannot tell;
I know the grass beyond the door,
The sweet keen smell,
The sighing sound,
the lights around the shore.

DANTE GABRIEL ROSSETTI

Growing up, Leslie had always been a tomboy at heart. She loved to play ball with the neighborhood boys. But because of her tall, slender build, sometimes they picked on her, calling her names like "Beanpole," "Olive Oil," and "Bird Legs."

Michael, a cute boy with dark eyes and hair, was different. He lived next door, and he didn't call Leslie names. In fact, he seemed to adore everything about her. One day when he was seven, Michael shyly gave Leslie a ring from a Cracker Jack box—and asked her to marry him.

Leslie never forgot his proposal, and for many years she continued to have a mad crush on Michael. In high school he excelled in sports and was popular with the girls. But it was obvious to Leslie that he didn't see his skinny childhood friend as girlfriend material.

During college Leslie lost touch with Michael, and then she learned that he'd been drafted by a professional football team in New York. She wasn't at all surprised when one day she read that he was marrying a well-known fashion model. A twinge of disappointment pinched her heart.

But the sadness didn't last. By the time her ten-year class reunion rolled around, Leslie had blossomed into a stunning beauty herself, and she was married to a wonderful man. When she saw Michael arm in arm with his lovely wife, she was sincerely happy for him. Everything had turned out as it should, she decided. *Childhood crushes are for kids, after all. Then you grow up and move on.*

Little did Leslie know that life was about to take a tragic turn. A few years after the reunion, her husband was killed in a plane crash. She had found love—only to have it snatched away.

Engulfed for some time in her grief, Leslie was out of touch with most of her friends by the time her twentieth reunion rolled around. As she mingled, she couldn't help but notice that hardship had visited many of her old acquaintances—including Michael. What her friends had told her was true. He, too, was alone, his wife having died of breast cancer years before.

At the reunion she and Michael cautiously began to renew their friendship. Michael had recently taken a job as an assistant coach for a professional football team. Soon they began to see one another regularly, and Leslie felt sure they were falling in love.

As months turned into years, however, Leslie began to wonder if Michael would ever want to marry her. Maybe she would forever remain his "best friend"—the girl next door.

One night the couple attended a Braves game together. The team was winning, the weather was perfect, and through Michael's great sports connections, they had the best seats in the stadium. After a few innings, Michael excused himself to get snacks. He returned with Cokes and Cracker Jacks.

Leslie smiled, but her eyes grew misty. Obviously Michael didn't recall his childhood Cracker Jack proposal. How silly of her to have treasured the memory—and the ring—all these years.

When she finished munching, she tossed her box into a trash bin behind her.

Michael jumped out of his seat. "Leslie! You didn't even get your prize!" He leaned into the bin to retrieve her box.

"That's okay," she said. "They don't have good prizes in them like they used to when we were kids."

"Wanna bet?" Michael asked. He handed her the half-empty box. When Leslie reached in for her prize, she pulled out an incredibly beautiful engagement ring!

A moment later a message flashed up on the stadium's giant screen. It said, "Leslie, I love you. Will you marry me? Michael."

Friends who attended Michael and Leslie's wedding agreed that Leslie, once called "Bird Legs," had never looked so beautiful. On her left hand sparkled a lovely diamond wedding set, and on her right the ring from the Cracker Jack box Michael had given her in the second grade.

As the groom leaned down to kiss the bride, Leslie's most cherished childhood dream had finally come true.

Some things, like beauty and love, just take a little time.

THE MYSTERY RING

The ring, so worn as you behold;
So thin, so pale, is yet of gold:
The passion such it was to prove—
Worn with life's care, love yet was love.

GEORGE CRABBE

My husband and I couldn't have been happier when our youngest son, Will, then a senior at Yale Law School, announced that he wanted to ask his college girlfriend, Jillian, to marry him. We'd met Jillian briefly on a couple of occasions, and she appeared to be a lovely young woman.

Will, ever the romantic, informed us that he'd already asked Jillian's father for permission to marry his daughter. And now he wanted to plan every detail of his proposal.

"I want this to be a big surprise," he said. "And I want her family there. Do you think Jillian's parents as well as her grandparents could join us at Christmas? She's an only child, and her family is really close."

My husband and I told Will we'd love to have them. As we chatted about the arrangements, I asked Will, "What are you going to do for a ring?"

"I wanted to talk to you about that, Mom. Jillian is an old-fashioned girl, and she loves antique jewelry. Does Grandma Margaret have any beautiful old rings she would spare?"

"Oh, honey," I said. "You know that Grandmother already gave her wedding ring to your brother when he got married."

"But perhaps she has some other family jewelry?" he asked.

"I'm not sure," I said, "but I'll ask her."

The truth was, I knew my mother had a ring set with a beautiful emerald that would be perfect. As a little girl I'd admired it whenever I snuck a peek into my mother's jewelry box. But I'd never seen my mother wear this ring. And once, when I'd asked her if I could borrow it for a special occasion, she'd curtly denied the request and refused to explain.

I was hesitant to broach the subject again, but for Will's sake, I decided it was worth the risk. The next day I phoned her and told her of Will's plans. Then I asked, "Do you still have that emerald ring you kept in your jewelry box all those years?"

"I don't think that will work," she said briskly. "He'll just have to buy her a ring."

It was clear by her tone that this was the end of the discussion. But I was now more curious than ever about the emerald ring.

The next day my mother came for supper. I was more than a little surprised when I saw her quietly place a blue velvet box in front of Will's plate. "Here's an engagement ring for Jillian," she announced quietly to her grandson.

When Will opened the box, there lay the antique emerald ring. He was beside himself with gratitude and excitement. "Thank you, Grandma Margaret! Jillian's going to love this ring. Did Grandfather give it to you?"

My mother ignored his question and said simply, "I hope your bride will enjoy it."

I spent the next few weeks decorating the house for Christmas. I wanted the holidays to be perfect for Will's engagement. He called numerous times from college, making sure I'd taken care of details, especially the Christmas angel.

It was our family's tradition to put the angel on the tree after dinner on Christmas Eve. As part of our little tree-topping ceremony we would sing "Angels We Have Heard on High." This year Will said he wanted Jillian to have the honor of placing our heirloom angel on the tree.

When Christmas Eve arrived, our families gathered around for the simple ceremony. That's when Will handed Jillian the angel—with the engagement ring dangling from the angel's wrist. Jillian was speechless when Will got down on his knees to propose to her as both families looked on.

After we sang "Angels We Have Heard on High," Will and Jillian basked in congratulations from their families and proudly displayed her ring around the room. But as Jillian held out her hand to her grandmother, Elizabeth, she let out a muffled cry. "Where did you get this ring?" she demanded of Will.

"It was my grandmother's," said Will, pointing to my mother.

"Would you mind taking it off, Jillian?" her grandmother asked. "I really must get a look at it!"

Everyone exchanged puzzled glances as Grandma Elizabeth held the ring up to the light. "I thought so," she exclaimed. "Look! My initials are intricately engraved inside this ring. Where did you find this? At an antique store?"

I glanced over at my mother, who was visibly shaken. "I've had it many years," she answered in a quavering voice.

"I don't believe I caught your last name, Margaret," said Jillian's grandmother.

When my mother couldn't seem to answer, I said, "It's Johnson."

"You must be joking!" Elizabeth exclaimed. "Was your husband by any chance named William Johnson?"

"Why, yes," I said, answering for my mother. "He was my father."

"There are lots of William Johnsons," my mother interjected. "It's a common name."

"Did your husband grow up in Indianapolis?" she asked.

"Why, yes!" I said. "Did you know him?"

"Did I know him? Your father and I were high school sweethearts. He proposed to me before he left for the war, and I accepted."

You could have heard a pin drop. Then Grandma Elizabeth, realizing there was nothing to do but explain, falteringly continued her story: "Bill was stationed in Italy. We wrote one another for about three months, but I was so young and fickle I—I found another—my husband, right here beside me. After the war, Bill's family left Indianapolis, so we never knew what happened."

"And you sent his ring back!" my mother suddenly said.

"Yes," Jillian's grandmother replied, "this is the same ring that I returned to Bill. Jillian's engagement ring is the ring I wore over fifty years ago!"

It was hard for any of us to grasp such a coincidence. No one in our family knew that my father had received a "Dear John" letter from his high school sweetheart when he was stationed in Italy during World War II. He'd met my mother in San Francisco after the war, where he'd taken a job. We never imagined there might have been any other woman in his life.

Suddenly it was clear why my mother had hidden that ring all those years. It was a painful reminder that she was not my father's first love. Now I was sure she regretted ever bringing that ring and her secret out of its hiding place.

Later that night when our guests had gone to bed, my mother and I were quietly doing the dishes together. I wanted to apologize for asking for the ring when suddenly she spoke. "All these years I've kept your father's first engagement a secret. I always felt like I was his second choice." I was about to protest when she held up her hand to stop me. "But God has given me the greatest Christmas gift of all tonight," she declared with a smile. "I finally came face to face with Elizabeth—the woman I envied my entire life!"

And then she began to chuckle. "All these years...all these years!" She kept repeating the phrase until gradually her chuckles grew into outright laughter—the first I'd heard from her since Dad's death three years before. Then she squealed, "She's not your father's type at all!"

From that night on, something softened inside my mother. In parting with the ring she'd kept hidden her whole adult life, she also parted with a fear that had kept her a prisoner. In its place she accepted the wonderful truth, one that her husband had known for years—his second choice had been the very best choice of his life.

AUTHOR UNKNOWN

MUSIC OF THE HEART

Journey's end in lovers meeting!
Every wise man's son doth know.

WILLIAM SHAKESPEARE

xcitement filled the air as young musicians from all over the world gathered in Radio City Music Hall to perform. Cathy, a blond girl from Louisville, Kentucky, was not the only one in the audience enthralled by the performance of the boy on stage. The applause was deafening as his concerto came to an end.

He made his way back into the audience, and Cathy was surprised when he took the empty seat beside her. She looked up and gave him a smile. Lee, the thirteen-year-old pianist from San Francisco, wanted to speak to Cathy, but the sight of this beautiful girl made him tongue-tied.

She spoke first. "You were wonderful."

Lee felt himself blush from ear to ear. "What do you play?" he asked after what seemed like an endless pause.

"I sing," Cathy said.

They shouldn't have been talking, but they were oblivious to what was happening on stage. Lee was desperate to find out everything about her. Cathy tried to concentrate on the program but kept stealing shy glances at the fine-featured boy beside her. They continued to whisper to one another while the performances continued on stage.

"I'm just so nervous," Cathy admitted.

"Here, maybe this will help." Lee took off a gold ring he had been wearing and slid it onto her slender finger. "Wear it now. You can give it back to me after your performance," he whispered.

Cathy stared at the heavy gold ring on her finger, which somehow made her heart feel as light as air. *What a lovely gesture,* she thought to herself.

Soon it was her turn to take her place on stage. She gave him a little wave as she headed into the wings. As she appeared on center stage, Lee was mesmerized by her lilting angelic voice. The feelings were unlike any he had known before. Could it be love at first sight?

Cathy was one of the last performers. When the program ended, Lee rushed toward the stage, but it was impossible to find her in the crowd of young musicians and their parents and teachers. He searched for her golden head among those of countless others, but the crowd swirled in all directions, and the noise was deafening. His heart plummeted as he realized he didn't even know her last name.

At the end of the evening, Cathy and her parents also searched the crowd to return the ring, but Lee was nowhere to be found. The only clue to the identity of the handsome young pianist were the initials "LS" engraved inside the gold ring. Cathy was distraught, and her parents were concerned about returning the ring before they flew back to Louisville, but their efforts were in vain.

In the ensuing years, the young pianist matured into an internationally recognized pianist, performing concerts around the world. He often thought of Cathy and searched for her face in a crowd. He prayed that God would somehow bring them together again.

Cathy, meanwhile, was also performing professionally, as a backup singer for a top artist. Her lovely voice was much in demand. Yet, the handsome, dark-eyed young pianist who once placed his ring on her finger remained in her memory, and her heart told her she would see him again. She too prayed that God would somehow direct her path to his.

While in Los Angeles, Cathy was invited to join a girlfriend at a Christmas cantata at the Dorothy Chandler Pavilion. As she took her seat and studied the program, suddenly a name jumped out at her—Lee

Smith, the pianist for the evening. Could he be her "LS," she wondered. When the program began, there was no doubt. Indeed, he was the pianist!

Will he even remember me? she wondered. She could barely contain herself until the performance ended. As soon as the curtain closed, Cathy was out of her seat and racing backstage. She found his dressing room and knocked.

"Come in," said the male voice.

Cathy put her hand on the doorknob and entered.

They just stared at one another. Then Lee caught sight of his gold ring on a chain around her neck. He was the first to speak. "What took you so long?" he said with a mischievous grin.

They flew into each other's arms in a warm and loving embrace.

Could two young teenagers, in one brief meeting fifteen years before, have somehow recognized God's plan for their lives? Lee and Cathy, now married a dozen years, will tell you yes. After they married, they decided to dedicate their talents and their music to God's glory. Today they serve as music ministers to a large congregation. Their lives overflow with the elements that brought them together—music and love. Cathy says, "I'm still wearing his gold ring—only now I wear it on my left hand. And what I took for a passing crush was really the first few notes of the love song of my life."

DARLENE RUBIN

Used by permission of the author.

A TALE OF TWO RINGS

❧

How charmingly sweet you sing!
Oh let us be married! too long we have tarried:
But what shall we do for a ring?

EDWARD LEAR

etty and I were both students at the Cincinnati Conservatory studying dramatic performance when we met. I was just out of the air force, so I was older than the rest of the students in the class. And I'll admit that, unlike most of the other fellows, I had marriage on my mind. I was ready to settle down and start a family. All I needed was the right girl.

The first time I heard Betty sing on stage I was taken aback by her gorgeous appearance and enthralling voice. I made a point of meeting her, and quickly I fell in love. I hadn't known Betty but a few weeks when I decided I'd finally found the girl I'd been looking for.

But there was one problem. Betty wasn't looking for me. Although she was friendly and kind enough, she made it clear she wasn't ready to go with just one boy yet. She was young, and she wanted to experience all that life had to offer. Marriage, she announced, was not on her mind at all.

But I was a man on a mission and not easily deterred. I pursued Betty at every opportunity, and now and then Betty would agree to go on a date with me. I would have a wonderful time, but then she would turn me down for several months. She insisted that she didn't like the idea of anyone getting serious over her.

After we graduated, both Betty and I headed for New York City, where we hoped to achieve success in the theater. I called her as often as possible, and I was thrilled when she began to accept dates with me regularly. After a couple of months of steady dating, I gave her a beautiful antique engagement ring and begged her to marry me.

She said she wasn't ready. She needed time. She needed to wait.

"Wait for what!" I pressed her. "If you love me now, why can't we get married?"

I persisted in arguing my case over the next few weeks. And when Betty finally agreed to marry me, I was the happiest man in New York.

We decided to hold the ceremony in Betty's hometown, Marietta, Ohio. Betty was a Methodist, but I had grown up in both the Roman Catholic and the Greek Orthodox Church, so we hired two priests to perform the ceremony. It's not easy to get a Byzantine priest, but my family arranged for one to travel over one hundred miles to the ceremony. My mother also chartered a bus to carry our five hundred wedding guests to my hometown for our wedding reception.

The morning of our wedding, three hours before our flight was to leave New York for Ohio, I arrived at Betty's apartment. She met me at the door, saying solemnly, "Greg, I've got some bad news for you."

I couldn't imagine what was wrong. "Did someone die? What can be so terrible?" I asked. "This is our wedding day—the happiest day of our lives!"

"This *was* our wedding day, Greg," she said quietly. "I'm just not ready to get married. I'm sorry." Then Betty handed me back the beautiful antique engagement ring. As she closed the door in my face, my heart shattered into at least a million pieces. I pounded on her door, but she refused to answer.

Sick with grief, I made my way back to my empty apartment. Just last week I had moved what few possessions I had into Betty's apartment.

When I called my mother to tell her the news, she was understandably shocked and distraught. "What am I going to do?" she shrieked. "What about all these people? All these presents? What am I going to tell people?"

I hung up and wept for hours, asking myself the same questions. This was a lot more drama than any of us had bargained for. I had no idea what to do. I'd already given notice on my lease. For a few days I slept on the floor of my apartment, but when the new tenants arrived, I bunked with friends all over New York. I wished that I had not pushed her so hard into marrying me. Now I had lost her.

Shortly afterward I got a part in a musical revue in Puerto Rico. I left New York, but I took my sorrow—and Betty's engagement ring—with me. Then one day as I was walking on the beach, I realized it was time to give Betty up for good. I took the ring out of my pocket and hurled it into the sea.

Several months later when I returned to New York, I began dating other women again. By chance one night I ran into Betty, who seemed genuinely happy to see me. Understandably, I felt extremely guarded. This was the woman who had all but torn out my heart.

However, at her suggestion, I agreed to a chat about old times over late-night Chinese food. Betty confided how much she'd missed me. She had never wanted to lose me, she said. Now that she'd finally seen me again, she realized that she'd only needed space. And time. "Is there still hope?" she asked.

She looked up at me with those beautiful eyes, and I knew I still loved her. Maybe I was equally responsible for what had happened. In my vigorous quest for marriage, I hadn't been sensitive to her fears and doubts. And obviously, I should have given her more time to be sure.

That night Betty and I agreed to give our relationship another chance. Several months later it was she who proposed—and I who hesitated. Could I survive another fiasco at the altar? "What ifs" crowded my mind.

Finally, I knew I had no choice but to say yes. I still loved Betty.

She had adored her one-of-a-kind antique engagement ring and asked for it back. I had to confess I'd hurled it into the ocean. And since I couldn't afford another engagement ring, I placed a simple gold band on Betty's finger, promising I would one day find a very special engagement ring to replace the first one. But in the back of my mind I added, *If you make it to the wedding.*

Our second wedding plans were similar to the first—minus the Byzantine priest, who declined. I suppose he didn't want to risk driving a hundred miles for nothing again.

I made a point of not talking with Betty the day before the ceremony. No pressure this time. No demands. The night before our wedding day, I didn't sleep one minute. I simply couldn't escape the thought, *What if she gets cold feet again?*

The next day as I stood in the front of the church waiting for my bride, I could hardly breathe. Never had I experienced such a combination of dread and anticipation. Finally the organist began the familiar tune "Here Comes the Bride." And there she was, starting down the aisle toward me on the arm of her father, radiating joy.

This time she was ready.

As she walked toward me, I felt as I had the first time I'd seen her on stage in New York—and she stole my heart all over again. It was the dramatic performance I'd been waiting for. Watching her walk into my life for keeps, I was certain it had been worth it to be her biggest fan.

And, as promised, on our twenty-fifth anniversary I replaced her "lost" ring.

AUTHOR UNKNOWN

BRAVE ENOUGH

The happiest day of my life,
When, thanks to God, your low, sweet "Yes"
Made you my loving wife!

WILLIAM C. BENNETT

Joe was a tall, soft-spoken young man who seemed to walk right into my heart. But after dating him for almost three years, I began to wonder if he would ever propose. Every time his parents or one of our friends would mention marriage, Joe would blush and change the subject.

Joe's two grown sisters sympathized with my dilemma. "It's so obvious that Joe adores you!" they'd say. "But you know Joe. He's always been so shy. He probably doesn't have the courage to propose!"

They were right. I did know Joe. And one of the first things that had attracted me to him was the sweet way he would divert attention from himself. I admit I always had a weakness for the strong, silent type. I'd even been warned that sometimes the "strong" part is just in a woman's imagination. But I decided that there's nothing like love for finding out, one way or the other.

One night Joe invited my parents, my brother, and me to attend the Broadway play *Crazy for You* at the Fox Theater in Atlanta. Joe and I especially loved this venue, in part because it has a marvelous old-fashioned orchestra pit and organ.

That evening our group arrived a little early. So I wasn't at all surprised when Joe suggested the two of us walk down front to check out the action in the pit. But when we reached the front, suddenly—inexplicably—the orchestra began playing our favorite love song. I turned to Joe in confused delight, but he had dropped to his knees in front of me and everyone! He held out an open ring box displaying an exquisite engagement ring and said quite loudly, "Denise, will you marry me?"

I was so stunned that I simply stood there in a daze, speechless. As our song filled the theatre, the crowd began to notice our little drama. Joe's face was glowing bright red by now, and finally he said firmly, "Please, Denise—take the ring!"

I quickly accepted the ring and placed it on my left hand. Then Joe stood up to embrace me, and I started crying tears of happiness. The theatre audience burst out in applause and cheers of "Bravo! Bravo!" We made our way back to our seats, arm in arm, where my family congratulated us with hugs and good wishes.

As the real program got underway, I was still trying to take in what had happened. My quiet Joe had set this all up. This was the same man who never wanted to draw attention to himself. *My Joe overcame his shyness in a big way to make this the most special night of my life,* I thought as I kept gazing happily at him.

But Joe seemed to be back to his quiet self. He leaned over and said something softly in my ear.

"What did you say?" I asked.

"Denise, honey," Joe whispered, "you still haven't given me an answer."

In all the sweet pandemonium, it was I who had failed to declare my intentions. "Oh, yes, Joe!" I exclaimed. "I would love to be your wife!"

Joe and I were married the following Christmas. My husband is still a little shy at times. But I know Joe. And now I can also tell you that he's the bravest man in the world.

TOLD BY DENISE MCDOW HUEY

"IF IT FITS"

Love comforteth like sunshine after rain.

WILLIAM SHAKESPEARE

ohnny let out a whoop. "Billy, here's the girl I was telling you about," he said. "It's Ruth Bell."

I straightened up, and there she was. Standing there, looking right at me, was a slender, hazel-eyed movie starlet! I said something polite, but I was flustered and embarrassed. It took me a month to muster the courage to ask her out on a date.

The Christmas holidays were fast approaching, and the combined glee clubs were presenting Handel's *Messiah*. One day in the library in Blanchard Hall, I saw Ruth studying at one of the long tables. Johnny Streater and Howard Van Buren urged me to make my pitch to her right there. The expression of the librarian at the desk turned to a frown as we whispered among ourselves. Undaunted, I sauntered nonchalantly across to Ruth and scribbled my proposal for a date to the concert. To my surprise and delight, she agreed to go.

That Sunday afternoon was cold and snowy. With Ruth Bell sitting beside me in Pierce Chapel, I didn't pay much attention to the music. Afterward we walked over to the Lane house for a cup of tea, and we had a chance to talk. I could not believe anyone could be so spiritual and so beautiful at the same time.

Ruth told me later that she went back to her room, got on her knees, and told the Lord that if she could spend the rest of her life serving Him with me, she would consider it the greatest privilege imaginable. So why did she make it so hard for me to get her to say yes out loud?

If I had not been smitten with love at the first sight of Ruth Bell, I would certainly have been the exception. Many of the men at Wheaton thought she was stunning. Petite, vivacious, smart, talented, witty, stylish, amiable, and unattached. What more could a fellow ask for?

Two things I felt sure of: first, that Ruth was bound to get married someday; and second, that I was the man she would marry. Beyond that, I did not try to pressure her or persuade her—that is to say, not *overly* much. I let God do my courting for me.

But as the months went by, I asked her at least to consider me. It would not have been right to let her assume that what seemed to be my heroic understanding of her concerns was a lack of interest or expectation on my part. We had lots of discussions about our relationship. I wouldn't call them arguments exactly, but we certainly did not see eye to eye.

In the meantime, Ruth enjoyed the social life at Wheaton, as I did, with many friends. One day she went canoeing on the Fox River in St. Charles, about ten miles west of Wheaton, with classmates Harold Lindsell, Carl Henry, and Carl's fiancée, Helga. Somehow the canoe capsized, and Ruth went under. Since both men were staunch Baptists, I suspected them of wanting to immerse the pretty Presbyterian missionary kids from China.

Because I was already an ordained Baptist minister, our divided denominational allegiance was another topic of conversation between us. Ruth stuck to her convictions.

"We've both got such strong wills or minds or something, I almost despaired of ever having things go peacefully between us," she wrote to her parents, "but I wouldn't want him any other way, and I *can't* be any other way. But you know, it's remarkable how two strong minds (or wills) like that can gradually begin to sort of fuse together. Or maybe we're learning to give in and don't realize it."

I was making some adjustments, certainly. At the Lane house one evening, I was so busy talking at the supper table that I ate three helpings of macaroni and cheese before I woke up to the fact that I had told Ruth I hated macaroni and cheese. That incident encouraged her to hope she could feed me anything and get away with it!

One Sunday evening after church I walked into the parlor of the Gerstung home, where I was rooming, and collapsed into a chair. That dear professor of German and his wife, with three young boys of their own, were accustomed to my moods and always listened patiently. This time I bemoaned the fact that I did not stand a chance with Ruth. She was so superior to me in culture and poise. She did not talk as much as I did, so she seemed superior in her intelligence, too. "The reason I like Ruth so much," I wrote home to Mother, "is that she looks and reminds me of you."

By now I had directly proposed marriage to Ruth, and she was struggling with her decision. At the same time, she encouraged me to keep an open mind about the alternative of my going to the missionary field. She was coming to realize, though, that the Lord was not calling me in that direction.

One day I posed a question to Ruth point-blank: "Do you believe that God brought us together?"

She thought so, without question.

"In that case," I said, "God will lead me, and you'll do the following."

She did not say yes to my proposal right then and there, but I knew she was thinking it over.

While I was in Florida, preaching in Dr. Minder's church, I got a thick letter from Ruth postmarked July 6, 1941. One of the first sentences made me ecstatic, and I took off running. "I'll marry you," she wrote.

When I went back to my room, I read that letter over and over until church time. On page after page, Ruth explained how the Lord had worked in her heart, and she said she felt He wanted her to marry me. That night I got up to the pulpit and preached. When I finished and sat down, the pastor turned to me.

"Do you know what you just said?" he asked.

"No," I confessed.

"I'm not sure the people did either!"

After I went to bed, I switched my little lamp on and off all night, rereading that letter probably another dozen times.

At the close of a preaching series just after that at Sharon Presbyterian Church in Charlotte, those dear people gave me, as I recall, an offering of $165. I raced right out and spent almost all of it on an engagement ring with a diamond so big you could almost see it with a magnifying glass! I showed it off at home, announcing that I planned to present it to Ruth over in Montreat in the middle of the day. But daytime was not romantic enough, I was told.

Ruth was staying part of that summer at the cottage of Buck Currie and his wife, whom she called uncle and aunt, and their niece Gay. Buck was the brother of Ed Currie, one of Ruth's father's fellow missionaries in China. Their house on Craigmont Road in Black Mountain was built near a stream and had swings that went out over the water.

As I turned off the main road and drove toward the house, which was some distance off, I saw a strange creature walking down the road. She had long, straight hair sticking out all over, an awful-looking faded dress, bare feet, and what looked to be very few teeth. I passed her by, but when I suddenly realized it was Ruth playing a trick on me—her teeth blacked out so that she looked toothless—I slammed on the brakes. She got in, and we went on to the Currie house deep in the woods.

I had the ring with me.

We went up to what is now the Blue Ridge Parkway. The sun was sinking on one side of us and the moon rising on the other. I kissed Ruth on the lips for the first time. I thought it was romantic, but she thought, or so she told me later, that I was going to swallow her.

"I can't wear the ring until I get permission from my parents," she said apologetically.

They were away, so she sent them a telegram: "Bill has offered me a ring. May I wear it?"

"Yes," they wired back, "if it fits."

BILLY GRAHAM

From *Just As I Am* by Billy Graham. Copyright © 1997 by Billy Graham Evangelistic Association. Reprinted by permission of HarperCollins Publishers Inc.

If we had no winter,
the spring would not be so pleasant:
if we did not sometimes taste of adversity,
prosperity would not be so welcome.

ANNE BRADSTREET

I Thee Wed

IT BEGINS WITH A SQUARE ON A CALENDAR. A LINE IN A DATE BOOK.

A POINT IN TIME. A MONTH. A WEEK. A DAY. AN HOUR. A MOMENT.

AT AN APPOINTED TIME, IN AN APPOINTED PLACE, BEFORE CHOSEN WITNESSES, A CEREMONY BEGINS. IT MAY BE IN A CHURCH, WITH SPECTRUM LIGHT STREAMING THROUGH STAINED-GLASS WINDOWS. IT MIGHT BE IN A STERILE OFFICE, DEVOID OF TRAPPINGS, BEFORE A SLEEPY-EYED JUSTICE OF THE PEACE. IT MIGHT BE IN A GREEN FIELD UNDER A WIDE BLUE SKY, WITH BANNERS FLYING IN THE WIND.

FROM THIS DAY, THIS WEDDING DAY, LIFE CHANGES. FROM THIS DAY, SOMETHING NEW BEGINS. FROM THIS DAY, TWO PATHS MERGE INTO ONE. FROM THIS DAY, THE STATUS OF A MAN AND A WOMAN TRANSFORMS, UNTIL THE END OF THEIR DAYS.

A GIFT FROM THE SKIES

&

*A woman can never be too fine
while she is all in white.*

JANE AUSTEN

When the young American soldier named Grover was sent to Germany for duty after World War II, he found a country ravaged by the effects of war and without hope. Allied bombers had dropped millions of tons of explosives on the town where Grover was stationed. Buildings had been flattened. Businesses were still closed. People stood in line for hours simply to buy a piece of horse meat.

But Grover found something unforgettable in the rubble of war. He met and fell in love with Elfriede, a beautiful dark-haired, blue-eyed German girl. When Grover proposed to Elfriede, her friends and relatives were elated. Now one of their own would marry and go to America, the land of opportunity! She could start a new life away from all this destruction.

But her parents' joy was dimmed by the knowledge that they lacked resources for even a modest wedding. Both their family home and church had been reduced to ruins. There were no dress or fabric shops left—and anyway, they didn't have money for soap, much less a wedding gown.

News of the family's plight spread quickly through the little town. One day, two former German prison guards knocked at Elfriede's family's door and presented a mysterious package. In the meantime, the use of a small church, the only one left standing in town, was offered free of charge for the wedding.

When Elfriede walked down the aisle, guests gasped in surprise. The young bride was radiant in the most exquisite silk gown the townspeople had ever seen. Even her veil was stunning, artfully laced with flowers and sprigs of ivy. Where could such an elaborate ensemble have come from?

At the happy reception, they learned the truth. Elfriede's mother had sewn the wedding gown using the silk parachutes of American airmen whose bombers were shot down by the Germans. The guards who knocked on the door had recalled where the parachutes were hidden and had come to offer them to the bride. The time of war was over, they said. Now it was time for love.

Her mother then found an heirloom bridal veil hidden away in a relative's trunk. But it was torn and full of small holes, so she wove the sprigs of decoration through the rips—because greenery in a veil is traditionally a sign of hope for European brides.

Hope followed the young couple to America. Grover, a coal miner, took his bride back to the hills of Kentucky where they raised their family. Like Grover and Elfriede's love, the wedding gown sewn from parachutes endured through the years.

Fifty years later, their granddaughter—looking a lot like Elfriede did on her wedding day so long ago—plans to wear the same gown for her walk down the aisle. And another generation of family and friends was moved by this beautiful reminder that even after terrible devastation, love can spring up new again, as can goodness in the hearts of men.

ELFRIEDE SAMONS, AS TOLD TO PATRICIA WATSON

THE PERFECT WEDDING

I chose my wife as she did her wedding gown,
Not for a fine, glossy surface,
but such qualities as would wear well.

OLIVER GOLDSMITH

I could hardly believe my wedding day had finally arrived. Gazing around the church, I sighed with proud satisfaction over the fragrances of roses and lilies and the strains of soft music that floated sweetly throughout the sanctuary. Hundreds of perfectly arranged candles stood ready to be lit.

I felt like a princess in a fairy tale. Not only was I marrying the man of my dreams, I was going to have the kind of wedding I'd wanted since I was a little girl. During the preceding year, I'd spared no time or money as I planned every detail. I desperately wanted to please my husband-to-be, Doug. He was inviting friends and business associates from all over the country to share in our blessed occasion, and I wanted them to talk about this perfect wedding for years to come.

As it turned out, they did.

The wedding was scheduled to begin at seven o'clock. As soon as my mother was seated, it was time for me to take my long-anticipated walk down the aisle. My big moment. But instead of making my grand entrance, I was back in the dressing room with my mouth hanging open. My bridesmaid had just informed me—very gently—that the minister was still "expected."

"Expected?" I almost shrieked. "He certainly is *expected!* You mean he's not here?"

"Well, yes—I mean, no, he's not," she continued. They hadn't wanted to upset me, she explained, so they'd waited until the last minute to let me know.

There was nothing to do but wait. As the guests began to grow restless, turning around looking toward the back of the church, my father decided to walk down the aisle—alone. From the back we could hear the wave of alarm rippling through the waiting crowd.

"Thank you for sharing this joyous occasion with us today," my father announced. "We are so sorry for the delay. Our minister from another state has just called to say that he took a wrong turn, but we expect him to be here within the hour. Two of the ushers have volunteered to meet and motorcade the lost minister to the church. In the meantime, is there a doctor—uh, I mean minister—in the house?"

A few doctors raised their hands but no minister.

Hours passed. People came and went. Children napped in the pews. Candles burned. I cried.

Finally at ten o'clock, three hours late, a flustered and embarrassed minister flanked by two ushers rushed into the church. The minister apologized profusely to the restless and famished crowd.

By now my picture-perfect wedding had turned into a huge fiasco. The hundreds of candles had burned to waxy nubs. Some guests had ducked out; many others looked like they should have. And the musicians were nowhere to be found.

Miraculously, Doug didn't seem the least bit embarrassed.

"Let's get married," my fiancé said, loud enough for everyone to hear. "I'm starving!"

That helped the audience get into the spirit of things. "Why doesn't the crowd just hum the wedding march?" someone suggested.

And so, with my dress a little wrinkled, my hair a little mussed, and my makeup a bit smeared, I finally walked down the aisle to a most unusual rendition of the wedding march. The minister performed the shortest wedding ceremony of his career, forgetting the special vows we'd written to each other. The wedding feast followed at the club next door, but most of the waiters had taken off, and the food was cold. Fortunately, the guests were so famished from sitting through the longest wedding of their lives, they overlooked the poor service and cold food.

At two in the morning, I tossed my bouquet to the faithful few who had endured the marathon. "At least we'll have lots of nice pictures," my mother reassured me as Doug and I made our getaway. That much would be true—the photographer had been there for hours by then, taking hundreds of pictures of everyone and everything.

Just before we were ready to depart, Doug drew me aside and whispered in my ear the most wonderful words I've ever heard. "I am so proud of you," he said. "How many brides could so gracefully endure such disappointment?"

When the photographer called a few days later to say his camera had malfunctioned and there would be no pictures, I managed to laugh as much as I cried. But I did get my wish. Doug's friends still talk about the wedding.

In the years since then, I've realized that my wedding day disaster was actually a gift. It helps me to remember that the real purpose of my wedding wasn't a picture-perfect ceremony. It was about a miracle invisible to the human eye—"And the two shall become one flesh." And that's as perfect as it gets.

DEE DEE MOORE

APACHE WEDDING
BLESSING

Now you will feel no rain,
For each of you will be shelter to the other.
Now you will feel no cold,
For each of you will be warmth to the other.
Now there is no loneliness for you,
For you are two persons, but there is one life before you.
Go now to your dwelling place
To enter into the days of your togetherness,
And may your days be good and long upon the earth.

A WEDDING AT THANKSGIVING

✑

Ah, love, let us be true to one another!
For the world, which seems
To lie before us like a land of dreams,
So various, so beautiful, so new...

MATTHEW ARNOLD

Our family calls it "the Thanksgiving when love showed up on our doorstep."

It was about three-thirty on a Thanksgiving afternoon. Our families were relaxing at my parents' home in rural South Carolina, following a wonderful meal, when the doorbell rang. My father, Marshall Williams, a state senator, attorney, and notary public, got up from his comfortable chair to answer the door.

"Senator, I'm sorry to bother you," a round-faced, early-fortyish man said, "but I was told that you would marry us." His bride-to-be blinked up wide-eyed at Daddy.

"You mean now—on Thanksgiving Day?" Daddy asked.

"Yes, sir, I do. If you don't mind, I mean," the man replied.

"Do you have a marriage license?"

"Yes, I do," he replied.

"Well, I'm happy to do this wedding." Daddy gestured to the couple to come into the house. "But may I say," he added, smiling, "that you have no idea what you are getting into." Most certainly, the two wedding candidates took him to mean marriage, but he did not, as you will see.

Charles, my brother and my father's law partner, was the man's attorney, we learned. The couple had first gone to Charles's house to see if he would perform the wedding, but Charles and a group of his friends were in his front yard suited up in camouflage to go hunting. Charles had begged off, and since in South Carolina a notary public can perform marriages, Charles had directed him instead to my parents' house a few hundred yards up the road.

"You'll get a better wedding up there at Daddy's house anyway," Charles had told him. "And if Mother is home, she'll throw in a reception to boot."

Now my parents stood in our living room, surrounded by their children and grandchildren, looking kindly upon the two nervous lovers. Mother turned to my older brother, Burns, who was watching a football game on television. "Burns," Mother said calmly, "let's straighten up the room a little because we are about to have a wedding."

"Wedding?" My sister Mary Ashley and I had the same reaction. "Goodness," I said with a laugh. "With all the weddings we've had in our family, a trip to the cedar-lined closet would outfit the bride."

The bride had appeared at the house wearing slacks, a knit blouse, and sandals. She didn't know it would be impossible for us to let her marry in such an outfit. In fact, my sister-in-law Karen had already been sizing up the blushing bride. "My mother just gave me her wedding dress," she offered, "and I believe that the dress is the bride's size! I'll go get it." She left to go to her house.

Mary Ashley said, "Let's go look at the wedding veil inventory to see what we could use." Off she and I went to fetch a suitable veil from the cedar-lined closet.

The round-faced man looked like a rabbit caught in the headlights. Or maybe he was just happy. All he and his fiancée could do was watch.

We led the bride to the guest room, where Mary Ashley tipped her face up and started applying makeup. "Honey, you're going to be lovely," she crooned as she worked.

Meanwhile Karen had returned with the dress, and she and Danielle, Burns's wife, set about mending and pressing the bridal gown. I went out in the garden to pick white camellias and cut ivy and greenery for a bridal bouquet. And Daddy was on the telephone with a local judge writing down the marriage ceremony so the vows would be legal and correct.

In a few minutes Mother announced, "When your father gets off the telephone, the wedding will begin."

Mary Ashley asked Mother to kindly get us a strand of pearls, some pearl earrings, pantyhose, and off-white evening shoes—in a size seven and a half if possible—which she happily did because it was Mother's shoe size!

When I was done with the bouquet, I set about to fix the bride's full head of hair into an old-fashioned Gibson look. Then I secured the Brussels-lace veil in place. Danielle painted the bride's fingernails a soft blush color as Mary Ashley sprayed her with a floral perfume, which made her sneeze.

And then we were ready for the wedding dress. The fit was...perfect!

My mother had called Karen's mother to tell her they had left too soon after lunch, because we were only minutes away from a lovely Thanksgiving wedding. When she inquired who the bride was, Mother said, "I don't know her name, but she is wearing your dress."

Mother invited Karen's mother and her husband to come back and bring some rice with them because she had cooked all of hers for the Thanksgiving meal. All she had left was grits. "We don't want to throw grits at the bride," Mother said. "But hurry. When Marshall gets off the phone, we'll start the ceremony."

About thirty minutes had transpired since the couple had knocked on our door. We took "our bride" upstairs so she could descend the stairway to the wedding march. Although quiet, she looked excited, happy, and sweetly alarmed.

Moments later, the music started. All the guests—our family, young and old—hummed the wedding march. Burns gave the bride away, which suited him fine because he didn't know her. Mother was the "mother of the bride" with a camellia corsage pinned on her jacket. All four of us daughters were bridesmaids, holding camellias from the garden, and all the granddaughters—four of them as well—were flower girls, sprinkling camellia petals in the bride's pathway.

Daddy performed an impressive ceremony in the finest Southern tradition. The bride cried tears of joy, and the groom's chest swelled in my father's coat. We were relieved to find out later that he had been thoroughly instructed by my mother in a marriage counseling session in the kitchen.

While we took pictures of the wedding party, the grandchildren decorated the groom's car with shaving cream and tin cans. As the bride and groom were about to leave, the grandchildren passed out handfuls of rice, followed by Daddy walking through the house with a broom in his hand. "I don't want anybody falling down on that rice," he said with lawyerly concern, "but it's a wedding, and I guess you have to throw it."

"Yes," we all said in unison. As we began to throw, he began to sweep.

We stood on the front porch waving good-bye to the newlyweds, the sound of rattling tin cans delighting the grandchildren.

A sudden stillness descended on our home.

"Well, now," Mother said, pausing. "That was a lovely wedding for thirty minutes, I do believe."

Mary Ashley looked around the room. "Did any of you think to ask the bride if she wanted us to fix her up in her wedding attire?"

"No!" everyone said in unison. Then we all burst out laughing. In fact, we could hardly recall anything the bride had said except "I do." Perhaps we had been a little too busy creating our Thanksgiving wedding to find out if the bride and groom even wanted it.

We were left wondering for about eighteen months. Then Daddy told us the couple had given birth to a son, whom they named Marshall—for him. And not long afterward, they appeared in my father's law office with a request. Would Daddy and Mother please be godparents to their son?

Daddy reacted sensibly. "Well, we probably don't have much time to do things for him," he said.

But Mother was thrilled. "That's the point, Marshall," she said. "Our

Thanksgiving couple isn't trying to *get* anything from us. They're trying to give back something precious from their hearts."

That's when we knew our Thanksgiving wedding had turned out to be the celebration we'd all hoped for. And that a family's love can—without notice—sweep even strangers into its wide embrace and leave everyone with stories to tell over turkey dinner for years to come.

ANN PLATZ

*Love is an irresistible desire
to be irresistibly desired.*

ROBERT FROST

GET ME TO THE CHURCH ON TIME!

God give us grace to accept with serenity
The things that cannot be changed,
Courage to change the things which should be changed,
And the wisdom to distinguish the one from the other.

REINHOLD NIEBUHR

My husband and I were thrilled when our youngest son, Brad, and his girlfriend, Anne, announced they were going to be married. But as the wedding plans got underway, I became nervous. Our family is from a small town outside of Los Angeles, but Anne comes from a very cosmopolitan family, many of whom are involved in the Hollywood entertainment industry.

How would our family handle a big-city, society wedding?

I wish I could say it came off without a hitch.

The last thing I worried about was Brad. He's a beautifully mannered, intelligent, prompt, reliable, and kind young man. And he was all smiles at brunch on the morning of his wedding day. The sun shone brightly, and the young couple radiated happiness. I was relieved. Everything seemed to be going perfectly.

Later that evening family members and wedding attendants began arriving at the church. Although it was still two hours before the wedding ceremony, I looked around for Brad but was told that he and Jeff, Anne's brother and the one who was to shuttle Brad to the church, hadn't arrived yet.

After making some further preparations, I glanced nervously at my watch. Now it was only an hour to the ceremony. Where was the groom?

Finally Jeff came rushing in. "Where's Brad?" I blurted.

Jeff looked surprised—and my heart sank. "He's not here?" he asked anxiously. "I had to run a couple of errands, so I gave him the keys to my car. He should have been here long ago."

Upon hearing this news, the bride burst into tears. Jeff quickly organized a search party of friends. Minutes ticked away. Jeff returned to tell us that he had found his car with the alarm malfunctioning. "Brad must have called a cab," he assured us.

The time to start the wedding arrived. But instead of filing into the church, Anne's family invited everyone into the church's courtyard. The minister brought out coffee, and an assistant found some juice in the preschoolers' refrigerator. We stood around giggling anxiously, trying to be polite. I was sure by now that our family had failed every social test Anne's family could possibly imagine. These were important people with better things to do than wait for a missing bridegroom. It was a mother's wedding-day nightmare come true.

Another hour passed, and still no Brad. By now giggles had turned to sobs. I went to the bride's side to hold her hand and dry her tears, but truthfully I wasn't in much better shape myself. Everyone reassured Anne that Brad hadn't changed his mind, which left only one other possibility. Something terrible must have happened.

And it had, as Brad explained later...

When Brad was ready to leave for the church, he went out to get into Jeff's car. An elaborate alarm system promptly went off. Brad tried to shut down the alarm but couldn't. Because the alarm was engaged, the car wouldn't start.

Lucky for Brad, he had his AAA card. He called for help, and eventually the road-service man arrived. While the repairman fooled around with the alarm, Brad wondered if he should call someone. Precious minutes ticked by. He had to get from his future brother-in-law's house to the church.

Brad went inside to call Jeff on his car phone but discovered the phone was out of range. He then dialed the church, only to be greeted by a recording.

Time had nearly run out. Brad was supposed to be standing at the front of the church, not in someone's kitchen. And it was clear by now that the AAA man was having no luck starting the car.

Brad knew he had to act quickly. Then he remembered there was a housekeeper on duty in the house. Surely she could give him a ride. When Brad located the housekeeper in the kitchen, he unfortunately discovered that she didn't speak English, and Brad spoke no Japanese. He explained his dilemma as best he could using sign language and talking very, very slowly. "Could...you...give...me...a...ride?" he intoned.

She nodded her head in agreement.

"Thank...you!...Let's go!"

But she only stood there looking puzzled.

In desperation, Brad resorted to leading her by the hand out to the car. She kept smiling. Seeing that the keys were in the ignition, he took them out and asked her, "May...I...borrow...your...car?"

She smiled again and nodded. In a flash, Brad hopped into the car and sped away as the housekeeper waved good-bye.

Brad was only a few miles from the church when he heard the sirens. Two unsmiling cops pulled him over. At first they wouldn't even tell him why they had stopped him. In spite of the fact that he was wearing a tuxedo, Brad was unable to convince the cops he was late for a wedding—his own!

The policemen demanded to see the car's registration, but it was nowhere to be found. When Brad insisted it was the housekeeper's car, matters got even more serious. Within minutes, the officers had Brad in the backseat of their squad car and were whizzing him off to headquarters.

Two hours after the ceremony was supposed to begin, Anne's parents finally gave up. The minister and all the guests should leave—there'd be no wedding today. But before they could make the announcement, two police cars, sirens wailing and lights flashing, came racing up to the church, and out jumped Brad.

"I'll explain later," he said. "Right now, I want to get married!"

So instead of sending guests home, Anne's parents invited them back into the church. The guests took their places, and step by step, note by note, vow by vow, a beautiful wedding proceeded as planned—except for being two hours behind schedule.

At the reception everyone wanted to hear Brad's story. He explained that after Jeff's car wouldn't start, he borrowed a car, which turned out to be the gardener's, not the housekeeper's. When the gardener saw Brad drive away in his car, he immediately called the police to report that a stranger in a tuxedo had stolen his car. At the police station it took considerable time and detective work before the mystery was solved. Finally the sympathetic cops gave the bridegroom a high-speed ride to his own wedding.

So you see, the wedding didn't quite go off without a hitch. But it was the beginning of a great friendship with Anne's family. Standing around the church courtyard that evening, sharing laughter and tears, worries and reassurances, was good preparation for being in-laws. Soon my concerns about social differences melted away.

These days, our families often get together for trips and events surrounding our children—and now, our grandchildren. But whenever a family wedding comes around, we always arrange for several back-up people to transport the groom—just in case.

IT'S NEVER TOO LATE

Grow old along with me!
The best is yet to be,
The last of life, for which the first was made,
Our times are in his hand.

ROBERT BROWNING

t is not good for man to be alone," the Scriptures say, but there are men and women who are called to singleness. Mother Teresa and Corrie ten Boom are fine examples of women called to serve. Another was the pretty and brilliant doctor, Margaret Jones, who grew up in a Quaker family in Maine. Margaret became a doctor in the 1920s when few women chose the medical profession. She attended Radcliffe, Yale, Cornell, and Harvard—quite an accomplishment, especially for a woman in that era.

After a disappointing romance, Margaret decided to dedicate her life to researching and treating cerebral palsy patients. She could have had her pick of eligible young men, but she chose instead to focus on her patients. Dr. Jones became world renowned for providing preschool education for children born with this affliction, enabling them to function at a much higher level. Her appreciative patients and their parents still visit her today.

Following her retirement, Dr. Jones continued her affiliation with UCLA, her travels, her hiking, and her work with young people in her church and community. She settled into what she thought would be a routine retirement. Little did she know what was about to happen to her in her golden years!

It all began when a new youth pastor, Jonathan, came to her church in Pacific Palisades. With her strong love for young people, Margaret graciously offered the young pastor room and board. When Jonathan moved into her home, he was amazed by Margaret's fine mind and her athletic abilities. In her eighties, she was still hiking and traveling all over the world, appearing to have more energy than someone half her age.

Later Jonathan met a widower and retired physician, Dr. Adrian Kanaar, in his church study group, and he was suddenly inspired. At age seventy-three, Dr. Kanaar had earned a place in the *Guinness Book of Records* for being the oldest gentleman ever to swim around Manhattan Island. He also had a passion for traveling. Now in his eighties, Dr. Kanaar would be the perfect match for Dr. Jones! This was a match made in heaven if the young pastor had ever seen one.

As soon as Dr. Kanaar was introduced to Margaret, he agreed with Jonathan. Dr. Kanaar began seeing Margaret on a regular basis. Something stirred deep in their hearts and souls. One evening as they were sitting at her dining room table, they exchanged a look that said it all. "It was just a look," Margaret explained, "but we both knew at that very moment that we were in love."

Margaret felt like a giddy schoolgirl. She considered her situation. After all, she was eighty-three years old. Should she consider marriage—if Adrian proposed? How fun it would be to have such a wonderful companion in her life and in her travels, she thought. Margaret had led a full and exciting life and was always one to take advantage of new experiences. She decided that she shouldn't miss the experience of marriage either, especially to someone as wonderful as Dr. Kanaar.

At the same time, Dr. Kanaar was busily planning his proposal. Wanting it to be very special, he enlisted the help of his family. His lovely daughter-in-law helped him pick out the ring, and they planned a beautiful dinner party for the family just before Christmas. Margaret was invited to join them.

Every family member took part in making the evening special. They brought out the candles, the china, and all the special touches. It would be an evening that no one would forget!

When the big night arrived, while everyone was seated at the table, Dr. Kanaar pulled out the beautiful ring and asked Margaret to be his wife. Without any hesitation, she uttered a resounding "Yes!"

Since Margaret had never had a wedding before, she approached it like any other bride. She selected flowers and music and had someone design her wedding attire, a long beautiful white silk gown and veil. The couple enjoyed parties, showers, and all the typical festivities. Dr. Jones was delighted when her women friends surprised her with a lingerie shower for her honeymoon.

Margaret's long-awaited wedding day finally arrived. A bride for the first time at age eighty-four. Margaret was radiant in her beautiful white gown and veil as she walked down the aisle on the arm of her brother, surrounded by an overflowing church of friends and family. When she looked into her bridegroom's eyes, she thought that Dr. Kanaar was the most handsome groom who ever stood at the altar. And no one was surprised that the young-hearted lovers were married by their matchmaker, Jonathan.

The couple shared four wonderful years of travel and companionship before Dr. Kanaar's death. "I've never known such happiness as in those four years," Margaret says. Her grief was lessened by the love and the family that Dr. Kanaar had brought into her life.

Today, still active and young-at-heart in her nineties, Dr. Jones-Kanaar will be the first to tell you, "It's never too late for love!"

From an interview with Dr. Margaret Jones-Kanaar. Used by permission.

To Have and to Hold

A HUSBAND AND WIFE MUST HAVE EACH OTHER...AND NOT IN A PHYSICAL SENSE ALONE.

WHEN THE REST OF THE WORLD IS AGAINST HIM, WHEN HIS FRIENDS TURN AWAY, WHEN HIS BOLD ENTERPRISES AND DREAMS FALL INTO THE DUST, A MAN MUST KNOW THAT HE HAS HIS WIFE. SHE IS THERE. SHE IS WITH HIM. SHE IS FOR HIM. SHE IS HIS.

WHEN A WOMAN'S HEART IS HEAVY WITH SORROW, WHEN HER CONFIDENCE EBBS, WHEN DOUBTS AND FEARS FILL HER THOUGHTS, ROBBING SLEEP FROM HER EYES, SHE MUST KNOW THAT SHE HAS HER HUSBAND. HER MAN. HER PRO-TECTOR. HER CHAMPION. HER LOVER AND FRIEND.

IT CAN BE A LONELY WORLD, AN INDIFFERENT, UNCARING WORLD, A WORLD WITH A HARD EDGE. YET WHEN A MAN HOLDS A WOMAN, AND A WOMAN HOLDS A MAN, THERE IS WARMTH, GREAT COMFORT, AND A DEEP SENSE OF RIGHTNESS.

NOTHING IS IMPOSSIBLE

Let those love now who never loved before;
Let those who always loved, now love the more.

THOMAS PARNELL

oor Virginia, she'll never get a husband with those four little children to raise," I heard my friends whisper more than once. After I lost my husband, the last thing on my mind was finding a new husband, but I was desperately praying for a job to support my children.

By the time Christmas rolled around, I was broke, had no job offers in sight, and was trying to raise four children under the age of ten on my own. I tried to keep up hope, but I had been asking God, *What will happen to us if I don't get help soon?*

My parents insisted we come to spend the holidays with them, and they paid for our airline tickets. Back in my hometown, I felt comforted by my family, but also smothered by the pity I was receiving from friends.

One day, as I was doing some grocery shopping for my mother, I turned into the produce aisle and found my sister racing toward me. "Guess who just phoned?" she panted. "John Lloyd! He heard you were in town."

I didn't know what to think. John and I had been high school sweethearts and continued to write for a time from our different colleges, but after a while the distance became too much for our relationship. We were sad to break up but remained friends. Years went by without seeing each other. We both dated others during college; then after graduation John accepted a job offer and I got married.

Although my parents told me that John visited them from time to time, I was happily married and didn't think about him. My father told me John had become a successful international businessman, and I was glad for him since I knew that had been his dream. My dream of becoming a wife and mother had also come true—until I lost my husband.

On Christmas Eve, my mother, my sister, and I were preparing dinner when we heard a knock at the door. When we peeked out the window, who was standing there but John Lloyd! I thought he might visit, but I hadn't expected him to arrive unannounced. My sister told me she'd stall him while I rushed upstairs to try to erase ten years from my face.

When I made my grand entrance, John and I stood staring at each other until I gave my chatty sister the signal to leave. Then John wasted no time. He walked toward me, swept me off my feet, and kissed me.

"I've never recovered from our breakup," he confessed, looking into my eyes. "I was crazy to let you get away! Virginia, I promise to love and care for you forever. Will you marry me?"

My heart melted. How could I say no?

When I told my sister later, she shrieked, "You're going to do what?"

"You heard me. John and I are going to get married."

"Have you lost your mind? You haven't seen one another in over ten years; you hardly know him anymore."

"What will people say?" Mother interjected.

"I thought you'd be happy for me," I said. "You've always loved John."

"Does he know you have four children?" my sister said pointedly.

Those words jolted me back to reality. Yes, John knew about the children, but he hadn't met them. And there were other concerns, such as the fact that I had become a Christian since John had known me before.

When he returned that evening, I tearfully explained to him about the children and about my faith. I told him I couldn't accept his proposal until we got to know each other better.

"But you've known me forever," he protested.

"I'm not the same person you knew before," I said. "God has changed my life." I shared with him my concern about his spiritual life.

For a moment John was silent, and then he said, "I haven't set foot inside a church since my teenage years, but if you'll wait for me, Virginia, I'll make every effort to find what you have."

John took his assignment seriously. He bought a Bible and a stack of theology books, attended church, and had regular discussions with a minister. It wasn't easy and it didn't happen overnight, but when John became a Christian his faith was strong and sincere.

And I knew that finally we could get married.

So, after all those years, that's how we came to be married. Our marriage was a testimony to all those friends who were convinced I'd never "get a husband," showing them that with God, nothing is impossible.

TOLD BY VIRGINIA LLOYD TO CHARLOTTE HALE

THE PRINCESS AND
THE ANGEL

God's in his heaven—
All's right with the world!

ROBERT BROWNING

As I was growing up, my family jokingly referred to me as "princess." I had to admit there was some truth in the name my family had given me. I wasn't terribly spoiled, but things always seemed to go my way. In the romantic realm, I always got the guy. I grew up with the false notion that whatever the princess wants the princess gets.

When I graduated from college, no one was surprised that I, the homecoming queen, married the football hero, who also happened to be the student body president. When our children were born, they, too, seemed to fit perfectly into our fairy tale—blond-haired, blue-eyed adorable kids. Life was good!

As the children grew older, my mother became concerned that God was missing from our lives. I had drifted away from church during college. "God!" I exclaimed to her. "We don't need God! It's the people who have problems that need God in their lives—certainly not us." Oh, Don and I believed in Him, but it was much more fun to spend our Sunday mornings playing golf or tennis, going to the beach, or sleeping in on weekends away. I brushed my mother off, assuring her that "Nobody goes to church anymore. Church is for religious fanatics or older people like you and Dad."

She managed to squeeze in one last sentence: "The day will come when you need God—everyone does sooner or later." Her words haunted me over the next few years, but I ignored those unwelcome thoughts.

Late one afternoon my husband and I were driving down Pacific Coast Highway to meet some friends at a restaurant for dinner. Suddenly there was a loud grinding crash, and I was pinned in the car and covered in blood. As I tried to lift my head, I noticed my husband was not beside me. Several Good Samaritans came to my rescue, including a young man dressed in a uniform who held my hand. I was shocked to hear his words. He was praying for me! I still recall his face. Not a handsome face like my husband's, but a kind face filled with compassion and love. As he attended to my wounds, he also kept me calm until the ambulance arrived. I felt safe in this stranger's hands.

When I awoke from surgery in the hospital, I learned that my husband had died in the accident. I was flooded with all the emotions that accompany tragedy—profound sadness, then denial, anger, guilt, and finally acceptance. My mother had been right. At some time in our lives, we realize we do need God, and did I ever need Him now! My fairy tale life was over.

As I grew spiritually, I wanted to make amends for all the years I'd lost. It suddenly became very important to me to thank the man in the uniform who had helped me through my darkest hour. I assumed the Good Samaritan in my life was a fireman or a policeman, so I began searching throughout the community. But too much time had passed, and no one at the police or fire departments recalled a stranger fitting that description. Finally I gave up. A woman at my church surprised me one day when she confided that she suspected my Good Samaritan was actually an angel sent by God. Wow! Did I feel special. I shared my miraculous story at church one Sunday, and someone even suggested I submit it to a popular inspirational magazine.

I began seeking God as never before. It's not easy being a widow at any age, but as many single parents will attest, it's particularly difficult raising children alone. So I prayed that God would bring me a husband and that all my problems would disappear. After all, He had sent an angel. He could easily send a husband!

However, it wasn't God's timing. I dated, and as the saying goes, "I kissed a lot of frogs," but not one of them turned into Prince Charming. When my fortieth birthday came and went, I struggled with feelings of deep self-pity.

On the morning of the tenth anniversary of Don's death, I found myself alone at the beach. I couldn't walk any further I was so overwhelmed with grief, loneliness, and self-pity. I walked down to the edge of the water and then collapsed on the beach, sobbing for what seemed like hours.

Suddenly I felt a firm hand on my shoulder. Startled, I lifted my head and looked into the eyes of the same kind stranger who had been there for me at the accident! I had found him—God had sent my angel back to encourage me!

"Is there someone I could call for you, ma'am?" he asked, snapping me out of my stupor.

"You're not an angel!" I cried.

"No, ma'am, I'm not. I'm a lifeguard, but I'm here to help you."

"You don't remember me, do you?" I asked.

"No, ma'am, I'm sorry. I don't," he replied.

I began to explain how he had helped me ten years before. Still, not a trace of recognition flashed across his face.

I kept babbling until he finally said, "I'm sorry, ma'am. There are a lot of serious accidents on this stretch of highway—I've helped hundreds of people." Still not sure that I wasn't a nut case, he insisted that I accompany him to the lifeguard station for coffee.

The coffee led to lunch and then to frequent visits to the lifeguard station on my daily walks until the lifeguard, Bill, and I got to know one another very well. We discovered that we not only shared our faith but other interests and values. My children absolutely adored him. Before we knew it, the lifeguard had fallen in love with the sobbing lady in the sand. A couple of years later, Bill and I were married on the beach. God didn't bring me a heavenly angel, but he brought me an angel on earth—a husband to have and to hold forever. Our marriage hasn't been a fairy tale, but through our faith and love for God, it's been something much deeper and more profound.

AUTHOR UNKNOWN

LITTLE RED BOOTS

Remember the Red River Valley
And the Cowboy that loves you so true.

AUTHOR UNKNOWN

ecently, when my daughter, Tate, turned five, I gave her a pair of red cowboy boots that had been mine when I was a little girl. I'd been saving them in a box until Tate was big enough to wear them. As soon as she saw the boots, Tate's eyes grew large, and she let out a whoop. "My first real pair of cowboy boots!"

As Tate pulled on the little red boots and began to dance around the room, I smiled to myself. Had I ever really been that young? Yes, I had. And the reason I'd saved those boots all of my life was only partly because they were my first pair of real cowgirl boots. The other reason was that the first time I ever wore them I made a special friend who happened to be a boy.

He'd been an older man—I was five and he was seven. I met him one day while he and his dad were visiting my grandfather's farm. I had just got my new boots and was sitting on the top fence rail as Grandfather saddled my pony. I was trying very hard not to get my shiny new red boots dirty when this boy from the city came over to say hello. He smiled at me and told me he liked my red boots. In response, I offered to let him ride my pony. I'd never let *anyone* ride my pony!

Later that year, my grandfather sold the farm, and I never saw the young man again. But every time I put on those red cowgirl boots, the memory of that sweet afternoon and the small crush I had on the older boy from the city came rushing back. When I outgrew them, I couldn't bear to part with them, and so my mother packed them away. And then recently, so many years later, I came across the boots again while I was cleaning the garage in preparation for a yard sale and realized they'd fit Tate.

Now, her laughter turned to squeals as my husband, Marty, scooped up his giggling daughter and danced her around the room. "I do like your new cowgirl boots, baby," he said. "They remind me of the day I had my very first ride on a horse. I wasn't much older than you are."

"Is this a true story, Daddy? Or a make-believe one?" Tate loved to listen to her daddy tell stories about when he was a little boy. "Does it have a happy ending?"

As Tate begged him to tell her about his first ride, I realized that even though my husband is a team roper in professional rodeos, I'd never heard this story. "Tell us, honey," I encouraged him. "When was your first time on a horse?"

Marty smiled at our enthusiasm as he sat down in the big, comfortable recliner. Tate climbed up into his lap.

"Well, actually it was a pony," he began. "Once upon a time when I was seven years old, I lived in a big city called St. Louis. That's in Missouri. I wanted a horse more than anything in the world, but we couldn't have one in the city. I told my dad that I wanted to be a real cowboy when I grew up, so that summer he took me to a friend's farm not very far from here. It was a beautiful sunny day. There was a little girl there, who had boots just like these. I'd been warned that she never let anyone else ride her pony. But for some reason, she let me, and it was my very first time."

I listened in stunned surprise. After asking Marty several more questions about the farm's location, we confirmed that it was true. We'd met when I was five and he was seven. I had been the little girl with the red boots in his childhood. He'd been the city-boy crush in mine.

Neither of us had ever forgotten that magical afternoon, or each other. And as we looked at our daughter sitting on her daddy's lap in those same little red cowboy boots, we both agreed. The story has a happier ending than we ever could have imagined.

JEANNIE S. WILLIAMS,
AS TOLD BY HER DAUGHTER AND GRANDDAUGHTER

The First Time

Each time we kiss, it's the first time
Like it never happened before.
The thrill of your touch
Means so much
As a million and one times ago.

You come to me, it's the first time
Like your heart just opened its door.
Our love is all new, I'm with you
Like it never has happened before.
In your eyes is the first surprise
That love could be like this,
Forever new, this me with you,
This touch, this love, this kiss.

Each time with us, it's the first time
This is ours forever to know.
No less time can be, you're with me.
Our good-byes will always and always and always
Be hello—hello!

KATE ORME DICKINSON EFURD

ENDURING LOVE

&

This is the very ecstasy of love.

WILLIAM SHAKESPEARE

velyn was not home when Joe called, but her answering machine took the message. When she returned and saw the blinking red light, she put down her purse and listened to the raspy but wonderfully familiar voice.

She hadn't heard that voice for fifty-seven years.

"This is your old friend Joe calling," the message said. "I'm sorry I missed you, but would you please call me collect when you get this message?"

Years rolled away for Evelyn. A whole lifetime. She and Joe had been sweethearts when World War II set them off on separate paths. In the decades since, they'd lost touch, married, raised families, and pursued and retired from careers. Now Evelyn was a widow living in Savannah, Georgia, a long way from their home state of Michigan.

Wondering what was in store, Evelyn returned the phone call. Both were nervous as teenagers on a first date, but they had a lot of news to catch up on. Joe told her that he, too, had been alone for several years.

"How in the world did you track me down?" she wanted to know. Joe confessed that since 1962 he'd held on to a copy of Evelyn's mother's obituary from the Ann Arbor newspaper. According to that, Evelyn lived in

Georgia. Then Joe explained that he had been an engineer with Michigan Bell for forty years. "Let's just say I still have connections in the phone business," he explained with a chuckle.

After that, Joe called almost every night. She and Joe reminisced about earlier times. They wrote to each other daily. And very soon, a romance was blossoming again.

Two months later Joe came from Michigan for a visit. Nervousness about how they would look to each other soon melted. "The minute I saw him I remembered our youth together," Evelyn recalls. "Nothing important had changed." The two spent hours going for walks on the beach, holding hands, and enjoying a warm relationship.

After two more trips south, Joe proposed to Evelyn—over the telephone, of course. "Evelyn, after all these years I think it is time for us to get married," he declared confidently.

Evelyn agreed.

On his next visit to Savannah, Joe, seventy-eight, took Evelyn, seventy-six, to a restaurant in the historic area on the river and presented her with an engagement ring. Shortly thereafter, they were married at St. Andrews Episcopal Church, Ann Arbor, Michigan, with their families in attendance. They honeymooned on a Hawaiian cruise. These days, Joe and Evelyn live in Savannah in the winter and Michigan in the summer.

"Our love story appeared in the *Savannah Morning News* on Valentine's Day," recalls Evelyn happily. "And we've received hundreds of cards and calls from both friends and strangers wishing us well. It has touched both of us that total strangers would find our love story to be an inspiration," Evelyn says. "It's more than just the miracle that we found each other after all these years. People know that a love that can be reborn after fifty-seven years is very special—a deep mystery."

Joe explains it in terms of phone lines. Once you've established a good connection, he says, you can hear and see the other person almost as if they're right next to you. No matter the time or distance.

So just put in your call, Joe advises, and let love bring you together.

EVELYN AND JOSEPH DEFORS

IT PAYS TO ADVERTISE

In my loving way, I am molding two hearts.
If they will only wait for Me in my special time,
Wait upon Me, the Master of the seasons of your heart.

DAVID HARBUCK

I had always known I would not marry early. I had too much to accomplish in my career to even think about a husband and children. But by the time I was thirty-one, I'd finished a graduate degree and was achieving career success in my field of education. Learning styles had become my area of specialty. I thought I could master virtually anything I set my mind to.

Except dating.

Suddenly I realized I didn't have a clue about how to have a normal social life. I hadn't really been paying attention. Where would a woman like me find eligible men who shared my values? I didn't frequent bars, and I had lived through enough church-sponsored singles functions for one lifetime.

So who was going to teach the learning expert how to find the right guy?

In the spring of 1985, I read an article about using the classified ads to meet eligible singles with mutual interests and goals. At first I dismissed the idea as totally absurd, but for some reason I remained intrigued. I noticed that most of the men who interested me read the same upscale newspaper, *The Seattle Weekly*. One day, on impulse, I picked up a copy and studied the Person to Person section.

A lot of groaning, gasping, and hooting followed, to be sure. But some of the ads struck me. They were like advertising masterpieces in only twenty words. The best ones were creative, clever, and amazingly non-threatening. I decided to give it a try. After all, I reasoned, I'm not advertising for a husband, just interesting friends—right?

Here's how my ad appeared:

> Professional SWF, 31, looking for a man committed to the solid values in life. If you're looking for casual sex, you're not looking for me. If you're interested in a friendship, let's explore the possibilities.

I got twenty-one replies, all from apparently sane, professional, Christian men. I went out with nine of them (lots of free lunches!). I decided I'd struck on the perfect social tool for a performance-oriented, career woman. No muss, no waste, and it put me in total control of who came calling. Perfect.

Until I met John. He was man number four. John was an attractive, stimulating man whose interests paralleled mine. We could spend hours talking. He was everything I'd been looking for, as my heart told me right away—and that was the problem. I felt my years-long tight grip on my life slipping away. Suddenly this stubborn, independent, career-oriented woman had let her heart walk right up to the edge of lover's leap and poise to jump.

After our first time together, I wrote in my journal: "Lunch today—I'm seeing him again. I just don't understand what I'm going through. My style promotes independence and variety, and yet here I am thinking how nice it would be to be committed to someone. There's no doubt that my heart feels more than ready to plunge into unknown waters. And me, who can't swim!"

Things happened fast—for both of us. It felt like we'd been walking toward the same destination for years and suddenly realized that this is where we became seat partners. John said we needed at least twelve months of relationship—"We have to experience every holiday together once," he announced—before we made any lifelong commitments. That sounded like an excellent career plan to me.

But my heart didn't cooperate much. In fact, I discovered I was in the middle of a war—between the plan-ful, hard-charging professional I'd become and a heart that seemed to be saying, "Time's up, Cynthia. You've met your match!"

I wrote in my journal: "I do think since he has custody of my heart that I should be entitled to frequent visitation rights. My heart has certainly not lost any time in drawing up the adoption papers. While it's spreading out the documents and handing John the pen, my mind is busily picking them back up and apologizing for the haste."

A few weeks later, John sent me a poem. It read:

> Do you and I tumble, or stagger, or stumble
> Or topple, or just fall in love?
> No, it's more like we fit like a ball in a mitt.
> And as planned as hand in a glove.
> Now for me to suggest that a test of the rest
> Of the best "Weekly" writers is due
> Would be near-cavalier; never fear: Here, my dear,
> Is the man in God's plan just for you.
> So if you're not afraid of the staid or delay
> And you prayed for a guy all your own,
> Slide all doubting aside, ride astride by my side
> I'm as near as your ear to the phone.
> With love (and apologies to Dr. Seuss!)
>
> JST

How could I argue with that? I realized that God had known all along what it would take to peel my fingers off my life and make me take that leap. And now I knew that God would help me learn how to swim.

I let go. John and I had a wonderful, two-year courtship and were married in 1987. Not once since then have I had to worry about what my heart is going to do next. Because I relinquished custody of my heart long ago to John Tobias—and love has taken care of all the rest.

CYNTHIA ULRICH TOBIAS

Used by permission of the author.

SANTA WITH THE
BLUE EYES

✍

His eyes how they twinkled!
His dimples how merry!

CLEMENT CLARKE MOORE

The year was 1945. World War II had just ended, and the YMCA was packed every weekend with handsome soldiers. This was terrific news for my sister, my best friend, and me. The three of us lived for the weekends when we would take the trolley downtown to the YMCA dances.

One December night as we jumped off the trolley and rushed up to the door, we almost collided with a uniformed man coming out. But this man wasn't wearing an army uniform. It was Christmas, and this soldier was dressed in a red suit, posing as Santa Claus.

Once inside, I breathlessly asked my sister and my girlfriend, "Did you see the blue eyes on that Santa Claus?"

"What blue eyes? And who's interested in Santa," my girlfriend demanded, "with all these good-looking servicemen around?"

I tried to tell myself she was right. I danced the night away with one soldier after the next. But I never really quit looking for those blue eyes among them.

The next weekend I was back—and more determined than ever to find Santa. All evening I searched for those twinkling blue eyes, but they were nowhere to be found. Then as I was leaving, I caught sight of a man behind the laundry counter at the YMCA, where many of the soldiers lived. His eyes captured me even across the room.

"There he is!" I whispered excitedly to my sister.

"Who?" she asked.

"Santa Claus! I'm sure—that man has the blue eyes I've been looking for!"

Never one to be shy, I walked right up to the counter to introduce myself. "Hi, I'm Polly," I said, smiling at the young man.

His name was Cy. He explained that he had just returned from the war and was helping his mother who ran the YMCA. He had little time for dancing, he said—but yes, he'd be honored if he could have one dance with me.

As I glanced at my watch, my sister grabbed my arm. "You can't!" she exclaimed. "We'll miss the trolley!"

She was right. I took a disappointed look at those wonderful eyes as my sister dragged me out the door.

"Maybe next time!" Cy called after me.

I thought the next weekend would never arrive. When it finally did, I found Cy waiting for me and for our dance. In fact, every weekend that winter I danced the night away with the dashing young man with the blue eyes. And today we're still dancing!

My family still teases me about marrying St. Nicholas. Our nine children have asked me again and again to tell the romantic story about how Cy and I met. And to their delight, fifty years later, that blue-eyed Santa Claus and I are still kissing under the mistletoe.

POLLY CHAPMAN

SAVE YOUR LAST DANCE
FOR ME

On with the dance! let joy be unconfined;
No sleep 'til morn, when youth and pleasure meet!

LORD BYRON

As the beautiful daughter of the Coca-Cola family, Rena was the toast of Atlanta society in the 1930s. Among the many admirers hoping to win her hand someday were William and Jack, two fine Southern gentlemen with impeccable manners. Each politely waited his turn to twirl the lovely Rena around on the dance floor or to escort her to teas, parties, and balls.

For her part, Rena was extremely fond of both young men. How could she ever choose between them?

Finally, when Jack was called away from town for an extended time, young William saw his chance and seized it. He proposed to Rena, and she accepted. Naturally, Jack was brokenhearted that he'd lost Rena. But ever the Southern gentleman, he graciously surrendered to William and even rallied to become a member of the wedding party.

Life, with all its twists and turns, went on. Jack eventually moved away, married happily, and raised a wonderful family. Meanwhile, three children were born to Rena and William.

Many years passed, and old age found Rena alone and confined to a wheelchair with multiple sclerosis. Friends from her glorious childhood days meant more to Rena now than ever. Two of them, Dottie and her husband, Johnny, were at her side as often as possible. The threesome spent many enchanted hours reminiscing about those bright years of dances and parties.

One day Dottie and Johnny heard that Jack was now a widower and also alone. It wasn't long before the two were scheming to reunite their old friend with Rena. And so they planned a lovely dinner party in their home without telling Rena or Jack that the other would be attending.

When Jack arrived, he saw the love of his youth in a wheelchair. But her brown eyes still sparkled, and she looked to him as beautiful as ever. That evening Rena got up from her wheelchair and danced all night. Taking up exactly where he'd left off forty-seven years earlier, Jack began courting Rena.

One bright spring day Jack took her to the park and insisted that she sit in the same swing where she had sat half a century earlier. He pushed his sweetheart high in the air as the two of them remembered the hours spent here together when they were young. And before they left the park, they both knew they wanted to spend whatever hours they had left together.

Soon, a wedding took place—much smaller but just as beautiful as the lavish wedding of half a century before. Jack and Rena shared five beautiful years before Rena died, on their second honeymoon. During that time, the couple relished telling their romantic story to waiters, bank tellers, the gardener, cab drivers—anyone who would listen.

Who could resist such a story? Or such a pair? As those who met them would often say with a sigh, "There's nothing so lovely as young love in old age!"

TOLD BY ELIZABETH CHAMBERS, RENA'S DAUGHTER

From This Day Forward

"FROM THIS DAY FORWARD." THERE IS MOTION HERE.

THERE IS A LEAVING BEHIND OF THINGS PAST, A SEVERING

OF OLD TIES, OLD HABITS, OLD LOYALTIES, OLD HAUNTS.

ON THIS DAY, SAY BRIDE AND GROOM, WE STEP ONTO A

ROAD NEITHER OF US HAVE WALKED BEFORE. THERE WILL

NOW BE TWO SETS OF FOOTPRINTS, SIDE BY SIDE. OUT IN

THE SUNLIGHT, TWO SHADOWS WILL BE CAST, BLENDING

INTO ONE AS DAY FOLLOWS DAY.

FROM THIS DAY FORWARD, LIFE BEGINS ANEW.

CANDY STRIPER

❧

Child of the pure, unclouded brow
And dreaming eyes of wonder!
Though time be fleet and I and thou
Are half a life asunder,
Thy loving smile will surely hail
The love-gift of a fairy tale.

LEWIS CARROLL

I was only fifteen years old when my mother was seriously injured in a car accident. While she was recovering at the local nursing home, the rest of the family struggled to cope with her absence. I was a depressed teenage boy if there ever was one. It seemed to me like everything that could possibly go wrong had.

Then one day when I was visiting my mother, an adorable candy striper walked into her room and made me forget how unfortunate I was. She had eyes that twinkled and the largest dimples I'd ever seen. She introduced herself as Susan and flashed a beautiful smile my direction.

Suddenly I could hardly think straight. I mumbled my name and was promptly propelled into a daze that I couldn't snap out of for days. All I could think about was the pretty, cheerful candy striper. I began to visit my mother more frequently. Susan chatted amicably whenever she stopped in my mother's room with magazines or flowers. Gradually a friendship began to blossom between us.

Before long my mother figured out why I was spending so much time at her bedside. "Jeff, shouldn't you be home doing your homework?"

she'd say with a sly smile. Or, "Did they cancel basketball practice?"

When my mother was finally able to come home, my dad, my brother, and I were overjoyed. But I was also unhappy about losing Susan's smile. You see, I was painfully shy, and so just dropping by the nursing home without an excuse was out of the question. As was giving Susan a call. Or simply telling her I was interested. In fact, when I learned that Susan went to the rival high school, I decided I'd probably never see her again.

But I couldn't forget her. Finally I grew desperate enough to take action. Not exactly brave action, mind you.

I called the nursing home—not to talk to Susan but to see if they had any job openings. The kitchen manager was puzzled why a teenage boy would be so excited about working in a nursing home washing dishes for very low pay. After he hired me, he discovered that I was the most enthusiastic dishwasher he'd ever had. And why wouldn't I be, since my new job meant I got to see Susan three times a week?

After a few months of growing friendship, I finally mustered the courage to ask Susan out—but only sort of. Since I didn't have a driver's license yet, I invited her to drop by the YMCA to watch me play basketball. The following weekend I asked a teammate if we could double-date so I could take Susan to a movie. He agreed, but only if I would pick up the tab for his tickets too.

For a moment I faltered. That would cost me five dollars—a fortune to a young guy in the sixties. But there was no stopping me now. Truth be known, I probably would have paid more. So I paid for all four of us to go out, and that night I finally got up the nerve to give Susan her first kiss in the backseat of my friend's '55 Chevy. That was five dollars well spent!

I planned to marry Susan after high school, but instead, I volunteered for Vietnam. Susan went away to college, and our relationship consisted of love letters back and forth.

When it was time for me to come home, I couldn't wait to see Susan and to finally ask her to be my wife. In order to get to the air base sooner and in hopes of getting home more quickly, a buddy and I hitched a ride with a local Vietnamese man. But instead of shortening our trip, the man pulled out a gun and demanded our money.

I couldn't believe it. After surviving the war, was I about to be killed on my way home? I handed over all I had, including the money I'd been saving for Susan's ring. But as I did, suddenly I saw her candy-striper smile in my mind. I had to get back to her—and this guy wasn't about to stop me. Without a plan, I lunged for the gunman. After wrestling for several minutes, I overcame him and even retrieved our money.

That was twenty-six years ago. Just seven years after I first saw the pretty candy striper with the great smile and cute dimples, the two of us were married. I still consider myself the luckiest guy in the world, and Susan looks just as beautiful today in her nurse's uniform as she did in that candy-striper uniform years ago.

This is the way I see it: whether you're fifteen or fifty, if you meet a girl whose smile lights up your entire being—even if you have to wash dishes, pay for someone else's date, and fight your way back from a foreign war—don't let her get away. Do whatever it takes to win her. Because—and I can promise you this—her smile is going to light up the rest of your life.

JEFF HIERS

THE PET-SITTER

All things bright and beautiful,
All creatures great and small,
All things wise and wonderful,
The Lord God made them all.

CECIL FRANCES ALEXANDER

know that these days a girl's not supposed to need a husband to feel fulfilled. But when I was a single woman approaching thirty, finding a husband was uppermost in my mind. I enjoyed my job teaching public school, but what I really wanted after spending seven hours in the company of twenty-five rowdy second-graders was to come home to the adult conversation and companionship of a man who loved me.

I'd already met every available man within my circle—handsome coaches, creative teachers, and kind church buddies. And so far, nothing had clicked.

As depression set in, I began to sleep too much. I even figured out a way to sleep until just twenty minutes before I had to be at school. I kept my coffeemaker on my nightstand and learned to pour without even opening my eyes.

That's when I realized I was in trouble. "God," I prayed, "You see that I'm deeply depressed. I know You want more for me. Help me to find a new hobby or a fun part-time job where I can make a little extra money and meet people over the age of ten." (God, of course, knew that this mostly meant nice single guys.)

That afternoon I pulled out the paper to look at job ads. But I only felt my depression deepen as I was reminded of all the things I didn't know how to do. Then I noticed the pet-sitting ad. I loved animals. My mother had bred dogs, and our family had always sheltered strays. Something like that would be great after school and on weekends. But how would pet-sitting introduce me to interesting men?

I laid aside the paper with a heavy sigh. Other people's pets? Was I *that* desperate for company?

A few days later—when I found myself scheming to get to school in only eighteen minutes—I decided I was.

First, I signed up to take care of Jedi, a simple-minded cocker spaniel whose one aim in life was to escape his happy home and bolt for another star system. Within a couple of months, I'd added Bo, Lefty, and a gang of other dogs to my list. Then there were fish, snakes, and Lily, a gorgeous Himalayan cat with extremely finicky tastes. Soon my life seemed taken up with either rowdy school kids or rowdy pets, with still no suitors in sight. In fact, some weekends passed without my seeing another human being.

However, keeping busy and earning a little extra money lifted my spirits considerably. In time, my business grew and several pet owners became regulars. One was Deborah, a lawyer who traveled frequently. She enjoyed the little notes I left for her, detailing the silly antics of her cats, Tiger and Tori. We became friends, and when Thanksgiving rolled around, she invited me to a get-together with her family and coworkers.

I had no other plans—involving people, I mean. So I accepted.

When I arrived at the gathering on Thanksgiving Day, the friendly man at the door introduced himself as Jerry, one of my clients. I'd never met Jerry before, only Lily, his aforementioned Himalayan cat. But before I could get acquainted with Jerry, Deborah appeared, chortling those words I'd come to both anticipate and dread—"There's someone here I want you to meet."

She introduced me to Don, who turned out to be good company. After all, he was neither a child nor an animal. But as the afternoon progressed, it became apparent to me that Don was not my type, even though he seemed to think I was his. Other than that little disappointment, the

Thanksgiving celebration turned out to be most enjoyable.

A couple of weeks later the phone rang as I was taping the oven buzzer to the Off position. (Sterling, my cat, had learned how to paw the timer knob until he got it to buzz.) I was only half listening as the man on the phone told me how nice it had been to meet me at Thanksgiving. Would I join him with the same group at the company Christmas party?

Don, I thought. Oh, boy. "No thanks," I began politely. "I have all these pet-sitting jobs. There's Jedi and Lefty and Lily and..."

I shudder now to think what would have happened if I had not mistakenly mentioned the high-brow Lily. Because the charming man on the phone wasn't Don at all, but Jerry, Lily's owner.

When that became apparent, I began fumbling for an apology. "Oh, Jerry!" I gushed. "We never really got a chance to visit at Thanksgiving, did we?" Then I told Jerry I'd be delighted to go to the Christmas party with him.

To make a furry story short, that first date led to the end of my career as a pet-sitter *and* my singlehood. Who would have guessed that my prayers would ultimately be answered through my services to a finicky feline?

Today, our family has grown to include one Brittany spaniel, two English cockers, and two fluffy cats. And whenever I remember how I found my husband, I thank God for His wisdom—and for all His creatures, great and small.

DEE ANN GRAND

FULL EMPTY NEST

There is no more lovely, friendly, and charming relationship, communion or company than a good marriage.

Martin Luther

As the bride and groom roared off on their shiny black-and-purple Harley-Davidson Heritage Classic, my heart skipped a beat. I waved, put my arm around Cynthia, and found myself drifting back thirty-seven years to our own wedding.

The Place: First Baptist Church in Galena Park, Texas. The Date: June 18, 1955. The Time: 8:00 P.M.

Within a matter of hours we, too, had been on our way to a lifetime of learning and growing, delights and disappointments, heartaches and laughter, and ultimately rearing a household of four busy kids.

Now, here we stood, watching our last child ride off into the sunset. I looked Cynthia in the eyes, wrapped her in my arms, whispered the three greatest words in the English language in her ear, and added, "Well, Hon…we're back where we started."

And so we are.

We started at ground zero, having never before known what it was like to be a husband or a wife. By God's grace, we discovered—and are still discovering—what that means. We started without knowing what the future held. We still don't. We started in simple faith, excited about God's leading. We're there again. If our God does not lead, we're still not interested in going. We started with hearts in tune to each other. Though young, we had no disagreement over who would have the final word. Our Lord, who had called us to become one, would remain preeminent. We started with a mutual desire to have a family and love each one with equal affection. We were determined not to let anything decrease the priority of our home—not school, not church, not the teenage years, not our own friends…still close…still committed.

I looked at Cynthia and smiled. Thirty-seven years rushed between us. Our primary job of parenting was done. Our roles of hands-on mom and dad were changing. Instead of telling our four what to do or how to do it, we would be available, keep our mouths shut, be willing to wait, happy to help, quick to affirm—but definitely would not get in their way. Or control. Or preach. Or manipulate. Their lives are theirs to live, free of our presence or counsel, unless requested. For Chuck and Cynthia, it's back to where we started.

According to the book *Passages of Marriage,* we have reached the fifth and final stage. "Transcendent Love"—"a profound and peaceful perspective toward your partner and toward life."

That sounds pretty good to me. Frankly, my wife still looks so great to me, has such depth of character, and fulfills my life so thoroughly, I get excited just thinking about cultivating this "transcendent perspective."

Our long-standing love, our museum of memories, and our track record of toughing it out through the hard times are all we need to rekindle the fires of intimacy.

CHARLES R. SWINDOLL

From *The Finishing Touch* (Nashville, Tennessee: Word Publishing, 1994). Used by permission of the publisher. All rights reserved.

LOVE BREAKS THROUGH

⟨⟨⟩⟩

Come live with me, and be my love,
And we will some new pleasure prove.

JOHN DONNE

By midlife, Atlanta businesswoman Carolyn Stradley had literally paved her way to success and national prominence. But along the way, something vital had been lost. Her heart felt as hardened as one of her million-dollar asphalt jobs.

Carolyn's blunt distrust of love was rooted in an impoverished upbringing in Appalachia. Violence, neglect, and alcohol abuse you could count on, she discovered; everything else was up for grabs. Orphaned at eleven, she raised herself with the help of an older brother. At thirteen, Carolyn came to Atlanta with her possessions in a cardboard box. For shelter, she slept in the bus station or her brother's one-room apartment.

"I went to high school, but I didn't smile or participate with others because my front teeth were missing due to neglect," Carolyn recalls.

Married at fifteen, pregnant at sixteen, she soon found herself caring for her husband, Arthur, who had become chronically ill with kidney disease. She worked several jobs just to make ends meet, cared for their daughter, Tina, and supervised her husband's twice-weekly dialysis sessions.

When Arthur died, Carolyn was twenty-six. By then she had worked for a paving company long enough to be seized with an unprecedented

156

idea. In a hard-edged business dominated by men, Carolyn decided she wanted to go it alone. She started her own paving business—on her kitchen table and out of the back of her pickup truck. "There I was—a young, single mom trying to buy dump trucks," Carolyn remembers.

Fortunately she was a quick study and a tireless worker. Within a few years her company, C & S Paving, was competitive enough to win the contract to pave the Olympic Stadium. Carolyn was honored at the White House with the Small Business Award for the state of Georgia and was second runner-up for the United States.

Carolyn thought she was too busy for romance. Everything she had learned to help her survive drove her further away from the comforts of love. She knew what it was like to have no parents, so she focused on raising her daughter. Only after Tina married and started a family of her own did Carolyn begin to think she might be interested in a relationship herself.

That's when she met Leon. The contractor he worked for sent him over to get a paving bid from "that tough redhead at C & S Paving." Tough was right. But so was Leon. And after four tries, Carolyn gave in to his request for a date. And then another. For the first time in years, she allowed herself to enjoy dating a man. And a good man too. Leon Thompson was a respected businessman in the Atlanta area.

However, their courtship was more like a collision of worlds than a meeting of minds. "Leon was from the old South," Carolyn explains. "His grandfather was a Baptist preacher, and his father was a deacon. Leon was warm and mannerly and had been raised in a loving Christian home. My experience had been the opposite. I had seen so much violence and cruelty. I wasn't really aware that things could be different."

This became dramatically clear one evening as they sat together in front of a beautiful fireplace. Leon leaned toward his striking red-haired lady friend and gently said, "Carolyn, I love you. What I want more than anything is for you to be my wife. Will you marry me?"

"Why in the world do I need a husband?" Carolyn retorted frankly.

Leon was devastated! But after a couple of weeks, he realized he wasn't wrong about Carolyn, just a little premature.

Unbeknownst to Carolyn, love was busily at work. Even though she was still afraid of marriage, she was beginning to sense something missing in her life. Leon and his family had shown her a better way, and her paved-over heart was beginning to soften.

A few days after Thanksgiving that year, Leon called Carolyn at work. "There's something we need to talk about, but we need some time alone. Can you get away?"

Carolyn agreed. The two of them drove to the mountains away from the demands of business. Leon began by telling her that he'd made a mistake. It wasn't fair to ask her to marry him, he admitted, without their talking through what marriage could mean—what it was intended to mean between two giving, caring people. "Honestly, I forgot, Carolyn, that you might have no idea of the tremendous possibilities," he declared.

Carolyn was struck again by this soft-spoken man's gentle wisdom and stubborn strength. What followed was a long and open discussion about married love.

"Before that day I had never heard any of what Leon told me," Carolyn admits now. "I thought that people got married to have children—and I had one and didn't need that anymore. My parents' marriage had been ruined by alcohol and violence. Leon gently opened my eyes to what could be—to what, without even knowing it, I so desperately wanted."

At their marriage two weeks later, Leon's father gave the bride away. Carolyn giggled, she smiled, she blushed, she cried—everything you'd expect a soft-hearted bride to do. That was fifteen years ago. Today Carolyn uses words like "blessed" and "complete" to describe her marriage with Leon. And she tells people that no matter how hardened life has made you, love can still break through to set you free.

From an interview with Carolyn Stradley. Used by permission.

ALL'S FAIR
IN LOVE AND WAR

✍

Love and war are the same thing, and stratagems
And policy are as allowable in the one as in the other.

MIGUEL DE CERVANTES

When Edward Howe went to school to become an engineer, the last thing on his mind was love—or war. But when the Civil War broke out in 1860, the ambitious young man was drawn into both.

Having grown up in Massachusetts, Howe was sympathetic to the Northern cause and decided to join the Union army. Because of his engineering skills, he was quickly promoted to captain in the cavalry, with twelve hundred men in his charge. His first orders were to take his troops from Massachusetts down to Chattanooga, Tennessee, to bring reinforcements to the military campaign near Chicamauga.

The ride was rough going. His troops had ridden for many hours by the time they reached Mount Sterling, Kentucky, about thirty miles east of Lexington. Howe was well aware that there were many Confederate sympathizers in the state, but what he didn't know was that he was about to meet one of the most passionate.

When Howe spotted a farmhouse in the distance, he ordered his hot and weary troops to halt. Here was the promise of rest and water for the men and horses. Captain Howe asked two men to ride up to the house to ask for assistance. Just as they were about to dismount, a lovely and petite young lady—she couldn't have stood more than four feet, ten inches—appeared on the porch.

"Get off this property right now!" she ordered. "Shoo! You boys just get back on your horses and go back where you came from!"

The soldiers were surprised but not amused. They'd never been screamed at by a Southern belle before. When one of them yelled to her that they just wanted water, she told him, "I'll die before I let any Yankee drink the water from our well!"

The young woman refused to back down or to help. The soldiers turned in their saddles to signal their captain that they had a problem.

Captain Howe ordered his staff aide to ride forward and resolve the disturbance, but his aide hesitated. Howe started to laugh. "My man, we haven't even seen the battlefront, and you're showing me that this little lady has put a fright into you! If that's the case, I believe that yonder lovely lady is right—we'd all better get back on our horses and go home!"

The captain's aide decided to approach the porch. Before peace returned to that farm scene—and horses and men had been watered—the farm girl had delivered several scratches to the aide's face and bruises to his shins, and the captain had made a big decision.

As the cavalry mounted to ride away, Captain Howe turned his horse around. "I'd better do the gentlemanly thing and apologize for causing the young lady so much distress," he told his aide. As he rode up to the veranda, the petite beauty was still standing guard, making sure every last Yankee left her property.

But when Captain Howe reached the porch, he realized that he wanted to say something else. "I don't know who you are, young lady," he said, "or for that matter where you come from. But I do know one thing. After this war is over, if I manage to get out of it alive, I'm going to come back to Mount Sterling, I'm going to find you—and I'm going to make you my wife. Any woman with the courage to take on an entire Yankee regiment is the girl for me!"

The young lady's eyes flashed with anger as she stomped her dainty foot and declared to Captain Howe, "Sir, I would die before I'd marry you!"

Captain Howe took his troops to Chattanooga where the Battle of Chicamauga ensued. Captain Howe was among the injured, wounded by cannon fire, and his recovery took many months. But as soon as he was discharged, he detoured to Mount Sterling. Dismayed to discover that the young woman was no longer living in the same house, he spent several days scouring the area for her. Finally he learned that she was the daughter of an Episcopalian minister, Vicar Thomkins.

Immediately he visited the vicar's home, but the vicar's daughter was anything but happy to see him. "I don't know why you even bothered to come," she said fiercely.

Howe smiled. He would have been disappointed with a lesser response. Here was a challenge, and a young woman worth pursuing! He proceeded to visit the vicar often and to woo his daughter at every opportunity. He gave her flowers, complimented her cooking, and responded graciously to her insults. And in time, his strategy seemed to be working. The vicar's daughter was softening toward Captain Howe.

Finally, Howe asked Vicar Thomkins for Juliet's hand in marriage. The vicar was by now quite impressed with the young Union soldier, but he wasn't willing to go against his daughter's wishes. "I'll put in a good word with the Lord for you," he told Howe. "And if you can persuade her, she's all yours. God help you!"

But when Howe proposed marriage to the vicar's daughter, she adamantly resisted. "It's not on account of it being you that's asking," she explained. "You've loved me more than I hated you. And now I don't hate you anymore. But I can't marry you because I just don't think I can survive up north."

Howe instantly made a counteroffer. He promised that if she was unhappy in Massachusetts, he would move her south one state at a time until she was happy.

She agreed to his terms, and Edward Howe, a gentleman and a man of principles, kept his promise to his bride. They started in Massachusetts, sure enough, and soon began moving south. But by the time this campaign was over, Edward and Juliet Howe had found happiness in Knoxville, Tennessee.

The story of Captain and Mrs. Howe has been passed down from generation to generation, with many warnings about tangling with a strong-minded Southern girl. But with the warning has come Captain Howe's wisdom about these things: "All is fair in love and war," he said, "but in love, no prize is worth winning without a fair pursuit!"

AS TOLD BY EMMET HOWE,
GRANDSON OF CAPTAIN HOWE

Editor's Note: Captain Edward Howe's uniform is proudly displayed at the Atlanta History Museum. Any Yankee who pursued a Southern belle with such vigor deserves an honored place in a Southern museum.

LOVE WITHOUT A NET

⌖

Now join your hands
and with your hands your hearts.

WILLIAM SHAKESPEARE

*A*nne Morrow was shy and delicate. Butterfly-like. Not dull or stupid or incompetent, just a quiet specimen of timidity.

Her dad was ambassador to Mexico when she met an adventurous young fellow who visited south of the border for the U.S. State Department.

The man was flying from place to place promoting aviation. Everywhere he went he drew capacity crowds. You see, he had just won forty thousand dollars for being the first to cross the Atlantic by air. The strong pilot and the shy princess fell deeply in love.

When she became Mrs. Charles Lindbergh, Anne could have easily been eclipsed by her husband's shadow. She wasn't however. The love that bound the two together for the next forty-seven years was tough love, mature love, tested by triumph and tragedy alike. They would never know the quiet comfort of being an anonymous couple in a crowd. The Lindbergh name didn't allow that luxury. Her man, no matter where he went, was news, forever in the limelight—clearly a national hero. But rather than becoming a resentful recluse or another nameless face in a crowd of admirers, Anne Morrow Lindbergh emerged to become one of

America's most popular authors, a woman highly admired for her own accomplishments.

How? Let's let her give us the clue to the success of her career.

> To be deeply in love is, of course, a great liberating force and the most common experience that frees—ideally, both members of a couple in love free each other to new and different worlds. I was no exception to the general rule. The sheer fact of finding myself loved was unbelievable and changed my world, my feelings about life and myself. I was given confidence, strength, and almost a new character. The man I was to marry believed in me and what I could do, and consequently I found I could do more than I realized.

Charles did believe in Anne to an extraordinary degree. He saw beneath her shy surface. He realized that deep in her innermost well was a wealth of wisdom, a profound, untapped reservoir of ability. Within the security of his love she was freed—released—to discover and develop her own capacity, to cultivate her own skills, and to emerge from that cocoon of shyness a beautiful, ever-delicate butterfly whose presence would enhance many lives far beyond the perimeter of her husband's shadow. He encouraged her to do her own kind of flying, and he admired her for it.

We're talking roots and wings. A husband's love that is strong enough to reassure yet unthreatened enough to release. Tight enough to embrace yet loose enough to enjoy. Magnetic enough to hold, yet magnanimous enough to allow for flight—with an absence of jealousy as others applaud her accomplishments and admire her competence. Charles, the secure, put away the net so Anne, the shy, could flutter and fly.

CHARLES R. SWINDOLL

THE WEDDING TRUNK

Hope like the gleaming taper's light
Adorns and cheers our way
And still as darker grows the night
Emits a brighter ray.

OLIVER GOLDSMITH

he day Oskar placed his grandmother's sapphire ring on Helga's finger, her mother's wedding trunk came down from the attic. As was the family custom, Helga would begin adding their names to the roster of brides and grooms embroidered on a silk petticoat in the trunk. From the time she was a little girl, she had dreamed of this special day and had practiced her exquisite stitch.

Just as Helga completed her own name and was threading the needle for Oskar's name, news came that the feared Gestapo had taken Oskar away. Even though Oskar had fiercely opposed the Third Reich, no one had believed such drastic action would be taken.

Inconsolable, Helga dropped her sewing with the unfinished names, and the gown was returned to the trunk in the attic. With it went the laughter and the joy of the young girl in love. As rumors of the death camps reached their city, everyone—even Helga—doubted that Oskar's name would ever be stitched upon the petticoat.

With each passing day, Helga retreated more deeply into her books, rarely speaking a word. But what could her family do? All their energies were devoted to surviving the war as the bombs one by one destroyed their city and then their home.

When the bombing ceased, the family gathered to sift through the rubble. Helga's mother spotted her wedding trunk, one of the few possessions that had survived the blast. When she pulled the contents from the battered trunk, the petticoat suddenly caught her eye. There was Oskar's name—someone had stitched it beside her daughter's name! Everyone stared at the petticoat in disbelief, fearing the sight of this would drive Helga deeper into despair. Instead, she knelt down beside the trunk and ran her fingers gingerly over Oskar's name. From that day on, the joy came back into Helga's life, despite her family's warnings that after all these years it was doubtful Oskar could have survived.

Liberation day came and went without any sign of Oskar, but Helga continued to watch and wait for him. Months later a lone Holocaust survivor hobbled into town. He stood before them, a skeleton of a man, beyond recognition to everyone but Helga. The smile was unmistakably Oskar's.

Throughout the years the trunk has been pulled out again and again for the weddings of the children and grandchildren of this devoted couple. It is far more than a reminder of their love—it is a symbol of hope.

No one ever discovered who stitched Oskar's name on the petticoat, but truly the faith and hope of that individual helped this couple's love to survive.

To Love, Honor, and Cherish

THERE ARE PLACES IN THE HEART WHERE YOU DON'T WEAR MUDDY SHOES. YOU ENTER CAREFULLY. YOU WALK QUIETLY. YOU SPEAK SOFTLY. THESE ARE THE TREASURE ROOMS...THE PLACES WHERE YOU KEEP ALL THAT YOU HOLD VALUABLE AND PRECIOUS.

ONLY CHERISHED THINGS BELONG IN SUCH PLACES OF THE HEART. AND THAT IS WHERE A MAN OUGHT TO KEEP HIS WIFE AND LIFE COMPANION. RIGHT THERE, IN THAT HIGH AND HOLY PLACE JUST BELOW (BUT NEVER HIGHER THAN) THE PLACE RESERVED FOR GOD. AND THAT WIFE MUST HOLD HER HUSBAND DEARER THAN HOUSES OR WEALTH OR CAREER OR EVEN CHILDREN.

WE HONOR THAT WHICH WE CHERISH.

WE PROTECT THAT WHICH WE CHERISH.

WE GUARD AND PRIZE AND TREASURE THAT WHICH WE CHERISH.

MARRIAGE SAYS, "I CHERISH YOU, MY LOVE, MOST OF ALL."

THE GARDEN OF LOVE

Live now, believe me, wait not till tomorrow;
Gather the roses of life today.

PIERRE DE RONSARD

efore I met my husband, John, every attempt I'd made to find and keep love had led to disappointment and heartbreak.

John knew this, and so when he proposed to me, he vowed, "Your life with me will be a bed of roses!"

I was deeply touched by John's sentiment, especially since I knew he would do everything he could to make good on his promise. But of course, hardships come in life no matter how wonderfully our spouses treat us. And by the time our tenth anniversary rolled around, we'd experienced our share of stress and difficulty. It had been the hardest year we'd encountered together so far. What if John actually forgot our anniversary? After all, I'd been disappointed by men so many times before.

I needn't have worried. John took me to a beautiful restaurant where he'd reserved a table with a lovely view. After a delicious, romantic meal by candlelight, we returned home and prepared for bed. In our bathroom, I brushed my hair a long time and applied some of John's favorite perfume.

When I came back into the bedroom, I noticed that John was smiling like an excited little boy. I couldn't imagine what he'd been up to. Then suddenly he folded the bedcovers back, and I gasped with delight and surprise. The entire bed was covered in rose petals, their fragrance filling the room.

"John, how did you do this? Where did you get all these roses?"

"Well," he said with a big grin, "I called the florist and ordered pale pink Oceana roses like the ones you carried in your bouquet when we married. I requested that the blossoms be full and that the roses not be arranged. Then I spent hours gently pulling the petals apart."

I was so overwhelmed by his gesture that my eyes spilled over with tears.

As John kissed them away, he gently held me and whispered, "Didn't I promise you a bed of roses when I proposed?"

"Yes, you did! But I never…"

That evening John and I celebrated our anniversary in a garden of love—and there were no thorns. I felt my wounded heart let go of old pains and lingering doubts. In their place, a healing peace engulfed me, and I fully understood the words from 1 John 4:18 (NAS) for the first time: "Perfect love drives out fear."

ANN PLATZ

Sweetheart, come see if the rose
Which at morning began to unclose
Its damask gown to the sun.
Has not lost, now the day is done,
The folds of its damasked gown
And its colors so like your own.

PIERRE DE RONSARD

HEALING HANDS

She watches over the affairs of her household....
Give her the reward she has earned,
And let her works bring her praise at the city gate.

PROVERBS 31:27, 31

When we first met, I knew Ellis's goal was to be a great heart surgeon, but I had no idea just how gifted my husband's hands were.

As his career flourished, Ellis began performing four or five surgeries a day. So many patients needed Ellis's skill and attention, and he was too compassionate to turn anyone away. He would rise before daylight and leave for the hospital and return home each night exhausted.

Over time, I became very concerned about my husband's stress level and inability to relax. I tried everything I could think of to help—little getaways, favorite meals—but nothing really worked.

Then one night Ellis came home with a stiff neck. "Is there anything I can do for you? How about a backrub?" I offered.

Ellis seemed delighted, and when I was done, he sat up and said, "Beth, I don't know what you did, but my neck is not stiff anymore!"

The next morning as I was praying for my husband, I suddenly got an inspiration. Ellis enjoyed his neck rub so much, why didn't I study the art of massage? Unknown to Ellis, I began taking classes in the morning while the children were away at school. After twelve weeks—with my family still totally unaware—I completed my course and immediately purchased a massage table. I could hardly wait to surprise Ellis!

That night Ellis again came home from work exhausted and tired. After dinner, I led him into the bedroom. "What is this contraption?" he asked.

"Let me demonstrate," I offered, inviting him to lie down on the table. That night I gave him his first professional massage. Ellis was blissful. And he was overwhelmed with gratitude when I told him what I'd done. "You took classes to learn to do this? For *me?*"

Now, whenever I notice that my husband is especially stressed and tense, I give him a loving massage. According to Ellis, these times on *my* table help him relax and do better work for patients on *his* table. "There are two people in this family with gifted hands," he says. "And both of them heal hearts!"

BETH JONES

MY FATHER'S CHAIR

*A good marriage is that in which each
Appoints the other guardian of his solitude.*

RANIER MARIA RILKE

When my parents said their marriage vows, my mother made sure that my father understood he had to protect her from her greatest fear—bugs, spiders, and snakes. Although this wasn't specifically a part of their vows, Mother wanted him to know this was one of his most important duties as her husband. Daddy had been a war hero, flying over thirty bombing missions in World War II, so Mother felt safe. If he could protect our country, he certainly could protect her from a few creepy crawlers.

Tucked away in my childhood memories are images of my father zapping insects as my mother stood on a chair, squealing in horror. Thankfully, we never had any snakes or mice in the house because I'm sure she would've gone right through the roof. In return for his chivalry, Mother always showed my father the utmost respect and made certain her children did too. She took great care to make Daddy's home—and especially his chair—his refuge from the storms of life. At least she did until the day he asked her to stop by the department store to see the new chair he wanted!

Mother's face went white and she could barely speak as he led her to the chair. The chair my father had his eye on didn't fit her coordinated home decor at all. Plus the monstrosity would take up half the room. My sister and I gasped in disbelief as we gazed upon the ugly contraption. Mother walked around the furniture showroom pointing out alternatives, but Daddy didn't lose his enthusiasm for the recliner. Mother fought back the tears and bit her lower lip when she saw that his heart was set on this chair. She knew that this was one small sacrifice she could make to show my father just how much she loved, honored, and respected him. It was also a special way she could show her gratitude for all the things he did for her—especially protecting her from all those bugs.

When the store delivered the chair, we discovered that Daddy had been right about one thing—it was the most comfortable chair in the house. The chair's ugliness didn't seem to matter anymore. Every time Daddy left the room, my sister, brother, and I made a mad dash for it. I confess there was a lot of pushing and shoving going on because we soon discovered that Daddy's change would fall out of his pocket into the side of the cushion. The coins made an excellent addition to our allowance. Even our beloved dog, Chip, would hop up in the chair when his master was out of the room. If Mother heard Daddy coming, she would rush into the family room to make sure his chair was vacant. After a while, she didn't even have to, because when we heard his footsteps, we'd run for another chair.

As the years went by and all the children left home, Daddy's chair remained. It had been reupholstered a few times, making it more attractive, but it was still Daddy's old chair. Now that he had retired, he often caught a nap in his chair in the afternoon.

When the first grandchild was born, Mother would sit on the arm of the chair as Daddy sat holding their precious granddaughter, Kimberly, and then later, Meg and Keith. As the grandchildren grew, it didn't take them long to discover all the joys of "Papa's chair." They, too, fought over sitting in the chair or hunting for quarters just as we had as children. But the moment Papa would appear, they'd hop down under their grandmother's watchful eye. Papa would often insist that they keep their seat, but they refused, not wanting to deprive their grandfather of his greatest pleasure.

There were other telltale events in the life of the chair. When I took my husband, Ken, home to meet my family for the first time, he plopped down in my father's chair. The neighbors, aunts, uncles, and cousins who had dropped by to meet Ken shrieked in unison, "That's Daddy's chair." Alarmed, Ken jumped up, thinking he'd sat on someone, but when my father insisted that he keep his seat, I knew instantly that he really liked Ken. Later when our family dog grew old and decrepit and deaf, Daddy would often take another seat so as not to disturb his faithful old friend.

My father is in his eighties now, and when we visit, the sight of his chair with his slippers, newspaper, glasses, and the bug swatter that mother has lovingly placed by the side evoke warm feelings of my childhood. I know immediately that I'm home. The last time we visited, Daddy told me that one more of his friends had died the week before. "I'm sorry, Daddy," I said quietly, sensing his grief at losing yet another friend. "Don't be sorry," Daddy explained. "He died in his chair—what a way to go!" Daddy's chair may have begun as just a small sign of respect, but the lessons learned about family, love, and marriage surrounding that chair will last for generations.

SUSAN WALES

*I love it, I love it; and who shall dare
To chide me for loving that old arm chair.*
ELIZA COOK

MAYNARD, MY LOVE

❧

We that are true lovers run into strange capers.

WILLIAM SHAKESPEARE

I never planned to have a career in politics. But right after I married Maynard, he told me that he intended to run for Georgia state office as prosecuting attorney—and he'd really need my help.

Me, campaigning in public? I balked. "Maynard, honey," I pleaded, "the only office I ever ran for was patrol leader in my Girl Scout troop."

But Maynard told me all I had to do was be my sweet self. The secret to success, he said, was to do as the voters did at the various functions we attended. If they ate watermelon, I should eat watermelon.

I was so madly in love with my new husband I would have done anything he asked. So I agreed. I followed his directions carefully, and soon I began to feel more comfortable. People were kind to me, and we attended every potluck and cakewalk possible. If two functions took place on the same night, Maynard would go to one, and I'd go to the other.

Then one weekend we were invited to South Georgia to the town of Wigham for the Rattlesnake Roundup. During our stay, we went to a Baptist church on Sunday and stayed until two o'clock in the afternoon. Afterward, Pastor Cooper and his wife invited us to join them for Sunday dinner at their house.

My husband was pleased about this and reminded me on the way over that this preacher's opinion was extremely influential in these parts. "This could be the most important dinner you've eaten in months," he told me.

There were thirteen children in the Cooper family. They were not the typical formal Southern folk we so often associated with, but the food was delicious, and I was genuinely charmed by the Coopers.

After lunch I offered to help Mrs. Cooper with the dishes. "Thank you, honey," she said. "Draw me some water out there on the porch."

I was from Virginia and had grown up in the city. Rustic living was unfamiliar to me. Mrs. Cooper seemed amused at my lack of experience and carefully showed me how to draw the water and heat it on the stove for the dishes. After we had finished our kitchen chores, she led me outside to the porch.

"Do you dip, Mrs. Smith?"

"What do you mean?" I asked.

"A little snuff now and then," she said.

Suddenly my whole life flashed before me. If I said the wrong thing, I felt certain I could lose the election for my dear husband. And so I fell back on his very clear advice: "Always take whatever is offered."

"I never have taken snuff before," I told Mrs. Cooper, "but if you would like for me to join you, I will."

Mrs. Cooper was a very short woman, and now she stood on her tiptoes and told me, "Pull your lip out, honey." Then she filled my mouth so full of snuff that I thought I was going to be asphyxiated right then and there.

"Don't spit it out now," she directed. "Just sniff it and enjoy it."

Maynard could hardly believe his ears when I told him what I'd done. "You took a dip?" he asked. "For me?" He hooted with laughter for some time. Then he hugged me, assuring me I'd done the right thing.

As it turned out, the Coopers personally saw to it that just about everyone in South Georgia voted for Maynard. He took the election and gave me all the credit when he won by a landslide in the Coopers' home county.

Maynard has passed on now, but never once in all the years of our marriage did he lose my vote. And as for Mrs. Cooper, she long ago became one of my best friends. She still likes to laugh about the first time we met.

"My lands, dear!" she says. "How could I not vote for a man who could inspire such devotion in a woman?"

And I have to agree.

HELEN SMITH

NOAH'S ARK

'Mid pleasures and palaces though we may roam,
Be it ever so humble, there's no place like home.

AUTHOR UNKNOWN

When my husband, Dan, and I built our dream house, we planned to live there for a lifetime. We imagined growing old, sitting in our rocking chairs on our sunporch to watch the grandchildren play in the garden.

All our hopes and dreams for the future ended when Dan suffered a heart attack and died. I was devastated, and no matter how hard I tried, I was unable to adjust to widowhood. My dear friends offered their love and support, but as the time passed, my grief remained as strong as ever.

One day a close friend, Eliza, stopped by to encourage me. "Joanne, it's time for you to live again," she said. I nodded as I had so many times before until she added, "I think you should begin dating."

I was stunned and replied, "You must be joking." I was hoping this would be the end of that silly dating nonsense, until another friend called to invite me to her Christmas party. "I've asked my friend Tal Dryman to escort you," she said.

I was pleasantly surprised when Tal and I enjoyed one another's company at my friend's party. When he asked me to dinner the next week, I promptly said yes. He took me to a lovely restaurant, but afterward the dancing was too much for me.

The next morning I was so traumatized by my return to the dating scene that I packed my car and my cat, Rita, and fled to South Georgia to the safety of my parents' home. I probably would have hidden out there forever if I hadn't had bills to pay, gardens to weed, and plants to water.

When I walked into my house, the phone was ringing. It was Tal Dryman asking me where I'd been. I accepted another date with him and then another. A year later Tal and I realized we had fallen in love.

When Tal proposed, we knew we had some difficult decisions to make. Just like Noah's ark, we had two of everything. We decided it was more practical for me to move into Tal's larger home. My friend Ann, an interior designer, helped us combine our belongings. As she worked on each room, she kept saying, "Your things fit together perfectly—it was meant to be." We all agreed the house looked beautiful.

In all the excitement of our wedding, I had not seriously considered the consequences of selling my dream home. After we returned from our honeymoon, the realization that I would never see my grandchildren play in my gardens suddenly hit me, and I was devastated.

Several weeks later Tal suggested, "Maybe we were too hasty having you move into my house. Would you prefer that I sell my home?" I was deeply touched by his kind offer, but I knew it wasn't practical to live in my smaller home, and I loved his home blended with our things. So the next morning I made the dreaded call to the real estate agent.

Later that night Tal's son called. Tal seemed to be involved in a serious conversation, so I left him alone. When Tal walked into our bedroom, he had a big smile on his face and said, "Guess what, darling? My son wants to buy your home."

"Sold," I said, as I gave my husband, the greatest salesman in the world, a smile and a big kiss!

Today Tal's son and daughter-in-law host our blended family gatherings at my former home. Tal and I often sit on that sun porch, drinking lemonade and happily watching our grandchildren play in the gardens of hope I planted years ago.

JOANNE DRYMAN

CELEBRATE THE MOMENTS

Love looks not with the eyes,
but with the mind.

WILLIAM SHAKESPEARE

Those who are wise romantics will realize that some special date or event every year can be used to fan the romantic flame. I recall one man who put together a very special celebration for his wife to honor her for a sacrifice she had made for him.

It was the eve of his graduation from a long, grueling master's degree program. Four years of intensive, full-time study had finally found him about to receive his diploma.

His wife planned a special party where many of their friends were to come and help him celebrate the long awaited "day of deliverance." There would be cake, refreshments, banners, streamers, a pool nearby, croquet, and other yard games. Many people had already accepted her invitation to come, and it looked like it would be a full house. Her husband, though, had other ideas. He secretly contacted each person who had received an invitation and told them he wanted to make the party a surprise in honor of her. Yes, there would be banners, streamers, and all the rest, but they would bear her name, not his.

He wanted to do something special to let her know how much he appreciated the years of sacrifice she'd devoted to his graduation. Working full-time to put him through and putting off her dreams of a house and family had, in many ways, been harder on her than the long hours of study had been on him.

When the day arrived, she was busy with preparations and last minute details, still convinced that all was going according to plan. He arranged to get her away from the party site, and while she was gone, he put up a huge banner with her name on it. During that time all the guests arrived as well.

She returned to be greeted with a huge "SURPRISE!!!" and when she realized what was going on, she could barely fight back the tears. Her husband asked a few people to share what they most appreciated about her. Then he stood before them and, with tender words of love and appreciation, expressed his gratitude for all she'd done for him. When he was through, they saluted her with an iced-tea toast.

The rest of the evening was a fun-filled fiesta of laughing, catching up with one another, water volleyball, yard games, and more food than anyone could eat. It was a celebration of an experience they both shared, and by commemorating it in a special way, this husband created a lifelong, romantic memorial to his wife's love and dedication.

GARY SMALLEY

From *Love Is a Decision* (Nashville, Tennessee: Word Publishing, 1989). All rights reserved.

TO MY DARLING WIFE, SHIRLEY

How do I love thee? Let me count the ways.
I love thee to the depth and breadth and height
My soul can reach, from feeling out of sight
For the ends of being and ideal grace.

ELIZABETH BARRETT BROWNING

I'm sure you remember the many, many occasions during our eight years of marriage when the tide of love and affection soared high above the crest…times when our feeling for each other was almost limitless.

This kind of intense emotion can't be brought about voluntarily, but it often accompanies a time of particular happiness. We felt it when I was offered my first professional position. We felt it when the world's most precious child came home from the maternity ward of Huntington Hospital. We felt it when the University of Southern California chose to award a doctoral degree to me. But emotions are strange! We felt the same closeness when the opposite kind of event took place, when threat and potential disaster entered our lives. We felt an intense closeness when a medical problem threatened to postpone our marriage plans. We felt it when you were hospitalized last year. I felt it intensely when I knelt over your unconscious form after a grinding automobile accident.

I'm trying to say this: both happiness and threat bring that overwhelming appreciation and affection for our beloved sweethearts. But the fact is, most of life is made up of neither disaster nor unusual hilarity. Rather, it is composed of the routine, calm, everyday events in which we participate. And during these times, I enjoy the quiet, serene love that actually surpasses the effervescent display, in many ways. It is not as exuberant, perhaps, but it runs deep and solid. I find myself firmly in that kind of love on this Eighth Anniversary. Today I feel the steady and quiet affection that comes from a devoted heart. I am committed to you and your happiness, more now than I've ever been. I want to remain your "sweetheart."

When even crises throw us together emotionally, we will enjoy the thrill and romantic excitement. But during life's routine, like today, my love stands undiminished. Happy Anniversary to my wonderful wife.

Your Jim

The key phrase in my statement is, "I am committed to you." You see, my love for Shirley is not blown back and forth by the winds of change...by circumstances and environmental influences. Even though my fickle emotions jump from one extreme to another, my commitment remains solidly anchored in place. I have chosen to love my wife, and that choice is sustained by an uncompromising will. "In sickness and in health; for richer or poorer; for better or worse; from this day forward..." This essential commitment of the will is sorely missing in so many modern marriages. I love you, they seem to say, as long as I feel attracted to you...or as long as someone else doesn't look better...or as long as it is to my advantage to continue the relationship. Sooner or later, this uncommitted love will certainly vaporize.

How, then, can real love be distinguished from temporary infatuation? If the feeling is unreliable, how can one assess the commitment of his will? There is only one answer to that question: It takes time. The best advice I can give a couple contemplating marriage (or any other important decision) is this: make *no* important, life-shaping decisions quickly or impulsively, and when in doubt, stall for time. That's not a bad suggestion for all of us to apply.

DR. JAMES DOBSON

For Better, for Worse

MARRIAGE IS A LONG JOURNEY THROUGH A CHANGING LANDSCAPE. IT ISN'T ALWAYS SCENIC. IT ISN'T ALWAYS PRETTY. IT ISN'T ALWAYS FUN. IT ISN'T ALWAYS EXCITING. ROMANCE MAY GO INTO HIDING. FEELINGS MAY LAG SO MANY MILES BEHIND DETERMINATION THAT YOU WONDER IF THEY WILL EVER CATCH UP. BUT ALL THE WHILE, THE ROAD IS LEADING SOMEWHERE. STAY ON THAT ROAD, ENDURE THE DESOLATE STRETCHES, CLIMB THE LONG HILLS TOGETHER, AND YOU WILL FIND VISTAS BEYOND WHAT YOU HAD IMAGINED.

THE ROAD TO "FOR BETTER" SOMETIMES TRAVELS THROUGH "FOR WORSE."

AND IT IS WORTH THE JOURNEY.

HEART'S FIRE

Keep the home fires burning,
While your hearts are yearning.
Though your lads are far away
They dream of home.

Lena Guilbert Ford

*S*arah was only a freshman when she met Jim, a popular upperclassman, at a church picnic. They began to date, and as time passed, Sarah's parents grew to like and admire the fine young man.

After Jim graduated from high school, he got a job and attended evening classes at the local junior college so he could remain near Sarah. The two spent every possible moment together dreaming of the day they would be married.

But their starry-eyed planning came to a sudden halt when the government announced the draft lottery for the Vietnam War. Jim and Sarah nervously sat in front of the radio as the birth dates were read. When Jim's was among the first ones drawn, he immediately hugged Sarah, who in turn burst into tears. There was little doubt that Jim would be sent to Vietnam.

Jim tried to be brave and was willing to fight, but the young couple spent hours anguishing over their approaching separation. They knew some people were skeptical about whether such a young love could survive the trials of war—or should even try. But when Jim was shipped out, Sarah vowed her eternal love. "I'll be praying every day that God will safely return you to me," she promised.

Jim went through boot camp and then on to Vietnam. Sarah wrote him every day and sent him tapes with news from home. She could hardly wait for school days to end so she could rush home to check the mailbox.

Then Jim's letters stopped coming.

Sarah panicked. Her family, as well as Jim's parents, tried to reassure her. "Sometimes the soldiers are on a secret mission," her father explained, "and they're forbidden to let anyone know their whereabouts."

Then one evening Jim's parents called to say they were coming over to see Sarah and her parents. As Jim's parents stepped out of the car, Sarah saw that his mother's eyes were red and swollen and his father's head was bowed. She began to scream even before her father, the local Baptist minister, could invite them in.

Jim, his parents explained, was missing in action—and feared dead.

His voice choked with emotion, Sarah's father prayed for Jim's safe return and God's comfort for all who loved him. But Sarah could not stop weeping and crying out Jim's name.

As the months wore on, Sarah's family and friends became increasingly concerned about the young girl. She carefully studied every news report and lingered over every soldier's face in the newspapers. She believed that Jim was alive and would come back to her.

Finally, one of Jim's buddies wrote to Sarah, telling her that he'd witnessed Jim's helicopter crash and explode. Even though the army had Jim listed as MIA, there was no way Jim could have survived that explosion.

Still, Sarah would not give up hope. She stubbornly persisted in waiting and praying for Jim's safe return.

A long, sad year passed. One Sunday in early summer, Sarah's father was preaching his morning sermon when he stopped midsentence. The minister turned pale, and several deacons rushed to his side. He pushed them away and shouted, "Praise God!" as he hurried down from the pulpit.

Every head in the church pivoted as he ran up the long aisle. There at the back of the church, in full dress uniform, was a handsome soldier. It was Jim.

Sarah screamed, "He's alive! He's alive! I just knew he was alive! Oh, dear God, thank you!" Then she dissolved into sobs as her father led Jim toward her. Jim reached out and wrapped his arms around Sarah as his parents rushed to embrace the pair. The organist began to play the "Hallelujah Chorus," and the congregation cheered.

A few weeks later the same congregation listened intently as Jim explained how God had saved his life. He'd been thrown from his helicopter minutes before it exploded. He had landed in the swamp below—inside enemy territory—and was soon captured by the Vietcong. He remained in a makeshift prisoner-of-war camp deep in the jungle for nearly a year before he attempted an escape.

"It was as though an angel was leading me back to the American line that night," he told them. "I just kept walking, and after two days and nights, I arrived at one of our camps. From there, I was airlifted to a hospital and then sent home. I am convinced it was Sarah's love and prayers that enabled me to survive."

Not long afterward Sarah and Jim were married by Sarah's father. Many of the guests wept openly throughout the ceremony. The nation had suffered so much loss. But this wedding was a sweet reminder that hope is worth hanging on to and that even through the tragedies of war, true love endures.

THE BEST OF TIMES, THE WORST OF TIMES

Fair or foul—on land or sea—
Come the wind or weather
Best or worst, whate'er they be,
We shall share together.

WINTHROP MACKWORTH PRAED

Caught up in a whirlwind of prewedding festivities, parties, and showers, I had never been happier in my life. There were those troubling sharp pains in my abdomen, but everyone assured me that was just prewedding jitters. Yet, as our wedding day drew closer, the pain intensified.

The next thing I knew, I was waking up in a hospital. I struggled to focus as my eyes met the eyes of the man I loved most in the world, my fiancé, Eric. Confused, I searched Eric's eyes, trying to remember.

Suddenly the memories came flooding back. A ruptured ovary had sent me into emergency surgery. I didn't have to ask—it was written all over Eric's face. We—I—would never have children.

Stoically I began the speech I had rehearsed so many times in the haze of anesthesia. "I know how much we—you—want children, so I can't possibly marry you now." Eric was silent, and with each passing second, I felt my plans for a life with him slipping away.

It had been our mutual love of children and family that had initially brought us together. Eric, a handsome and successful lawyer, clearly was

the most eligible bachelor in our circle of friends. I was flattered and surprised when he focused his attentions on me. He confessed that what
attracted him to me were not only the qualities he wanted in a wife but
also those he desired for the mother of his children. As he slipped the
sparkling engagement ring on my finger, we vowed to have at least five
kids.

Those happy thoughts were abruptly interrupted by the sound of
Eric's voice calling my name, propelling me back into the stark reality of
the hospital room. Knowing our plans for a family, and possibly even a life
together, had been cut away by the surgeon's knife, I braced myself for the
devastating blow.

"Ellie, you're right. I do want to have children—"

"Fine," I pretended. "You have no obligation—"

"But," he interrupted, as he held his fingers to my lips to silence me,
"not as much as I want you to be my wife."

Tears of relief rolled down my face.

"We'll adopt," he assured me.

On our wedding day when we recited the words "For better, for
worse," our family and friends cried. We knew that storms come with any
marriage, but we had endured disappointments before we had even spoken our vows. For this reason we were confident that our love would sustain us through the dark clouds that would float in and out of our future.

After a couple of years of marriage, we began to seriously discuss
adoption. We had no idea just how complicated the process was until we
met with an adoption counselor. We had fully expected to have a baby in
our arms within days. But each time we were rejected, I sank deeper into
despair. Eric would lovingly pull me out as he held me tenderly in his
arms and reassured me that "God's timing is perfect. He has a special child
for us. We just have to wait." I so wanted to believe my husband, but with
each rejection, my doubts grew stronger.

A year later we abandoned our adoption efforts when Eric's mother,
Anna, was diagnosed with terminal cancer. Once again, our love grew
stronger as we endured these painful circumstances. When the hospital
summoned us in the middle of the night, we knew the end was near.

Expecting the worse, we were stunned when we found Anna sitting up. Although she was very weak, she firmly clasped both our hands and prayed for the Lord to bless us with children, and then she slipped away peacefully. We left the hospital arm in arm and knew in our hearts that God would give us a child.

Just four months later our counselor announced that a teenager had chosen us to be the parents of her baby! "There are some complications," the counselor hesitantly explained. "The child will most likely have some developmental delays." Our hearts sank, but as we looked into one another's eyes, we saw that our love had grown strong enough to endure the circumstances. We knew without a doubt this was the child God had for us.

We could hardly contain our joy and our love when the baby appropriately arrived at our home on Thanksgiving Day. My parents had just come from the East Coast to spend the holidays with us. They were amazed but overjoyed when we introduced them to their new grandson, whom we named Will for my father.

God used the years that Eric and I spent waiting and praying for a baby to strengthen us. This strength coupled with our love has sustained us through the best and worst times of our lives together. As we have successfully weathered the storms, Eric's words have proven true many times over: "God's timing is perfect!"

AUTHOR UNKNOWN

OUR RAINBOW FAMILY

❧

Two faces o'er a cradle bent:
Two hands above the head were locked:
These pressed each other while they rocked,
Those watched a life that love had sent.
Solemn hour! O hidden power!

GEORGE ELIOT

My life changed the day I met a young army captain named Jerome Duffy. He was ramrod straight, handsome, and serious. I felt my heart sinking right out of sight. As I got to know him, I loved Jerome's strength and his caring nature. And I guess something happened in him too, because we fell hard for each other.

We'd both grown up around large families—and we both loved kids. I couldn't think of another man on earth I'd rather marry and raise a family with. The more time we spent talking about our hopes and dreams, the more God seemed to be saying, "You're exactly right for each other."

We were married within six months. Nine months and one day later the first of our dreams came true when I delivered a beautiful baby at the Queen of Angels Hospital in Los Angeles, where I worked as a nurse. Jerome and I were blissful.

Then the unthinkable happened. Our precious baby lived for only two days. We both felt like our dreams had suddenly crashed down on our heads.

Fortunately we had our faith to lean on. My mother, who had been raised by nuns in a convent in New Orleans, had taught her children to trust God in all circumstances. She'd say to me, "Honey, God always has a plan for you. He's always working it out—and it's gonna be good!"

Jerome had also been raised in a loving Catholic family. His steadfastness at this time meant the world to me. He'd take me in his strong arms and say, "Darling, it's going to be okay. We're going to get through this together."

We decided to try again. Within months I was pregnant, and our hopes soared. But then I lost our second baby. And, unbelievably, our third.

Between our shock and our grief, we had a hard time grasping what was happening. We felt as if our faith had been tested and our future had been ripped away. How were we going to have the family of our dreams if I couldn't deliver one healthy baby? Short of a miracle, we'd never have children of our own—it was that simple.

The nuns at the hospital where I worked tried to encourage me. "God has another plan," they'd tell me. "Just keep praying." But I wasn't so sure anymore.

Jerome was as strong as ever. "Juanita, honey," he'd say. "I still love you with all my heart. We don't have to have kids to be happy." No one uderstood more than Jerome—that's what I loved so much about him. He also wanted a baby just as much as I, and he completely empathized with me.

By then the Korean War was raging, so the U.S. Army sent Jerome overseas. Now, of course, even the possibility of pregnancy was gone. I lived with my parents in Los Angeles and continued working as a nurse. I missed my husband terribly. It was a lonely time of trying to think up another kind of life I might want.

Jerome tried to be there for me, even from a distance. When he wrote, he told me about his company's new campaign—which didn't have a thing to do with guns. Captain Duffy would line up his troops every Sunday and proceed to a nearby orphanage. He'd put everyone to work, doing chores, playing with the kids, and building "hot floors"—raised floors that could have fires underneath to provide the children with warmth.

Jerome also explained how hard it was for these orphans to fit into

Korean life, especially those of mixed race. Because of all the soldiers in Korea at that time, thousands of children of mixed race were being born. My husband had a special sensitivity about this issue, because he was of mixed Puerto Rican and black descent. Other kids had often been tough on him growing up.

One day I got a letter that changed everything. Jerome told me he had met an eighteen-month-old boy at the orphanage who wanted to spend every minute with him. "Darling, I want you to know that I do not intend to leave Korea without him."

His words stunned me. He felt that strongly? No one understood a mother's longing for a child like Jerome did. He felt exactly the same way as I felt. Finally I could see how his strength was bringing him closer to me, not further away. Our marriage was stronger than ever after trusting God in spite of what we had been through.

It was the beginning of months of struggle to get the boy to the States—piles of red tape and endless medical tests. Jerome and I prayed for one miracle at a time, and they happened. Since Jerome had to remain in Korea, he finally found two Korean students who agreed to fly the child to San Francisco, where they were enrolling in college. I would meet them at the airport.

Imagine my delight when the two Korean students got off the plane with Vincent—and he ran right into my waiting arms. He clung to me as if he knew I was his mother. In no time at all, Vincent was running around like any healthy toddler. I couldn't have loved this child more if he had been my own baby.

Before long, it dawned on me. He was.

And that was just the beginning of our family. A few years later we adopted another racially mixed child, a three-year-old girl we named Maria. Then a mixed-race girl from Taiwan became our Vickie.

We'd lost three babies, but God had given us three beautiful children of our own to love and cherish—children who needed us desperately. The nuns had been right. God did have a plan, and it was good!

And it got even better. Somehow my own body had been healing. Soon I was pregnant again. I sailed through two pregnancies and delivered perfectly healthy boys, Billy and Jerome Jr.

By the time that army colonel of mine retired in 1970, we were sur-rounded by kids on every side—children, grandchildren, nieces, and nephews. And every one of them still reminds Duffy and me that right behind the disappointments in life stands a good God—and the dreams of a lifetime.

And love can help us bring them home.

JUANITA DUFFY

In loving memory of Colonel Jerome Duffy, United States Army, retired. 1921–1998.

THE LOVEBIRDS

‿

For the years fleet away with the wings of the dove.

LORD BYRON

By the time I reached my early thirties, I'd spent my entire life looking for a love that would last. After a failed marriage and a series of broken relationships, I'd come to the sad and bitter conclusion that love never came to stay. Best to try to live without it.

About this time I was offered an exciting job with an impressive salary in a nearby city. This seemed like a new beginning for my young daughter and me. We found a charming cottage in a family neighborhood near my office, and after several inquiries, I enrolled my daughter in a good school.

But I had one more hurdle to climb before I could totally relax. Since I had no family and knew no one in our new city, I was forced to run an ad to arrange for after-school child care for my daughter. Selecting the person who would spend so much time with Margaret was more than a little frightening.

I prayed that God would send the right person, and I took great care with the ad. But as I began interviewing the menagerie of applicants who responded, I wondered if we shouldn't pack our bags. First came a guy with a tongue ring so large that he spoke with a lisp. Next a retired military man with ideas about discipline that curled my hair. Then a sharp-tongued grandmother who refused to climb my stairs.

None were exactly the role model I had in mind for my daughter. I was on the verge of tears when the last applicant arrived. She was a friendly young art student, dressed in a crisply starched white shirt and black suit. As we began to talk, my hopes gradually soared. There was something special about this young girl. And before the interview was over, I knew God had brought Julie to us.

Margaret adored Julie as much as I did. So much so, that in time she liked to pretend that Julie was her big sister. After a few weeks, Julie confided that her parents had divorced when her sister was killed in an accident. I could see the pain in her eyes. I comforted her and told her it is not unusual for couples to be pulled apart over that kind of loss. "Maybe, in time, your parents will get back together," I said.

"It's too late—I have a stepfather now," she told me. And I realized that Julie needed our love as much as we needed hers.

Things continued to run smoothly. A few weeks later Julie explained that her father was coming to town for a visit and wanted to take us all to dinner. Being Julie's first time away from home, I understood why her father wanted to meet the woman with whom his daughter was living. And I agreed to go along.

As soon as Julie, Margaret, and I walked into the restaurant, a smiling man approached us with an outstretched hand and introduced himself as Jerry. Noticing that we were the same height, I thought, *At least I won't be attracted to him. I like tall men.*

But after chatting with Jerry for a few minutes, I became enchanted by him and forgot about his height. And he seemed to like me, too. The next weekend Jerry flew to Atlanta to see Julie—and me—again.

Over the next few years, Jerry and I saw each other often. But I'll admit that my fear of losing at love got in the way. I was afraid that if I gave him my heart, my *whole* heart, he'd fly away with it and I'd never recover. Our girls were as patient and respectful of us as possible.

Then tragedy struck. First, Jerry's mother developed Alzheimer's. He had always been extremely close to her, and so he moved home to care for her. Then my own mother, whom I spoke to weekly and adored, suffered a heart attack. Within months of each other, both Jerry and I lost our mothers.

The next time Jerry and I spoke he asked the question I had grown to dread. "Life is too short," he said. "Please, let's give our love a chance and become a family. Will you be my wife?"

To my own great shock, I said, "Yes, I will!" Without knowing it, I had changed. Perhaps with my mother's death something stubborn and untrusting in my heart had finally been put to rest. Jerry was right. I needed to love as I needed to breathe.

Margaret and Julie were ecstatic when they heard our news.

We decided to get married by the ocean on Sea Island, Georgia. Before my mother had died, she'd read about a wedding where the bride and groom released doves when the minister pronounced them man and wife. She thought this was a lovely idea and told me that if Jerry and I married, I should do this especially for her.

After checking with the bird sanctuary located on the island where we planned to marry, Jerry agreed it was a marvelous idea. "We'll do it in honor of both our mothers," he said.

A close friend decorated the birds' cage with white tulle and ribbons for the wedding. As Jerry and I finally stood before the minister, overlooking the ocean and surrounded by close friends and family, I was overcome with happiness. As our lovebirds cooed, we spoke our vows to one another with tearful tenderness.

When the minister pronounced us man and wife, we opened the cage door and released our two lovebirds. Our guests marveled as they flew side by side, soaring high above the palm trees and toward the coral sunset over the ocean. For a brief moment the lovebirds hovered over the waves with sparks of sunlight reflecting off their white wings.

Then, as if God was sending us a promise, suddenly the birds swooped down and flew back toward the wedding party. One gently landed on my shoulder; the other on Jerry's. Many of our surprised wedding guests, including Margaret and Julie, were moved to tears. Jerry and I wept openly.

Amazingly, the two birds returned home with us. And to this day their gentle cooing reminds us that, this time, love has come to stay.

MARGARET DICKINSON WATKINS

THE MIRACLE
OF THE DIAMOND

Whatever a man prays for,
he prays for a miracle.

IVAN SERGEYEVICH TURGENEV

A lthough Charlie and I had been married for over thirty-five years, we were struggling with problems in our health, as well as our marriage. I was beginning to doubt that God heard my pleas for healing. When the weekend approached, I was determined that we would enjoy ourselves and forget our problems for a while.

Charlie and I had gotten up early and planned our day over morning coffee. He would mow the lawn and tend the gardens, while I entertained three of our grandchildren. Afterwards, we'd all spend the rest of the afternoon out on our deck grilling hamburgers and playing in the hot tub.

My husband got the tractor out of the barn while I drove over to our son's house to pick up the children. Ryan, Kyle, and Krista greeted me with big smiles and their bathing suits in hand. The children were so anxious to get wet that they helped in the garden to speed things along. Finally the chores were done, and all five of us headed out to the deck to splash away the rest of the afternoon.

After our grandkids had gone home, Charlie and I sat down at the kitchen table with sighs of exhaustion and contentment. But then, gazing at my husband's hands, I noticed something that brought our lovely afternoon to a screeching halt. The diamond from Charlie's ring—the one that once belonged to his mother—was missing! How could I tell him?

Charlie was an only child, and his mother had died just before his thirtieth birthday. That Christmas, his father had his mother's beautiful diamond set into a new brushed gold mounting and presented it to his son. The ring immediately became Charlie's most treasured possession.

Finally I said in a quiet voice, "Honey, look at your hand. Your mother's diamond is gone."

Charlie stared at the empty gold mounting in painful silence. He seemed unable to even speak.

"I will look for it!" I cried. "I will try to find it."

"Glenna, do you realize what an impossible task that would be? I have mowed an acre of grass, worked on the gardens, cleaned the car, and played with the grandchildren. No, honey, it's just gone. Let it be."

After Charlie quietly left the room, I sat at the table and wondered what to do. It was an easy decision. I headed out the door to search before darkness took over. First I searched the car. Next I checked the tractor and the barn. From there, I walked the yard.

I was about to give up when my five-year-old friend from across the street came over.

"What's the matter, Miss Glenna?" Brenton asked. "Can I help?"

As I smiled at my little neighbor, I was reminded of my grandkids. And then it hit me. "Of course! The hot tub!" I shouted.

I asked Brenton to wait while I ran into the house and put on my bathing suit. Brenton sat on the edge of the tub and cheered me on while I searched for the diamond. One, two, three times I reached beneath the water and felt with my hands all over the smooth surface of the tub. No diamond. It was growing dark. I took the filter out and checked it. Still no diamond.

Finally, I cried out to God. "Oh, Lord, please help me find this diamond. You know how very special it is to my husband. If it is in this water, please direct my hand to it!"

At that moment, my hand felt a point. I grasped it and brought it up to the surface. It was the missing diamond!

Brenton and I cheered loudly enough for the whole neighborhood to hear us. Then I took the treasure of my husband's heart and presented it to him. He was obviously moved—not only that I'd found his diamond, but that I'd searched for it even when he'd given up hope.

The next day I took the diamond and the setting to the jeweler. She had worked on the ring on two other occasions and was quite familiar with it. Now, as she carefully examined it through her jeweler's loupe, she declared in surprise, "Glenna, this stone is perfect! No chip!"

Somehow, a small old chip on the diamond had disappeared.

At home, Charlie and I marveled together over the news. It was hard to decide which miracle was greater—that I'd found the diamond, or that the diamond had been "healed." From that moment on, our marriage began to heal, too.

Finally we decided that the greatest miracle of all was what the ring represented. After all, diamonds chip. Gold tarnishes. Rings are lost and found. But love—like that of my husband's parents, and now like ours—lasts forever.

GLENNA GEBAUER

THE CHRISTMAS TREE

But let it whistle as it will.
We'll keep our Christmas merry still.

Sir Walter Scott

'd known Beth all my life, but it wasn't until I ran into her after college that we fell in love. I was thrilled when she agreed to marry me, especially in light of my career plans. Immediately following our wedding, we flew to Japan, where I intended to study the Japanese language in anticipation of becoming an international lawyer. I could offer Beth no white picket fence, at least not for a while.

Japan was exciting for me, but for Beth, who had never been away from home, it was a difficult adjustment. She knew no Japanese and couldn't find a job. Our apartment was smaller than the bathroom we have today! Even though Beth was a great sport about it all, I knew she was very lonely and homesick.

Late that fall Beth's spirits seemed to lift as she began planning our first Christmas together. She busily made ornaments, centerpieces, and stockings. "I'm going to make our first Christmas the most memorable ever!" she proclaimed.

When I came home each night, she'd proudly display a new Christmas ornament for our tree. She was so happy about them I didn't have the heart to tell her there were no Christmas trees in Japan! In fact it was against Japanese law to cut down trees.

As the season drew closer, I began praying every day for a Christmas tree for my wife. "Nothing is impossible with God," I reminded myself. I asked everyone I knew or met if they could help me. I tracked down every lead I was given, but I couldn't produce a single tree.

One night Beth announced that she was ready for her tree, and I was finally forced to explain there wouldn't be one. My sweet wife was so gracious about the news. But I could see the disappointment in her eyes even as she declared, "We'll still have a wonderful Christmas!"

Christmas Eve found me dejected about the tree, but I was also happily anticipating the evening with my Beth. When I got off the bus, I began to run toward our apartment. Yes, I was going home empty-handed, but I was going home to the most wonderful wife in the whole world!

Then I saw it. At first I rubbed my eyes to make sure I wasn't hallucinating. There in the gutter was a beautiful Christmas tree, tinsel still sparkling in its branches! Surely someone had thrown it away. But how could that be, since it was Christmas Eve?

I scooped up the tree and took it home to my bride. Beth squealed with delight when she greeted me at the door. It was a miracle!

After eating the delicious dinner Beth had prepared, we spent the evening decorating our tree and marveling together over God's kindness to us. We kept the tree up as long as we could, discarding it only after it became a fire hazard.

Today we live in America, and getting a Christmas tree is as easy as a trip to the woods or the supermarket. But we've never found another tree quite as beautiful as that first one. Beth was right. Our first Christmas was the most memorable ever.

FRED BLUMER

For Richer, for Poorer

SOME COUPLES BEGIN MARRIAGE EXTREMELY POOR, AND EXTREMELY HAPPY. AND THROUGH THE YEARS, SOME OF THOSE SAME COUPLES GAIN A GREAT MEASURE OF PROSPERITY... BUT ADD TO THEIR HAPPINESS NOTHING AT ALL.

CARS AND HOMES AND FURNISHINGS ARE NICE, TOYS AND BOATS AND RVS ARE FUN, STOCK PORTFOLIOS AND MUTUAL FUNDS GIVE A PLEASANT ILLUSION OF SECURITY...BUT WHERE DID THE LAUGHTER GO? WHERE'S THE SPONTANEITY? WHERE ARE THOSE TIMES OF LEANING ON EACH OTHER, COVERING FOR EACH OTHER, CRYING WITH EACH OTHER, AND DEPENDING ON EACH OTHER AS IF THERE WERE NO TOMORROW?

WEALTHY OR POOR, A HUSBAND AND WIFE MUST FIND AGAIN THOSE THINGS THAT MADE THEM RICH IN JOY, RICH IN ADVENTURE, RICH IN THE DELIGHT OF ONE ANOTHER.

TIMING

Give what you have to someone.
It may be far better than you dare think.

HENRY WADSWORTH LONGFELLOW

In September, Terry Shafer was strolling the shops in Moline, Illinois. She knew exactly what she wanted to get her husband, David, for Christmas, but she realized it might be too expensive. A little shop on Fifth attracted her attention, so she popped inside. Her eyes darted toward the corner display. "That's it!" she smiled as she nodded with pleasure. "How much?" she asked the shopkeeper.

"Only $127.40."

Her smile faded into disappointment as she realized David's salary couldn't stand such a jolt. It was out of the question. Yet she hated to give up without a try, so she applied a little womanly persistence.

"Uh, what about putting this aside for me? Maybe I could pay a little each week then pick it up a few days before Christmas."

"No," the merchant said. "I won't do that." Then he smiled. "I'll gift-wrap it right now. You can take it with you and pay me later," he said. Terry was elated. She agreed to pay so much every week, then thanked and thanked the man as she left, explaining how delighted her husband would be.

"Oh, that's nothing at all," the shopkeeper answered, not realizing the significant role his generosity would play in the days ahead.

Then came Saturday, October 1. Patrolman David Shafer, working the night shift, got a call in his squad car. A drugstore robbery was in progress. David reacted instantly, arriving on the scene just in time to see the suspect speed away. With siren screaming and lights flashing, he followed in hot pursuit. Three blocks later the getaway vehicle suddenly pulled over and stopped. The driver didn't move. David carefully approached the suspect with his weapon drawn. When he was only three feet from the driver's door, two things happened in a split second. The door flew open as the thief produced a .45-caliber pistol and fired at David's abdomen.

At seven o'clock that morning a patrolman came to the door of the Shafer home. Calmly and with great care, he told Terry what had happened.

Her husband had been pursuing a robbery suspect. There had been gunfire. David was hit. Shot at point-blank range.

Stunned, Terry thought how glad she was that she had not waited until Christmas to give her husband his present. How grateful she was that the shopkeeper had been willing to let her pay for it later. Otherwise, Dave would have surely died. Instead, he was now in the hospital—not with a gunshot wound, but with only a bad bruise.

You see, David was wearing the gift of life Terry could not wait to give—his brand-new bulletproof vest.

There are times that the timing of something is as remarkable as the thing itself. Sometimes more so.

CHARLES R. SWINDOLL

From *The Finishing Touch* (Nashville, Tennessee: Word Publishing, 1994). Used by permission. All rights reserved.

LIGHTNING STRIKES TWICE

☙

Nobody knows the trouble I've seen.
Nobody knows my sorrow.
Nobody knows the trouble I've seen.
Nobody knows but Jesus!

NEGRO SPIRITUAL

I never had any question about what I wanted to do with my life. I would marry, major in advertising at the University of Minnesota, and then open my own ad agency.

Right out of college I tasted success. Soon my company was billing in the millions. I bought an airplane, a boat, a Mercedes, a limo. I entertained my clients at lavish dinners and events. There seemed to be no limit to my bank account. I married Karla. Everything was going according to plan.

Then desktop publishing arrived on the business scene—and disaster struck. I watched many of my clients depart as they opened their own in-house agencies. Slowly I began to lose financial ground, and the toys started to disappear. I sold my Mercedes and my Fiat on the same painful day, and four months later I watched as someone drove my limo away. Soon I was forced to find a buyer for my four-seater airplane and then, at last, my boat.

While the money had flowed, Karla and I had collected so many things, some useful, others useless. Now my wife recommended that we sell many of these possessions at weekend garage sales to cover our living expenses. "We don't really need them anyway," she declared.

It wasn't long until I was stripped of everything—except Karla. I figured soon she'd be disappearing too because most of my focus had been on money and not her.

Then, just when I figured things couldn't get much worse, they did. In the next six months, most of my staff left, taking chunks of the business with them. My wife and daughter were rushed to an emergency room after a near-fatal accident. My father died of cancer. And finally, our house was struck by lightning and, shortly after that, attacked by giant ants (I'm not kidding!).

I felt like a modern-day Job. I'll never forget the day I came home from work feeling everything was at an end. I sat at the kitchen table, my face in my hands. All that remained was for Karla to leave.

But unlike Job's wife, who said, "Curse God and die!" Karla encouraged me. "Honey, I believe in you," she said. "And what's more, this is probably the best thing that has ever happened to us."

I looked at her as if she had lost her mind. But that was the turning point. The years that followed proved she was right.

Today Karla and I view our past adversities as a valuable learning experience—not a hard-luck story. All those losses drew us closer together and closer to God. I gave up my fantasy that I could actually control the world. And with Karla's sweet help, I learned all over again how to enjoy simple pleasures in life—the smell of toothpaste on my child's breath at bedtime, the sight of a single flower in our garden, my wife's loving touch on my arm.

I always thought that the "poorer" in "for richer or poorer" was something terrible a spouse promised to endure. But now I know the truth. Less is often more. And a husband's true riches are best measured by how much love remains when everything else is taken away.

STEVE GOTTRY

LOVE NEVER FAILS

❧

[Love] always protects, always trusts,
always hopes, always perseveres.
Love never fails.

1 CORINTHIANS 13:7–8

In the early '70s, my husband and I were young and our money was scarce. I'd taken a job as a nurse working the night shift to try to make ends meet. One night as I was preparing to leave for work, Tommy was crouched over his desk, going through a stack of bills. He stood to kiss me good-bye and gave me a reassuring hug. "When you're rich in love," he said, smiling, "you don't need a lot of money."

I tried to smile, but I couldn't help thinking, *Since when does love pay the bills?*

While I drove to the hospital through a steady rain, my vision was blurred by my tears as I indulged in a bout of self-pity. Why couldn't my life have turned out more like the lives of my childhood friends? They told me of college graduations, trips to Europe, and promising careers, and here I was, weighed down by the responsibilities of a husband, two babies, and the graveyard shift.

By the time I arrived at work I was feeling more depressed than ever, and it didn't help that one of the nurses going off shift was in a bad mood as well. When I sat down with her to review the patient records, she told me about a young couple whose newborn daughter had just been diagnosed with Down syndrome. "The husband is refusing to leave, but you'll have to make him go home," she barked. "Those are the rules!" In those days, husbands were banned from the delivery room, were not allowed to hold the newborn, and could only visit in limited hours.

I ached for the new parents, and my eyes grew moist as I thought again about my own problems, which now seemed so small.

"Did you hear me?" the nurse repeated. "Make him leave."

I nodded, then took a deep breath and headed down the hall. When I entered room 712, it was dark, but I could make out a young man sitting on a chair, embracing his wife in the bed next to him. They looked up at me.

"They tell us our child has Down syndrome," the woman said in a frightened voice. "It can't be true!" She began to sob.

Her husband gently comforted her and said with authority, "It isn't true."

I sat down at the end of the bed and spoke a few words of encouragement, then tried to discuss the baby's condition with them. But they refused to listen. Finally, I got up and excused myself. "I'll be back in a few minutes."

I walked down to the nursery and located their daughter. She looked like a tiny cherub sleeping peacefully in her bed. I asked the attendant to hand her to me.

"Where are you taking her?" she asked. "Surely not to see the parents. They're already so upset. And you need to get the husband—"

"Please," I interrupted, "just hand me the baby."

The attendant stared at me for a moment in silence, and I suddenly realized I could be putting my job and much-needed paycheck on the line. But then, still speechless, she picked up the baby and gave her to me.

I returned to room 712 and paused briefly to pray before entering. When I sat down on the bed and held out the baby for the parents to see, their eyes grew wide. One by one, I pointed out the beauty of the baby's features: her rosy skin, her tiny hands, her perfect feet, and every other precious part of her tiny body.

Suddenly, a stream of light from the hallway shone through the darkness onto the infant's face. The baby's eyes opened, and she looked directly into the loving eyes of her mother and father. At that moment, God's love and peace seemed to descend upon the room like a warm blanket.

After I returned the baby to the nursery, I looked again into room 712. The couple was smiling as they talked about their beautiful daughter. Then the husband kissed his wife good-bye and left for home.

As I drove home at sunrise, at the end of my shift, the burdens from the night before seemed to lift from me. Tommy had been right—we truly were rich, and I could hardly wait to share my renewed hope and joy with my husband.

Through the years since then, whenever Tommy and I encounter a dark moment, we remember those young parents and wait for God's light to shine through. His love has never failed—and neither has ours!

SUSAN HENRY LOVELL

LOVE AT ALL COST

☙

For there is nothing greater and better than this—
When a husband and a wife keep a household
in oneness of mind.

aking money was the goal of Millard Fuller, and he was very successful at it. From his days in college, his entrepreneurial skills were outstanding. In fact, it was these same skills which led him to meet his wife. One afternoon while he was pounding the pavement in Tuscaloosa, Alabama, selling advertising, he stopped at a movie theater and asked for the manager. While waiting for someone to bring the manager, he chatted with the girl in the ticket window. She was good-looking and friendly, and Millard was just about to ask for her phone number when his business appointment appeared. By the time that Millard had signed him up for an ad and returned to the front of the theater, the shift had changed and the pretty, young ticket seller was gone.

Millard asked of her whereabouts. He learned what her name was and asked those who worked there if they knew her telephone number. The response was, "We are not allowed to give out that information." He persisted and asked for her address. The response came, "We can't give out that information either." Millard even went back to the manager to ask about the young lady, but he too would give no information.

He was pretty sure of her last name, so the next thing that Millard did was to check the telephone book and call every number in the directory with the last name of Caldwell. "Hello, is Joan Caldwell there, please?" "No." "Thank you." Then he would try another number and inquire, "Do you know Joan Caldwell?" "No." "Thank you."

The third call produced another girl on the line. "Is this Joan Caldwell?" "No." Millard then explained his problem. The young lady was sympathetic and tried to be helpful. She offered one suggestion and then another, and as she talked, Millard began to lose interest in Joan because this girl sounded so nice over the phone. Finally, he could contain himself no longer. "What's your name?" he blurted out. "Linda," came the answer. They continued chatting, discovering in the process that they had several mutual friends, and Joan receded further and further into the background. Suddenly, Linda asked how tall Millard was, and he responded, "Six feet, four inches." "I'm five feet, ten inches," said Linda, and immediately Millard could tell by Linda's voice that she was now much more interested in him.

He inquired as to whether or not he could drive out to meet her. Linda said yes, gave him directions, and a few minutes later, he was knocking on Linda Caldwell's door. A year later, in August 1959, the lovely Linda Caldwell became the wife of Millard Fuller.

The first years of life together were rather phenomenal, from a business standpoint particularly. Millard's goal was to make "a pile of money." He didn't much care how he did it; he just wanted to be independently wealthy.

As a student, he had sold advertising for desk blotters and a student telephone directory, and he had developed a birthday cake service by mailing a letter to the student's parents right before the student's birthday, offering to deliver a cake to the student on that important day. He had a million ideas and most of them worked, whether he sold trash can holders, doormats, or holly wreaths by mail, or tractor cushions to the Future Farmers of America, or favorite recipes of home economics teachers. Millard Fuller was, by every stretch of the imagination, a successful entrepreneur. He also worked at rehabilitating houses, then renting them or leasing the rooms.

When the company treasurer marched into his office in 1964 and announced that Millard was worth one million dollars, he started immediately thinking ahead to his next goal: ten million dollars.

With Millard's success, there came a price. As he relates, his personal integrity began to slip. As the years went by, while being honest with customers, he made sure that he was always making "the best deal" for his company. His health began to suffer; he had neck pains, back pains, and kidney problems, a sore ankle that wouldn't heal, and an episode of not being able to breathe. The biggest price was paid in his relationship with Linda. Millard said, "I'm an ardent believer in free American enterprise, but it's like dessert: 'If you eat too much, you get sick.' By age twenty-nine, I was getting sick. I am the kind of person who is totally consumed, totally focused. I had no concept of balance, and I could not see past my lifelong goal. Linda, though, saw what I could not see, that our marriage was also sick from my incessant drive to make money. I ignored all the signs and pushed ahead toward making the next million, until Linda walked into my office and announced that she didn't love me anymore. I was astounded, thinking, 'I bought you a Lincoln; I bought you two thousand acres of land, two speedboats, a cabin on the lake; I'm paying for your college education. I got you a maid. You have so many clothes you can't get them in the closet! I've done everything for you! How could you not love me?' But before I could say anything, she was speaking again. She told me that what I wasn't giving her was myself. She said she never saw me. I promised to spend more time with her and the kids, and I meant it. Linda wanted to believe it, too. The matter calmed down and a year passed. But nothing had changed. I was still working from dawn to the wee hours of the next morning, which prompted Linda to approach me with the grim news that she was considering a divorce."

Millard couldn't believe that Linda was serious, but Linda decided to leave and went to New York City to seek counsel from a pastor that she and Millard had known from a brief stay in New York a couple of years earlier. Millard tried vainly to dissuade her, but Linda asked, "How do you know you love me?"

"I just love you, that's all," responded Millard. "I love everything about you, I—"

She didn't let him finish. "I'm not sure whether or not we have a future together. I just have to get away and think about it."

On a Sunday after her announcement, Linda drove to the airport in her car and caught a plane to New York City. The week that followed was the loneliest in Millard's life, and the most agonizing.

On the first night of their married life, Linda and Millard had signed an agreement in which they promised to "outlove" each other. "We promised not to keep secrets and to keep a right relationship with God. We proposed this covenant the week before our wedding, she writing one word and then handing me the pen to write the next. We had the document framed, and we hung it over the bed in every place that we lived." During a week of sleepless nights, Millard took down the agreement and reread it again and again. They had promised to outlove each other, and she was off to New York deciding if they had a future together. He was in Montgomery, feeling miserable and desperate.

Linda called on Thursday night and told Millard to come to New York the following Tuesday. "I wanted to go immediately," said Millard, but she said no. She had planned more counseling sessions and wanted more time to think. By the weekend, he knew that he couldn't sit at home any longer, so Millard arranged for his parents to keep the children, called the pilot in from his company, and had him fly to Niagara Falls, New York. The plane trip itself was hazardous and almost ended in a crash. By the time Millard finally got to New York on Tuesday, he had already realized that God was intervening in his life in clear, unmistakable ways.

"Linda and I began our time of reconciliation. My momentous decision was already beginning to be made. The pastor had told Linda she could love me again if she had ever loved me. I certainly wanted our marriage to work. I loved Linda so much and loved our son and daughter. I desperately wanted us to stay together as a family." They went to Radio City Music Hall to see the Rockettes perform. Then came the movie *Never Too Late,* making Millard smile and suggesting hope. Standing in the refreshment lounge during intermission, Linda began to sob. They left and walked together, stopping to sit for a while at the steps of St. Michael's cathedral. Then they walked again, and as they walked, they cried and shared and cried some more.

Love began to be reborn. A light rain began to fall. "We hailed a taxi. As it rolled along the wet streets, there was a sensation of light in the cab. It wasn't anything spooky. Perhaps it came from a conviction I felt," said Millard, "concerning what I was about to say. But I turned to Linda, and I told her I felt we should totally change our lives. We should make ourselves poor again, give all our money away, and start over. 'What do you think?' I asked. I saw the glimmer of hope in her eyes, and I knew she agreed.

"Later that evening, I called the pastor who had been counseling Linda. His reaction was one of surprise. He was glad about our reconciliation but cautioned us about making such a radical decision so quickly. 'Wait until the morning. Think it over,' he suggested, 'and come see me.' But we had decided. The following morning we hailed another taxi, this one in front of our hotel, and the first one we saw stopped and picked us up—a miracle in itself. We climbed in. 'Congratulations,' said the cabby. 'This is a brand-new taxi. Nobody has ever ridden in it.' This time we both laughed and cried. We felt that God was confirming us in our radical, crazy decision. A shiny new taxicab—a fresh start. How exciting!"

DR. STEVEN E. BERRY

Editor's note: Millard Fuller is the founder of Habitat for Humanity International. The Fullers have served as missionaries to Africa as well as to inner cities of America. They have traveled worldwide in the interest of Habitat for Humanity, inspiring volunteers to stamp out poverty housing around the world. From giving everything they owned away, they started a vision for the human family that has impacted millions of lives for the building of God's kingdom.

Used by permission of the author.

FOUND TREASURE

In the spring a young man's
fancy lightly turns to thoughts of love.

ALFRED, LORD TENNYSON

In 1965 I was a single, young career woman living on very little income in Atlanta, Georgia. Because I was no better at budgets than I was at cooking, I ate quite frequently at local restaurants. I tried to stick to those that served low-cost meals, but I still managed to get into what I considered a lot of debt.

One morning I decided it was time to get my life in order. I added up what I owed to creditors and could not make ends meet. My parents had always taught me to live debt-free, and I knew I hadn't been careful enough. "Forgive me, God," I prayed. "And show me a way out of this debt!"

At noon that day I went over to the Dixie House Diner where I could get a ninety-nine-cent, blue-plate lunch special, which was about all I could afford. After I finished my meal, I went to the ladies' room, where I noticed something green lying on the counter. It was a full money clip! I quickly unclasped the bills and counted them. They totaled exactly the amount I needed. I couldn't believe it. God had answered my prayer!

Then I came to my senses. Surely this money belonged to someone— and the right thing for me to do would be to turn it in. God doesn't bless stealing. I hesitated for a few moments, and then mustering my resolve, I gave the money to the cashier, explaining where I'd found it. *Why did I have to be so honest?*

"Why, how good of you to turn it in, honey!" she exclaimed with a heavy Southern drawl. "I tell you what. If no one claims it in three days, we'll give you a call."

I wrote down my name and address on a piece of paper, and she put it in the cash drawer along with the money clip.

Three days later I hadn't heard anything. Disappointed, I stopped by the Dixie just to make sure.

"Oh, yes!" the cashier exclaimed. "That was the restaurant owner's money. She was so happy you turned it in that she said to give you a free lunch if you came back."

Sighing in resignation, I took a seat and tried to enjoy my lunch on the house. The restaurant was empty except for a young man sitting across the room. I noticed he was kind of cute, but I was so disappointed about the status of the money that I didn't have the heart even to try to catch his eye.

Several days later I got a call from the Dixie cashier. "Hi, honey," she said. "Remember me? I took your name and phone number when you turned in that money."

Yes, I told her, I remembered.

"Well, a fellow was in here that day you were here for your free lunch," she explained, "and after you left, he asked if I knew who you were. I told him no, I didn't. But then I remembered I still had your phone number in the drawer. He's back again, and he wants your telephone number. Can I give it to him?"

Great! Now some weirdo from the Dixie House was stalking me! "No, I don't think so," I said. "I don't give my number to strangers."

"But, honey," the cashier persisted, "if you ask me, I think you're making a mistake. I checked on this guy myself 'cause I thought he was kind of cute. He's twenty-nine, and he's a dentist. He used to be a captain in the air force. And I asked around—"

"Okay, okay," I finally said. I'd never heard anything so ridiculous. A cashier matchmaking for a customer! "But after you give him my number,"

I said, "then maybe you could kindly toss it?"

I think that comment hurt her feelings a little, but she agreed. Within an hour I got a phone call from a man I'd never met, asking me to have dinner with him—"somewhere other than at the Dixie Diner."

That was a good start. A nice dinner appealed to me. And hey, it was one way to save money. In fact, by now I'd gotten a free lunch *and* a free dinner out of that money. Not too bad.

Little did I know that this wasn't all I was going to get. I met the mystery caller for dinner, and we hit it off immediately. The man who got my number has been my husband now for over three decades. I absolutely adore him! And in the end, I owe it all to a matchmaking cashier—and choosing to do the right thing.

Who says honesty doesn't pay?

MARCIA WILLIS

DREAM GIRL

✑

Beautiful dreamer, wake unto me,
Starlight and dewdrop are waiting for thee.

STEVEN FOSTER

*T*ed, fresh out of law school, was preparing to work full-time for a prominent New York law firm. Before he could start, he received an offer for a movie he had written. The son of 1930s Hollywood movie stars, Evelyn Peirce and Bob "Tex" Allen (Ted Baehr), who after World War II went on to star in many Broadway plays, Ted decided to follow in his parents' footsteps and choose a life of creative adventure.

One night just before setting out on a yearlong, cross-country trip to develop his script, Ted had a powerful dream about a woman he'd never met. Since he felt content in his relationships, Ted didn't think too much about the dream—until he dreamed about the same woman again. And again.

Each time, Ted told his partner about his vision with a vivid description of the girl in his dream—a woman who was very unlike the women he usually dated.

Then, nine months and many miles later in Houston, Ted's partner rushed into the room and breathlessly announced, "I think I've found her—the girl in your dreams!" He described the girl in detail. Ted was stunned. Her name was Lili, and she sounded a lot like the girl he'd described.

Curious, Ted left messages all over town for this dream woman.

Normally, Lili, a successful architect and beautiful socialite who graced magazine covers and dallied with the rich, would not answer calls from people she didn't know, but Ted's name, Teddy Baehr, made her think that he might be a friend playing a joke. So she called back. Ted convinced Lili to meet him, another woman, and his partner for dinner.

When they met, they talked throughout the evening, and the next night and the next.

A week later, driving across Texas together, the scene in Ted's dream occurred.

When he proposed marriage, Ted told Lili, "I can offer you nothing but love and adventure."

"But, Ted, that's exactly what I have always wanted!" she declared. And she said yes—to the man of her dreams.

THE GIFT OF THE MAGI

*Grant that I may not so much seek to be loved
as to love. For it is in giving that we receive.*

ST. FRANCIS OF ASSISI

One dollar and eighty-seven cents. That was all. And sixty cents of it was in pennies. Pennies saved one and two at a time by bulldozing the grocer and the vegetable man and the butcher until one's cheeks burned with the silent imputation of parsimony that such close detailing implied. Three times Della counted it. One dollar and eighty-seven cents. And the next day would be Christmas.

There was clearly nothing to do but flop down on the shabby little couch and howl. So Della did. Which instigates the moral reflection that life is made of sobs, sniffles, and smiles, with sniffles predominating.

While the mistress of her home is gradually subsiding from the first stage to the second, take a look at the home. A furnished flat at eight dollars per week. It did not exactly beggar description, but it certainly had that word on the lookout for the mendicancy squad.

In the vestibule below was a letter-box into which no letter would go, and an electric button from which no mortal finger could coax a ring. Also pertaining thereunto was a card bearing the name, "Mr. James Dillingham Young."

The "Dillingham" had been flung to the breeze during a former period of prosperity when its possessor was being paid thirty dollars per week.

Now, when the income was shrunk to twenty dollars, the letters of "Dillingham" looked blurred, as though they were thinking seriously of contracting to a modest and unassuming D. But whenever Mr. James Dillingham Young came home and reached his flat above he was called Jim and greatly hugged by Mrs. James Dillingham Young, already introduced to you as Della. Which is all very good.

Della finished her cry and attended to her cheeks with the powder rag. She stood by the window and looked out dully at a gray cat walking a gray fence in a gray backyard. Tomorrow would be Christmas Day, and she had only $1.87 with which to buy Jim a present. She had been saving every penny she could for months, with this result. Twenty dollars a week doesn't go far. Expenses had been greater than she had calculated. They always were. Only $1.87 to buy a present for Jim. Her Jim. Many a happy hour she had spent planning for something nice for him. Something fine and rare and sterling—something just a little bit nearer to being worthy of the honor of being owned by Jim.

There was a pier glass between the windows of the room. Perhaps you have seen a pier glass in an eight dollar flat. A very thin and very agile person may, by observing his reflection in a rapid sequence of longitudinal strips, obtain a fairly accurate conception of his looks. Della, being slender, had mastered the art.

Suddenly she whirled from the window and stood before the glass. Her eyes were shining brilliantly, but her face had lost its color within twenty seconds. Rapidly she pulled down her hair and let it fall to its full length.

Now, there were two possessions of the James Dillingham Youngs in which they both took a might pride. One was Jim's gold watch that had been his father's and his grandfather's. The other was Della's hair. Had the Queen of Sheba lived in the flat across the airshaft, Della would have let her hair hang out the window some day to dry just to deprecate Her Majesty's jewels and gifts. Had King Solomon been the janitor, with all his treasures piled up in the basement, Jim would have pulled out his watch every time he passed, just to see him pluck at his beard from envy.

So now Della's beautiful hair fell around her, rippling and shining like a cascade of brown waters. It reached below her knees and made itself almost a garment for her. And then she did it up again nervously and quickly. Once she faltered for a minute and stood still while a tear or two splashed on the worn red carpet.

On went her old brown jacket; on went her old brown hat. With a whirl of skirts and with the brilliant sparkle still in her eyes, she fluttered out the door and down the stairs to the street.

Where she stopped the sign read: "Mme. Sofronie. Hair Goods of All Kinds." One flight up Della ran, and collected herself, panting. Madame, large, too white, chilly, hardly looked the "Sofronie."

"Will you buy my hair?" asked Della.

"I buy hair," said Madame. "Take yer hat off and let's have a sight at the looks of it."

Down rippled the brown cascade.

"Twenty dollars," said Madame, lifting the mass with a practiced hand.

"Give it to me quick," said Della.

Oh, and the next two hours tripped by on rosy wings. Forget the hashed metaphor. She was ransacking the stores for Jim's present.

She found it at last. It surely had been made for Jim and no one else. There was no other like it in any of the stores, and she had turned all of them inside out. It was a platinum fob chain simple and chaste in design, properly proclaiming its value by substance alone and not by mercilous ornamentation—as all good things should do. It was even worthy of The Watch. As soon as she saw it she knew that it must be Jim's. It was like him. Quietness and value—the description applied to both. Twenty-one dollars they took from her for it, and she hurried home with the eighty-seven cents. With that chain on his watch Jim might be properly anxious about the time in any company. Grand as the watch was, he sometimes looked at it on the sly on account of the old leather strap that he used in place of a chain.

When Della reached home her intoxication gave way to prudence and reason. She got out her curling irons and lighted the gas and went to work repairing the ravages made by generosity added to love. Which is always a treacherous task, dear friends—a mammoth task.

Within forty minutes her head was covered with tiny, close-lying curls that made her look wonderfully like a truant schoolboy. She looked at her reflection in the mirror long, carefully, and critically.

"If Jim doesn't kill me," she said to herself, "before he takes a second look at me, he'll say I look like a Coney Island chorus girl. But what could I do—oh! what could I do with $1.87?"

At seven o'clock the coffee was made and the frying pan was on the back of the stove and was ready to cook the chops.

Jim was never late. Della doubled the fob chain in her hand and sat on the corner of the table near the door that he always entered. Then she heard his step on the stair away down on the first flight, and she turned white for just a moment. She had a habit of saying little silent prayers about the simplest everyday things, and now she whispered, "Please, God, make him think I am still pretty."

The door opened and Jim stepped in and closed it. He looked thin and very serious. Poor fellow, he was only twenty-two—and to be burdened with a family! He needed a new overcoat and he was without gloves.

Jim stopped inside the door, as immovable as a setter at the scent of a quail. His eyes were fixed upon Della, and there was an expression in them that she could not read, and it terrified her. It was not anger, nor surprise, nor disapproval, nor horror, nor any of the sentiments that she had been prepared for. He simply stared at her fixedly with that peculiar expression on his face.

Della wriggled off the table and went for him.

"Jim, darling," she cried, "don't look at me that way. I had my hair cut off and sold it because I couldn't have lived through Christmas without giving you a present. It'll grow again—you won't mind, will you? I just had to do it. My hair grows awfully fast. Say 'Merry Christmas!' Jim, and let's be happy. You don't know what a nice—what a beautiful, nice gift I've got for you."

"You've cut your hair off?" asked Jim, laboriously, as if he had not arrived at that patent fact yet even after the hardest mental labor.

"Cut it off and sold it," said Della. "Don't you like me just as well, anyhow? I'm me without my hair, ain't I?"

Jim looked around the room curiously.

"You say your hair is gone?" he said, with an air of almost idiocy.

"You needn't look for it," said Della. "It's sold, I tell you—sold and gone, too. It's Christmas Eve, boy. Be good to me, for it went for you. Maybe the hairs of my head were numbered," she went on with a sudden serious sweetness, "but nobody could ever count my love for you. Shall I put the chops on, Jim?"

Out of his trance Jim seemed quickly to wake. He enfolded his Della. For ten seconds let us regard with discreet scrutiny some inconsequential object in the other direction. Eight dollars a week or a million a year— what is the difference? A mathematician or a wit would give you the wrong answer. The magi brought valuable gifts, but that was not among them. This dark assertion will be illuminated later on.

Jim drew a package from his overcoat pocket and threw it upon the table.

"Don't make any mistake, Dell," he said, "about me. I don't think there's anything in the way of a haircut or a shave or a shampoo that could make me like my girl any less. But if you'll unwrap that package you might see why you had me going a while at first."

White fingers and nimble tore at the string and paper. And then an ecstatic scream of joy; and then, alas! a quick feminine change to hysterical tears and wails, necessitating immediate employment of all the comforting powers of the lord of the flat.

For there lay The Combs—the set of combs, side and back, that Della had worshipped for long in a Broadway window. Beautiful combs, pure tortoise shell, with jeweled rims—just a shade to wear in the beautiful vanished hair. They were expensive combs, she knew, and her heart had simply craved and yearned over them without the least hope of possession. And now, they were hers, but the tresses that should have adorned the coveted adornments were gone.

But she hugged them to her bosom, and at length she was able to look up with dim eyes and a smile and say: "My hair grows so fast, Jim!"

And then Della leaped up like a little singed cat and cried, "Oh, oh!"

Jim had not yet seen his beautiful present. She held it out to him eagerly upon her open palm. The dull precious metal seemed to flash with a reflection of her bright and ardent spirit.

"Isn't it a dandy, Jim? I hunted all over town to find it. You'll have to look at the time a hundred times a day now. Give me your watch. I want to see how it looks on it."

Instead of obeying, Jim tumbled down on the couch and put his hands under the back of his head and smiled.

"Dell," said he, "let's put our Christmas presents away and keep 'em a while. They're too nice to use just at present. I sold the watch to get the money to buy your combs. And now suppose you put the chops on."

The magi, as you know, were wise men—wonderfully wise men— who brought gifts to the Babe in the manger. They invented the art of giving Christmas presents. Being wise, their gifts were no doubt wise ones, possibly bearing the privilege of exchange in case of duplication. And here I have lamely related to you the uneventful chronicle of two foolish children in a flat who most unwisely sacrificed for each other the greatest treasures of their house. But in a last word to the wise of these days let it be said that of all who give gifts these two were the wisest. Of all who give and receive gifts, such as they are wisest. Everywhere they are the wisest. They are the magi.

O. HENRY

In Sickness and in Health

MARRIAGE IS A RELATIONSHIP BETWEEN TWO ETERNAL SOULS TEMPORARILY HOUSED IN FRAGILE, FAILING BODIES. SOLOMON, WHO KNEW A FEW THINGS ABOUT MARRIAGE, ONCE WROTE: "TWO ARE BETTER THAN ONE, BECAUSE THEY HAVE A GOOD RETURN FOR THEIR WORK: IF ONE FALLS DOWN, HIS FRIEND CAN HELP HIM UP. BUT PITY THE MAN WHO FALLS AND HAS NO ONE TO HELP HIM UP!" (ECCLESIASTES 4:9–10).

MARRIAGE SAYS, "NO MATTER WHAT…"

"NO MATTER WHAT HAPPENS TO YOU, I WILL BE THERE AT YOUR SIDE."

"NO MATTER WHAT YOU MUST ENDURE, BE IT PAIN, OR DREAD, OR WEAKNESS, OR SORROW, OR LOSS, OR INDIGNITY, I WILL ENDURE WITH YOU. I AM ONE WITH YOU."

"NO MATTER WHAT PATH YOU MUST WALK, HOWEVER LONG, HOWEVER DARK, HOWEVER DIFFICULT, YOU WILL NOT WALK IT ALONE."

I WILL LOVE YOU FOREVER

❧

I love thee with the heart,
Smiles, tears, of all my life!

ELIZABETH BARRETT BROWNING

My fiancé, James, and I were engaged less than twenty-four hours when we received the staggering news that he had been diagnosed with pancreatic cancer. His prognosis was terminal, and he was given only months to live.

For two people consumed with love for one another, this was an indescribably devastating blow. But after several tearful discussions, we decided we still wanted to marry. Surrounded by loving family and friends, we were married at James's home in a beautiful ceremony scheduled between radiation and chemotherapy. Our anticipated honeymoon trip to Paris was replaced with a majestic view of the Grand Canyon at the IMAX Theater.

But we were happy to be together.

In the following months, which miraculously stretched into three years, we learned very quickly to treasure every moment and to create our own happy days and enchanted evenings. Our romantic interludes were spent dancing in the garage, clad in old flannel nightshirts. One evening when James was in the hospital, we brought along a music tape and listened to Ella Fitzgerald sing our favorite love songs while the chemotherapy dripped into James's veins.

Eventually my husband's condition dramatically worsened, and physicians told us that his death was imminent. Our wedding anniversary was only two days away. Within hours of hearing this news, James tenderly took my hand and asked if we should celebrate early—in case he didn't survive that long.

I agreed, but I couldn't help thinking how wonderful it would be if James could live to see our anniversary. And what if celebrating earlier somehow released him to let go of life sooner?

Laying aside my qualms, that very night James and I joyfully celebrated three years of marriage. We repeated our marriage vows, we prayed together, we shared Communion, and of course, we cried.

James lived through that day and the next. As midnight finally arrived on the eve of our wedding anniversary, he motioned for me to help him sit up in bed. Then, in a sweet whisper still audible in my memory, he said, "I wanted to show you my devotion by living long enough to say, 'I'll love you forever. Happy anniversary.'"

The next morning James went to be with the Lord. But he left me more cherished memories of love than many wives experience in a lifetime of marriage.

DESIREE LYON

Morning without you is dwindled dawn.

EMILY DICKINSON

JUST ONE KISS!

❧

Oh love, thy kiss would wake the dead!

ALFRED, LORD TENNYSON

r. Baumann's doctors had warned him and his wife that he was at high risk for a heart attack. But when the attack actually came, Mrs. Baumann still wasn't prepared. Gripped with shock, fear, and panic, she rode by her husband's side in the ambulance, repeatedly crying out to God to save him.

At the hospital the nurses had to pull Mrs. Baumann away from her husband so the doctors could examine him. After they had successfully stabilized his heart, Mrs. Baumann rushed down the hall to the telephones to call each of their seven children. With tears of exhaustion and relief, she told them of their father's heart attack, assuring them that his condition was now stable.

But when Mrs. Baumann returned to her husband's room, she gasped at the sight before her. Two nurses stood over her husband. Tubes ran in and out of his trembling body, and machines and monitors were humming and beeping. His face was bright red, and he was gasping for breath.

"What have you done to my husband?" she cried.

One of the nurses explained, as sympathetically as possible, that he had suffered a massive stroke.

A stroke! On top of the heart attack! Mrs. Baumann couldn't control her emotions. Overcome with grief and blinded by tears, she grabbed her husband's head off the pillow. She held him tightly in her arms, calling out his name and kissing his lips.

At that very moment, the doctor walked in and demanded, "Mrs. Baumann, what do you think you're doing?"

She turned to the doctor and hotly declared, "The question is, Doctor, what have you done to my husband?"

The doctor shook his head and chuckled, "Mrs. Baumann. That is not your husband!"

For a moment Mrs. Baumann was so stunned she couldn't speak. Then she looked more carefully at the man on the bed.

"He's…he's…not!" she cried, turning a dark shade of crimson. "Oh no! Oh dear! Oh no!"

Gently a nurse escorted the mortified Mrs. Baumann into the hall.

"Why didn't that man try to stop me?" asked Mrs. Baumann.

"Because of his stroke, he's unable to move or to speak," the nurse answered.

Mrs. Baumann gasped. "And now he must be wondering why that strange lady kissed him!"

As soon as they entered her husband's room, Mrs. Baumann rushed to her husband's side and kissed him. Then, still shaken, she related her mistake. "He had so many tubes and…and…I hope I didn't hurt him, Bernie!"

Mr. Baumann smiled and assured his wife that the man was probably feeling better than ever. But Mrs. Baumann decided she better go down to the chapel to pray for both Bernie and the man she'd kissed—and perhaps made worse!

A few days later the doctor dropped by Mr. Baumann's room for his final checkup. "Mrs. Baumann," he said, "you'll be glad to know that your husband and my patient across the hall have both made miraculous recoveries. Do you suppose it was my good doctoring, your prayers, or your passionate kisses?"

"Why, why…" she fumbled.

"Maybe it was all three!" the doctor added with a wink.

MRS. DORTHEA (DOTTI) BAUMANN

A NEW HEART, PLEASE

❧

Give, oh give me back my heart!

LORD BYRON

Like many single women, I spent my early twenties waiting to meet that special guy—and being disappointed. But by the time I was twenty-seven years old, I'd finally learned to be content as a single person. If God never brought me a husband, I knew I would still enjoy my life.

As is so often the case, that's exactly when I met Scott. Within weeks I knew that I wanted to share the rest of my days with this wonderful man. I couldn't imagine how I'd ever gotten by without knowing him. He felt the same, and we began planning our wedding and dreaming of the children we'd have someday.

Then, out of nowhere, Scott began to experience excruciating pain in his abdominal area every time he ate. When his internist diagnosed gall bladder problems, we were relieved, having feared a more serious medical problem. His doctor decided to change his diet, but the pain persisted, and he determined that surgery was necessary.

After Scott's operation, we expected him to go home in a day. We were anxious for him to be on the mend so we could continue our wedding plans. But he did not recover as planned. The concerned doctor explained that he would have to perform a second exploratory surgery to determine why Scott wasn't improving. Once more, I kissed Scott good-bye and said a prayer as they wheeled him down to the operating room.

During this surgery they discovered that the surgeon had cut his bile duct by mistake, and his entire body was poisoned. Scott was not expected to live.

I couldn't believe my ears. Wasn't this supposed to be just a simple gall bladder operation? Scott remained in intensive care several days as his family and I prayed and kept a vigil by his side. Three weeks later he seemed to respond to treatment, and doctors cautiously released him from the hospital.

When Scott continued to feel ill, we decided to seek another hospital's opinion. We traveled to Emory University in Atlanta, Georgia, where he was diagnosed with cardiomyopathy, an unexplained weakening of the heart tissue. We were astonished to hear that Scott would not live unless he had a heart transplant. The doctors were amazed that Scott was even able to walk into the hospital.

A heart transplant? Scott was a large, strong man who had played semipro football, worked an eight-hour job, and exercised at the gym at least five days a week. He was a young, seemingly healthy man, who had just received his second death sentence!

Doctors explained that it would be difficult to acquire a suitable heart for Scott. Size and blood type were major factors, and with Scott weighing three hundred pounds and being six feet, seven inches tall, finding a match would be no easy task. Meanwhile, Scott's employer thought it would be best if he took a medical leave. This part of his life was torture as we sat waiting for a heart to become available. Some days we talked of death, and other days we were optimistic. But my heart ached constantly. And every day I grew more angry with God. Why, just when I had decided to be content as a single, had God brought a man I loved—only to take him away?

Eventually Scott began to talk again about getting married in spite of our desperate situation. Part of me was delighted. I longed to be married to the man I loved. But something inside my heart also held back. By entering the most intimate relationship possible, wouldn't I just be setting myself up for a greater loss? For days I battled my fear of loving more only to lose more.

I'm not sure what changed my mind. Perhaps it was Scott's prayers. I only know that one morning I woke up and knew that Scott and I needed to be married. We put together a small wedding with immediate family members and a few close friends. It was the happiest day of my life. And as the groom kissed the bride, I prayed that God would grant Scott a new heart so we could spend our lives together.

Three months later, as Christmas neared, we reflected more than usual on God's sacrifice of His Son to bring us new spiritual life. And we were keenly aware that new physical life for Scott also could come only at the cost of another's life.

Still, we prayed and prayed. And if anyone asked Scott what he wanted for Christmas, he replied, "A big heart."

Two days after Christmas a phone call came at 5:30 A.M. A heart was available, and we needed to get to the hospital as soon as possible. On the way we felt a jumble of elation and terror. Always, in the back of our minds, lurked the question of Scott's surviving this dangerous operation.

But Scott did survive. And today he has recovered and is leading a normal life. Every day we are thankful to God, as well as to the family that donated their twenty-three-year-old son's organs after he was killed in an accident.

Today, as I remember my hesitation about marrying Scott and my anger at God, I see how making a covenant "for better or worse, in sickness and in health"—in the very midst of sickness—deeply strengthened our marriage commitment, as well as my faith. You see, when God gave my husband a big heart, he helped mine grow bigger as well.

CATHY PUTNAM

UNFORGETTABLE LOVE

Thou art my life, my love,
My heart, the very eyes of me,
And hast command of every part
To live and die for thee.

Sir Walter Scott

The old man slips out of his jacket and Ivy League cap and into the routine.

"How're we doing today, Mother?" he asks the woman in the wheelchair.

He pauses just for and instant—expectantly, as if she might actually answer him—but as always she stares straight ahead without speaking or acknowledging his presence. He runs a hand gently through the close-cropped white hair and remembers a time when it was different: long, luxurious, the color of fire. A lifetime ago, when everything was different....

In the beginning, theirs was a forbidden alliance. Her staunch, Scotch-Irish father disapproved of the young, handsome Italian who had gone to work as a laborer right after grade-school to support his mother and five siblings after his own father's death. Yet, despite the obstacles the two of them faced (or perhaps because of them), their love bloomed. Wanting desperately to be together, they stole away one night and found a sympathetic priest to marry them.

In due time they were blessed with a son (the image of his father) and a daughter (the image of Shirley Temple). Having secured a steady job with the local gas company to provide for his family, he had earned the respect of the community (and at last, his father-in-law), and life was good.

But life doesn't always stay that way, and one spring afternoon in 1944 tragedy struck. Walking home from school through an alley with her brother, "Little Sister" (age six) was hit by a truck and killed. He was forced to assume the grim task of identifying his daughter's body; his wife was much too distraught. On the brink of despair, she withdrew from the world. But he, ever the strong one, cajoled her into going about the business of living again. God blessed them with more children: another son and daughter, fourteen months apart. And, though they would never completely forget the pain of loss, happiness once more filled their home.

Happiness and heartache—over the years they would have their share of both. The sorrow of sending a son off to war; the joy of welcoming him back. The horror of having their remaining daughter badly injured in an accident; the pulling together as a family as they helped her convalesce. And then there were the weddings, the children-in-law they would embrace as their own, the arrival of grandchildren and, eventually, great-grandchildren—and through it all they cherished each other with the same unwavering devotion as when they first fell in love.

Knowing she'd always hated her given name—Armenta—he had taken to calling her "mother" almost as soon as she became one. And though she sometimes called him "dad" for the benefit of the children in her heart, he would always be "Jimmy," a term of endearment reminiscent of their shared youth. Jimmy. It was possibly the last word she ever said— in her final lucid moment, before the cruel affliction known as Alzheimer's robbed her of her memory and her speech.

Occasionally some well-meaning person would question him about his daily pilgrimage to the home, where his uncommon faithfulness had made him something of a legend.

"Why do you do it, day after day? She doesn't even know who you are."

And his answer was always the same: "Maybe not. But I know who she is."

As he looks into her dark, shining eyes, the only vestings of the woman she used to be (his wife, his partner, his dearest friend), he searches for a sign that perhaps on some level she still recognizes him. But, finding no such sign, he sighs.

"What do you say, Mother? Are you ready to eat?"

And, as he has done every morning for the past five years, he tenderly fastens a bib around her neck and begins to feed her breakfast.

MARY JEANNET LEDONNE

In loving memory of my father-in-law, James V. LeDonne, who passed away on December 8, 1997. He was utterly devoted to my mother-in-law for the nearly sixty-six years they were married.

KRICKITT AND ME

✑

In the depth of winter, I finally learned that
Within me there lay an invincible summer.

ALBERT CAMUS

heir spirits were soaring as the newlywed couple, Kim and Krickitt Carpenter, headed toward Phoenix to spend Thanksgiving with her family. They were driving their new Ford Escort and chatting about the Cowboys, the university baseball team that Kim coached back in their hometown of Las Vegas, New Mexico. With them was Milan Rasic, Kim's assistant coach.

It was pitch-dark at 6:30 P.M., and by then Krickitt had taken the wheel. Kim, who had a head cold, had gotten in the backseat of the car so he could lie down. Six miles west of Gallup, New Mexico, on Interstate 40, a flatbed truck traveling ahead of them at about thirty miles per hour was obscured by exhaust smoke. Kim woke to Krickitt's scream of terror and Milan's shout, "Watch out!"

Krickitt hit the brakes and attempted to swerve left, but collided with the flatbed. A pickup truck that had been behind them slammed into the driver's side of the Escort. The little car flew through the air and came down on its roof, skidding more than one hundred feet before it stopped.

Kim was squeezed against the roof of the car, which was underneath him. He couldn't move his legs, and the pain in his back was excruciating.

"Krickitt!" Kim screamed. There was no answer. He couldn't see that

Krickitt was suspended above him, held by the seatbelt and the steering wheel, her head swelling grotesquely as fluid flooded her brain.

It took a half-hour for rescuers to extract Krickitt from the crumpled metal. Since she was critically injured, the first ambulance took her to Rehoboth McKinley Christian Hospital in Gallup. Shortly after, a second ambulance followed with Kim and Milan, who was not badly injured. Krickitt was then flown to University Hospital in Albuquerque.

Kim Carpenter and Krickitt Pappas had met by phone, a chance business call in September 1992. As head baseball coach at New Mexico Highlands University, Kim, twenty-seven, received lots of catalogues for customized sportswear. When something caught his eye, he dialed the toll-free number, and in Anaheim, California, a sales associate answered. Her voice was animated, sparkling with laughter.

"Your name is really Krickitt?" he teased.

"And you're from Las Vegas, but not Nevada?" she responded laughing. She explained that her real name was Krisxam, a Greek name, pronounced "Kris-ann," and that an aunt nicknamed her Krickitt when she was two because she never stood still.

Over the next three months, Kim's interest in sportswear increased remarkably, but only if a certain twenty-three-year-old sales associate was available to answer his calls. A gymnast, Krickitt knew a lot about sports, and she seemed genuinely interested in Kim's team.

Pretty soon their conversations turned deeper. Both were dedicated Christians who believed marriage vows were a sacred promise. It seemed that, at every turn, each was finding something more to love in the other.

In April 1993, Krickitt accepted Kim's invitation to visit New Mexico and see his team play. Two weeks later Kim met Krickitt's friends and parents.

Kim asked Krickitt's father for his daughter's hand that June, a formality she insisted upon. "You have our blessing," Gus Pappas said.

Kim then flew to California and went to Krickitt's apartment. Dressed in a suit and tie despite the sweltering heat, he called her name until she came out on her balcony.

"Well, will ya?" Kim yelled.

"Will I what?" Krickitt responded, then raced down to him. Kim knelt on one knee and held out a bouquet of flowers. "Will you be my lifetime buddy?" Kim asked.

"Yes!" she said. "Yes, I will."

On September 18, 1993, Krisxam Pappas and Kim Carpenter were married in Scottsdale, Arizona. The couple honeymooned in Maui, and on their return squeezed into Kim's small apartment in Las Vegas.

Only ten weeks later, Kim listened in shock as a doctor told him that Krickitt was in a coma, completely unresponsive. There was possible brain damage. She might die.

Around 5:00 A.M. Kim, despite his own severe injuries, had arrived in Albuquerque to see Krickitt. She had a plastic hose in her mouth and a device stuck in her head to measure intracranial pressure. Plastic bags hung on metal stands, all draining fluids down clear tubing into her arms. *This can't be Krickitt!* Kim thought as he felt the room sway and go dark.

Krickitt's athletic body started fighting back. Though still comatose, she was able to breathe on her own by the first week in December. She was transported by air ambulance to Barrow Neurological Institute in Phoenix, deemed the best place for her recovery.

Krickitt gradually came out of her coma, and three weeks after the accident it was time for a professional assessment of her mental abilities. Kim stood by anxiously as a therapist asked Krickitt questions.

"Where does the sun rise?" the therapist said.

Answer, babe, Kim urged silently. *Show us you're getting well.* Krickitt looked puzzled, then satisfied. "North," she said with certainty.

"Who is president?" "Nixon."

"Where do you live?" "Phoenix."

Phoenix was where she had lived before she was married. Kim was encouraged. *Yes, babe! We're going home soon, and everything will be all right.*

"Who are you married to?" Krickitt's blue eyes drifted around the room. Her voice was flat, emotionless, and her words stabbed at Kim's heart: "I'm not married."

Stunned, Kim backed out of the room. In the hallway he wept openly, slamming his fist against a wall. *God, help me! Help Krickitt and me.*

As Krickitt became more responsive, it gradually became clear that she had lost all memory of the year before the accident. She didn't remember their courtship, wedding or honeymoon, or their short time together as husband and wife. Kim Carpenter was a complete stranger to the woman he had fallen madly, hopelessly in love with.

For the next month her parents and friends would ask, "Who are you married to, Krickitt?"

She would seem to concentrate, but then say any of a half-dozen men's names—her gymnastics coach, old friends, a doctor.

Once Kim showed her a video of their wedding. When the camera panned on Kim's face, he said gently, "That's me, Kimmer. And the girl is you, Krickitt." But Krickitt showed no reaction.

Every day Krickitt worked with a physical therapist, speech therapists, and others at Barrow. Once an accomplished gymnast, she had to be taught to walk. At first, she would jerk her right foot forward and drag the left foot, unable to lift it even an inch off the floor. Her brain had sustained injuries in the frontal lobe, which controls personality, emotions, and decision making, and in her parietal lobe, which governs language and mathematical comprehension.

Krickitt's memory of being a child, a teenager, and a college student gradually returned. But Kim continued to be "that guy," just one more person who made her try to walk, feed herself, and hit a ball with a paddle.

Often her reaction to him was anger and rejection. "Why don't you go back to Las Vegas?" she said more than once.

"Because I love you" was Kim's unwavering response.

In February 1994 she was able to move into her parents' house and go to Barrow as an outpatient. In March Kim began a physically and emotionally exhausting commute, flying to Las Vegas to coach the college baseball team half the week and back to Phoenix on Sundays to prod Krickitt the rest of the time.

Sometimes there were clear signs of improvement, like the day when Kim pitched a ball to her. Instead of missing it by several feet, she scored a direct hit. In her sudden laughter Kim could hear the echo of the Krickitt he'd fallen in love with.

There were comical moments too. One day after Kim had returned to Las Vegas, she told a Barrow therapist, "I miss that guy who was here." When she got home, her mother phoned Kim and said, "Krickitt wants to talk to you."

Kim was thrilled that she'd thought of him. "How are you?"

"Fine," she said. "I gotta go now."

Her short attention span was evident when people visited her too. She'd greet them warmly with "Hi, how are you? I'm glad to see you" and follow it with "Well, bye now" in the next sentence.

For the most part, however, Krickitt had to cope with confusion, unfocused anger, and physical pain. Kim turned to the Bible and to prayer for strength. *Lord, please let Krickitt remember me. Please, God, bring her back to me.*

On March 12, 1994, Kim and Krickitt went to their apartment for an "orientation" visit. In the small living room, Krickitt picked up an eleven-by-fourteen-inch photo and studied it with a quizzical look. It was their wedding picture, but it didn't mean a thing to her.

A month later Krickitt went "home" to stay. It was not easy. Her brain injuries didn't heal like a broken leg mends, with steady improvement. Her continual confusion over where to find things in the apartment, how to find her way around, her anger at Kim for being tough about her therapy—all this caused temper outbursts that were completely unlike the woman Kim had known and loved.

This new Krickitt was like an unruly adolescent, not caring about anyone's feelings. A young woman known for patience and compassion before the accident, she now lacked both.

For the first time they got into arguments, and after one of these Krickitt ran out of the apartment. Worried, Kim drove around until he found her outside a fast-food restaurant. "You promised me you would not run off!" Kim scolded her.

"I can't promise anything," she cried, as dismayed by her erratic behavior as he was.

"I can't live like this anymore," Kim said. "I can't see me without you, and I can't see you without me, but maybe that's the way it has to be."

There was one promise that was bred in Krickitt's bones: She had grown up believing that marriage was forever. It was a promise that she had made to God before she had ever met Kim. And when neither of them felt they could go on as they were, that promise kept them together.

In the fall of 1995, Kim went to see a professional counselor. During one session the therapist asked him, "What made Krickitt fall in love with you?" At first he gave the counselor a glib answer, describing himself as "funny, clever, handsome." But then he took the question seriously. *What made Krickitt fall in love with me?*

He thought of all the love and affection he'd shown her during their courtship. He was her sweetheart. Then he considered how he had acted since her injury. He was more like a parent or coach. Finally it struck him: *Start over! Win her back!*

"Would you like to go to a movie tonight? We could get some pizza afterward." It felt awkward courting Krickitt again, but Kim made "Date night" a part of their weekly routine.

They tried golfing together, but they often didn't make it past the second hole. Kim had to learn patience, to let go and not criticize. They knew they were on the right track when they could laugh and say, "Wow! We made it to the fourth hole without fighting!"

Although Kim set out to reawaken love in Krickitt, he couldn't foresee the result of their dating. She was the same woman, and yet different. Kim came to love her as the person she had become.

Krickitt began to notice how compassionate and generous Kim was. Gradually, she felt herself "growing into love," which she described as "sort of like falling in love, only better."

Kim's counselor planted the seed of an idea: Would it be meaningful to renew their vows?

"Oh, yes!" was Krickitt's reaction. "But if we're going to have a wedding, I want a proposal, too," Krickitt said with her jaw set.

On Valentine's Day, 1996, Kim once again went down on one knee and, with a bouquet of flowers in one hand, asked Krickitt to be his bride.

"People think we're getting married a second time to make my memory come back," Krickitt would say. "But I have accepted that that part of my life is erased."

The reason for the wedding ceremony, Krickitt adds, was because "every woman should have that moment to remember."

On May 25, 1996, Krickitt Carpenter held out her hand to Kim. "I thank you for being true to your original vows," she said, "and I pray that I might be the wife you fell in love with."

They gave each other their original wedding rings. Then, unaware of the other's plan, each brought a second ring to commemorate this second vow of love.

Kim and Krickitt emerged from the chapel, posed for photos, and then made their way through a crowd of family and friends. It was the beginning of a new life for them, a moment that, now, Krickitt could remember and treasure forever.

LYNNETTE BAUGHMAN

A WINNING TEAM

There is in every true woman's heart
a spark of heavenly fire,
which lies dormant in the broad of prosperity;
but which kindles up, and beams and blazes
in the dark hour of adversity.

WASHINGTON IRVING

Imagine not being able to kiss your wife, or make love to her, or even hold her hand. Lou Gehrig's disease has robbed Charlie Wedemeyer of all the pleasures that most men enjoy and take for granted in their marriage. And yet, Charlie and his wife, Lucy, share a deeper and more meaningful intimacy and happiness in their marriage than most couples.

Their love and romance had all the makings of a fairy tale—living happily ever after. In high school Lucy, the blond, blue-eyed cheerleader, fell in love with the native son, who just happened to be the football hero, the athlete of the decade for the entire state of Hawaii. He received a scholarship from the University of Michigan, where he made the All Star college team and married his high school sweetheart, Lucy.

Charlie and Lucy then moved to San Jose, where he was offered the head coaching position at Los Gatos High School. They had two beautiful and talented children, a girl and a boy, Carri and Kale. Charlie also led his young team to a winning season. Life couldn't get any better than this.

Then tragedy struck. Actually, it crept up on the Wedemeyers. When Charlie couldn't hold on to a piece of chalk in his classroom, he attributed it to clumsiness. But eventually he was diagnosed with Lou Gehrig's disease, a disease that destroys the tissue in the neuromuscular system. With the insulation gone, the nerves are unable to function, and the victim becomes increasingly paralyzed. Ultimately, in the final stages of the disease, even the muscles and nerves required for breathing stop functioning. The doctors gave Charlie only a year to live.

When Charlie told Lucy his diagnosis, her world was shattered. "We cry out to God, 'Why, why, why?' Sometimes there are no answers," Lucy explains. She struggled to remain positive and do what wives are supposed to do in adversity. Lucy was confident that their deep love for one another would see them through this crisis. She even refused to let anyone see her cry. Of course, this proved totally unrealistic. God sent a messenger to sustain them—their son, Kale, who shared his faith.

"One afternoon I felt I couldn't take it anymore as I was trying to load Charlie into a borrowed van. I just yelled out to God, 'I need some help down here! I can't do this by myself anymore, you know!' He obviously heard me because I was suddenly filled with this enormous strength. I can't explain it. It's like you have this void in your inner being that is suddenly filled."

Stripped of all his physical abilities, Charlie prayed that God would still use him, and his prayers were answered. In spite of his illness, Charlie's high school football team compiled an incredible record, and Charlie was named "Coach of the Year" for the third time in his short career. More importantly, Charlie has a public speaking career which offers encouragement to hundreds of thousands of people each year—and yet he cannot speak. Lucy reads his lips and speaks for him.

After Charlie lost the ability to speak, Lucy would join her husband on the sidelines, reading his lips and relaying the plays to his assistant coaches. As Charlie led the Los Gatos Wildcats to the championship with Lucy as his voice, there was not a dry eye in the stadium. The fans witnessed the true meaning of the vow "in sickness and in health."

When Charlie Wedemeyer was first diagnosed with Lou Gehrig's disease, the doctor told him he had only a year to live. Now, over twenty years later, still coaching, he credits his survival to his wife. "I wouldn't be here today if it weren't for Lucy," Charlie admits. God knew this beautiful woman would love Charlie Wedemeyer unconditionally. When she spoke her wedding vows, "For better for worse, in sickness and in health," Lucy wrote them on her heart—happily ever after!

LUCY AND CHARLES WEDEMEYER

I know only one duty and that is to love.

ALBERT CAMUS

MOVING LOVE

*And ruined love, when it is built anew,
Grows fairer than at first, more strong, far greater.*

William Shakespeare

I got up and I walked across the room and had this really strange sensation. Then it came to my mind about people walking on air when they're in love."

These were the words of the eighteen-year-old dancer Margot Fonteyn the morning after she met a handsome nineteen-year-old law student, Roberto Arias, at a party at Cambridge University. Sadly, their two-year romance ended abruptly when Roberto was called home as World War II erupted.

Nearly twenty years later Margot had made her mark in the world of ballet and was performing with the Royal Ballet in New York when Roberto unexpectedly walked into her life again. At breakfast the next morning he told her, "You know, you're going to marry me and be very happy." Margot responded, "You're crazy," but after their marriage, she wrote in her diary, "Roberto rescued the human heart trapped inside the ballerina."

While her husband was the Panamanian ambassador to Great Britain, Fonteyn continued to dance as well as perform her duties as the ambassador's wife. Whenever she danced, there were always red roses waiting from her husband. It was a storybook romance later marred by tragedy when at the end of one of her performances Margot learned that Roberto, who was waging a political campaign in Panama, had been shot five times by a rival and was paralyzed from the neck down.

Devastated, though stoically accepting their fate, Fonteyn rushed to her husband's bedside, where she helped nurse him through a 108 degree fever. Friends later said that it was Margot who kept him alive and put the will back into him. When his wife danced with Rudolf Nureyev in *Romeo and Juliet* in London, Roberto watched his beloved from a stretcher in the wings.

When Dame Margot Fonteyn finally retired at age sixty from her extraordinary career as a prima ballerina, the devoted couple and their beloved five dogs settled in a simple, four-room house on a cattle ranch in Panama City. In spite of their tragic circumstances, their blissful retirement was spent doting on one another until they died.

Many of Margot's friends pitied the couple's tragedy, but Margot said of their marriage, "I feel it's rather a fair division. He thinks; I move. You see, I love him. I took my wedding vows seriously, for richer, for poorer, in sickness and in health."

As Long As We Both Shall Live

LOVE BETWEEN TWO CHILDREN OF GOD OUTLIVES THE

UNION, OUTLIVES FAILING BODIES, OUTLIVES THE EARTH

ITSELF. LOVE, IN WHATEVER CELESTIAL FORM IT TAKES IN

HEAVEN, LIVES ON AFTER THE EARTHLY SHELL HAS PASSED

INTO DUST.

FOR THE ONE WHO BELIEVES, DEATH CHANGES "GOOD-BYE"

INTO OTHER, MORE HOPEFUL WORDS.

I WILL SEE YOU SOON, MY LOVE. I CANNOT BRING YOU

BACK TO ME, BUT I CAN COME TO YOU.

AND I WILL.

THE GOLD WATCH

'Tis the last rose of summer
Left blooming alone;
All her lovely companions
Are faded and gone.

THOMAS MOORE

*W*hen my husband, Henry, retired from his job as a mechanic, the owners of the Ford dealership where he had worked gave him a gold watch inscribed with his name. Henry was so proud of that shiny gold watch that it became his greatest treasure. "Now I have something special to leave my son," he beamed.

But the gift our son wanted was for us to relocate. Violence had been on the rise in the Los Angeles community where my husband and I had raised our family, and now our grown children urged us to enjoy our retirement years in a beautiful, safe place. But Henry refused. He said the right thing to do was to stay put and try to make a positive difference.

One small way to do this was with our roses. Every day, Henry and I worked in the rose garden in front of our house. Soon it was one of the few bright spots on our street. If someone in the neighborhood had a birthday, a graduation, a birth, or a death in the family, Henry would deliver a bouquet of our roses to the family. Before long, Henry and I became known as the "Rose couple."

One night around 10:00 P.M. a friend called, asking Henry for help. "Charlie's broken down at the corner of Thirtieth and Crenshaw," Henry explained, heading for the door. "It sounds like the carburetor. Shouldn't take me too long."

"How about picking up some milk on the way home?" I asked.

"Sure," Henry said, "but don't wait up, honey."

When I hadn't heard from Henry by 11:30, I began to worry. Henry always called if he was delayed. I began to pace the floor and pray while I waited. After an eternity there was a knock on the door.

"Lucille," a familiar voice called out. Through my peephole, I saw our pastor.

I can scarcely recall the rest of that evening. My worst fears were confirmed. During an apparent robbery attempt, Henry and Charlie had been gunned down by neighborhood gang members. Both were dead.

Our son, Ed, went to the morgue to identify his father and collect his things. When he arrived home, Ed informed me that the killers had not only taken Henry's wallet but the gold retirement watch.

In the weeks following Henry's death, my grief was indescribable. Ed also grieved deeply for his father. He tried to reassure me that the loss of the gold watch didn't matter. "Daddy gave me so much good stuff that I keep tucked away in here," he said, pointing to his heart. "I don't need the watch, Mama."

But for some reason, I did. I couldn't be comforted about Henry—or the watch. Often I prayed, "Please, dear Lord, help the police find Henry's killers. And please, I beg you, help me get back my Henry's watch!"

Weeks passed with no arrests. Still I couldn't let go of the idea of recovering the watch. Perhaps it was my way to hang on to hope. Or to Henry. As I walked to church or the market or visited a neighbor, I would instinctively check the wrist of everyone who passed by. I even browsed through the local pawn shops.

Eventually my children decided to offer a $250 reward for the return of the gold watch. Six months passed, and no one responded. The owners of the Ford dealership presented me with another gold watch just like the first one. Although I was touched with their kindness and generosity, it wasn't the same as finding the watch Henry had owned and worn so proudly.

Meanwhile, my roses had fallen into gross neglect. It was too painful for me to garden without my Henry.

One weekend Sharon, our oldest daughter, came to stay with me. She suggested we get up early on Saturday to prune. "Mama, you've got to live again," she told me as we trimmed the roses and pulled weeds.

As we worked that morning, I noticed a young African American man walk past our garden two or three times. He paused as if he wanted to say something.

Finally I spoke to him. "Son, would you like some of my roses?"

"Are you the Rose Lady?" he asked.

I nodded and replied, "I am. And who might you be?"

"Name's Jared," he mumbled. He hesitated a moment before he reached out and took the bouquet I was holding out to him. Then he left without a word.

The next Saturday afternoon the young man appeared again. "You sure like my roses, son," I laughed as he stood staring. He appeared so nervous and jumpy that I suddenly became afraid.

"Rose Lady," he finally said, "I need to talk to you. It's important."

We sat in silence on my porch for a few minutes. Suddenly he reached in his pocket and pulled out a handkerchief. He cleared his throat and said, "Got something here that belongs to you."

In the folds of the handkerchief was Henry's watch. Tears streamed down my face as I lifted the precious gold timepiece and held it close to my heart.

"I didn't kill him," he declared. "I swear. You believe me, don't you?"

"Well, I don't suppose you did. No killer would bring this watch to me," I said.

Then Jared told his story. He was with his gang when they decided to rob Henry and Charlie. But Jared was shocked and angry when one of the gang members pulled a gun and killed the two men. "They told me to go over and get their wallets and check for jewelry," he explained, "but when I was unfastening the watch, your husband...he said something, ma'am. He whispered, 'Get my watch to the Rose Lady. Tell her I love her.'"

The young man was trembling, and tears filled his eyes. "I hid the watch from them," he continued. "I was going to bring it to you sooner, but I was afraid. Are you going to turn me in to the police?"

I thought for a moment about what Henry would do and then spoke. "I'm going to ask you to do the right thing."

"It's not that easy, you know. If I go to the police, those boys will relocate me to the cemetery," he responded.

"I'm sure it's not easy," I agreed, "but I've always found that when you do the right thing, God will take care of the rest."

I never saw that young man again. He did go to the police, and his friends were eventually arrested for the murders, but Jared was not charged. It seemed to me at the time that, just as he had given me back Henry's watch, God had given Jared back his life.

Sometime later I ran into one of Jared's relatives. "Where is the young man these days?" I asked.

"Oh, he's in college now!" she said proudly.

"You tell him the Rose Lady said hello," I told her.

After I got Henry's watch back, I finally began to heal. Years later I heard the good news that young Jared had graduated from college. Suddenly I had an idea. I found the duplicate gold watch the Ford dealer had given me, boxed it up, and sent it to the new graduate with best wishes from the Rose Lady.

My roses, and my heart, were in bloom again.

SUSAN WALES

FLOWERS FROM HEAVEN

*But there's nothing half so sweet in life
As love's young dream.*

THOMAS MOORE

n old man got on a bus one February 14, carrying a dozen red roses, and sat beside a young man. The young man looked at the roses and said, "Somebody's going to get a beautiful Valentine's Day gift."

"Yes," said the old man.

A few minutes went by, and the old man noticed that his young companion was staring at the roses. "Do you have a girlfriend?" the old man asked.

"I do," he replied. "I'm going to see her now. I'm taking her this." He held up a Valentine's Day card.

After riding in silence for another ten minutes, the old man rose to get off the bus. As he stepped into the aisle, he suddenly placed the roses on the young man's lap and said, "I think my wife would want you to have these. I'll tell her that I gave them to you."

He left quickly, and as the bus pulled away, the young man turned to see the old man enter the gates of a cemetery.

AS TOLD BY BENNETT CERF

LOVE LETTER
FROM HEAVEN

What greater thing is there for two human souls
than to feel that they are joined...
to strengthen each other...
to be at one with each other in silent
unspeakable memories.

GEORGE ELIOT

Several years ago my husband, George, died of complications follow-ing an automobile accident. Ours had been a long, happy marriage, and his death left me deeply depressed. As time passed, instead of being grateful for all the wonderful years we'd shared, I became engulfed in self-pity. Often I prayed, "Lord, why didn't you take me first?"

When I broke my leg a few weeks before my ninetieth birthday, I felt more confined—and alone—than ever. "If only George were here," I despaired, "he would chase away this sadness with words of wisdom and encouragement."

On this particularly blue day, I decided to call a friend and ask her to visit. Unfortunately, she was leaving on a trip and couldn't come.

I understood. But as I hung up the phone, tears started to flow. I moved to the window to sit in my favorite chair with Duke, my beloved cat, curled up in my lap. "Dear God," I prayed, weeping, "please give me the strength to get through this hour."

Get your Bible, a quiet voice inside me nudged. But my Bible was in the bedroom, and with my leg in a cast, it would be too hard to retrieve. Then I remembered my small travel Bible. Hadn't I seen it in the living room bookshelf? I found it and opened it, surprised to discover that it was George's old travel Bible instead of mine. They looked alike, and I thought I'd given his Bible away.

I turned the pages until I reached my favorite Scripture. Suddenly a letter fell into my lap. Carefully I unfolded the yellowed pages. It was a love letter from George. In it, he expressed his deep affection for me. His words of comfort went straight to my lonely heart.

My cheeks wet with tears, I continued to leaf through the Bible. In the back pages I found more notes from George. According to the date, he'd written these in the hospital prior to an earlier surgery. He must have feared that he would not return home. After he recovered from the surgery, the letter and notes were forgotten.

But no, I realized. They were *never* forgotten. God knew exactly where George's words of comfort were hidden—and exactly when I'd need them most. Laughing some and crying some, I spent the rest of the afternoon basking in the company of both my husband and my Lord. I never felt less alone, and now I knew for certain that I never would be.

LUCILLE HEIMRICH

MY HUSBAND'S HANDS

Chiefly the mold of a man's fortune is in his own hands.

FRANCIS BACON

is smallest gesture was the purest expression of love.

Paul's hands were twice as long as mine and half a hand wider. His fingers did not taper; they were long and square, laced with fine veins all the way to the tips. His nails squared off the ends of his fingers, with clearly defined moons and white edges. He took great pride in keeping them neat.

My husband's hands had a fine firm feeling, warm, never cold, never moist. And in his final days, when he pressed them together around one of my hands, I closed my eyes and concentrated on memorizing the feeling.

Had I remembered to tell him that I found his large hands beautiful? Did I ever explain that in his clasp in a movie, in church, I felt pure and honest expressions of his love?

Those hands gave our newborn daughter her first bath and did the same for the five babies who followed. They gave haircuts to three sons and toweled three daughters' hair after showers. Those hands were not tough hands, or soft either. They were the hands of a college professor, and they traced patterns in the air as he taught marketing students at the university where he himself had studied so many years earlier.

261

Those hands stripped and refinished furniture. They cut and refashioned the metal sides of an outgrown children's swimming pool, then used them to mend fenders and rust spots of secondhand cars. They manipulated suitcases atop station wagons for twenty-eight summer pilgrimages to visit grandparents in Pennsylvania.

Those hands reached for mine through months of chemotherapy and radiation. They clasped mine in the deepest, darkest moment when he whispered into the curve of my neck, "I wonder how it is to die. I wonder if it hurts."

And those hands flailed in unconscious confusion as he spoke to his own father who had died years earlier: "Daddy, I can't lift my legs. Daddy, I can't move my arms. Daddy, sometimes I'm hot and sometimes I'm cold."

I asked, "Is your father trying to help you through this?" There was no answer but the stillness of his listening as all movement stopped.

"I'll be all right," I said. "We'll be all right. I think you should take your daddy's hand and let him lead you."

Early Wednesday morning, in a state of nervous anxiety, I clipped, filed, and whitened his fingernails. There was no movement, no recognition, no response as I laid his hands across his chest. Within an hour the hospice nurse checked him with her stethoscope, and there was nothing left for me to do but close his luminous green eyes and lay my hands on his for the last time.

For seven and a half months my grief had been frozen like an icy presence that would not yield. Then one Sunday I opened the top drawer of Paul's dresser and reached in for one of his clean, pressed handkerchiefs—I like to use them now. What I touched was an opened pack of emery boards. I was undone. Tears came as I closed my eyes and tried to remember the clasp of Paul's hands. My grief brought to mind the funeral, when the children left to return to their own homes: Cathy to Milwaukee; Bill to San Francisco; Mary and her husband, Joe, to Sterling, Illinois; Terri and her husband, Don, to Huntington Beach, California; Michael to New York City. And Stephen, the youngest, to Bloomington, Illinois.

Stephen had kissed me good-bye and then, impulsively, had taken my hand in both of his. It was as though his father's long, graceful hands had clasped mine once again.

HELEN TROISI ARNEY

Used by permission of the author.

SUNSET

Sunset and evening star,
And one clear call for me!

ALFRED, LORD TENNYSON

ecause Elizabeth Franz and her husband, Ed Binns, were both actors, they often worked in separate cities during their many years together. They missed each other terribly at such times and deeply cherished every evening spent in each other's company when they were both home. Watching a sunset became their special way to celebrate the joys of just being together.

One day when they were feeling particularly happy to be home together, they enjoyed a long conversation, reminiscing over the joys and difficulties of their many years of marriage. Ed had recently survived a serious bout with cancer and was feeling victorious. The trials, they agreed, had made them stronger in their faith and in their love for one another.

Later that afternoon Elizabeth was delighted when Ed asked, "How would like you to go for tea and scones in the country, my dear?"

"Oh, yes!" she replied. He knew this was one of her favorite simple pleasures in life. Ed always loved to plan these little surprises, and though small, such gestures were dear to his wife's heart.

As they drove off together, she was bursting with gratitude. But as they approached an intersection in the little village, Ed suddenly slowed the car to a stop.

"Elizabeth!" he exclaimed. "Have you ever seen such a magnificent sunset in your entire life? Just look at those colors!"

She looked over at him in questioning surprise. She could see in his eyes that he was feasting on a sunset. Then Ed put his head back and sighed deeply. It was his last breath.

You see, it was a gray, rainy day outside. There was no sunset—only Ed's sun was setting. And from the look on his face, it must have been spectacular!

Editor's note: Elizabeth Franz, considered by many to be one of America's greatest stage actresses, also appears in film and television. She is best known for her roles in Mary Sister Ignatius, Brighton Beach Memoirs, *and* Death of a Salesman. *The late Edward Binns was a renowned actor on stage and in films. His film roles included* Twelve Angry Men *and* Judgment at Nuremberg.

&

If I had thought thou couldst have died,
I might not weep for thee;
But I forgot, when by thy side
That thou couldst mortal be:
Yet there was round thee such a dawn
Of light ne'er seen before,
As fancy never could have drawn,
And never can restore!

CHARLES WOLFE

From an interview with Elizabeth Franz. Used by permission.

HAPPY TRAILS

❧

Oh, give me a home where the buffalo roam,
Where the deer and the antelope play,
Where seldom is heard a discouraging word
And the skies are not cloudy all day.

AUTHOR UNKNOWN

*E*arly in the morning before the museum opens, Dale and I go in the back entrance and walk around in private. It's quiet and the only footsteps we hear are ours. We walk past all the glass cases and displays. We see Robin's baby toys and the folded American flag that covered Sandy's coffin. There are fading pictures of Debbie that make us remember how happy she was for the years God let us have her before He called her home. We see the old battered car that took my family out of Ohio to the promised land of California. There's Pat Brady's Jeep, Nellybelle, and pictures of Gabby Hayes when he was a serious young actor, and a shot of Art Rush helping me get ready for our wedding on New Year's Eve nearly half a century ago. There's Dale wearing fancy hats for her first photo session, and me, in overalls, standing next to my first horse, Babe.

Sometimes we stop to read some of the piles of letters that little pardners wrote us through the years, asking our advice and telling us about the good deeds they did. I get a little choked up when I see ol' Trigger, rearing high and looking down at us when we walk past; his saddle looks so shiny and inviting. We stroll past memories of the good times and the bad times and the hard times, and we think of all that we have shared.

I guess Dale and I know pretty well, as her song says, that "some trails are happy ones and others are blue"; and we also know that when we have to part, it will be only "'til we meet again." And that time, our happy trails will be for all eternity.

ROY ROGERS

Editor's note: A tribute to the marriage of Roy Rogers and Dale Evans, and in memory of Roy, who died in August 1998. Roy and Dale maintained a personal museum together—memories of their lives, their children, and Trigger—which they moved to their ranch in Victorville, California, in 1976.

Reprinted with the permission of Simon & Schuster Adult Publishing Group from *Happy Trails: Our Life Story* by Roy Rogers, Dale Evans with Jane and Michael Stern. Copyright © 1994 by Roy Rogers, Dale Evans with Jane and Michael Stern.

A Match Made in HEAVEN

Volume Two

SUSAN WALES & ANN PLATZ

Guideposts®

CARMEL, NEW YORK 10512

www.guidepostsbooks.com

A MATCH MADE IN HEAVEN, VOLUME II
published by Multnomah Publishers, Inc.
© 1999 by Susan Huey-Wales and Ann Williams-Platz
International Standard Book Number: 1-57673-658-X

Cover photograph by Victoria Yee/Tony Stone Images
Cover design by Kirk DouPonce

Scripture quotations are from:
The Holy Bible, New International Version
© 1973, 1984 by International Bible Society,
used by permission of Zondervan Publishing House

Also quoted:
The Holy Bible, King James Version (KJV)

Multnomah is a trademark of Multnomah Publishers, Inc.,
and is registered in the U.S. Patent and Trademark Office.
The colophon is a trademark of Multnomah Publishers, Inc.

For information:
MULTNOMAH PUBLISHERS, INC.•P.O. BOX 1720•SISTERS, OR 97759

Library of Congress Cataloging-in-Publication Data:
Match made in heaven–volume two. / [compiled] by Ann Platz and Susan Wales.
    p. cm.
    ISBN 1-57673-658-X (alk. paper)
    1. Love—Religious aspects—Christianity. 2. Love—Anecdotes.
    3. Marriage—Religious aspects—Christianity. 4. Marriage—Anecdotes.
    I. Platz, Ann.   II. Wales, Susan.
    BV4639.M334 1999
    242'.644—dc21

                                                                98-46112
                                                                CIP

To the joys of our lives, the wind beneath our sails, and the colors in our rainbows, we lovingly dedicate this book to you, our darling daughters,

MEGAN CHRANE (SUSAN),

COURTNEY NORTON (ANN),

AND MARGO CLOER (ANN)

To Megan and Margo
we pray that God will bring you a Match Made in Heaven.
To Courtney, we thank God for your Match Made in Heaven,
Dr. Michael Norton.
We thank you for embracing our beloved husbands,
Ken Wales and John Platz, as your stepfathers,
with the joys, and sometimes tears, of having daughters.

CONTENTS

CONTENTS

With This Ring

I Thee Wed

To Have and to Hold

CONTENTS

From This Day Forward

To Love, Honor, and Cherish

For Better, for Worse

To love what you do and feel that it matters—
how could anything be more fun?

KATHARINE GRAHAM

To Don Jacobson and our Multnomah family,
thank you for your monumental efforts and for believing in us!
A special thank-you to our editor Tracy Sumner, for his guidance.
To Penny Whipps, Cliff Boersma, Ken Ruettgers, Kirk DouPonce,
Jennifer and Steven Curley, Judith St. Pierre, Jeff Gerke,
Heather Kopp, and Holly Halverson, thank you.

Ken Wales and John Platz for your love, patience,
and support throughout this project.
To Dorothy Altman and Fran Beaver,
thank you from Ann Platz. You are great!
To Pam Zelek, thank you from Susan Wales.

For the gift of storytelling:
Susan's parents,
Mr. and Mrs. Arthur J. Huey Jr.,
and Ann's parents,
Mrs. Margaret Williams and
the late Senator Marshall Williams.

Dear Readers, Family, and Friends:

What joy God has blessed us with by entrusting this collection of inspirational love stories to present to you! Do you believe that marriages are made in heaven? We do, wholeheartedly! As the pages of this book unfold you will see how God miraculously reaches down into our lives when we allow him to direct us. He will not only make your paths straight, but he will lead you to the road of love and romance. Along the way we can guarantee that you will encounter storms, rocky roads, and thorns, but we can promise you that the trip will make your journey worthwhile as you encounter the joys along the way to where only God can take you.

As we've walked through the joys and sorrows of our own marriages; the pain, rejection, and loss of divorce; and, at last, discovering the blessing of finding love again; we have not been alone. The difficulties of life have taught us to trust God with all our hearts and not to lean on our own understanding. He has been with us every step along the way in both our joy and in our pain. It was through stories much like these in our book *A Match Made In Heaven, Volume II*, that God gave us encouragement, instruction, comfort, laughter, and hope.

We present this book with our love to offer encouragement to single men and women everywhere who desire to have someone special with whom to share their lives. God is waiting for you to relinquish your hopes, dreams, and desires to him so he can bring his best to you.

We present this book with joy to invite married couples to take their own walk down memory lane to rekindle the love, sense of humor, and romance in your marriage as the stories in this book remind you of those glorious days when you first fell in love.

We present this book with comfort to offer hope for those men and women who have loved and lost as a gentle reminder that one day you will meet again for all eternity.

We present this book to our husbands, Ken and John...*if we never met again in our lives I should feel that somehow the whole adventure of existence was justified by my having met you* (Lewis Mumford).

And most of all we thank the lovers in our book who have shared their hearts and their love with us and our readers. And once again, we thank God for a friendship that endures while celebrating the delights and tribulations of birthing yet another book of love!

When love finds you, send us the miracle of your love story to share with others so that we can continue to spread God's love, joy, hope, and comfort to the hearts that need it the most.

The minute I heard my first love story
I started looking for you,
not knowing how blind that was.
Lovers don't finally meet somewhere.
They're in each other all along.

RUMI

Divine Appointment

The Lord God said,
"It is not good for man to be alone.
I will make a helper suitable for him."
GENESIS 2:18

IMAGINE WHAT IT MUST HAVE BEEN LIKE FOR ADAM IN THE GARDEN OF EDEN.

THERE WAS ADAM, THE FIRST HUMAN, AS GOD BROUGHT THE BEASTS AND BIRDS IN A PARADE BEFORE HIM. ADAM GAVE THEM NAMES AND MARVELED AT THE ENDLESS VARIETY OF CREATURES GOD HAD MADE. BUT AT THE END OF THAT DAY ADAM MUST HAVE BEEN TIRED AND LONELY. HE WATCHED THE LION SAUNTER OFF TO ITS CAVE WITH HIS LIONESS. THE WHITE DOVE PERCHED IN AN OLIVE TREE WITH ITS MATE. THE STALLION THUNDERED ACROSS THE MEADOW WITH A MARE.

FOR ADAM, NO SUITABLE HELPER WAS FOUND (GENESIS 2:20).

PERHAPS ADAM LOOKED AROUND, FEELING THAT SOMETHING WAS MISSING BUT NOT KNOWING WHAT IT WAS. BEFORE DRIFTING OFF TO AN EXHAUSTED SLEEP, HE MAY HAVE DARED TO ASK GOD, "HAVEN'T YOU FORGOTTEN SOMETHING?"

WAS GOD WAITING FOR ADAM TO EXPERIENCE A SENSE OF SUBTLE LONGING BEFORE HE FINISHED HIS WORK? WE DON'T KNOW, BUT WE DO KNOW GOD WAS NOT FINISHED YET. IN THAT DEEP AND QUIET NIGHT, GOD CREATED WOMAN FOR MAN. SHE WAS EVERYTHING ADAM NEEDED, AND WOULD BECOME HIS INSPIRATION.

AT DAWN, AS ADAM AWOKE TO THE SLEEPING FORM BESIDE HIM, SO DIFFERENT YET THE SAME, WHAT THOUGHTS MUST HAVE RACED THROUGH HIS MIND? HOW SURPRISED HE MUST HAVE BEEN. HOW SWEET THE ENCOUNTER. BUT IT WOULD TAKE A LIFETIME TO DISCOVER ALL THE WAYS WOMAN WAS THE COMPLETION OF GOD'S DIVINE DESIGN. "THEREFORE A MAN SHALL...BE JOINED TO HIS WIFE" (GENESIS 2:24).

AND GOD HAS BEEN DESIGNING SURPRISE ENCOUNTERS EVER SINCE.

THE MAN IN CHARGE

✍

"For I know the plans I have for you,"
declares the Lord.
"Plans to prosper you, and not to harm you,
plans to give you a hope and a future."
JEREMIAH 29:11

As a young man I had big plans for my life. The war was raging in Europe, and, wanting to serve my country, I enlisted in the Navy Air Corp. As a young cadet, with dreams of flying military aircraft, I found the competition among the men was fierce. When the grades were posted, I was relieved to discover that I had made a high B, until a mentoring officer pulled me aside and gave me a dose of reality.

"Ray, you're a good soldier," he said, "but there's so much competition in the navy that you most likely won't make the cut with a B." Sensing my disappointment, the officer suggested, "Why don't you go back home and apply for Army Air Corp? You'd make an excellent pilot, and there's not as much competition in that branch. They'll be lucky to get you."

Those words were music to my ears. With renewed hope, I headed back home. Fortunately, I knew the lady who ran the draft board in my hometown of Columbus, Ohio. After I explained my situation, she promised me that she would put a hold on my papers until the next crop of recruits was admitted into the Army Air Corp. It would only delay my plans for a matter of weeks. I was flying high on hope.

I was shocked a few days later when I went to the mailbox and found the letter with the news: I was about to be drafted into the army. My entry into the Army Air Corp was only days away. *How could this have happened?* I wondered. I figured a trip down to the draft board was all I needed to straighten this mess out. I found out that while my friend at the draft board was away on vacation another woman in the office had processed my papers. Now there was nothing that could be done. I was drafted.

My hopes and dreams of becoming a pilot were permanently dashed when I was assigned to the Infantry Division of the United States Army. "Why, Lord?" I questioned. Despair flooded my being. And yet I was strengthened knowing that God had a plan for me. Maybe it wasn't the plan I had in mind, but I knew without a doubt that I had to trust him. My family rallied around me lending their support and prayers.

After basic training, I was shipped off to Europe just after D-Day. I arrived on French soil and was immediately placed on the front lines, where we faced combat every day. Through all that, my faith in God sustained me. I prayed often and kept the New Testament the Army had issued me in my pocket, close to my heart, often seeking it for words of comfort and faith.

My days on the front line were filled with the horrors of war. Death was all around me. Each time I watched the American planes overhead from my foxhole, my heart broke a little more. I wondered if God realized I was supposed to be up there and not down here on the front line. *Did God forget me?* I wondered.

Our division was assigned to General Patton and we fought through Normandy and the Saint Lo breakthrough. During the siege, my hands were wounded with shrapnel and I was taken away to have them bandaged. This injury probably saved my life, because when I returned to the outfit, I was horrified to discover that only three men—including me—were left in my platoon.

From Saint Lo we marched into Paris and liberated the city. It was obvious to me that God had intervened to spare my life. I was then assigned to another platoon. Next we headed for the Hurtegn Forest in Germany. We dug foxholes and put covers over them because artillery shells were hitting the treetops and crashing down on us. Again, as I looked up at the planes fighting in the sky above me, I cried out, "Lord, don't you know that I'm supposed to be up there and not down here? Why didn't you give me my dream of flying?"

I went on out to check on my men, when suddenly, an 80 shell, a weapon used by the Germans, came close and barreled me over. I felt a sting. The shrapnel had gone through the front of my right thigh. I was treated in the field by my platoon sergeant. As he walked me back to the aid station, I had to step over the dead soldiers lying in the forest. I was thankful to be alive.

The medics transported me to a hospital in Belgium for surgery, but before I could undergo the procedure, the hospital was bombed. My fate again was suddenly changed when all the patients had to be transported to Paris, where we were scheduled on a flight to England. When we arrived in Paris, a thick, heavy fog hung over the airport and our plane couldn't take off.

Once again, I found out how God had intervened. While we waited for a train to the hospital in Cherbourg, France, I saw one of the fellows from my platoon and asked, "How did we do on our attack of the village?"

"There's nobody left but you and me, Sarge," he told me.

Our entire platoon was wiped out. I was awestruck that God had spared me.

The first morning I awoke in the Cherbourg hospital, an attractive American Red Cross nurse with a beautiful smile and a pen and paper in her hand greeted me with a smile. I rubbed my eyes, wondering if she was a figment of my imagination. But then she spoke.

"Write to your wife," she instructed me, "and tell her you're alive and safe and sound in a hospital in France."

"I don't have a wife," I confessed.

"Well, write to your girlfriend, then," she prodded.

There was a girl back home, but I quickly forgot her as I gazed into the beautiful hazel eyes of the nurse before me. I was sure I wasn't the first soldier to look wistfully into those eyes, but I wanted to be the last. The nurse, whose name I learned was Betty, was very professional and a bit standoffish. But she was simply obeying orders. All the nurses had been warned not to fraternize with enlisted men. Their major had sternly warned them, "You'll be sent to the hospital in the Philippines." While the pretty nurse's mannerisms said no, her eyes told me that she had an interest in me. I was not about to give up easily.

Betty and I became better acquainted each day as she nursed me back to health. One day when she appeared she noticed that I was reading my New Testament. We were both delighted to discover that we shared the Christian faith, and we began talking about the Lord. I relayed to her how God had miraculously spared me time and time again in the battlefield. Our Christian fellowship strengthened our relationship, and I then knew without a doubt that God had orchestrated all those circumstances to bring me to this place to meet this special woman.

The hospital at Cherbourg was only allowed to keep a patient for thirty days, and as I watched the pages on the calendar change each day, I knew I had to work quickly to win the pretty nurse's heart. I was being sent to England to recuperate and would be sent back to battle as soon as I regained my strength.

When the time came for me to go to Oxford to recuperate, I was saddened to tell Betty good-bye. I presented her with a gold wedding band that I had found on the battlefield, and she promised to wear it around her neck on a dog tag chain in remembrance of me. I managed to get a promise from her that she would write to me in Oxford.

Our letters crossed the English Channel with speed and regularity. We were becoming better acquainted through the mail. With each letter we were falling more and more deeply in love.

I knew what I felt for this woman, and I knew it was real. But it was going to take a miracle of God to keep us together.

When I recovered from my injury, I was sent back into the battlefield in Germany. One night when we were advancing, I became disoriented and separated from my group. Because of the shadows in the German forest, I thought the trees were my men. I suddenly found myself in a small German village. Praying all the while that God would protect me, I finally made my way to a home of a farmer about three miles behind our line. I'll never forget the look on his face when an American soldier appeared at his door. In broken German I tried to explain to the farmer and his terrified family that I was there in peace, that I was lost and exhausted and needed a place to sleep. Eventually, the farmer led me to his barn where I prayed for a safe night of sleep. It was not to be.

I was later awakened by a group of German soldiers the farmer had led to me. I was terrified as I cradled my New Testament close to my heart. *There will be no more letters to Betty now*, I thought.

The Germans didn't know quite what to do with me, so I traveled with them. All the time I was with them, American forces were attacking them—and me—from all sides. *How ironic!* I thought. *I'll be killed by my own men*. When we reached the POW camp in Munich, they handed me over as an escaped prisoner. When I embraced the other prisoners, both French and American, they took care of some minor wounds I had incurred along the way. That night, the camp was bombed so we had to be transported to the dreaded Stalag VII A in Munich.

I was aware that Munich was one of the targets that American forces had planned to bomb, so I expressed some concern for our lives.

"What are you worried about?" a fellow prisoner asked. "You're listed as an escaped prisoner. You're scheduled to be shot at dawn with a group of us."

"Were these the plans you had for me all along, Lord?" I prayed. "Is this how my life is going to end?"

With the stark realization that I was about to meet my Maker, my thoughts traveled to home, family, and Betty, the pretty nurse who, unbeknownst to her, I'd planned to make my wife. I knew I would never see her again. I spent the night on my knees praying and seeking solace from my battered New Testament. I prayed that God would somehow intervene in this hopeless situation. The men surrounding me were encouraged to have a Christian among them. I was their *ray* of hope.

Back in France, Betty had been devastated when one of her letters to me was returned marked "killed in action." At that moment she realized just how much she loved me. She was numb with grief as she went through the motions of caring for her patients. The news of losing me was more than she could bear.

But Betty's spirits soared when the next morning another letter arrived marked "missing in action." Hope flooded her as she prayed every moment for my safety. She was very much in love with me...as I was with her.

Perhaps it was Betty's prayers that night, but the Americans chose on the eve of my death watch to bomb Munich. Amid the rubble and confusion I was spared, and in a matter of days American soldiers marching through Munich liberated us. The war was over.

I was sent to France to recover and then sent home. When I returned home my mother received a letter from Betty asking if she had heard from me. I answered the letter myself but somehow it had the wrong APO (post office) box. But as Betty was leaving for home, someone ran up to her and handed her my letter just as she boarded the ship. She has since said she was surprised that I hadn't heard her scream all the way to America.

Betty and I were reunited back in the States, where we finished out our duties after brief furloughs. We finally rendezvoused in New Orleans, where I was stationed. That is where we became man and wife.

The bride didn't wear a white gown but her uniform. I also wore mine. We were proud to wear our military dress, and it was also our tribute to the armed forces, which God used to bring us together.

As I look back over my wartime service, I realize that God was in charge all along. Without God's divine appointment, my path would never have crossed with Betty's. If I hadn't been wounded, I would have never met her.

God had led me into the battles through the long and winding path that led me to the woman he had for me. My disappointments were transformed into joy through these difficult circumstances. I am still in awe at how God had his hand on me and carried out his plans for my life through some bitter disappointments.

He had a plan all along. Little did I realize when I was so devastated over not realizing my dream of flying that God had something better in store for me.

Since the day I left the service, the Lord has been in charge of my life. I have learned to remember that when the going gets rough during the courses of our lives, he still has a plan.

He is the man in charge!

BETTY AND RAY WHIPPS, AS TOLD TO SUSAN WALES

THE FEAST OF
ST. STEPHEN

❦

I live with those who love me
whose hearts are kind and true
GEORGE LINNAEUS BANKS

What do you want for Christmas?" my mother asked. So many answers swelled in my throat, but none of those were possible.

With a lopsided smile, I replied, "I'd really like a man on my Christmas tree."

In July of that year, my husband had drowned while lobster fishing off our small village in a remote corner of Maine. A young fisherman on his way home had discovered the wreckage of the boat, and divers had searched for three days before finding my husband's body.

My husband had just finished college and I had been teaching for three years. We were anticipating the day we would move from the parsonage we rented from the church to a home of our own. Our dream was to buy and restore an old cape cod house and raise children in the nurturing intimacy of small-town life. Now at twenty-five, I felt cheated of the future we had planned. My husband's self-confidence and ambition had made him the decision maker in our marriage. Alone, I felt adrift on an ocean of uncertainty.

The house we rented had an old piano, and I decided that music lessons would take me outside myself and demand my total concentration.

Though I had no ear for music and an appalling lack of rhythm, I doggedly practiced scales and simple songs. By Christmas I could labor through my favorite carol, "Good King Wenceslas." I liked the medieval imagery of Wenceslas the Holy looking out upon the Feast of Stephen. The tune replayed itself in my head as I tied ribbons, baked cookies, and tried not to examine how I felt about the approaching holiday.

I spent Christmas Day at my parents' house. Their attempts to give me a generous Christmas must have stretched their meager resources. Among their gifts to me was a cloth ornament my mother had stitched—a little white doughboy wearing a chef's hat and a smile. It appeared that my wish for a man on my Christmas tree had been answered.

On December 26, aching to escape the post-holiday slump, I settled into my easy chair for a nap. When I heard a knock at the door, I did not feel at all hospitable. *Probably the chairman of the parsonage committee, here to take more measurements for the furnace,* I thought. "Come in," I called out.

The chairman's son stood in the doorway with a package in his hand. He was about my age, but I had seldom had occasion to speak with him. I knew that he was a lobster fisherman and that his passion was baseball. My grandfather, an avid baseball fan, often praised this young man's pitching ability. In a fleeting flashback to the previous summer, I saw him drive past my house, wearing his red and white uniform and a smile on his face after winning his game. At that time I had thought idly, *I wonder what he lives for besides baseball?* He never dated, and I couldn't imagine a life of just baseball and lobstering.

"I've brought you some scallops," he said, while I stared at him as if he were a genie who had materialized from a bottle. My cousin was visiting me, and since her father and his mother were cousins, I assumed that he was bringing the scallops to her. He continued to stand. I continued to stare. At last it occurred to me that he expected me to ask him in. I croaked a feeble invitation, offered him some Christmas cookies, and strained to make my knowledge of baseball last for a twenty-minute conversation. When the door finally closed behind him, I thought I had figured out the reason for his visit. Everyone in our small town had been particularly thoughtful to me, and no doubt his family had dispatched him on this kind errand.

The following evening, he phoned to tell my cousin and me that he had a surprise for us, and he soon arrived with a pail of lobsters. This time the conversation was easier, and we talked of our love for our town and its way of life, our extended families, and the pristine beauty of our harbor.

We saw each other every day for two weeks, then he said, "I would ask you to marry me if I thought you were ready."

Offhandedly, I replied, "If I thought I was ready, I would say yes."

That August, the church next door to the parsonage overflowing with our extended families, we began a marriage that is now in its twenty-fifth year.

Every Christmas the doughboy occupies a place of honor on the tree, and on the day after Christmas, our thoughts turn to our first awkward visit. We later discovered that, according to the church calendar, December 26 marks the Feast of St. Stephen, and we remark on the fact that he shares his name with the feast day. We seldom dwell on the fact that Stephen was the fisherman who discovered the wreckage of my first husband's boat some twenty-seven years ago.

Stephen and I built a traditional Cape overlooking the harbor. There we raised two children who grew up surrounded by loving aunts, uncles, cousins, great-aunts, great-uncles, and grandparents.

The life that I had thought lost to me returned with an abundance I never could have imagined.

PAULINE CATES

MOM'S LAST LAUGH

Oh happy living things! no tongue
Their beauty might declare:
A spring of love gushed from my heart,
And I blessed them unaware.

SAMUEL TAYLOR COLERIDGE

Consumed by my loss, I didn't notice the hardness of the pew where I sat. I was at the funeral of my dearest friend—my mother. She finally had lost her long battle with cancer. The hurt was so intense, I found it heard to breathe at times.

Always supportive, Mother clapped loudest at my school plays, held a box of tissues while listening to my first heartbreak, comforted me at my father's death, encouraged me in college, and prayed for me my entire life.

When Mother's illness was diagnosed, my sister had a new baby and my brother had recently married his childhood sweetheart, so it fell to me, the twenty-seven-year-old middle child without entanglements, to take care of her. I counted it an honor.

"What now, Lord?" I asked, sitting in church. My life stretched out before me as an empty abyss.

My brother sat stoically with his face toward the cross while clutching his wife's hand. My sister sat slumped against her husband's shoulder, his arms around her as she cradled their child. All so deeply grieving, no one noticed I sat alone.

My place had been with our mother, preparing her meals, helping her walk, taking her to the doctor, seeing to her medication, reading the Bible together. Now she was with the Lord.

My work was finished, and I was alone.

I heard a door open and slam shut at the back of the church. Quick footsteps hurried along the carpeted floor. An exasperated young man looked around briefly and then sat next to me. He folded his hands and placed them on his lap. His eyes were brimming with tears. He began to sniffle.

"I'm late," he explained, though no explanation was necessary.

After several eulogies, he leaned over and commented, "Why do they keep calling Mary by the name of 'Margaret'?"

"Because that was her name, Margaret. Never Mary. No one called her 'Mary,'" I whispered. I wondered why this person couldn't have sat on the other side of the church. He interrupted my grieving with his tears and fidgeting. Who was this stranger anyway?

"No, that isn't correct," he insisted, as several people glanced over at our whispering, "Her name is Mary, Mary Peters."

"That isn't who this is."

"Isn't this the Lutheran church?"

"No, the Lutheran church is across the street."

"Oh."

"I believe you're at the wrong funeral, sir."

The solemnness of the occasion mixed with the realization of the man's mistake bubbled up inside me and came out as laughter. I cupped my hands over my face, hoping it would be interpreted as sobs.

The creaking pew gave me away. Sharp looks from other mourners only made the situation seem more hilarious. I peeked at the bewildered, misguided man seated beside me. He was laughing, too, as he glanced around, deciding it was too late for an uneventful exit. I imagined Mother laughing.

At the final amen, we darted out a door and into the parking lot.

"I do believe we'll be the talk of the town," he smiled. He said his name was Rick and since he had missed his aunt's funeral, asked me out for a cup of coffee.

That afternoon began a lifelong journey for me with this man who attended the wrong funeral, but was in the right place. A year after our meeting, we were married at a country church where he was the assistant pastor. This time we both arrived at the same church, right on time.

In my time of sorrow, God gave me laughter. In place of loneliness, God gave me love. This past June we celebrated our twenty-second wedding anniversary.

Whenever anyone asks us how we met, Rick tells them, "Her mother and my Aunt Mary introduced us, and it's truly a match made in heaven."

ROBIN LEE SHOPE

*Marriage is the gold ring in
a chain whose beginning is a
glance and whose ending is eternity.*
KAHLIL GIBRAN

Reprinted by permission of Robin Lee Shope.

AN ARRANGED MARRIAGE

It may be those who do most, dream most.

STEPHEN LEACOCK

When people ask me how Roger and I got together, I tell them that ours is an arranged marriage. I say it's an arranged marriage because I know beyond any doubt that God arranged it.

Roger didn't catch my eye, at least not at first. We attended the same church and the same singles class. He remembers meeting me through a mutual friend, but my earliest recollection meeting him was at a singles class party at my sister's apartment. It wasn't a moment that stood out in my mind, even to this day.

Roger was sitting away from the action at the party, looking as if he felt out of place. Since we were at my sister's home, I felt as though I should help her out with hosting and making people feel at home. I approached Roger and tried to make him feel welcome. We chatted for a while, and he seemed like a nice guy. But I felt no interest in him.

Roger, on the other hand, knew from our first meeting that he was interested in a romantic relationship with me.

I met Roger during my first year of teaching, a year in which nothing seemed to go right for me. I was having a rough time with my new job, and it didn't look like things were going to turn around for me anytime soon. It turns out that the struggles I was enduring gave Roger just the "in" he needed to get to know me better.

Roger had volunteered to call and encourage the members of the singles class each Monday, and he always saved his last call for me. He must have sensed that I needed a shoulder to cry on for as the conversation slowed each week he would ask the question: "So how is work?" That would usually prolong the conversation another thirty minutes. It was good to have someone to talk to about my troubles.

I enjoyed talking to Roger and I appreciated his concern over how I was doing. But we didn't communicate much except over the phone. Obviously, if we were going to get together, God was going to have to arrange some help for us. He did just that.

Not long after we met, Roger decided to volunteer to help Wallace, the maintenance man at our church, on Saturday mornings. It just so happened that I lived across the street from the church and would often walk over to talk to Wallace. And, as long as I was there, I would visit with Roger.

One day, after one of my visits, Roger asked Wallace if he knew me. Wallace replied that he reckoned he knew me—pretty well, in fact. You see, Wallace is my father, and, with an intuition only a father could have, he could tell that Roger liked me…*really* liked me. Daddy approved of Roger's feelings for me too, and not only did he approve, he encouraged me to come visit him and Roger whenever I had the chance. Roger looked forward to the visits, and I began to enjoy being around him. I liked how easy it was to talk to him, and sometimes we would flirt with one another.

Roger was always careful not to seem pushy or overbearing, but I began to notice that things I said—even to other people—were getting his attention. I once remarked to a group of people that a pair of suspenders on any man makes him look more handsome. The very next week Roger showed up at church sporting a pair of suspenders! In fact, he made sure to take off his jacket when I was near so that I would notice them.

Roger was in the full-time Air National Guard and was often out of town for various trips. When Roger was away on one long trip—to Central America—our singles leader asked us to write him. I wrote once (I later learned that he read my letter many times a day) and was going to write again to ask him to bring me a rock from Central America for my rock collection. I never wrote the letter, but instead prayed that Roger would bring me a rock.

Roger, I would later learn, was making his own request of God.

Roger called me long distance from Central America. He claimed that he was homesick and that my number was the only one he could remember other than his brother's. I knew that wasn't true. This was when I became aware of Roger's feelings for me.

At Thanksgiving, after Roger had returned home from Central America, Daddy decided to invite Roger to dinner to thank him for his help at the church. My parents assured me that they were not setting me up, but I still called Roger that evening to see how he felt about spending the holiday in our home. He was not home, so I left a message.

I did not speak to Roger until his usual Monday call. This call was not like the others. There was something different in his voice. After the usual chitchat, I asked him what was wrong. He then told me of his feelings for me, feelings he had had from the time we met. Although he hadn't come close to proposing, I heard the word *marriage* going off in my head. I told Roger that I liked him, but that I wasn't sure how much or in what way, and that if he was going to buy wedding rings, the conversation was over.

Yet, by that Friday, I somehow knew that Roger would be my husband. Sometimes it's that way when God arranges something.

After that week, Roger and I started dating with the understanding that we knew that we would be married. On one of our first dates, Roger came over to my house to pick me up, and when he arrived, he said that he had something for me. It was a rock. No, not the kind fastened to a ring. It was the rock from Central America that I had prayed for Roger to bring.

Roger reached into his jacket and pulled out a heart-shaped rock. It was very unusual, particularly since there were so few rocks in that area. As strange as it may sound, Roger told me that the Holy Spirit had prompted him to pick up the rock and give it to someone special. He had been holding on to the rock for almost two months and now was giving it to me (I still keep that heart-shaped stone on the stand next to my bed).

Even though I knew Roger was the one for me, I was nervous about how fast this relationship was moving. Roger had already told me that he loved me, but I really did not know how to respond. After talking to a good friend, she explained that love is a decision, not a feeling. She said that Roger was waiting for me to make the commitment. I realized that the time had come for me to do just that.

I made plans and set up the perfect place to tell him I loved him. I asked him to drive us to the Marietta Square. I had planned for us to walk to a special spot I had picked out, but as we were getting out of the car, it began to rain—hard. I was crushed. My romantic moment was ruined. When we got back into the car, Roger saw the expression on my face and asked if I was okay. He asked several times and I finally told him that I had planned for everything to be perfect when I told him I loved him. He was quiet a moment, then smiled and said, "I want you to see something. I have kept this since we met."

He took a wrinkled, aged piece of paper from his wallet. He'd obviously carried it with him for quite a while. He handed it to me and I read these words:

God, please let me marry Melinda Ward.

At that moment, I didn't care about the rain. I didn't care that the moment hadn't unfolded according to my plans. This moment was far more wonderful than anything I could have imagined. This moment was perfect. We both knew that God had arranged this moment, and we knew that he had arranged for us to be together. Forever.

That's how it is with an arranged marriage—arranged by God, that is!

MELINDA ATKINSON

THE PUZZLE FITS

Take away love and our earth is a tomb.
ROBERT BROWNING

*L*ife is like a puzzle with thousands of tiny, fragmented pieces. Sometimes the pieces fit easily together; sometimes it takes time for the picture to make sense. So discovered Norma and Lon Day, whose puzzle pieces found an amazing fit.

Norma lost her husband of forty years, her high school sweetheart, Tom, when he suddenly died of a massive hemorrhage. One week later, Lon lost Dot, his wife of forty years, in a plane crash. Both Norma and Lon were steadfast believers who took comfort in God's grace and abundance. He had blessed both with wonderful marriages and three children each.

Both couples had belonged to the same church. When Norma lost Tom, Lon and Dot attended the funeral. A few days later, Lon and Dot presented Norma with a photograph album commemorating Tom's military service. Tom had been one of the Marines to make the initial assault on the beaches of Iwo Jima. Lon thoughtfully made three sets of copies for Norma's children.

Still grieving when her friend Dot died, Norma didn't attend the funeral. She sent flowers and mailed a note of condolence. She remembered Lon's kindness to her and her children and promised herself that later, when time had passed and her heart ached a little less, she would reach out to him and offer him the comfort he had first extended to her.

Months later, Norma's children urged her to do two things: first, to go to Palm Springs on the vacation that she and Tom had planned weeks before his death. And second, to call Lon to see how he was doing. They liked Lon and felt he could be a comfort to their mother.

Lon was incredibly happy that she called. A friendly, encouraging phone call led to a brief visit. Then Norma asked Lon to dinner.

When he came over, they laughed, cried, and reminisced about their marriages. Both felt relieved to talk freely about their experiences and the heaviness of grief. Two days later, Norma left for Palm Springs.

While she was away, Lon wrote several letters. He kept her abreast of the local news. He also asked if he could meet her at the airport, along with their pastor and his wife. As Norma came to the gate, their pastor gave Lon a little friendly nudge forward. "Go on. Give Norma a hug to welcome her home," the pastor urged. Lon did, and the courtship began with their pastor's blessing.

At Tom's funeral, Norma had promised herself to take a European trip. She and Tom had discussed the possibility before his death. Norma thought this was the perfect opportunity to remember her beloved husband while simultaneously going on with her own life. While she was on her trip, Lon called Norma first in London and then in Paris. By Paris, she realized she was falling in love with him. With this realization, Norma immediately cut her trip short and returned to see this man whom she believed was God's choice for her—her missing puzzle piece.

Norma and Lon courted for more than a year before they married. They both felt sure that their love, commitment, and trust in the Lord had brought them together and took the time to affirm it.

In the beginning, when Norma and Lon lost the ones they loved, the pieces in their lives just didn't seem to fit. But with time, healing, and God's abundant provision, they realized that God held all the pieces of their puzzles, and he alone could make them fit. And he did.

NORMA AND LON DAY

MR. WONDERFUL

Love is the gift of oneself.

JEAN ANOUILH

new friend and I once asked the Lord to send her a husband. It's not as bizarre as it sounds. We didn't ask God to direct a certain individual her way; we asked him to send someone into her life who would bless her and bring much happy companionship into her life. She had been divorced quite a while and was lonely so we prayed very earnestly. We talked a long time afterward about how God loves to bless his children and restore to us the things we have lost. I felt strongly that her prayer would be answered and that her husband was on the way. Little did I know....

Not long after this prayer session, a friend invited me to a Presbyterian renewal program in Jonesboro, Georgia. I was living in Nashville, Tennessee, and I was Methodist, but something told me that I should definitely attend the renewal. Almost as soon as I arrived, I figured out why: I found him! I met "Mr. Wonderful"! I was so excited. His name was Joe and he was kind and gentle, a devout Christian and an elder in the church we were visiting. He told me that he had lost his wife after a prolonged bout with cancer. He spoke with great pride and love of his two grown sons and his love for God. Mr. Wonderful he definitely was.

Now all that remained was to get him together with my new friend and all prayers would be answered. Sounds easy, doesn't it? Guess again.

Joe invited me to breakfast one of the last days before the renewal ended. I took that opportunity to casually mention my friend, to illuminate her good points, and showcase her various talents. I even went so far as to hand him a piece of paper with her name and phone number, but he never seemed to take the hint. He just smiled and tucked the phone number in his pocket.

After the renewal, Joe came to visit me in Nashville. More and more, I began to notice and appreciate his unique qualities. We enjoyed getting to know each other better and after a short time, we realized that we were falling in love. Not long after, we were married.

I still call Joe Mr. Wonderful because that is who he is, and he always will be the answer to my truest heart's desire. God answered my unspoken prayer with a vast gift.

Months after Joe and I married, my friend called, wanting to know whatever happened to that Mr. Wonderful guy who was supposed to call her for a date. I had to laugh as I admitted to her that I had married him.

"Well," she said, "keep praying for me." We both kept praying and before long, my friend found herself married to her own Mr. Wonderful!

AS TOLD TO ANN PLATZ

I arise from dreams of thee
In the first sweet sleep of night,
When the winds are breathing low,
And the stars are shining bright.

PERCY BYSSHE SHELLEY

AN OLD-FASHIONED GIRL

The fleeting promise, chased so long in vain:
Ah, weary bird! thou wilt not fly again:
Thy wings are clipped, thou canst no more depart,
Thy nest is builded in my heart!

BAYARD TAYLOR

My wife, Sarah, and I both looked for a long time for that special someone to spend our lives with. We had both been praying for spouses when we met and fell in love.

One evening not long after we had gotten engaged, I was visiting Sarah at her home. We had just finished dinner and we were cuddling on the sofa watching television when a show came on that we decided to watch. When a lovely girl appeared on the screen, I remarked to Sarah that when I had seen this very rerun years before, I prayed that God would bring me a wife just like the woman on the television…old-fashioned, pure, and kind.

My fiancée's eyes suddenly filled with tears.

"What's wrong, Sarah?" I asked, concerned that I had made my sweetheart cry.

"Fred…." She paused. "That's *me* on the screen…. I was the star in that television show."

You see, Sarah was not only soon-to-be my wife, but she *was* the actress on the screen. We both wept as we realized how God had answered my prayer! He didn't just give me a girl *like* the girl that played that part.

He gave me that *very* girl, a girl who is as old-fashioned, pure, and kind as the one on the television screen.

SARAH AND FRED BOVA, AS TOLD TO SUSAN WALES

How do I love thee? Let me count the ways.
I love thee to the depth and breadth and height
My soul can reach, when feeling out of sight
For the ends of Being and ideal Grace.
I love thee to the level of everyday's
Most quiet need, by sun and candle-light.
I love thee freely, as men strive for Right;
I love thee purely, as they turn from Praise.
I love thee with passion put to use
In my old griefs and with my childhood's faith
I love thee with a love I seemed to lose
With my lost saints, I love thee with the breath,
Smiles, tears, of all my life!—and, if God choose,
I shall but love thee better after death.

ELIZABETH BARRETT BROWNING

THE GREATEST CATCH

Ask me no more: thy fate and mine are seal'd:
I strove against the stream and all in vain:
Let the great river take me to the main:
No more, dear love, for at a touch I yield;
Ask me no more.

ALFRED, LORD TENNYSON

When I was growing up, my mother would often finish my sentences for me—and rarely the way I intended. If I started to complain about homework, she'd pipe in, "But it sure is great to have teachers who want me to grow up smart." If I worried about my prospects for finding true love, she'd recite Psalm 37:4, "Delight yourself in the Lord, Nell, and he will give you the desires of your heart."

As a teenager, I sometimes felt she had my life all planned out before I even had a chance to live it. But by the time I went off to college, I'd learned to take comfort in knowing how much she cared about my future.

After college, I took a teacher's job in my hometown so I could live near my mother. I'd only been home a few months, however, when my father died suddenly of a heart attack. Now Mother wanted me to move even closer. For weeks on end she begged me to move in with her.

With more than a little reluctance, I finally agreed. To my surprise and relief, it worked out well for both of us. I enjoyed my mother's company, and on my modest salary, I was also quite happy to save on rent.

Having me around again seemed to give Mother new purpose. She had someone to cook for and fuss over on a daily basis. But above all, she was now in a better position to marry me off. "Nell, you just delight yourself in the Lord, and…," she'd begin. Of course, I would finish the verse for her. I tried to convince her that, actually, I was perfectly content being an old maid school teacher, but she wouldn't hear of it. In her mind, I definitely needed to be married, and besides, her plan called for grandchildren.

Toward this end, my mother would invite another potential victim over for dinner at least once a week. The fact that pickings were extremely slim in our little town or that I wasn't terribly cooperative didn't give Mother a second's pause. Each of the young men was cordial, polite—and smart enough to know what Mother had in mind. Most ran for the door before we served dessert, even though my mother was famous for her homemade pies.

I was close to forty when we learned that mother had cancer. She was very brave. "I've had a wonderful life," she assured me. "My only regret is that I won't live long enough to see you married—and me a grandmother."

By that time, I agreed with her wish completely. But since I never let on, she had no idea how much I wished I could give her the desire of her heart. And I never let her know that I sometimes doubted her seemingly matter-of-fact faith in answered prayer. Hadn't I read in an article that women over forty were more likely to be abducted by terrorists than to meet a man and marry?

Never one to give up hope or put aside her mothering role, Mother spent our last conversation telling me how to tend to certain details in my life—and especially how to plan my wedding.

At Mother's funeral, more than one thousand people arrived to celebrate her extraordinary life. No one was surprised to learn that Mother had planned her own funeral down to the smallest detail. For example, she had arranged for a helium balloon to be given to everyone in attendance. We were to write a prayer request—the desires of our heart—on a little card attached. When the minister prayed the final prayer at her gravesite, we were to release the balloons.

I wrote down the only thing I could think of. *Lord,* I wrote, *You know the desire of my heart. I want a husband. Nell.*

What a sight it was to see all those hopes floating up, up and away. For a few seconds, I believed that my prayer request would somehow reach heaven. Then I went home to pick up the pieces of my life.

About two months later, I received a phone call. "Nell? Is that you?" inquired a familiar voice.

It was Horace Van Heusen, the man who owned the pharmacy in our little town. Mother had had this confirmed bachelor over for dinner dozens of times it seemed. He and mother would talk all evening while I listened, probably with a pout etched across my face. Mother just couldn't see that Horace—cautious and mild-mannered—was definitely not my type.

Horace cleared his throat and asked how I was getting along.

"I'm fine, Horace," I told him. "But I'm rather busy grading papers. Thanks for calling."

I was preparing to hang up, when he exclaimed, "Wait! There's something I've got to tell you." After a long pause, he finally spoke up. "Last week I was fishing down by Mabreys Creek—"

"Catch anything?" I interrupted, trying to be more friendly.

"Oh, I caught something all right," he muttered.

"And what might that be?"

"Looks like I might of caught myself a wife," he said.

"You're getting married, Horace?" I tried to hide my surprise. "I'm so happy for you. Who is she?"

"Listen, Nell, this is too important to discuss on the phone. May I come over? Right now?"

I tried to say no, but the words wouldn't come out. In less than ten minutes, Horace was ringing my doorbell clutching a small velvet box. He must have read on my face the sudden dread I felt. But he plunged ahead anyway.

"When I was fishing, I caught the remnants of a balloon," he said. "Inside, there was a prayer request for a husband." He paused in his speech to place the box in my hands. "It seemed to me like the answer to my prayers, too."

I couldn't imagine being married to Horace. My heart softened a little as I looked into the eyes of this shy, blushing man, but he had to know that I couldn't entertain such an impossible idea.

"Horace, you can't think that…but really you don't think.... That's ridiculous!"

Horace calmly told me that he didn't think it was ridiculous at all. He had accepted the balloon as a sign from God, and he wanted me to pray about it.

In the months that followed, I did pray. And if I forgot, it seemed that my mother completed my sentences from the grave. *I need to pick up milk, stop at the dry cleaners…and pray about Horace.*

To my surprise, each day the idea of Horace and me seemed less ridiculous than before. Finally, I invited him over to dinner, warning him that I couldn't cook like my mother had. What I didn't say was that I needed to see if my feelings really had changed.

They had. In his patience, I thought I saw courage and steadfastness. In his shyness, I suspected a humble heart.

We cautiously began to date. By the time our wedding day arrived, Horace and I were madly in love. Who would have ever thought?

At our wedding reception—you guessed it—everyone released a helium balloon with the desires of their hearts attached. This time as I sent my balloon up to heaven, I asked God for a baby girl.

A year later we had our precious baby girl. I named her May, for my mother. Horace brought me a big bouquet of pink balloons.

Today whenever I see a balloon, it reminds me to teach my daughter, like my mother taught me, *Delight yourself in the Lord, and he will give you the desires of your heart!*

NELL VAN HEUSEN, AS TOLD TO SUSAN WALES

SING ME A LOVE SONG

Those who bring sunshine to the lives of others
cannot keep it from themselves.
JAMES M. BARRIE

I found my husband at the Steak and Ale. It's not as easy as it sounds.
To reach the point when I was ready to commit the rest of my life
to someone special, I had to travel a long, hard road that was confusing
and sometimes terrifying. But through the grace and love of God, I made
it and learned many valuable lessons. And when I did finally make it to
that Steak and Ale I was ready to meet Tom and for him to meet me.

I was born and raised in Murray, Kentucky, the oldest of three children. My mother insisted that I attend college and earn my degree. By the
time I was a junior in college, I had been seriously dating a young man for
almost four years. We planned to get married, so I dropped out of school.
But two days before the wedding, I got cold feet. I called off the wedding
and returned all of the presents.

I decided then to fly to Atlanta and try to make my way in the big city.
I had exactly one hundred fifty dollars in my pocket and a suitcase filled
with all the clothes it could hold. A girlfriend offered me a room in her
apartment—so much for glamour in the big city!

I went to Atlanta with the goal of pursuing a career as a professional
singer. Once again, though, cold feet foiled my plans. Instead I became an
executive secretary with General Motors. Not surprisingly for someone

who loves to sing, it was a disappointing job. I added to my misery by suffering through a bad relationship and then found myself at rock bottom, where I even considered suicide. At that point, the only place for me to go was back to Kentucky. I knew my family would welcome me and I would find my balance again.

Back home, I finished my schooling in the college's new television and communications department. I earned my degree with honors. When I stood at graduation, tears of joy and gratitude clouded my eyes as I located my parents in the crowd.

I moved back to Atlanta, this time with the resolve to do things right. I was determined to follow my heart and pursue the job I really wanted. I returned to my love of singing and got my first job at a supper club. One evening, a nice-looking man dressed in a yellow sports coat and white pants approached me during a break.

"My name is Vic Varconi and I am really enjoying your singing," he said. "But I have to ask, and I know it sounds clichéd, but what's a nice girl like you doing in a place like this?" He smiled.

"Singing and making money to pay my bills," I replied. "What's a nice guy like you doing here?"

Vic told me that he was a Presbyterian ministerial student at the local seminary and that as part of his psychology project, he was visiting clubs trying to find out why people went there in the first place. I laughed when he told me his answer. Soon after, we became really good friends. He was just the kind of friend I needed.

He introduced me to a new church, Mount Paran Church of God. The very first time I went there, the entire church sang "Hallelujah" in rounds. I must have cried buckets of tears. The sound was so beautiful and seemed to fill my soul. I knew I had found my church. I felt that God was making sure that this time around, my life was going to work. He was leading me in the best possible direction.

I started praying with Charlotte, a wonderful woman from Mount Paran. I told her that I wanted to be married and that this time I was ready. Charlotte prayed that God would send me the right man; she added that he needed to be tall because I was. I laughed at the last part of her prayer.

Enter the Steak and Ale, where I got a singing job. One night, as an introduction to my next song, I asked the audience if they had heard of Elton John. A man answered my question with, "Yes, but have you heard of Tom McGarey? He's at the end of this table and he is dying to meet you." Tom was six-feet, four inches and wonderfully handsome. I decided to make the most of the opportunity!

I sang a love song to him and a friendship bloomed, then blossomed effortlessly into true love. We were married in October of 1979 in the beautiful Blue Ridge Mountains.

Even twenty years later, the sight of a Steak and Ale makes us smile and squeeze each other's hand.

DIANNE McGAREY

Across the threshold led,
And every tear kissed off as soon as shed,
His house she enters, there to be a light,
Shining within, when all without is night;
A guardian angel o'er his life presiding,
Doubling his pleasure and his cares dividing.
SAMUEL ROGERS

IT STARTED WITH
TOMATOES

*To Love is to place our happiness
in the happiness of another.*

GOTTRIED VON LEIBNITZ

In 1941, a pretty blond thirteen-year-old named Mary Ellen Shives saw more tomatoes in any one day than a girl could possibly count, more tomatoes than a girl had minutes in a day, or dreams to fill them with.

You see, she was working at a tomato cannery near her family's farm in Fulton County, Pennsylvania. The job brought Mary Ellen extra money after her farm chores were done at home. Besides, it was wartime, men were scarce, and energetic young women more than welcome in the work force.

One day, Mary Ellen impulsively wrote her name and address on a label and packed it carefully among cans of tomatoes about to be shipped. People sent notes across the seas in bottles, didn't they? But she was nowhere near the sea, so tomato cans would have to do.

That night she lay in bed wondering and dreaming where her label might end up. Would a handsome, decorated soldier find it? Or just a crabby cook in some elementary school cafeteria? There was no way to know. Probably the label would disappear without a trace.

Weeks passed with no response, and Mary Ellen decided it had been a silly, immature thing to do. In the coming months, her attentions shifted to important teenage concerns—clothes, social events, and new crushes. In time, she forgot about the label.

Meanwhile, across the Atlantic, a teenager named Nick Tyssens was suffering through the war in German-occupied Netherlands. After working as a slave laborer in Germany, he was sent to a concentration camp where he became desperately ill and frail. By the time the war ended in 1945, Nick weighed only ninety pounds.

After he recovered, Nick became one of the first men to enlist in the newly founded Dutch Marine Corps and he was sent to Camp Lejeune, North Carolina, for training. That summer, he offered to help out a buddy who had mess hall duty. When they opened a crate of canned tomatoes, both soldiers spotted a label with a girl's handwriting on it. It had been in the crate for four years.

In their eagerness to grab the label, the two men tore it in half. But Nick's half had the girl's name and address. Anyway, unlike his buddy, Nick was fluent in speaking and writing English.

Nick decided to write to the girl. Or, for all he knew, perhaps "Mary Ellen Shives" was an old woman.

One day in September Mary Ellen Shives stopped to get the mail as she came in from working in the fields. She was surprised to find a letter written in red ink addressed to her. The envelope contained a photo of two young men, one of whom was circled in red.

The enclosed letter was short. The writer, Nick Tyssens, explained that he was a Dutch marine stationed in America for training. He told her he'd found her label in a case of tomato cans. *What kind of girl would do such a thing?* he wondered. If she was interested, he'd like her to write back.

Mary Ellen felt a shiver go up her spine. She had always wanted to visit Holland. That evening, she stared at the photo for at least an hour. In the morning, she eagerly returned his letter with her own, along with the most flattering picture of herself she could find.

Before Nick's return letter reached Mary Ellen, he had already been whisked off to the Pacific for more training. Each week for two and a half years, Nick and Mary Ellen corresponded. Through their letters, they became friends and confidants. Then friendship turned to love. Nick concealed a ring in a bar of soap and sent it to Mary Ellen, asking her to marry him.

Delighted, she accepted, even though she knew that Nick was about to be shipped back to the Netherlands. When and how would she ever meet her new fiancé?

Nick decided to go to his commanding officer and try to persuade him to let him return to America. The officer listened impassively to the obviously love-sick soldier—until Nick told him the part about the tomato can label. Then he burst out laughing—and decided to grant Nick permission.

Nick traveled by freighter for more than fifty days before finally disembarking in New York City. He set off for Pennsylvania by bus. By the time he arrived at Elwood Shives's farm, he was in a taxi and completely broke. His future father-in-law had to pay his cab fare.

In front of Mary Ellen's family (and quite a few family friends who just had to witness the event), the nervous couple finally met for the first time. Mary Ellen had planned to stay back, look calm, and keep her poise. But as soon as Nick stepped out of the cab, she flew into his arms. They didn't let go for a very long time.

Nick had only a two-month visitor's visa and had to be out of the country by September 24. Everyone wondered if the adventurous couple would still want to marry after they'd met, and if so, wouldn't a wedding date by the twenty-fourth be too soon?

The answers were yes and no, respectively. Mary Ellen Shives and Nick Tyssens were married on September 22, 1948, in the parsonage of St. Paul's Methodist Church in Hagerstown, Maryland. They spent their wedding night riding a bus to New York City in order to catch the ship that would carry them to the Netherlands.

To Mary Ellen's surprise and amazement, Nicky's hometown of Maastricht, Holland, welcomed them with a banner and music. Both of them agreed, however, that America would become home. Six months later, the couple sailed back to America with a stowaway—Mary Ellen was expecting their first child.

The Tyssens, who now live in Hagerstown, recently celebrated their golden anniversary. They enjoy a large family of children and grandchildren. But Grandma Mary Ellen is always dismayed when she hears of a new little Tyssens who doesn't like tomatoes. "Doesn't like tomatoes!" she cries. "They should eat tomatoes for dessert. How do you think all this began?"

DENISE TYSSENS, DAUGHTER-IN-LAW

A Dedication To My Wife

To whom I owe the leaping delight
That quickens my senses in our wakingtime
And the rhythm that governs the repose of our sleepingtime,
The breathing in unison

Of lovers whose bodies smell of each other
Who think the same thoughts without need of speech
And babble the same speech without need for meaning.

No peevish winter wind shall chill
No sullen tropic sun shall wither
The roses in the rose-garden which is ours and ours only

But this dedication is for others to read:
These are private words addressed to you in public.
T. S. ELIOT

THE FIRST NOEL,
BUT NOT THE LAST

Christmas is the kindling of new fires.
GLADYS TABER

Once again my fellow workaholic and I were the last lawyers to leave the office. "Merry Christmas, Sister Scrooge! You'd better get outta here before Santa Claus comes!" Jack warned.

"Happy holidays to you, too, Ebenezer. See you next year," I replied.

After Jack was gone, I turned back to some work on my desk. I was in no hurry to get over to my parents' home to celebrate the holiday weekend with my family. My two married sisters and their families and my brother and his family had arrived earlier in the day. I knew they would all greet me with their yearly barrage of questions: "Met anybody interesting, sis?" "Why don't you got out with Ralph again?" "Why don't you join a dating service?"

I had prayed feverently throughout the year that this year would be different, and that God would provide a special guy for me to invite to my parents' for Christmas dinner. Up until the last week, I'd still felt hopeful, somehow sure that God was going to grant me a positive answer to this prayer.

But once again, Christmas was almost here and I was alone.

At thirty-five I was beginning to believe that I might never marry. I had plenty of friends who love being single. But I longed to meet someone to share my life with—and have children with. By now, my biological clock was clanging for all the world to hear, especially my younger siblings who were all married with children.

When the clock struck six-thirty, my work was finally finished. I gathered all the gifts I had received from my coworkers and headed for the elevator. As I hopped on, I was not surprised to find myself the only one going down. Everyone else was probably at home with their families preparing for Christmas Eve by now.

Down, down I went from the forty-seventh floor—until the elevator stopped suddenly on the thirty-ninth floor and another holiday workaholic joined me. "Merry Christmas," the stranger said.

I barely got a glimpse of him over my stack of packages but I returned his greetings with as much enthusiasm as I could muster.

Down, down the elevator continued until it jerked to a sudden stop. I looked up at the monitor. We were on the twenty sixth floor and presumably another late worker was about to join us. But when the doors didn't open, I exchanged a nervous look with the man next to me.

My companion began to punch the buttons on the panel. Nothing happened and suddenly the entire elevator car went black. I was seized with a sudden panic. *What if I am trapped in an elevator in the dark with an ax murderer on Christmas Eve?* I thought.

We both began trying to dial our cell phones in the darkness even though we knew we couldn't get service inside the elevator.

My companion spoke first. "You wouldn't happen to have a match?" he asked.

We both laughed, realizing I was holding an armload of packages— and he had just uttered a clichéd come-on line.

I knelt to put my packages on the floor. Lucky for us, I collected matchbooks from restaurants. I retrieved several small boxes and smiled in the darkness when I realized I could do even better that. "I even have a couple of candles," I offered.

"You're kidding! That's great," he said.

I began going through my boxes and bags of gifts and retrieved two large scented candles. I lit one and held it by his side as he groped for the elevator phone to call the service company. He gave them our location and looked over at me as he hung up.

"Everyone's away for Christmas, so they're running a skeleton crew," he said. "I'm afraid it will be a couple of hours before they can get here." Then he tried to reassure me. "I'll sound the alarm in the meantime and someone is sure to find us even before the elevator folks get here."

"On Christmas Eve?" I blurted. "You really think anyone's left in the building?"

"Sure," he said confidently. "We can't be the only crazy people working late on Christmas Eve."

While the alarm blared, I began to make myself comfortable in my corner of the elevator. I lit the other scented candle. *Thank you for the gift, Jill,* I murmured, and placed it in the middle of the floor. He held onto the other candle checking the controls on the panel until he finally decided he'd done all he could. Finally he turned and sat down.

"I'm Chad Hunter," he said with an outstretched hand.

"I'm Greta Green," I replied.

"I don't know about you, but I'm a praying man," Chad announced. "Would you like to pray with me that we will be rescued soon?"

I couldn't believe my ears. Here was a guy, a successful businessman —and he prayed! I wondered if he was single. I sat there dazzled as he prayed the most beautiful prayer I'd ever heard.

We exchanged pleasantries and I mustered up my courage to ask, "Your wife and children are probably worried and waiting for you at home?"

"Nope, I'm single," he replied. My heart began to beat a little faster. As we kept talking, I learned that he was unable to go back East to spend the holidays with his family because of a new client he had acquired for the firm. "I was planning a quiet Christmas Eve at home," he confided, "so no one is going to come looking for me until tomorrow when I don't show up for dinner at one of my partner's homes."

"Don't worry," I assured him, "my family's expecting me for a Christmas Eve supper tonight. Of course, they'll expect me to be late as usual. But in a couple of hours they'll probably send out the National Guard."

Chad then observed that our situation was nothing compared to what Mary and Joseph must have felt when there was no room at the inn on the first Christmas Eve. He regaled me with funny stories of his childhood Christmases back in New England. And he laughed at my own tales of Christmases past.

Over an hour had passed and I hadn't even thought about how hungry I was until Chad suddenly pulled out a bottle of wine. "I bought this for tomorrow to take to my partner's house for dinner, but there's no reason that we shouldn't celebrate Christmas right here and now." He pulled out a Swiss Army knife and pulled the cork out.

Okay, I can match that, I thought. So I shuffled through my bags and retrieved a coffee mug and an assortment of Christmas goodies the girls at the office had prepared—cheese straws, cookies, fruit, and even homemade bread and jelly. We enjoyed our Christmas Eve feast by candlelight. At one point we sang his favorite Christmas carol, "The First Noel."

For the first time in years, my heart was filled with the Christmas spirit and hope. And when the elevator service people arrived, shouting to tell us they were going to get us out soon, my heart sank. I felt like Cinderella must have felt when the clock struck twelve. I didn't want this Christmas Eve to end.

Hours after the elevator first stopped, the doors opened and my brother and my father were standing there waiting. As we hugged, I sniffled back a few tears. They assumed I was emotional because of my ordeal. But the real reason for the tears was that I didn't want to say goodbye to Chad.

When we exchanged farewells, Chad handed me his card and I gave him mine. "Merry Christmas," he said and disappeared out into the parking lot.

The next morning, our family attended our church's Christmas service as usual. But I hardly heard a word the minister said. I couldn't stop thinking about the stranger who'd become my friend in an elevator. When the organist began to play the "The First Noel," my eyes filled with tears.

As I walked up the aisle after communion, I glanced up to see Chad sitting on the right side of the church. I was stunned. *My eyes must be playing tricks on me!* I thought. But there he was, smiling broadly as he waved.

It was almost impossible to sit through the rest of the service. At the close, he rushed over to greet me.

"Merry Christmas, Greta," he said.

"I didn't know you went to church here!" I exclaimed.

"I don't," he said. "I came to see you."

"How on earth did you know you would find me here?" I asked with amazement.

"Remember, you told me that your family comes here every Christmas morning. I knew I'd find you here," he said.

My heart was beating wildly, and my sister began smirking and poking me in the side. My father leaned over and gave me a wink while my mother mouthed, *Invite him for dinner.* I just stood there speechless but beaming.

"I don't know about you," Chad began, "but after spending Christmas Eve with you, I couldn't wait. I just had to see you again."

Chad cancelled his dinner plans to join me and my family for Christmas dinner. God had heard those prayers I had prayed throughout the year. I was not alone that Christmas. Nor have I been alone any Christmas since then. Chad and I were married on Christmas Eve the following year. The next year, our first child was born on Christmas Day. We named her Noel.

To this day, whenever Chad and I find ourselves in an elevator together, we still hum "The First Noel." And we give thanks to God for the many wonderful Noels that have followed.

GRETA HUNTER, AS TOLD TO SUSAN WALES

The Moment We Met

God knew his chosen time:
He bade me slowly ripen to my prime,
And from my boughs within the promised fruit,
Till storm and sun gave vigor to the root.
BAYARD TAYLOR

"I KNEW THE FIRST TIME I SAW HER..."

"I'D KNOWN HIM AS A FRIEND FOR THE LONGEST TIME, THEN ONE DAY..."

"TO TELL YOU THE TRUTH, AT FIRST WE DIDN'T REALLY LIKE ONE ANOTHER THAT MUCH. THEN, OUT OF NOWHERE..."

TALK TO ONE HUNDRED HAPPILY MARRIED COUPLES AND YOU'LL GET ONE HUNDRED DIFFERENT STORIES ABOUT HOW TWO PEOPLE RECOGNIZED THERE WAS SOMETHING SPECIAL BETWEEN THEM. GOD MAKES MATCHES THE WAY HE MAKES SNOWFLAKES: NO TWO ARE EXACTLY ALIKE.

WE ALL KNOW COUPLES WHO MET, KNEW THEY WERE RIGHT FOR EACH OTHER ALMOST INSTANTLY, AND MARRIED AS A MATTER OF COURSE. THEN THERE ARE THE TWO PEOPLE WHO FOR THE LONGEST TIME HAD NO ROMANTIC FEELINGS ABOUT ONE ANOTHER, BUT ENDED UP CRAZY IN LOVE. OTHERS HAVE

HAD TO OVERCOME INSURMOUNTABLE OBSTACLES LIKE DISTANCE, OR DIFFERENCES IN CULTURE AND FAMILY BACKGROUND IN ORDER TO MAKE IT TO THE ALTAR. WHAT A VARIETY OF STORIES THERE ARE ABOUT THE TRIUMPH OF RELATIONSHIP WHEN GOD BRINGS A MAN AND A WOMAN TOGETHER.

THE LORD KNOWS EXACTLY WHO BEST SUITS YOU AS FRIEND AND LIFELONG LOVE. HIS WAYS ARE MYSTERIOUS AND FULL OF GRACE. BEFOREHAND, YOU HAVE NO WAY OF KNOWING WHAT BEAUTIFUL MOMENT HE IS DREAMING FOR YOU. BUT WHEN TIME, CIRCUMSTANCE, AND YOUR INWARD PREPARATION ARE JUST RIGHT, HE CONSPIRES TO DO THE IMPOSSIBLE—IGNITING THE FIRE OF INTEREST AND ATTRACTION.

HE LEAVES IT UP TO YOU TO GENTLY FAN THE FLAME.

A CHRISTMAS REMEMBERED

❧

Love took you by the hand
At eve, and bade you stand
At edge of the woodland,
Where I should pass;
Love sent me thither, sweet,
And brought me to your feet;
He willed that we should meet,
And so it was.

J. B. B. NICHOLS

My youngest brother Joe had dreamed of serving his country since he had been a young boy. When Joe graduated from high school, he immediately joined the armed services—much to our family's concern, since our country was at war. Our fears were confirmed when soon afterward, he was shipped to Vietnam. Joe convinced us that he felt it was his calling and his duty to serve his country.

It was 1968, and large numbers of Americans were protesting the Vietnam War. As I read the letter from Joe, my heart began to break. The news of the unrest and the antiwar protests had slowly swept across the ocean to our soldiers. The men in his platoon who were bravely serving their country and fighting the war were not only discouraged, but deeply hurt by their country's reaction to the war they were fighting and many of their friends were giving their lives for.

The young men were also painfully lonely and heard little from the folks back home. A few of these men didn't receive any letters or packages from home.

I was outraged by the lack of support our country was showing our men. A large number of these soldiers had no choice in the circumstances that took them to Vietnam.

After receiving my brother's letter, I worked hard to persuade the city council of San Mateo, California, to adopt my brother's company, which was made up of men who were virtually orphaned by their country's protests.

The town joyously reacted, and patriotism and appreciation soared. Little old ladies were baking cookies, and teenagers were corresponding with the men. Each one of the men in my brother's company was adopted by a citizen of our town. By a proclamation of the city council, the town officially adopted Company A of the 1st Battalion, 327th Infantry, 1st Brigade, 101st Airborne Division known as the famed Screaming Eagles.

In mid-March of that year, Joe wrote an enthusiastic letter of thanks to both my mother and me for organizing the outpouring of love in the San Mateo community. But that was about the last we heard from Joe, because less than two weeks later, we received the devastating news that my brother's company had been ambushed and that many of the young men were killed, including Joe.

The entire town of San Mateo went into shock. Joe was the town's first adopted son and the news of his death brought the reality of the war to our doorstep. Our family was shattered, but I dealt with my grief by plunging into the Company A adoption with more vigor than ever before. I would not allow my brother's life to be lost in vain. I would make a difference in the lives of others!

When Christmas approached, the city of San Mateo agreed to send me to Vietnam to represent the town bearing gifts for the platoon. I was excited about meeting Joe's buddies.

The city had struck medallions for the platoon and asked me to personally deliver them to their adopted sons. The money was raised and provided for my trip. I was eager to go and talk to the members of the platoon.

Joe had been halfway around the world when he was killed. It was not only important for me to witness the spot where he'd died, but to talk to the men who had been with him when he was killed. I knew this would provide enormous comfort to my family and me.

When I landed in Vietnam, Joe's platoon leader was called to escort me to the men's camp. The platoon leader had only two more weeks left in Vietnam, and escorting a woman into dangerous territory was not exactly what he wanted to do. He thought my coming there was the most ridiculous thing he'd ever heard of, and he let me know it. He was irritated when the call came, but he grudgingly made his way to meet me at the airport.

This was his second tour of duty in 'Nam and he had been gravely injured during this last tour. I learned later that he was injured in the same ambush that had killed my brother. He was literally counting the hours until he could go home, so he was grumbling all the way of his journey to greet me.

No one could have prepared either of us for the moment we met. Steve's attitude took a 180-degree turn, much to the amusement of the soldiers around him. We bonded the very moment our eyes met, and his enthusiasm increased remarkably. It's impossible to describe what happened, but it was obvious to us and all the men that something special was occurring between the two of us, something almost magical. My hopes soared. The entire experience was just too special to put into words.

I soon learned that Steve had not only been my brother's platoon leader, but he had been there helping a soldier who was wounded in the process of trying to save my brother's life. Steve was wounded while he aided that soldier and still bears the scars today. It seemed like a miracle to me at the time that Steve was able to give me every detail of my brother's last days and more importantly, his last hours.

When we arrived at our destination and I first saw the young soldiers, tears moistened my eyes as I was struck at how very young they were. As I looked into their eyes, I saw the look of love, and some shyness, loneliness, and fear. I saw my brother. Every one of them looked like my brother.

It was Christmas Day when I arrived and the company held a memorial service for Joe, followed by the soldiers singing "Silent Night." No Christmas before or after has ever touched my life like that one.

When Steve drove me back to catch my plane back to America, my life had changed. I had changed. I was fighting my emotions and the strong feelings that had developed for the young lieutenant who had accompanied me.

When Steve saw me off, I knew he had feelings too, because to my utter surprise, he kissed me good-bye. "I'll call you when I come home," he promised. I knew in my heart that he would. Just the same, it was painful to leave him.

My heart was heavy as I left Steve standing there. He finally disappeared from my sight as I flew away. As I sat back in my seat on the plane I knew that the trip had been a tremendous healing process. My visit with the appreciative soldiers changed my life.

Company A became an extended family for me and my city. I am still in touch with those surviving men today. When I returned home, I received a hero's welcome. I reported all the details of my trip to the city but held secretly in my heart the love I felt for the young lieutenant I had met.

Just as he promised, weeks later I received a phone call from the young lieutenant who had escorted me. He was home from Vietnam and wanted to see me. My heart fluttered at the mere sound of his voice.

Steve eventually settled in my area, and proposed soon afterward, but we weren't married for eight years. It never bothered me that we had such a long engagement because I was aware that Steve required a lot of healing from his experiences in the war. He had witnessed a lot of his men dying—young men—and desperately needed to come to terms with the war before he could be made whole and ready for marriage. I am thankful that we were both mature enough to accept this.

We were also faced with the dilemma that Steve wanted to get as far away from the war as he could. He didn't want to talk about it, hear about it, or think about it, and yet the woman he loved was still attached to and heavily involved in her adopted Company A.

After we were married and the years went by, Steve healed and eventually got involved in my adopted platoon as much as I had. When Desert Storm began, I began organizing again and my ideas soon grew into a national organization.

While I realize that my efforts have made a difference in the world—especially with the young men and women who serve our country—the greatest gift was that I was blessed with the most wonderful husband. Steve has become my life's partner and the love of my life.

Since that time, there has not been nor will there ever be a Christmas like the one I spent in Vietnam. My brother Joe's short life not only had a great purpose, but it brought such meaning to my life in so many ways. I made the Christmas trip to Vietnam to seek the gift of healing, but in addition, I returned with the gift of love for a lifetime.

What could be more fitting at Christmastime considering the ultimate gift of love that mankind received on that very first Christmas.

CAROL, AS TOLD TO ANN PLATZ AND SUSAN WALES

THE HEALING DREAM

I have found the paradox that if I love until it hurts,
then there is no hurt, but only more love.

MOTHER TERESA

I was having breakfast at a local drugstore in Palm Beach, Florida, when I first saw her. She came in with an older couple and needed directions. They were lost, but suddenly I felt quite found. They got the directions they were after and left. But I couldn't get her out of my mind. I wanted to know everything about her. I wondered what she did, what her voice sounded like, what her favorite hobbies were. I had it bad.

Driving home about a week later, I saw her crossing the street in front of the Palm Beach Elementary School. I thought my heart was going to explode. I was positive that God had brought me to this place, just as he had brought her to the drugstore that day. This was it. It required some detective work on my part, but I convinced the sister of a good friend of mine, who happened to know the mystery woman, to introduce us.

I arranged for my friend's sister to bring her to my office. She could introduce this attractive lady to me sort of by accident. The meeting was magnetic. We started dating immediately and were married two years later in 1966. Our daughter was born in 1969. Life was perfect.

In 1970, perfection was interrupted. My wife was diagnosed with breast cancer. Being a teacher, she taught our daughter everything she could get into her head until she died, at age thirty-two, in 1974. My wife was an outstanding woman, beloved by her community, her colleagues, and her students. She was an inspiration to all who knew her.

When we were in the hospital for the last time, she told me she loved me and that she trusted me to do the best I could for our daughter. She knew I would love our daughter enough for the both of us.

My wife was far too young to die. It took me a long time to accept her death—thirteen years, in fact. It was then that I dreamed about her. In this dream, she and I were walking through a shopping mall together. You see, my wife loved clothes. She had been a beauty queen in high school and college. She made most of her clothes. Easily, she could have been a dress designer. She would see an evening gown in the window of a shop, go straight home, and make it herself.

In the dream, I was so happy to be with her, so content to be holding her hand. I had almost forgotten what that felt like. She was dressed in a blue double-knit pantsuit circa 1970. I laughed and told her, "Darling, you need some new clothes!" She smiled at me.

I jerked awake from the dream. I reached for her beside me. I had to remind myself that she wasn't there except in my imagination. I thought a long time about that dream. *Why now?* I wondered. The dream haunted me, and slowly I began to understand its healing value.

My mind was telling me that both my wife and our relationship belonged to the past. I had never let her go and so I was still stuck with one foot in the present, the other planted firmly in the past. I had to move forward. I had to continue with my life. So in my mind I finally told my wife that I had loved her from the first moment I saw her in the drugstore that morning, that I loved the way she used to make me laugh and how she looked at me with love in her eyes, that, most important, she always seemed to teach the people around her the greatest lessons. And I told her good-bye.

Sometime later I was having a business lunch when I noticed a woman sitting a few tables away. She was seated with a group of six people and she appeared to be in charge of the meeting. I couldn't stop watching her. I wanted to meet her. But how could I? I was about to leave. I couldn't interrupt her meeting. I decided to jot a short note inviting her to a lunch or dinner. I included my office and home telephone numbers on the note. As I left the restaurant, I slid it under her plate. When I arrived at my office, I told my secretary that if a woman called to inquire about me, patch her straight to me.

Nothing happened.

I waited and waited. I waited a little more. Nothing. Then a call came from a lady who asked my secretary, "Would you tell me who Bill Smith is?" My secretary told her my position in our company. "Thank you very much," she replied, then hung up.

Two weeks later, she called me at the office. We agreed to meet, but she lived in Charlotte, North Carolina, and I was in Atlanta. We were trying to get our schedules together and finally we saw that we were both going to be in Florida at the same time. I was to be in Boca Raton and she would be in Miami. So we made a date for dinner in Miami.

We were both kind of nervous when we first saw each other. It was more or less a blind date. After dinner, I heard music coming from the lounge so I asked her to dance. After dancing with her one time, I knew she was right for me. It felt so natural.

She eventually told me about her response to my note. She put it straight into her purse without even reading it. The president of her company was sitting to her left and she didn't want him to think that people were flirting with her when she was out of town, so she acted like it didn't happen. At the airport, the president asked her if she was even slightly curious about the note. "Let's look at it," he said. She pulled it out and they all read the note. The president commented that he liked a man with strong handwriting.

We dated for about two years and I took her back to the same restaurant where I met her and asked her to marry me. We were wed at my house with our children and relatives present. My wife and I now go back every year to that restaurant to celebrate our anniversary. Our children, all three of them, get along wonderfully. We made a new family full of people and full of love.

And it was all because of a healing dream. Had God not helped me to let go of my beloved first wife, I might never have met the woman who fills my life with blessings now. With my history, I don't believe in "chance" encounters—at drugstores, restaurants, or in dreams. God's plan is wonderful.

AS TOLD TO ANN PLATZ

SEND MIKEY
RIGHT OVER!

I'm glad it cannot happen twice,
the fever of first love.

DAPHNE DU MAURIER, *REBECCA*

The blond-haired blue-eyed kindergartner surveyed her classmates on the other side of the playground. Who should she choose? Who should she call? She studied the faces of each one of the gangly boys and then she surveyed the group of giggling girls.

There stood Mikey, tall and proud. Diane was drawn to Mikey's big blue eyes and smiling face. Her decision was made: she would choose Mikey. Shyly, Diane called out, "Red rover, red rover, send Mikey right over."

The young boy grinned with a smile that stretched all the way across his face, and ran across the lawn to her.

Later that year, when Mike fell off the swing at Diane's birthday party, it was she who came to his rescue and nursed his scrapes (and bruised pride). Her tenderness made Mikey feel all better.

After kindergarten, Mike and Diane went to different elementary schools. They did not meet again until the sixth grade. But even after all those years, they hadn't forgotten one another. They continued to exchange glances in class and the cafeteria.

In the seventh grade, Mike's parents allowed him to have his first boy-girl party. Mike invited Diane as his special date. Throughout high school, they were rarely apart again.

Diane proudly wore Mike's class ring their senior year. The couple enjoyed all the fruits of their young first love. Sadly, after graduation, Diane and Mike, like many other high school sweethearts, parted ways.

Diane was leaving for Macalester College and Mike had been accepted at Yale. They were both ready to experience all college had to offer, but that didn't lessen the pain of their farewell. As they walked away, they both knew in their hearts that their relationship probably would not survive. They agreed to cherish the memories but look to the future.

College was an exciting adventure for the two of them. "I was very active on campus and began dating immediately," Mike explains. "It was a very exciting time in my life. I was meeting people who were so sophisticated and attractive. My ego swelled with all the choices of outstanding women to go out with.

"There were many times when I would begin to get serious about a certain girl—until I would compare her to Diane. The answer was always the same, no matter how special the new woman in my life might seem: *No one* could hold a candle to Diane!

"Diane's character, intelligence, kindness, and gentle ways were always a cut above the rest. She also had such a deep and genuine faith in God. At the time, I was considering going into the ministry, so that was one of Diane's most important assets. Diane was all a man could ever hope for in a wife. She exuded so much self-confidence and such strong values that I never felt I was competing with her, as I did with so many of the other women I was seeing.

"Plus, I knew I wanted to marry and have a family. I was dating with that goal in mind. Whenever I dated someone seriously and got to know her, I would ask myself: 'Would I want this woman to be the mother of my children?' I highly recommend this litmus test for any potential marriage partner. The only woman I could ever answer 'yes' to that question was Diane.

"I could hardly wait to get home that summer to tell Diane that I knew without a doubt that she was the girl I wanted to marry. I had played the field for a year and Diane was the only one left standing!

"When I arrived home, my first stop was Diane's house. Unfortunately, there she stood at the door with a guy she'd met at college who had dropped by to meet her parents. My heart began pounding in my chest. I was devastated. Worse yet, he had a shiny new Corvette standing at the curb. How could I ever compete with that?

"I got out of my old clunker and went up to the door. What I really wanted to do was punch the guy, but instead I extended my hand."

Here Diane takes over the narration. "As I watched Mike's behavior in comparison to my college friend's I thought, 'This guy is history!' I asked him to leave the next morning. I knew then without a doubt that Mike was the man with whom I wanted to spend my life."

Just before his senior year of college, Mike proposed to Diane. They were married following their respective college graduations. The entire town of Estherville, Iowa, turned out to see the hometown sweethearts become man and wife.

Mike and Diane have been married thirty years. They love to show their faded kindergarten class picture in the hallway of their home. It's like many of the black and white photos from the fifties: Davy Crockett coon-skin caps and cowboy hats with chin straps rest on the heads of the boys, and the girls are adorned with big bows and hair ribbons. Pretty Diane is standing next to the wide-eyed young boy who even at five is making eyes at her. And who would have dreamed that Diane's Red Rover choice would become a lifetime partner?

DIANE AND MIKE RHODES, AS TOLD TO SUSAN WALES

Editor's note: Mike and Diane Rhodes live in Pacific Palisades and have two daughters, Sarah, a teacher, and Katie, a missionary in Russia. Mike is an award-winning director and producer for many television shows and movies including the CBS series, Christy, China Beach, and the Fox series Beverly Hills 90210, as well as several television movies of the week and the feature film, Dorothy Day.

HAMBURGER
HEAVEN

He that is of a merry heart
hath a continual feast.
PROVERBS 15:15

From time to time they bumped into each other in the library, the cafeteria, and other spots around campus, but they rarely exchanged anything more than a brief greeting.

One night after the dinner meal on campus, Jim and Shirley found themselves standing near one another in a circle of friends. Capturing the moment, Jim sidled up to Shirley and said, "See this nickel? I'm gonna flip it in the air. If you can call heads or tails correctly, I'll buy you a hamburger. But if you lose, you'll owe me one."

How's that for a new approach? Jim would be a winner either way because he got a date out of the arrangement. Shirley liked the idea and said, "It's a deal." She called heads as the nickel went into the air, but it landed tails.

"Good," said Jim. "when do you want to pay off?"

"Hey, wait a minute!" Shirley protested. "Give me a fighting chance. Let's go double or nothing."

Jim flipped the coin and Shirley lost again.

"Great," said Jim. "I like hamburgers. Now I get two of them."

"Let's go one more time," she demanded.

Jim checked the nickel. "You now owe me four hamburgers," he said.

Before they had completed the game, Shirley owed him one hundred twenty-eight hamburgers, and she's been frying them ever since.

SHIRLEY AND DR. JAMES DOBSON

Thou art my life, my love,
My heart, the very eyes of me,
And hast command of every part
To live and die for thee.

ROBERT HERRICK

Excerpted from Dr. Dobson: *Turning Hearts Toward Home*, Rolf Zettersten,1989, Word Publishing, Nashville, Tennessee. All rights reserved.

MAN'S BEST FRIEND

☙

A door is what a dog is
perpetually on the wrong side of.
OGDEN NASH

Jimmy Stewart was one of the biggest stars as well as the most eligible bachelor in Hollywood in the late '40s. Women everywhere were pursuing the charming bachelor but at forty he appeared in no hurry to marry.

One night when he attended a dinner party at the home of his friend Gary Cooper and his wife the matchmaker, Rocky, he was seated next to the lovely Gloria McLean. Obviously interested, he offered to drive Gloria home and as he walked her to her door, he invited her for a golf date.

Their courtship is vividly described below from *Jimmy Stewart, A Wonderful Life* (Pinnacle Books, Kensington Publishing Company).

When the two played golf, Gloria beat Jimmy and he didn't seem to mind at all. When he drove her home he declined her invitation to come in but not because he didn't want to! He was afraid of her enormous dog who growled at him at the door.

"Only as I drove away did I realize how smitten I was by Gloria. I wanted to see her again but I knew I would have to win that dog over because Gloria was obviously devoted to it," Jimmy recalled.

To woo Gloria, he had to woo her dog, too. Jimmy went about schmoozing both with typical thoroughness. He would show up for a date with a steak from Chasen's under his arm as a peace offering for the German shepherd. The dog was no gourmet and continued to growl at him. He tried talking baby talk to him, patting him, praising him. "It was terribly humiliating, but I finally got to be friends and was free to court Gloria.

"It took me a year to get her to say yes." He didn't say how many chateaubriands from Chasen's it took to get the German shepherd to agree to the union.

Maybe the dog never became Jimmy Stewart's best friend, but the marriage was a success! The Stewarts' long and happy marriage was legendary and one of the great role models in Hollywood.

LETTERING IN LOVE

Your letters are always fresher
to me than flowers
Without fading so soon.

<small>MARY RUSSELL MITFORD</small>

It was the spring of '42 and they were two kids living on two continents when pen and paper—and a school assignment—brought
them together.

She was fourteen, a student in Miss Frady's class here, when the
eighth-graders were asked to select a pen pal from a list of kids in
England. It was a small way of uniting teens during the war.

He was fourteen, too, a grocery errand boy outside London when he
began writing her.

They had little in common but the two found enough to write about
for years.

When the war ended and he was in the Royal Navy, he wrote to say
he wanted to visit her in Iowa. She told her fiancé, who quickly laid down
the law: No more letters.

It seemed the pen pals would never cross paths again.

Dear Sir or Madam,
I am writing to see if you can help me in my plight. During the war
years, I was writing to a girl (as a pen friend). Her name was then

Miss Colleen Lee. If you could by any chance trace her for me, I would be very grateful.
Yours truly,
Geoffrey W. Lake

The letter was dated October 19, 1989, and now, almost ten years later, Geoffrey still can't say precisely why he decided to look up his old pen pal.

He was sixty-one, happily married for decades to his wife, Eileen, with a grown son, Michael. But something tugged at the retired factory worker.

He didn't remember Colleen's address but couldn't forget her hometown's distinctive name: Soldier.

With just 250 souls in Soldier, there are no strangers. It turned out Colleen was now Colleen Straight, having long ago married her childhood sweetheart, Harvey, and their three children were adults.

Geoffrey and his wife were planning to visit the United States when his note arrived in Soldier.

Dear Geoff,
What a surprise! I believe it's been forty-five years since we corresponded.

Where to begin? Colleen dashed off a breezy three-page letter describing her family and where they had lived over the years. She also invited Geoffrey and Eileen to Soldier.

And so, they began corresponding again. They always signed their letters as couples.

Then in December 1992, Colleen had sad news.

This is not an easy letter to write. I lost Harvey…I know I must not dwell on his passing, but I do think of it a lot.

Geoffrey responded with a condolence card, and one each year on the anniversary of Harvey's death.

Geoffrey and Eileen's plans to visit Colleen the next year fell through, but the letters continued.

Then in November 1997, Geoffrey's wife of forty-five years died. This time, Colleen did the consoling.

Dear Geoff and Michael,

It's difficult at this sad time to find the right words to comfort you. You will find yourself thinking of all the things you have done together and that helps a lot…just be thankful you had a good life together.

On a January night a year ago, a downcast Geoffrey dialed his phone. He was tempted to hang up before a little girl answered.

"Grandmother, somebody I can't understand wants to talk to you," ten-year-old Ashley said.

"Hello, Colleen, do you know who this is?" the caller asked.

For the first time in fifty-six years, the childhood correspondents spoke to one another.

They talked for a while and at the end, Colleen recalls, "He said, 'Good-bye, love.' I really took that to heart. I thought, boy…he means business!"

Geoffrey wanted to visit her, though Colleen felt it was too soon for the new widower. So she delicately put him off.

But their calls and letters picked up.

"We more or less—" Geoffrey begins

"Struck up a romance," Colleen finishes his sentence.

My darling Colleen,

It sounds a bit ridiculous the way we feel about one another. Here we are, both approaching the age of seventy and carrying on as though we are teenagers, but honey, I've got a young heart and cannot express my feelings any other way. I love it and I love you, honey. Roll on May 28!

That was the date they agreed to meet in New York.

"It was love at first sight," Geoffrey adds.

They spent three days touring New York before heading to Iowa, where he met her family. Then it was off to Mount Rushmore—where they bought friendship rings decorated with hearts.

Everything clicked. There was no tension, no shyness, no awkwardness.

In no time, Geoffrey decided to move to Iowa. He returned home to settle some personal matters, then on his first night back last September, he bent on one knee and proposed to Colleen.

"I said yes!" she recalls, turning to Geoffrey as they sit at their kitchen table. "I didn't even stop to think about it, did I?"

On November 28, the wartime pen pals became husband and wife. They sent out word to friends and family: "A reception honoring the newlyweds Colleen and Geoff will be on Saturday…"

It was their first joint correspondence.

SHARON COHEN

LOST AND FOUND

❦

Marriage is a sweet state,
I can affirm it by my own experience,
In very truth, I who have a good and wise husband
Whom God helped me to find.

CHRISTINE DE PISAN

ou're going to bring home a nice man from Korea to marry!"
This prophecy relayed by a well-meaning neighbor frustrated
twenty-four-year-old Susan as she prepared for her first overseas missions
trip. *I'm NOT going halfway around the world to look for a husband,* Susan
thought indignantly. And indeed, she wasn't. She was traveling the long
distance to serve God and the people of South Korea as a medical missionary. Susan had received God's call to serve him overseas at the young
age of ten. And now, fourteen years later she was embarking on this exciting adventure to a foreign land. Looking for a husband was the last thing
on her mind!

Susan's tenure in Korea was filled with great challenges and great
rewards. All too quickly, her two-year project had come to an end. As she
packed a very large steamer trunk full of her belongings and all her
mementos from her Korean experience, she chuckled as she recalled her
former neighbor's good-bye. *How many people will be disappointed that I
didn't find a husband here?* Susan wondered. After all, it was the hope of
most women of her mother's generation to see the next generation of
young women married. And two years in Korea didn't produce that result.

Susan arrived back in the United States without incident—almost.

She arrived safely, but her steamer trunk was MIA (missing in action). Somewhere on the way from Asia, the shipping company had lost the trunk including any clue to its whereabouts. Susan anguished over the fate of her trunk but kept praying it would turn up. Why would God have allowed all her belongings and all her personal treasures to get lost? Meanwhile, she began her next adventure—pursuing a master's degree in missions at a small Christian college in South Carolina.

Almost a year had passed when, out of the blue, Susan received a phone call from the shipping company. They had located her long-lost trunk. Susan's heart leaped with joy and thanks.

"When can you get it here?" she asked excitedly.

"It's on its way as we speak," the man informed her. "Ought to be pulling up there in about thirty minutes, ma'am."

"Thank you, thank you!" Susan gushed.

"But ma'am," the man said, "you'll need to get someone over there to unload it."

"Can't the driver—?" Susan suggested.

"Nope," said the man. "The union doesn't allow the driver to do that work, and besides that trunk is the size of a refrigerator. It will take several big guys to get it off the truck and into your house."

Susan panicked. She had only recently moved to the small college town. How in the world could she recruit three or four "big guys" in a matter of minutes? As soon as she hung up, she feverishly dialed an acquaintance, Paul, who lived in one of the college dorms. The small college did not have private phones in the dorm rooms. Instead, it had only one phone in each dorm hallway. Understandably, the residents were loathe to answer the phone as this invariably involved the time-consuming activity of tracking down or taking a message for the person for whom the call was intended.

On this particular day, when the phone rang Dave Hedberg was alone in the hall on his way to class. He heard the phone ring and ring. He hesitated, but, having a few minutes to spare (this day anyway), he decided to pick up the phone.

"Hello."

Susan was relieved when the phone was answered. "Is Paul there?" she asked breathlessly.

"No, Paul has moved off campus," came the response.

"Moved? Really? Do you know where he lives now?" Susan inquired anxiously.

Sensing how distraught the caller was, Dave replied, "No, but is there anything I can do to help you?"

Susan knew she must sound desperate, but she was. "I hate to ask this of a perfect stranger, but...how big are you?"

"How big am I?"

Knowing how strange the question she posed was, Susan quickly explained her predicament to the stranger she had just met on the phone a few seconds before. Always one to help whenever he saw a need, Dave assured her that he and the friends he would recruit were big enough to help. They arranged to meet on the steps of the campus student center.

As he told it later, when Dave arrived at the student center and got a glimpse of the attractive blond who had been at the other end of the phone, he was especially delighted that he'd answered the dorm hall telephone earlier that day.

Sure enough, Dave's muscles proved big enough to help Susan move her newfound trunk of treasures. But ultimately, it was his love for Christ and his love for Susan that were big enough to win her heart.

Two years after their first meeting, Dave proposed on the same steps where he first laid eyes on Susan. And so, while Susan didn't bring home a "nice man from Korea to marry," she did find true love through the misadventures of her steamer truck and its journey to South Carolina from Korea.

SUSAN HEDBERG, AS TOLD BY HER SISTER PAM ZELEK

Editor's note: Susan Zelek and David Hedberg were married, and today serve as missionaries to South America.

LEFT INSTEAD
OF RIGHT

✎

*A man's heart plans his way
but the Lord directs his steps.*

Why did I turn left instead of right in the alley that Friday night? Was there an angel blocking my path as I came out of the underground restaurant, causing me to walk up inexplicably toward Harvard Square, rather than downhill toward my apartment?

I had begun graduate school only a few weeks before. While I enjoyed the John F. Kennedy School of Government and was learning to survive on fewer hours of sleep than I had dreamed possible, I was aching for the family and friends I had left behind in my hometown of Washington, D.C. I missed my church and the close bonds forged in our single-adults group. I missed singing and my ego was still bruised by my almost comically horrible audition and subsequent rejection from the Harvard Collegium choir just two days before. Harvard was an experience of a lifetime—but it was also new territory, sometimes cold, and often lonely.

That crisp fall evening, I had looked forward to the first meeting of the Harvard Graduate School Christian Fellowship (HGSCF), a monthly gathering of all the Christian fellowship groups within the university's many graduate programs. For three years, my relationship with God had been the most important thing in my life, and I was yearning to find others who shared that priority. I was also looking for friends among my classmates, and that day I had jumped at the opportunity to go waterskiing with three of them.

Tired and disheveled, I returned late to my apartment, realizing there was no way I would make the HGSCF meeting before it ended. For some unfathomable reason, I showered, changed, and walked the two miles to the campus meeting site anyway, arriving just as the last few people were turning out the lights.

I recognized Virginia, a second-year student at the Kennedy School. She mentioned that some of the others had asked her to get a big table at a nearby underground restaurant, where they would meet for a late dinner. Would I like to join her?

I was thankful that after all I would get to meet people from other graduate programs, but when the whole group arrived en masse at the restaurant, there were too many. From across the room, I could see them crowded on the steps down into the restaurant, talking to the hostess, who was regretfully shaking her head. My eyes fell on one particularly good-looking guy in a striped shirt. Because Virginia and I were both tired, we elected to stay at the restaurant while the others went elsewhere, but I grinned and told her that I sure would have loved to have met a few of the nice young men in that group!

It is funny how things work. For the next ten minutes, Virginia and I tried unsuccessfully to be served. Waiters bustled all around us but would not stop and give us menus, take our orders, or bring us water. After our fifth fruitless attempt to flag down someone, we joked that we must be invisible and decided to call it a night.

We walked up the steps and said our good nights at the entrance to the restaurant. Virginia's bike was parked in Harvard Square, which we could see at the end of the alley to our left. My apartment was on the campus of the business school, downhill and to the right. I turned left.

Unbeknownst to me, as I was walking up the alley, another person was walking down an intersecting street toward me. On Friday nights, Harvard Square is as crowded as Grand Central Station at rush hour, and suddenly I found myself nearly bumping into someone. I recognized the striped shirt. We both looked at each other and said in unison, "Say, weren't you just at the restaurant?"

He introduced himself as Jeff. He was in his last year at the law school, had been in the HGSCF group that left for a less-crowded restaurant, and was out looking for anyone who'd lost the group. He pointed me toward the new restaurant. An hour into dinner, the topic turned to singing. Jeff was in the Law School Christian Fellowship's a cappella singing group, which was looking for a soprano! A friendship was born, and a romance followed.

Almost exactly two years later, Jeff and I were married at my church in Washington, D.C. We both look back on that fall night with amazement. Events had to have been perfectly synchronized for us even to have met. Because of his schedule, Jeff did not attend another HGSCF meeting until right before he graduated. If I had given up on going to the meeting despite the late hour; if Virginia had left the building one minute earlier; if a waiter had served us; if I had turned right instead of left; if Jeff had been ten seconds earlier or later on his path through crowded Harvard Square—Jeff and I would never have met. God did it all, and he did it well.

A man's heart may plan his way, but thank goodness, the Lord truly does direct his steps.

SHAUNTI CHRISTINE FELDHAHN

And the fruit that can fall without shaking
Indeed is too mellow for me.
LADY MARY WORTLEY MONTAGUE

SHE ROPED
HIM IN

Twice or thrice had I loved thee,
Before I knew thy face or name.

JOHN DONNE

I spent the summer after my high school graduation with my sister and her husband at the campground in Cedar Falls, Iowa. My sister had invited me to come and help care for her new baby, and I was thrilled to enjoy a summer vacation by the river.

Every afternoon when the baby napped I enjoyed the luxury of swinging out on the front porch in the hammock, reading a good book. I was relishing my last few months of freedom before I began school at the local college.

Every day, a dashing young man would hurry by the house on his way to work and I would peek up from my book to get a glimpse of his handsome face. I later learned that he was responsible for firing up the stove in the dining hall and that was why he came by our house each afternoon. How I longed to catch his eye so that we could meet!

As the summer wore on, I observed him watching me as he passed by, but it took several weeks before he finally smiled and said hello, but there was no other contact. I longed to meet the stranger with the friendly face but I was much too shy to initiate a conversation. I wished that he would.

One sunny afternoon just at the very moment the young man passed by, I had an opportunity to meet him, as the rope on the hammock suddenly broke and I tumbled out onto the floor of the porch. What a stroke of luck! My knight-in-shining armor immediately dashed up on the porch to rescue me.

At last, we met. His name was Leon Krafft and he told me that he attended the local college where I would be going in the fall. From that day forward we chatted every time he came by. I found myself looking forward to his brief visits that became the highlight of my afternoons.

Much to my disappointment, though, the summer romance that I'd been dreaming of never developed. Leon never invited me to go out.

After the summer ended, college began and I would run into Leon occasionally. He was always smiling and friendly, but he still didn't ask me out. I kept praying that he would.

One Friday afternoon when we ran into one another on campus, he asked me if I would like to go to a party with him that evening. "Yes, I would love to go with you!" I answered breathlessly. I had daydreamed about going out with him every afternoon as I swung in the hammock when he walked past me. My dream had finally come true!

I practically floated home on a cloud that afternoon to get ready for my date that evening, But when I announced to my mother that I was going to a party with the boy I had met over the summer at the campground, she promptly extinguished my enthusiasm. Mother was not pleased and she delivered a scorching lecture to me.

"Don't you know that a proper young lady never accepts an invitation for the same evening? You are obviously his second choice."

I frankly didn't know if I was his first, second, or third choice, but it was too late to do anything about it now…and was I sure glad it was!

Leon and I had a wonderful time that evening, and when I told him that my mother had scolded me, he confessed to me that I had, indeed, been his second choice. He had been seeing the campus queen, but she was suddenly called away for the evening. When he ran into me, his problem of finding another date at the last minute was quickly solved. Too bad for the campus queen, because after that evening, Leon never left my side.

A year later we were married and remained happily so for more than fifty years. My dear husband always teased me about tampering with the rope so the hammock would fall at the exact time he walked by. For the rest of our lives, Leon told everyone the story of how I roped him in. Truthfully, I couldn't have planned it that way if I'd tried!

I would tell anyone that it's not necessarily a bad thing to be second choice, just as long as you're the *right* choice. And, as in my case, with a little help from above, you can be roped right into first place before you know it!

RUTH KRAFFT, AS TOLD TO SUSAN WALES

There is a garden in her face
Where roses and white lilies blow;
A heavenly paradise is that place,
Wherein all pleasant fruits do flow;
There cherries grow which none may buy
Till "Cherry-ripe" themselves do cry.
THOMAS CAMPION

Will You Marry Me?

Prithee, pretty maiden
will you marry me?
SIR WILLIAM SCHWENCK GILBERT

HE HAS BEEN FEELING OUT THE EMOTIONAL ENVIRONMENT WITH THE ONE HE LOVES. THEY HAVE TALKED ABOUT WHAT THEY LIKE, WHAT THEY WANT, WHAT THEY DON'T. THEY HAVE TALKED ABOUT WHO THEY ARE AND HOW THEY BELIEVE. THEY SHARE A COMMON COMMITMENT TO WALK IN GOD'S WAYS. HE IS CERTAIN THAT HE WANTS TO SPEND THE REST OF HIS LIFE WITH HER. HE IS SURE THAT THE INTENTION IS MUTUAL.

HE IS READY. IT IS THE CULMINATION OF MONTHS—OR YEARS—OF GETTING ACQUAINTED, PRAYING FOR DIRECTION, NURTURING A RELATIONSHIP, LEARNING THE GIVE AND TAKE OF LOVE, AND SEEKING THE WISDOM OF FRIENDS AND FAMILY.

HE HAS REHEARSED THIS MOMENT IN HIS MIND A THOUSAND TIMES, AND IS NOT ABOUT TO ASK THE ALL-IMPORTANT QUESTION ON A WHIM.

WHY, THEN, DO HIS LIPS QUIVER AND KNEES KNOCK? WHY IS THIS MAN'S HEART POUNDING?

A CHRISTMAS
PORTRAIT

Christmas isn't a season.
It's a feeling.
EDNA FERBER

Steve and I met and fell in love while we were in law school. We often talked about marriage, and I fully expected Steve to present me with an engagement ring at graduation. But the only thing presented that day in May were diplomas.

I brushed off my disappointment, convinced that Steve would propose to me on my birthday in July. That would be much more romantic anyway, I decided. I looked forward to the day with great anticipation. The night before, I could hardly sleep. I was too busy planning how I would accept the proposal—happily, of course, but not too desperately.

Sure enough, when Steve handed me my gift, it was in a small jeweler's box. I opened it with baited breath—to discover a beautiful gold locket. "It's beautiful, Steve!" I gushed. But honestly, it was a struggle to hide my disappointment. *What was he waiting for?*

It didn't help that my little sister had gotten engaged the year before. Not only that, but her fiancé planned the most romantic proposal. He took her on a scavenger hunt and at the end of the evening she discovered the sparkling diamond tied to the stem of a pink rose—her favorite kind.

Steve, a more serious type, probably wasn't capable of such creativity. But I did expect a proper proposal. Not that I needed to worry about that.

Raised in a Southern family, he had impeccable manners and always knew the proper thing to do. He would certainly ask my father for my hand in marriage. But *when?*

Now with Christmas fast approaching, I mustered up my courage and asked my father if Steve had mentioned anything.

"Like what?" my father asked.

"Like my hand in marriage," I replied.

"I've hardly laid eyes on Steve since he began working at the law firm," Father said. "You two aren't still serious are you?"

My heart sank. It looked like Christmas, too, would pass without a proposal. I began trying to drop subtle hints—like dragging him past the window of jewelry stores, or asking him what style of decorating he'd prefer in a home. But I only received blank responses. "I don't know," he'd say, and change the subject.

My best friend, Betty, suggested that I try a little something to wake him up. "Tell him you think the two of you should date other people," she suggested. The thought devastated me, but maybe Betty was right. If he thought he was losing me then just maybe he'd propose. Then again, I didn't want to manipulate something as important as a marriage proposal.

I finally decided that if the ring didn't appear at Christmas, I'd have a heart-to-heart talk with him about my feelings. In the meantime, I had a hard time getting into the Christmas spirit. Each year, since my sister Sarah and I have been little, our entire family has gotten dressed up, and with our dog, Puddin', in tow, marched off to the mall to pose with Santa. Mom puts the picture on our Christmas cards and sends them to family and friends all over the world.

But this time when Father announced that we were having our annual Christmas photo taken on Saturday morning, I balked. "Dad," I protested, "aren't we all getting a little too old for this? Why can't we just have our picture taken in front of the Christmas tree like normal people?"

Dad pretended not to hear me, and Mom was oblivious. "This year," she gushed, "your sister's fiancé, Ted, is coming along. So you'll have the honor of sitting on Santa's lap all by yourself."

"Oh, yippee," I moaned.

"And next year," Mom added, "maybe Steve will be in our picture."

"I don't think so, Mom," I said. *Maybe,* I thought, *Steve has realized that I have a wacky family and that's the reason he hasn't proposed yet.*

When I saw Steve that Friday night, he invited me to accompany him to pick out his mother's Christmas present the next morning, but I had to decline.

"I have to have my picture taken with my family," I told him. I was sorely disappointed because helping a guy buy a present for his mom is quite a wifely chore.

"They aren't still going to see Santa, are they?" he asked.

"Yes, I'm afraid so," I confessed, "but maybe I can meet you afterward."

"I doubt it," he said, "Have you ever seen those lines waiting to see Santa on Saturday mornings? You'll be lucky if you make our date at eight."

The next morning when Sarah's fiancé arrived we all crowded in the family car along with Puddin', who was decked out in his finest Christmas sweater.

"Are you sure you want to marry into this crazy family, Ted?" I asked my sister's fiancé.

"Sure," he replied, "I think this is really cool!"

At least my father had arranged for us to arrive early and have our pictures made before the line of screaming children descended upon Santa Claus. As we waited for Santa to be escorted by an elf to his throne surrounded by a gaudy miniature toyland, I glanced at this year's Santa.

"Wow, they sure picked an awful Santa this year!" I whispered to my sister. "He's a puny looking thing and that beard is about as fake as any I've seen."

Sarah looked him over and disagreed. "I think he's kinda cute," she replied.

My parents were making cheerful chatter with one of the elves as I stood alone pouting. "Let's get this over with," I complained a little too loudly. The other elf must have heard me because we were immediately invited up to Santa's throne.

"Ho, ho, ho!" bellowed Santa as he looked in my direction.

Our dog, Puddin', took one look at this ridiculous Santa Claus and began to growl.

"My sentiments exactly, Puddin'," I whispered.

"Ho, ho, ho!" Santa hollered again, louder this time because of Puddin's growling and yapping. "Come sit in Santa's lap, little girl," he said in a fake Irish accent, looking in my direction.

"Isn't Santa taking this a little too far?" I protested. My mother shot me a look that could kill. So I climbed up in Santa's lap praying I wouldn't squish the skinny impostor.

The elves arranged my mother and father behind Santa. Sarah and her fiancé sat at his feet holding onto Puddin', who had finally calmed down. And there I sat, a twenty-four-year-old on Santa's bony lap. The children in line started to giggle. It seemed as though the photographer would never get the camera adjusted. We all waited.

"Ho, ho, ho!" said Santa. "There seems to be a problem. In the meantime, why don't you just tell Santa what you want for Christmas."

"You've got to be joking," I objected.

"Go on, tell me," he said.

"Well, if you must know," I said, "I want an engagement ring. If you can arrange that, Santa Claus, I actually might believe in you."

"I think I can manage that," he mumbled, "and who's the lucky bloke so I can put a wee bug in his ear?"

"My boyfriend, Steve," I answered. "But good luck, Santa—I've been waiting forever."

The photographer was finally ready again and I managed to smile through several photos. It was finally over, or so I thought. Santa reached down into his big bag and pulled out some presents for my parents, my sister and Ted, even a bone for Puddin'. Next he handed me a Christmas stocking bulging with candy.

"Well go on, darlin'," he insisted, "look inside."

Amid the candy canes and chocolate kisses, I spotted a tiny box. "It can't be!" I screamed. The photographer was snapping away as I opened the dainty satin box. It was the most beautiful engagement ring I had ever seen in my entire life. "But where is Steve?" I asked.

"Ho, ho, ho!" Santa said again, dropping his accent. "Will you marry me?"

It was Steve! I couldn't believe that my sweet, prim and proper Steve was disguised as Santa Claus!

"Aren't you going to get on your knees, Santa Steve?" I teased.

"I would but you're sitting on them," he said. So to the cheers of all those waiting in line, I turned around and gave Santa a big kiss, polyester beard and all.

Today our children squeal with delight when they see the pictures of Mommy on Santa's lap, kissing Santa. I must confess, every Christmas season without fail our whole clan still dresses up in our finery and meets at the mall for our annual photo. And right before the camera goes pop, I always turn to Steve and give my sweet, skinny Santa a well-timed kiss.

AS TOLD TO SUSAN WALES

O my Luve's like a red, red rose
That's newly sprung in June;
O my Luve's like the melodie
That's sweetingly played in turn.
As fair art though, my bonnie lass,
So deep in luve am I;
And I will luve thee still, my dear,
Till a' the seas gang dry.

ROBERT BURNS

WHAT ABOUT FRED?

❧

He used to say to me in his soft language:
"God brought you to me,
Sweet Lover, and I think he raised me
To be of use to you."
CHRISTINE DE PISAN

hen I was single and not in a relationship, which was more often than not, I often bemoaned to my friends, "There's nobody for me to go out with!" My friends were always sympathetic, knowing how much I wanted someone to share my life with.

I hung out with a crowd of actors and musicians in Los Angeles who were committed Christians. There was one guy in our group named Fred Bova. I'd only met him once, but we had friends who suggested that we go out. I'm an actress, Fred's a musician, and our friends prayed for both of us that God would bring someone special into our lives. They would often suggest my name to Fred just as they suggested his to me, as a possible date, but Fred would always say, "I don't really know Sarah." And I would say, "He's definitely not my type."

During the time Fred and I hung out in the same crowd, we rarely saw one another. We both were in other relationships. But just as a special boyfriend dumped me on Christmas Eve, my friend Daisy insisted that I come to her party alone. She told me that Fred was going to be there, playing his guitar.

There's nothing worse than to have just broken up with your boyfriend at Christmastime. Also I was so distraught that I was almost crying my eyes out, and I didn't want to make a spectacle of myself. So I sat in a corner and held my personal pity party, crying buckets of tears. I never heard from Fred.

After that disastrous romance, I decided to give up dating and concentrate on my career. I wasn't looking for anyone, but during those next two years, my friends kept asking, "What about Fred?" I would protest, telling them I'd given up dating.

That following summer I got a leading role in a play in Pittsburgh. Before I left, I promised my friends I would get to know Fred when I returned. They didn't forget, either, and I agreed to go to a party where I would have a chance to chat with Fred.

"Everyone's saying that the two of us should get to know one another," Fred said cautiously.

"I know," I told him, "they've told me that, too."

"Would you like to go to lunch?" Fred asked.

We met for lunch several times, but there was something wrong. I finally confessed, "I just can't do this anymore…I'm too nervous."

Fred told me he felt the same way and that really broke the ice. For some reason, both of us knowing that the other one was nervous put us both at ease. At that moment, he asked me for a real date.

We went to dinner, and as the evening unfolded I was mesmerized by this kind and gentle man. He appeared to be enchanted with me, too.

When my birthday rolled around a few days later, Fred gave me a vintage birthday card. He had no way of knowing that I'm an old-fashioned girl, so I was overjoyed to discover that he, too, shared my passion for antiques and, more importantly, my faith in God. We were discovering what our friends had known all along…it had just taken a us a few years!

We had dated little more than a few months when Fred asked me a shocking question: "Is it too soon for me to propose?"

I became all tongue-tied because it *was* too soon. Fred could sense my apprehension and said, "Maybe Christmas?"

He didn't wait for Christmas but proposed in November. At Christmas, Fred gave me a lovely antique engagement ring. Celebrating this happy Christmas with Fred made me think about how three years earlier I was crying over a guy who wasn't right for me when God had my future husband right there under my nose.

Less than a year later Fred and I were married surrounded by our friends—our matchmakers. But there is more to this story, much more.

When I was helping Fred move out of his apartment into our new home, he took me by the hand and pointed out something on the sidewalk. There scrawled in concrete obviously written years ago, the name, *Sarah*.

"God has been trying to tell us and show us this for a long, long time," he grinned as he took me in his arms. Fred had lived in the apartment quite a while and had walked over the name *Sarah* several times a day.

"I thought about you every time I walked past your name. It was only a few months later that I realized there was another name there, too." We looked down at the sidewalk and there in plain view above my name, Sarah, was the name *Fred* faintly visible.

It seems that God was not only trying to show and tell us something when he brought Fred and me together; he made sure what he was telling us was written in concrete.

SARAH RUSH AND FRED BOVA, AS TOLD TO SUSAN WALES

TIME IN A BOTTLE

⌒

The voice of the sea speaks to the soul.
The touch of the sea is sensuous,
enfolding the body in its soft, close embrace.

KATE CHOPIN

Every August of my childhood, my family gathered at my grand-parents' beach house on the North Carolina coast. It was two weeks that I looked forward to each year, especially being with my cousin Marilyn from Connecticut. She and I were the same age.

From morning till night Marilyn and I played in the sea. As children we loved riding the waves and building sand castles. When we became teenagers, we loved the romance of the ocean as we took long walks down the beach, daydreaming about our future. The summer we celebrated our sixteenth birthdays we decided it would be wildly romantic if we tossed a bottle filled with a note from each of us into the sea. We spent days composing our letters for our bottles. Marilyn wrote the following:

> *When you open this bottle and discover my letter*
> *I hope you'll agree that fate has brought us together.*
> *Write me and we will see*
> *If our love is meant to be!*

"Clever, don't you think?" she asked.

I, on the other hand, decided to be very daring. I wrote: "Will you marry me?" I also included my name, address, and phone number. The evening before we left for home, we went to the beach where we tossed our bottles into the sea at sunset. We staged quite a little ceremony that evening on the beach.

For years afterward, we talked about who would find our bottles. I told Marilyn that I hoped he would have blond hair and blue eyes. She was hoping her Prince Charming would be tall and dark.

To our disappointment, there was no news from our bottles. "They're probably somewhere on the ocean floor," I speculated.

The years went by. I moved to New York where I shared an apartment with Marilyn until she married. My advertising career was flourishing but my social life seemed to be at a standstill. My parents, knowing I had a little extra money and some time off, convinced me to spend my vacation with them at my grandparents' beach house.

When I arrived a couple of days before my parents, it was lonely and I longed for the days of my youth when the house was full of cousins and laughter. My grandparents had passed away and the rest of the family rarely made time to visit the beach house. Everyone had busy lives and all my cousins had their own families now—except for me.

I was feeling incredibly lonely as I walked the beach each morning. My parents arrived a few days later and my mother announced that a mysterious letter addressed to me had arrived at their home.

"Debbie, I didn't know you knew anyone from Charlotte," she said.

"I don't." I thought it might be someone I'd met at college.

"Does the name Tom O'Neil sound familiar?" my mother asked.

"Nope. Don't know any O'Neils."

"Well, don't just stand there," my father urged. "Open it!"

I ripped into the letter. As I read it, a wave of emotion swept over me. I was both embarrassed and intrigued at the same time.

"Well?" Mom asked. "Aren't you going to tell us who it's from?"

"I…It's…oh, no!"

"What? What?"

"Somebody found my bottle!"

"Your what?"

"My bottle! The bottle I threw into the ocean ten years ago."

"What?"

I made myself read the words. "It's this guy, Tom O'Neil. He found my bottle, and—"

"And what?"

I looked at them woodenly. I'm sure my face was white. "He's accepted my marriage proposal."

Two mouths fell open.

"And he wants me to call him. Here's his number."

Mom and Dad made me go back to the beginning and explain everything. I told them I'd imagined the bottle had made its way to Spain or some exotic island. "Can you believe it only made it down to the next beach?"

The next morning, at my parents' urging, I dialed Tom O'Neil. There was no answer (thankfully), so I left my name and the number at the beach house on his voice mail. *It's all some prank,* I told myself.

He called me the next evening.

"Hi Debbie," a strong male voice said. "This is Tom O'Neil. I'm not at home. I called and checked my messages. You're not going to believe this, but I'm here at the beach, too! Want to have dinner at the Crab Shack tomorrow night?"

I was so shocked I could hardly speak. But before we hung up, we agreed to meet for dinner the following evening. I mean, how could I not?

When the hostess led me to his table, I was stunned. There sat this handsome young man—with blond hair and blue eyes.

Meeting Tom was just too good to be true. It turned out he worked as an attorney in Charlotte. He had been coming to the neighboring beach with his family for his entire life, just like I had. He had found my bottle ten years before, but never contacted me until now.

"I was just getting to the point in my life where I wanted to meet someone," he said. "I figured you would be a good place to start. I always knew I would contact you one day—when I was ready to get married. For ten years I've dreamed about the girl who put the note in that bottle."

I was suddenly self-conscious. "I hope you aren't disappointed."

"Absolutely not. You're far more than I ever dreamed. Besides, you've already proposed! That makes things a lot simpler."

We laughed like old friends.

Over the next two weeks, we had a lot of fun getting to know one another. Our friendship grew, but didn't progress beyond that. My parents referred to the experience as my "summer romance." But that was pushing it—we hadn't even held hands.

When I returned to New York, I didn't really expect to hear from Tom. I figured I'd see him next summer if we were both still available, but I knew long-distance relationships were impossible. I did find myself thinking about him, however. Often.

Two weeks later, I came home from work and found a letter from him. "He misses me," I reported to my cousin Marilyn. I'd called her about the mystery man right away.

Tom came to New York to visit me a couple of times. And we ran up a sizable long-distance phone bill. *And* we wrote letters once a week.

We met at the beach again the next summer. The night before we were leaving, we walked down the beach at sunset. Tom had brought a blanket. When we got a spot near my family's beach house, Tom insisted that we pause so that I could dig in the sand for a surprise.

I dug where he indicated and found the same old bottle I'd thrown in the ocean eleven years before. There was a note inside. It read, "Will you marry me?" And that wasn't all. At the bottom of the bottle was a beautiful engagement ring!

Exactly two years from the time Tom first contacted me, we were married at the little church in the beach community with my cousin Marilyn as my matron of honor. Every summer we bring our children to the beach house.

Next summer our daughter turns sixteen, and she's already working on the letter that she plans to place in her bottle.

MARGARET O'NEIL

SILVER JUBILEE

Brief is life, but love is love.

ALFRED, LORD TENNYSON

arper and I were approaching our silver wedding anniversary. We'd had twenty-five years of wedded bliss and we both felt the desire to share our joy with our closest friends and family. We decided the perfect way to celebrate our love was to get married for a second time.

We invited our original bridesmaids and groomsmen to attend. Our guests—friends and family we had collected through the years—came from all over the country. I felt like a young, blushing bride again in a beautiful gown with silver thread woven through it. In my hair, we used silver gray net for a small veil. I carried a bouquet of white calla lilies down the aisle.

For the most important part, the vows, Harper and I carefully repeated the ones we'd made to each other twenty-five years before. We promised to love and cherish each other all over again. The best part of our second wedding was that we weren't the least bit nervous. We enjoyed our meaningful ceremony to the fullest and were thrilled that we could share it with all our friends and family.

Our daughter came home from college to help us celebrate. She thought we were joking about taking a second honeymoon. We kept trying to tell her we were serious and she kept rolling her eyes and laughing.

She stopped laughing when we waved good-bye to her from the car, leaving her to entertain all of the guests at the reception.

Marge Piercy wrote, "Life is the first gift, love is the second, and understanding the third." Our second wedding honors all three: the life God gave us, the depth of feeling that joins us, and our realization of both as gifts. Twenty-five years marks a very important anniversary. We've come through so much, learned so much, and loved so much. Harper and I both think that marriage should be celebrated, so why limit yourself to just one wedding? Who knows—we may even get married a third time!

DR. ANNE GASTON

I arise from dreams of thee
In the first sweet sleep of night,
When the winds are breathing low,
And the stars are shining bright.
PERCY BYSSHE SHELLEY

ONE DAY YOUR PRINCE WILL COME!

☞

An engaged woman is always
more agreeable than a disengaged.
She is satisfied with herself.
Her cares are over, and she feels
that she may exert all her power
of pleasing without suspicion.

JANE AUSTEN

At the age of five, many girls love playing with dolls and imagining the joys of having a family. But how many of them start praying for their fantasies to come true?

At five years old I was already eager to meet Prince Charming, get married, have kids, and live happily ever. And even at that young age, every time I kneeled to pray I asked God to send me a husband.

Through all my growing-up years, the prayer remained the same. By the time that I graduated from college at twenty-three, I had kissed a lot of frogs but none had turned into Prince Charming. I decided my fairy tale was probably still en route, but for the time being, I'd better get serious about a career.

I pursued another goal, this one to become an agent in Hollywood. As the years passed I found success in my career but faced failure in the dream department. I discovered that Hollywood was not the place to find husband material. Few men of faith crossed my path. Friends who knew how much I wanted to get married were astonished when I ended promising relationships, turned down dates and even a couple of marriage proposals because the men involved weren't believers. My friends thought I was being too picky, but as much as I wanted to marry, I refused to compromise on the faith issue.

By the time I turned thirty, I accepted the fact that I might never marry, and I relinquished my hopes for marriage to God. After much prayer, I did finally find peace and contentment as a single career woman. The deep desire in my heart for a husband was not removed, just dormant, so I figured I couldn't do any harm by continuing to pray for a husband…just in case!

When I was thirty-three I was in a hotel lobby just before attending the Golden Globe Awards. An attractive young man approached my dear friend, Cathy Brown, and asked to see her program. They begin chatting and he happened to mention that he was a Christian. Hearing those words, Cathy grabbed him by the hand and led him in my direction.

Cathy was so proud of herself. She thought she had found "one." I was interested and amused until I learned that Will was only twenty-six and was a guest at the hotel from Oklahoma City. I politely gave him a business card and walked off to rub shoulders with Kevin Costner, Brad Pitt, and the other movie stars that had assembled for the Golden Globes.

Cathy, though, both a relentless matchmaker and a genuinely nice person, was not about to let this Christian guy—a rarity in Hollywood—get away! She arranged for him to get into the Golden Globes and the aftershow parties.

After those events, almost a year passed before I thought of Will Rogers again. Cathy called one day and said, "Remember the cute guy from Oklahoma City? He's in town for the week—wants to know if we can get together with him!" I flipped through my calendar; it was jammed, so I suggested that she invite him to hike with a group of our friends on Saturday.

Everyone enjoyed the hiking trip except Cathy, who was busy darting between Will and me. She whispered, "Victorya, you should go out with Will. He likes you!" and "Will, you should ask Victorya out."

Neither of us knew she was coaxing the other.

Later that evening Will joined Cathy and me and my parents for a concert. When Cathy went to the ladies' room with my mother, she announced, "This is the one—just watch. Victorya is going to marry Will Rogers."

My mom just humored her and said, "Yeah, sure, Cathy."

But something had clicked. Will and I began e-mailing one another every day and within three weeks, he came back to Los Angeles to see me. After that, he visited every few weeks. I began to hope and pray that maybe Cathy was right. When Will invited me to fly out to meet his family for Thanksgiving, I knew things were getting serious.

That weekend, my hopes began to soar when Will told me that he wanted to marry me one day, but when he didn't officially propose, I was devastated. Afterward I prayed: "Lord, why did this guy have to come along who apparently cares for me but isn't ready for marriage? I've waited for so long to meet the right person. If he knows he wants to marry me, why doesn't he just propose?"

The next time I saw Will, I honestly told him how much I wanted to get married. Much to my disappointment, he replied, "Victorya, I love you and I know without a doubt that one day I want to marry you, but I'm just not ready yet. Trust me, when the time is right—I'll propose!"

Yeah, yeah, yeah, I thought. *I'd better get used to being single again!*

From then on, I grew exceedingly anxious every time Will came to Los Angeles. I always wondered if this would be the time he'd propose. By the time he arrived, I was so uptight that it began affecting our relationship. Every moment I was with him I expected him to pop the question, but he never did. Each time he left without a proposal, I was in tears. To make matters worse, when I showed up at the office on Monday morning, everyone was anxiously waiting to see if I was wearing a ring!

Will always apologized and explained that he felt bad, but he just wasn't ready to get married. One week he called to say that he wanted to come for the weekend, but he didn't want his visit to cause any anxiety. "I'll just tell you up front that I'm not going to propose," he said, "so if you would prefer I not come, I won't."

"Of course I want you to come," I assured him. Knowing not to expect his proposal actually took a lot of pressure off, and we had one of our best visits ever. Just before we left for an Angels baseball game, Will began acting a little strange. He asked me to sit down on the couch and after a dramatic pause, he finally spoke. "If I were to propose to you without a ring, would you still consider us engaged?"

I asked suspiciously and anxiously, "Is that a proposal?"

"Maybe, but answer the question," he ordered.

"Of course we'd be engaged. I don't need a ring," I assured him.

Then he said again, "Even without a ring, we'd be engaged?"

By this time I was so excited I could barely whisper, "Yes."

Will continued, "So, will you marry me even without a ring?"

I had a big ear-to-ear grin and my eyes begin to tear up as I answered, "Yes!"

Suddenly, Will whipped out a ring and said, "Well, how about with the ring?"

At that moment I totally lost it—I shed a gallon of tears. It was finally true: I was officially engaged!

After I had cried for a few minutes, Will laughed and told me that I could look at the ring. It was so gorgeous that it took my breath away!

I became Mrs. Will Rogers on January 31, 1998, at the Crystal Cathedral in Garden Grove, California. It was the happiest day of both of our lives.

As we drove away to our honeymoon destination, Will took my hand and tenderly revealed, "When I was a little boy about five years old, I dreamed about the girl I would marry. And when you walked down the aisle today—do you know that you were that girl in my dream?"

Then I told Will how I'd prayed for my husband since I was five years old and now he was there...by my side! Will and I both cried as we saw with clarity that God hears and honors the prayers and dreams of even the youngest of hearts.

VICTORYA MICHAELS-ROGERS, AS TOLD TO SUSAN WALES

PEN PALS

Submit yourselves one unto
the other as unto the Lord.

PAUL'S ADVICE TO CHRISTIAN COUPLES
EPHESIANS 5:21

When do you ask a girl to marry you?"

The man remembered asking his mother long ago, and her answer came again to his mind: "When you can't live without her."

This was now that time, but the question still caught in his throat.

He had met her years before at a Christian student conference in New Mexico. At the time, he was an undergraduate student in Mississippi. She was from Texas, and was attending school in Massachusetts.

For the next three years after they met, they saw each other just once a year, staying in touch by writing back and forth. While each believed God had a special partner for them, and while both had prayed to be led to a Christian spouse, they simply regarded each other as pen pals. Through monthly letters they exchanged thoughts and began to discover special qualities in each other. It was a sort of correspondence course in companionship.

He finished college and began graduate school in Kentucky. That same year, she began her junior year abroad in Geneva, Switzerland. While there, she was led to a student retreat in the Swiss Alps. The retreat was led by a yet-unknown theologian, Francis Schaeffer. The exciting spiritual and intellectual atmosphere lured her back many weekends to the place called *L'Abri* (The Shelter), where she felt close to her special friend across the Atlantic.

Upon the completion of her year in Switzerland, she and her pen pal reunited and discovered, much to their own surprise, that their relationship had advanced to a deeper level.

Although still separated by hundreds of miles, they saw each other on holidays until her graduation from college. As a graduation gift, her parents presented her with a trip to a Christian student conference in the Holy Land. She chose the tour group led by her pen pal!

At the end of the tour, she took him to visit *L'Abri*, where he met Francis and Edith Schaeffer and saw the place that had been so special to her. That weekend, Schaeffer led a worship service in his chalet for the people of the village of Huemoz. That evening there was a communion service with students from five continents sitting cross-legged in a circle. Afterward, the young couple took a walk alone in the crisp alpine air. On that bright night, with the moon shining off the snowcapped Mont Blanc and the hint of Swiss cowbells in the higher pasture, they walked along, hands clasped, in a seemingly serene silence. Actually, he was nervously rehearsing the question that he had been considering for many months, and she was wondering if that "feeling" she had that he might propose was more than wishful thinking.

Completely unaware of their surroundings, they found themselves back in the chalet kitchen sipping hot chocolate. She had perched herself on top of the running washing machine.

Suddenly, he got up, positioned himself in front of her as if to block her escape, and blurted out, "Will you marry me?"

There! He had finally said it! He could breathe again, but the words had seemed too puny for the commitment it expected and inadequate to demonstrate the devotion he felt toward her. Before she could respond, he blurted again, adding the words his father said had worked for him thirty-five years earlier: "I mean it. This is not a trial. This is forever."

She only smiled. It was a tender smile, but it revealed nothing affirming. Then she shook her head slowly and told him, "I always wondered what this would be like." Holding his hands and looking into his eyes, she said nothing for almost five minutes—perhaps considering each option, or relishing the moment, or even wondering how to say no painlessly. He listened to the washing machine begin its spin cycle and held his breath again.

"Yes, yes, I will," was the long-awaited answer. It came so simply that he couldn't believe that it was settled. She jumped down from the washing machine and smiled again. They embraced as the spin cycle stopped and rushed off to share their joyful news with their hosts.

The next morning after breakfast they sat in the grass of the high pasture, praying together. He showed her a letter that he had written to her parents back in Texas, asking for their daughter's hand in marriage. He was struck again by the description of real commitment that his own parents' words had shown him. Thirty-six years later, that commitment, first made during a moment in Edith Schaeffer's kitchen, is remade daily in deeper and broader dimensions.

DORSEY AND PAM DEATON

Kindness in women,
Not their beauteous looks,
Shall win my love.
WILLIAM SHAKESPEARE

BEGINNING TO BEGIN AGAIN

❧

*A diamond is a chunk of coal
that did good under pressure.*

A MOUNTAIN SAYING

had been married a few short years when my husband walked out
on me, leaving me alone with little money and a young daughter to
support. We had been living in California, where my husband was a cin-
ematographer/director in the movie industry. Then, suddenly, this world
stopped. After the divorce, things turned from bad to worse for me. I
thought long and hard about what to do, and leaving California seemed
to make the most sense. So, I packed up my daughter and moved to New
York in the hopes of making a new start. To escape the world and life of
the West Coast, I fled across country to the world I had once known.

In New York, my daughter and I temporarily lived with friends of the
family. But you can only be a guest for so long. I knocked on many doors
trying to find a place to live. Apartments are hard to find in New York.

Because of my mother's social connections, I was invited to the many
parties that New York society held, but I felt loneliness even in the midst
of this sophisticated world. Something was missing in my life, but I didn't
know what. Since the divorce, I felt like I'd been floating, just barely going
through the motions of life. This was definitely the lowest point of my
life...I couldn't get a credit card. I was ready for a change.

It was about then that my friend, Lee, took me to a prayer group that she attended. I was busy trying to start my own business as a personal shopper and a fashion consultant. I was working very hard, and what few moments I had at the end of the day I happily gave to my daughter. However, I forced myself to make room for the growth of my faith. I wanted a place to live and more importantly, a purpose for my life. After the first meeting at the prayer group, I prayed to accept the Lord. I could immediately feel things in my life start to change for the better. After such an exhausting period, I finally felt rejuvenated. I felt alive.

My life began to turn around. I found an apartment and my business prospered. But the biggest change happened when I surrendered my life to the Lord. The leaves and the flowers even looked different. It seemed that I could see, taste, smell, hear, and touch life for the first time.

Lee wanted me to meet a gentleman from Georgia. I kept saying no, that the timing was all wrong, but Lee wouldn't listen. She persuaded me to go out with him. "He's only here for two days. You'll like him and be doing me a huge favor at the same time."

Lee had done so much for me. I owed her at least this small favor. But, the timing was still awful. Oh well, I thought to myself, what could it possibly hurt. I knew I wasn't interested in a relationship at this point. In fact, I had completely given up on the idea of marriage at all and my life was going so well that I didn't really know if I wanted a serious relationship.

Guy was a true Southern gentleman and I liked him right away. He made me feel comfortable and spending time with him was a pleasure. He made me laugh, which I needed so desperately. He just seemed to fit into the new picture of my life. I could tell immediately that Guy was an incredible Christian. He was definitely one of the good ones!

We went to dinner both nights that he was in New York. After that, he'd fly up to see me and go along with me to my prayer group. I was amazed at how easily and effortlessly our lives seemed to fit together.

We had dated for a year when Guy invited me to join his mother, aunt, sister, and children at his North Carolina mountain house. I remember that it was pouring down rain. I was busy baking an apple pie, complete with an apron tied about my waist, when Guy suggested we go for a ride.

"I've got flour all over me," I laughed.

"It doesn't matter. Come on," he whispered. I quickly tried to dust most of the flour off me and then followed him out the door.

We had been driving for a few minutes when he looked at me and smiled. "Ginny, I can't live without you. I don't want to live without you," he said. "I want you to marry me. I want you to be my wife."

I was absolutely speechless. "Can't we keep dating?" I asked, feeling panicked.

Guy smiled. I suppose he had already anticipated my anxiety. "I don't want to rush you. Take as much time as you need. A week? A month? How long do you need? I'll wait."

I couldn't breathe and my ears were burning. I was so excited. I felt like a schoolgirl. I realized that I was smiling at him then. I knew that I was really in love with him. I had known it for a while but I hadn't expected a proposal that afternoon. But as I looked into his eyes, I knew that he was the one God had for me. "Okay," I agreed. "I'll do it!" That was Labor Day weekend and we were married that December in New York.

It's been eleven years now and we are still madly in love. When I look back on the tough times in my life, I realize that the struggles, those dark and confusing times, make us who we are meant to be. They make us grow stronger. I am so thankful for those lessons.

When I least expected it, God sent a husband to me. Looking back, I can see the hand of God working in my life at that time. God placed the people I needed the most at the right time and place in my life. Even in the darkest moments of my life, God was always with me, urging me forward to fulfill his plan for my life. He made sure that I met the people who would help me along my path until I was indeed ready to meet the most wonderful Guy in the world.

GINNY MILLNER

THE APPLE OF HIS EYE

What greater thing is there
for two human souls
To feel that they are joined...
so strengthen each other...
to be at one with each other in
silent unspeakable memories.

GEORGE ELIOT

Clothed in rags, the emaciated form of a young boy, in an effort to stay warm, shuffles back and forth in front of the barbed wire fence of a Nazi concentration camp in Germany. Like so many Jews before him, he wonders, "Will I survive?" The year is 1943 and I am that young boy.

As I look across the barbed wire, I suddenly catch sight of a young farm girl hurrying by. Her eyes are drawn to my sad figure. Embarrassed, I struggle to turn away, but our eyes are destined to meet. Without any words, a connection is made through our shy glances.

Bravely, I call out to her, "Do you have anything to eat?" The girl searches for any sign of the guards, and seeing none, she reaches in her pocket, pulls out an apple, and tosses it over the fence. My heart leaps with joy as the shiny red apple flies through the air, bringing with it both nourishment and hope. Food has become only a faint memory for me. How long has it been since I had tasted an apple? As I hold the fruit in my hands it seems to thaw my frozen fingers as well as my soul.

"Come back tomorrow," I ask.

The same time the next afternoon, I make my way to the fence. I wait.

In the distance the tiny speck grows larger. As she comes closer, our eyes embrace. She tosses another apple in my direction. I can see by the look in her eyes that she, too, is being fed by our stolen moments.

The next day she came again bringing with her another apple, and then the next day a crust of bread. Our secret rendezvous continued for seven months, and the young girl became the apple of my eye. Through my pain and sorrow her visits supplied the hope that I needed to carry on.

Then one day I overhear that we were being moved to another concentration camp. My heart breaks knowing that I will never see those eyes again. When we meet that afternoon I tell her I'm going away and not to come again.

The next day I am shipped to another camp. The endless days pass by and then the months stretch into years. Each night when I am awakened by the recurring nightmares filled with the horrors of all I have endured, I weep for I am alone. My mother and father have died. But then I am comforted by the memories of the young girl's eyes as I dream of the precious moments we shared.

At last the war is over. The Russian Army descends upon our camp and frees us.

The years go by and I am living in New York City. In 1957, a good friend arranges a blind date for me with another immigrant. Reluctantly I go, and as I chat with my date in the back seat of the car on the way to the restaurant, she asks me the question often shared by immigrants, "Where were you during the war?"

"A concentration camp in Germany," I reply. "And you?"

"My family and I were spared. We had Aryan (Christian) papers and were fortunate to work on a farm in Germany," she answered. Then a faraway look came upon eyes.

"What is it?" I ask.

"Oh, nothing," she replied, "Just a memory."

"Go on," I encourage her.

"Our farm was located near a concentration camp," she explained, "and every day I visited a young boy there and secretly tossed an apple over the barbed wire to him. We rarely spoke a word...but I can tell you, there was love between us. One day he was gone and I never saw him again. I assume he was killed but I cherish the memories of those months we shared.

"Were his feet covered with rags?" I ask. "And did he tell you one day not to come again?"

"Why...why, yes," she replied. "How do you know that?"

I felt as though my heart would explode as I took her hand in mine. I composed myself and spoke, "You fed me when I was hungry, you gave me hope when I had none. It was you who saved my life. Destiny has brought us together again. This time we are free...no longer separated by the barbed wire, and I never want to be separated from you again. Will you marry me?"

Without any hesitation she replied, "Yes," I will marry you." Roma suddenly knew, too...that I was that young boy, as I knew that she was the apple of my eye.

AS TOLD TO SUSAN WALES BY HERMAN ROSENBLAT

Used by permission of Herman Rosenblat. Mr. Rosenblat tells his life story in *The Will To Live*, published by Adam's Media Corporation, Holbrook, Massachusetts.

With This Ring

Go little ring to that same sweet
That hath my heart in her domaine.
GEOFFREY CHAUCER

IT'S THE MOST RECOGNIZED SYMBOL OF COMMITMENT IN OUR CULTURE. IT IS THE ULTIMATE TOKEN OF LOVE BETWEEN A MAN AND A WOMAN. IT IS THE VISIBLE MESSAGE TO ALL THAT THIS WOMAN OR THIS MAN IS NO LONGER LOOKING, BUT NOW AND FOREVER BELONGS TO A CERTAIN SOMEONE. THE WHITE OR YELLOW BAND OF METAL, SOMETIMES SET WITH BRILLIANT STONES, IS A TREASURE WHOSE VALUE FAR EXCEEDS ITS PRICE TAG.

YOUR WEDDING RING, ADORNING THE THIRD FINGER OF YOUR LEFT HAND, SAYS TO FRIENDS, FAMILY, AND THE REST OF THE WORLD, *I HAVE FOUND THE LOVE OF MY LIFE. I HAVE MADE UP MY MIND THERE IS NO ONE ELSE FOR ME.*

THE DAY A HUSBAND AND WIFE PLACE A RING ON EACH OTHER'S FINGER, IN THE PRESENCE OF GOD AND WITNESSES, ITS PERSONAL MEANING OUTWEIGHS ITS BRILLIANCE AND BEAUTY. AS YOU WALK WITH THE ONE YOU LOVE INTO THE FUTURE, YOU WILL NOT ALWAYS BE AT THE SAME PLACE IN THE SAME PATH AT THE SAME TIME. ALL KINDS OF WEATHER WILL

FIND YOU. THERE WILL BE STUMBLING BLOCKS. OBSTACLES MAY BRING DOUBT AND FEAR. LET YOUR RING ALWAYS REMIND YOU OF THE DAY YOU SEALED YOUR DECISION TO CLEAVE TO ONE ANOTHER, BE FAITHFUL, BECOME ONE FLESH.

YOUR RING IS YOUR SYMBOL OF FOREVER-AFTER SHINING COMMITMENT.

A COSTLY KISS

&

Pussy said to the Owl, "You elegant fowl!
How charmingly sweet you sing!
O let us be married! too long we have tarried;
But what shall we do for a ring?

EDWARD LEER

One thing was obvious as they approached married life. They needed a newer car. For years Jim had been driving a dilapidated heap he called "Ol' Red." This 1949 Mercury convertible was a disaster on wheels. The top wouldn't go up or down, the electric windows didn't work, the lights sometimes went out unexpectedly, and the engine dozed off every now and then. Jim never knew if he would get where he was going. A typical scene around town was Shirley steering the wreck while Jim pushed it. Once they got it started, people would drive alongside and point frantically at the wheels, which appeared to be falling off. It was a humiliating experience.

Furthermore (and most frustrating to Shirley), the front seat of the car was disintegrating. Springs stuck up at various angles, snagging her clothes and puncturing her backside. Shirley hated that car with a passion, but Jim didn't want to go into debt to buy a newer one. Tension was obviously brewing between Dobson and Deere over the pile of junk he used to transport her.

This conflict culminated one day as Jim came to the dorm to get Shirley. They had scheduled important job interviews that day, and she had spent two hours getting dressed. She was wearing her best outfit—a black suit she had just retrieved from the cleaners. So off they went. As they flew down the road at fifty miles per hour, the rotted old convertible top suddenly blew off. Bits of string and canvas beat them about the head and shoulders, and dust settled everywhere. The remnants of the top hooked onto the back of the car and flapped outward like Superman's cape.

Shirley had absolutely had enough. She screamed at Jim from the floorboard, where she crouched to escape the flogging. Jim was angry, too, not just at his car but at Shirley. For Pete's sake! It wasn't *his* fault. So he just kept on driving, with the ribs of his convertible top glistening in the sun, the ragged canvas flapping out the back, and his fiancée yelling at him from under the dashboard. Passersby must surely have thought these folks were crazy.

Given this background, it was a minor triumph for Shirley to get Jim to agree to buy a newer car. They picked out a gleaming white, 1957 Ford with white sidewall tires and a hard top. They drove Ol' Red up to the used car lot, where the engine sighed once and gave up the ghost. Somewhere in a salvage yard sits a lonely red Mercury with no top. On a spring protruding from the front seat are tiny woolen fibers ripped from a coed's skirt.

But that inconvenience was finally over for them. Jim and Shirley climbed into their shiny new (three-year-old) car and patted the dashboard. They could not have been more proud if they had just bought a new Rolls Royce. Down the road they drove in their chariot, feeling like a king and queen. They had gone only five blocks when Jim leaned over and kissed Shirley to celebrate the happy moment, but just as he did, the two cars in front of them made an unexpected stop in the middle of the block. Jim was on top of them by the time he looked up. He slammed on the brakes, but it was too late.

The events of the next few seconds have been preserved in their minds like an old videotape. "I can still hear my tires screeching and then the awful sounds of metal crunching against metal, and breaking glass tinkling as it fell to the pavement," Jim recalls. "I can see the hood and fenders of my beautiful car rising in slow motion toward me. At the same time,

Shirley and I are falling forward as our heads hit the sun visors."

It was actually a three-car collision since Jim knocked one car into the next in line. Fortunately, no one was hurt. The stunned couple got out of the car and surveyed the wreckage. They were sick over what they had done. Moreover, they were afraid someone might have seen the careless kiss that caused the accident. They weren't afraid to admit their fault in the matter; they just didn't want the whole world to know that an untimely kiss was really to blame.

While Jim was exchanging information with the two irritated drivers, Shirley overheard two little boys talking on the sidewalk.

"What happened?" one of the lads asked.

"Oh, that guy over there kissed the girl and hit two cars in front of him," the other responded matter-of-factly. Shirley held her breath!

Then the boys rode off on their bicycles, thereby concealing until this moment the embarrassing truth.

Although the damages were covered by Jim's insurance policy, he had to reckon with a one hundred dollar deductible—precisely the amount they were planning to spend for Shirley's wedding ring. On the wedding night she had to settle for a silver band, but Jim surprised her on their first anniversary with the ring she should have received twelve months earlier.

From *Dr. Dobson: Turning Hearts towards Home,* Rolf Zettersten, 1989, Word Publishing, Nashville, Tennessee. All rights reserved.

POP THE QUESTION,
NOT THE CORK!

❧

T'isn't beauty, so to speak
Nor good talk necessarily
It's just It.
Some women'll stay in a man's memory
If they once walked down the street.

RUDYARD KIPLING

What a difference a day can make! When I woke up that morning, I never dreamed that I was about to meet *Mr. Right*. I had almost given up on love when *he* walked into my life. It happened when I least expected it. The distinguished film producer was expected in Atlanta for a fundraiser. It was a miracle that our paths even crossed.

Ken had been an eligible bachelor for many years and was an unlikely candidate for the husband I had prayed that God would one day bring into my life. I was a far cry from the women he usually dated. Ironically when we met, I was wearing no makeup, my hair pulled back with a ribbon. There I stood before this handsome man, looking far from my best. "Why hadn't I at least put lipstick on?" I chastised myself.

I knew it was a special moment and feared I'd lost it because of my appearance. And yet when our eyes locked, we knew. It was as though God reached down from heaven and placed my hand in Ken's. There was never any doubt after that moment. I'm convinced that I could have had a paper bag over my head, and he still would have fallen in love with me.

That's because God was our matchmaker. It didn't matter to Ken what I looked like, what I was wearing, or even what I said. God revealed our hearts at that special moment. Our lives would never be the same. My head was spinning and my routine life suddenly took off on an exciting adventure.

Our fateful meeting was the beginning of a great romance followed by many crosscountry flights for both of us. I knew it was just a matter of time before Ken would propose. Ken was a professional at making beautiful films, and I knew he would plan an unforgettable proposal with the same thought and creativity that he planned his movies.

At Christmas I found the airline ticket he'd secretly sent to my mother to place in my Christmas stocking. When I called Ken to thank him, he explained that he wanted me to be in Los Angeles for Valentine's Day. *This must be it!* I told myself.

When February 14 arrived, Ken, every woman's dream of a romantic, had planned a very special evening for me at Saddle Peak Lodge, a romantic out-of-the way restaurant nestled in Malibu Canyon. Ever the producer, Ken drove me up the coast along the ocean's edge just as the sun was setting while Ken played our favorite love song, Rachmaninoff's Second Piano Concerto. Mesmerized by the beautiful setting, I must admit that I had to pinch myself to make sure I wasn't dreaming. Ken made me feel as though I was his star in a very romantic movie he was producing. I just couldn't wait to see what happened next in his script.

When we arrived at our destination and I stepped inside the 1929 hunting lodge, my fairy tale began to unfold. The maître d' seated us in front of the massive stone fireplace. The crisp white tablecloth held two dozen of my favorite Sonya roses. Ken had remembered. We just sat there gazing into one another's eyes and basking in the warm glow of the fire and the candles. Because of the distance that separated us, this was a rare opportunity for the two of us to be alone. I never wanted this evening to end but we were suddenly interrupted by the maître d'.

He reappeared at our table with waiters carrying a bottle of champagne from the restaurant's renowned vintage collection. "This is a rare champagne," he announced, "and I want to share a glass with the two of you for Valentine's Day."

Not wanting to break the romantic spell, I politely refused, but when Ken and the man insisted I try the rare champagne, I accepted. The maître d', the wine steward, and the waiters lingered as if they were waiting for me to comment on the taste. I decided if I was ever going to get rid of the entourage and be alone with my sweetheart that I would have to take a big sip. *They're going to stand there and watch me drink this whole glass,* I thought, so I purposely took a big gulp this time.

The look on Ken's face, and the faces of the little group that had congregated around us, suddenly changed to horror as the sparkling engagement ring that Ken had arranged for the restaurant to place in the champagne disappeared. I never even saw the ring. My mind was on making eyes at Ken!

Thanks to a quick little cough, the ring resurfaced. Everyone was greatly relieved that I hadn't choked to death or worse yet, swallowed my beautiful ring. In all the confusion, Ken momentarily forgot to propose. When he recovered, he uttered the most beautiful proposal ever offered to a woman in my opinion.

Mother always told me to look before you leap. I had looked into my heart and knew that God had brought Ken into my life. Mother forgot to add...look before you sip!

Today when we celebrate our anniversary, the two of us reserve our same table at Saddle Peak Lodge and reflect on all the miracles God has brought into our lives—especially the miracle of his matchmaking. And when the waiter comes round, Ken says, *No champagne for Susan, please!*

SUSAN WALES

THIS TOO SHALL PASS

Young bride, a smile for thee,

To shine away thy sorrow;

For Heaven is kind today, and we

Will hope as well tomorrow.

MARTIN FARQUHAR TUPPER

My girlfriend, Rebecca, and I had struggled through the worst year of our lives. My mother died in January, Rebecca was laid off from the job she loved in February, and a fire destroyed my apartment building in March. When April arrived, my company downsized and I assumed the duties of three employees; in May Rebecca discovered a lump in her breast (fortunately, it was benign).

Trial after trial, we leaned hard on our faith and it sustained us. As we sought solace in the Lord we developed a motto: "This too shall pass."

Though I had planned to propose to Rebecca for some time, after such a tragic year I wanted to create a moment so fabulous and overwhelming that it would erase all our bad memories. I began to plan the perfect romantic proposal.

I considered all the ways my friends had proposed to their wives. My college roommate had hidden his wife's engagement ring in a box of chocolates. One friend hired a pilot to write his proposal, along with puffy hearts, in the sky. Another friend rented a billboard for a day and painted his love in huge block letters. My friend Joey's proposal beamed from a baseball field's scoreboard lights. All those proposals were memorable, but none seemed appropriate for Rebecca and me.

When I dropped by Rebecca's apartment one evening after work in June, I found her in tears. It seemed our tough times weren't ended yet. She explained that her dog, Buzzy, had been hit by a car earlier that afternoon and had died. She was inconsolable. Buzzy had been my pal as well, so I didn't feel much better. As I kissed Rebecca good-bye that night, I promised that we would visit the pound and get her another dog over the weekend.

As I was driving home feeling despondent over Buzzy's death, I had a sudden inspiration. I now knew exactly how I would pop the important question! The next morning I hurried over to the pound and found an adorable black lab puppy. I promptly adopted him for Rebecca and took him home for safekeeping until the weekend.

When Saturday finally arrived, I loaded a picnic basket with a catered lunch, flowers, and a blanket. Then I attached the engagement ring, an heirloom that had belonged to my mother, to a gold ribbon and tied it around the puppy's neck. I put the puppy in a second picnic basket and packed everything in the car.

I picked up Rebecca that morning for a day at the beach. Still grieving over Buzzy, she asked, "Jessie, when are we going to the pound?"

"Monday," I told her with a straight face.

"I won't feel better until I get another dog," she said sadly. "There's such a big hole in my heart."

"I know," I replied. "I feel the same way, but remember: This too shall pass."

When we got to the beach, I took the two picnic baskets from the back of my car. Fortunately the puppy was asleep. I prayed silently that he wouldn't wake up until we arrived at the water's edge.

Placing the flowers in a vase in the center of the blanket that I had spread out on the sand, I brought out my boom box to play some of Rebecca's favorite romantic songs. The setting was perfect as the waves lapped along on the sand with their own special melody.

"Oh, Jessie," Rebecca said, "this is so sweet of you, to try to make me feel better about Buzzy."

I smiled. *You just wait,* I thought gleefully, *you're going to be the happiest girl in the world.* I knew that when I gave Rebecca the new puppy she'd feel better, but when she saw the ring and I proposed, she'd be ecstatic.

It couldn't have been a more beautiful day. There was a cool ocean breeze and the sun was shining as we sipped lemonade. Suddenly I heard the puppy whining and I knew it was time.

"What's that?" Rebecca asked innocently.

I opened the picnic basket and brought out the puppy.

Rebecca jumped up and down as she cried, "Oh, Jessie! I love you! Just look—he's the cutest dog I've ever seen. And you—you're the greatest guy in the whole world."

My heart pumping, I placed the dog in Rebecca's outstretched arms and waited. As she cuddled the dog, I put my arm around her. "Rebecca, there's something very special for you tied around the dog's neck."

She looked up at me quizzically. "There's nothing around the dog's neck," she replied.

"It's on the gold ribbon," I said.

She felt along the ribbon. "There's nothing here."

My heart sank. I grabbed the dog and looked all through his fur. Nothing! Inside I panicked. *So much for my perfect proposal,* I thought. *Now the ring is missing!*

After a frantic search of the sand, I confessed to Rebecca that her engagement ring had been tied on the ribbon. She started to cry. I felt like crying too, but I said, "Don't worry. We'll find it."

"Oh, I'm not crying because you can't find the ring," she said. "I'm crying because you were going to propose to me."

"That ring's worth crying over!" I informed her. "Without it, I can't propose to you. And besides, it belonged to my mother."

Sensing my distress, Rebecca knelt alongside me in the sand and helped me search again for the diamond. It was hopeless. The ring was nowhere to be found.

"The dog must have bitten the ring off the ribbon," I told her as I turned the picnic basket upside down.

"He's only a puppy," she reminded me. "What did you expect?"

Through tight lips I told her, "I thought you'd think it was romantic."

Great, I thought. *What was supposed to be the happiest day of our lives is turning into a heated discussion.*

In unison we realized what had happened and said together, "He ate it."

Gathering our belongings, we left the beach and raced to the vet's office. The doctor laughed as I described our dilemma—until he noticed that neither of us was laughing. Without another word he took the puppy to X-ray.

When the vet returned, he held up the film for us to see. There inside the puppy's tummy was my mother's ring. "Oh, no," we moaned.

"Don't worry about a thing," the vet assured us. "Leave the puppy with me and I'm sure we'll have your ring back by the morning—maybe sooner."

"Will you have to operate?" Rebecca asked sheepishly.

"No," the vet answered, chuckling.

Rebecca then asked, "Then how will you—"

"This too shall pass," the vet assured us.

We burst into laughter. Our familiar words of comfort were to be applied to yet another amazing circumstance.

"I'll call you," promised the vet.

Later that afternoon the vet did call and I picked up the ring. I proposed to Rebecca over a candlelight dinner. She said she'd love to be my wife.

With our troubles finally behind us, a year later we were married. When the minister asked our attendants to "pass the rings," Rebecca and I exchanged a knowing smile. I spoke the vow on cue: "With this ring, I thee—" Then I burst out laughing, remembering the journey of the ring. Rebecca couldn't keep a straight face either when she said the same vow. The minister, puzzled by our reaction, frowned.

Throughout our marriage God has been faithful. Each time we run into to trouble, we gaze upon Rebecca's ring and remind each other that our troubles will pass…one way or the other!

And by the way, we named our black lab Ringo.

AS TOLD TO SUSAN WALES

WITH THIS RING

"With this ring…"
your strong, familiar voice
fell like a benediction
on my heart, that dusk;
tall candles flickered gently,
our age old vows were said,
and I could hear
someone begin to sing
an old, old song,
timeworn and lovely,
timeworn and dear.
And in that dusk
were old, old friends—
and you,
an old friend, too,
(and dearer than them all).
Only my ring seemed new—
its plain gold surface
warm and bright

and strange to me
that candlelight...
unworn—unmarred.
Could it be that wedding rings
like other things,
are lovelier when scarred?

RUTH BELL GRAHAM

Ruth Bell Graham, *Ruth Bell Graham's Collected Poems*, Baker Book House Company, © 1995. Used by permission.

FOLLOW YOUR HEART

❧

The best and most beautiful things in life
Cannot be seen or even touched...
They must be felt with the heart.

HELEN KELLER

After graduation from college I moved with two of my friends, Megan and Leslie, to Kansas City, where we were seeking jobs and—more truthfully—where we each hoped to find our Prince Charming.

I found a great job as a marketing assistant in a large company. One of my coworkers arranged a blind date for me with Carl Young, a salesman with a telecommunications firm. Carl had just arrived in town and needed a date for a company function.

Carl and I had a wonderful time and I was greatly encouraged when I learned that Carl also shared my faith in God. When he saw me to my door, I realized that Carl was very shy, so I mustered up my courage and said, "I'd really like to see you again." That's when Carl gave me the news—news to me anyway!

Carl blushed and said, "Katie, I have a girl back home, but I'd really like to be friends."

Fat chance, I thought to myself. We said good-bye and I mumbled, "Have a nice life."

The next weekend Carl and I showed up at the same party, and we had a chance to chat. Carl told me he had tickets for the ball game and asked me if I'd like to join him. My head said no, but my heart said yes. My heart won the argument, and, against my better judgment, I agreed to accompany him.

Once again I had a wonderful time with Carl, and I invited him to a party. Megan and Leslie both chastised me. "If you want to get married, you're wasting your time." I reasoned that having a friend like Carl wasn't such a bad thing. Maybe he would introduce me to some nice guys.

I enjoyed Carl's company and it was easy for us to talk for hours about our faith in God. Before long, we were seeing one another every week. The weeks of seeing one another turned into months. Being a very forthright kind of guy, on several occasions Carl tried to bring up the subject of the girl back home, but I would always say, "Let's not discuss it...let's just have fun and enjoy our friendship."

Carl and I continued seeing one another on a regular basis until November rolled around, and he told me that he was going home to Tennessee for Christmas. His announcement brought me back to reality. I was then reminded of the girl back home. I stopped accepting his invitations. The time had come to use my head and not my heart.

Carl kept calling but I made up every excuse imaginable not to see him, even though I missed him terribly. He was persistent and said that he just wanted to talk, but I prayed that God would give me the strength to refuse him every time. Megan and Leslie were applauding my newfound courage to say no to him, but unbeknownst to them, my heart ached.

Just before Christmas, Carl called to invite me to dinner. When I refused, he asked me if he could drop by to give me a Christmas present before he left for home. Megan and Leslie gave me a hard time for letting him come by, but I couldn't refuse. This time I listened to my heart!

I had spent months knitting Carl a cashmere sweater for Christmas, but the wrapped package now sat under my tree with my brother's name on it (luckily they were the same size). I scurried around and put Carl's name on a tin of cookies, my standard Christmas gift for my friends, and told him he could come over one Saturday afternoon.

"Katie, you look spectacular," he said when I answered the door.

I knew I looked good because I had spent hours getting ready since my female pride wanted to show him what he was missing when he went home to his girlfriend.

"I'm going home tomorrow and I wanted to see you before I leave," he announced.

Because I knew he'd be seeing *her*, those words pieced my heart. I felt shattered at the thought.

We sat on the sofa and I handed him the tin of cookies. "My favorite," he replied politely. "Chocolate chip."

"They're everyone's favorite," I said sarcastically.

He then reached inside his coat and pulled out a beautifully wrapped package. He handed it to me, and when I opened it, I gasped at what was inside. It was a velvet box containing the most beautiful strand of pearls I'd ever seen. I was speechless. And puzzled.

"They're my grandmother's," Carl told me.

"Carl," I said, "I can't possibly accept these!"

"But my grandmother wants you to have them," he said.

"But your grandmother doesn't even know me!"

Carl dropped his head for a minute and then continued, "Katie, my grandmother wants the girl I marry to wear these on our wedding day."

My heart began to beat wildly. *The girl I marry? Is this a proposal?*

"But what about your girlfriend back home?" I asked.

"I've been trying to tell you for months," he explained. "After our second date, I knew that God was showing me that you were the girl that I wanted to spend my life with. I was just too shy to tell you, but then when I realized that I was losing you…I couldn't wait any longer. I love you."

With those words it was as though God reached down from heaven and knitted all the pieces of my shattered heart back together again!

I was stunned. I couldn't hold back my tears as Carl reached down and fastened the pearls on my neck and then got on his knees and proposed. "I had hoped for a more romantic proposal, but when I couldn't talk you into going out with me…well, this will have to do!"

When Carl returned from the holidays, he invited me to a romantic dinner at our favorite restaurant and presented me with his grandmother's ring. The next Christmas we were married.

After years of marriage, with my encouragement and God's help, Carl eventually outgrew his shyness.

I have learned a lesson of my own, too: There are times when it's better to keep listening to your heart!

AS TOLD TO SUSAN WALES

If ever two were one, then surely we.
If ever man were lov'd by wife, then thee;
If ever wife was happy in a man,
Compare with me ye women if you can.
I prize thy love more than whole Mines of gold,
Or all the riches that the East doth hold.
My love is such that Rivers cannot quench,
Nor ought but love from thee, give recompense.
They love is such that I can no way repay,
The heavens reward thee manifold I pray.
Then while we lived, in love let's so persevere,
That when we live no more, we may live ever.

ANNE BRADSTREET,
FROM "TO MY DEAR AND LOVING HUSBAND"

A HEART OF STONE

In courtesy I have chiefly learned
that hearts are not given as a gift
but hearts are earned.
WILLIAM BUTLER YEATS

It was Valentine's Day and also our first anniversary. I had planned a romantic candlelight dinner for my husband, Tom, that evening to celebrate our love and our first year of wedded bliss. I had rushed home from work to make his favorite dish, lasagna, and brought out our wedding china and my grandmother's silver. The candles were on the table and the stereo was playing our song as I soaked in a fragrant bubble bath waiting for Tom to come home from work. Just as I heard the door open, I squirted Tom's favorite perfume behind my ears and rushed down to greet him.

It was the perfect evening, at least until I glanced down at my left hand when I was clearing the table. I let out a cry of distress, "Tom, my diamond is missing from my engagement ring." We both left the table to frantically search everywhere for the tiny stone: the kitchen, the dining room, and the bathtub. I worried that it had gone down the drain.

"We'd better call the plumber," Tom resigned himself.

"But honey, it's nighttime. Do you know how much a plumber charges after hours?" I was torn with indecision.

"Believe me, we'll pay a much higher price if we don't find your diamond," he told me, unleashing the guilt.

I thought back to the day when Tom had purchased my ring. He had wanted it to be a token of our love that I would treasure for a lifetime so he had stretched to spend far more than he could comfortably afford. Truthfully, I would have been satisfied with the pop top off a soft drink can—I was just so happy when he asked me to be his wife. But when I first looked at the beautiful diamond, it took my breath away, and I knew that the sacrifice that he had made was worth every penny. It was an exquisitely cut heart-shaped diamond. We had had our first date on Valentine's Day so the ring had great sentimental value for both of us. In fact, after we set a date, we were married on the next Valentine's Day.

At the time my husband had purchased the ring, he was a college student, and I knew he had made a great sacrifice to buy this ring for me. He had sold his ancient Volkswagen bug for a few hundred dollars in order to purchase the ring. After the proposal, he was forced to take the bus everywhere until he graduated and landed his first job and could buy another car.

We had insurance but we had a very large deductible. So large that it would be impossible for us to replace the diamond. We continued to search high and low, but no diamond. Tom shrugged his shoulders and dialed the plumber.

While we waited for the plumber to arrive, I cried until my eyes were swollen shut while we continued to look for the diamond. It was nowhere to be found. When the plumber finally arrived, he spent a couple of hours taking the drain apart. No diamond but a bill that could have probably paid for another ring. Tom was forced to pull out his VISA card.

By now it was almost midnight but I decided that we had to salvage what was left of our disastrous first anniversary dinner. I brought out the beautiful heart-shaped strawberry cake that I had made for our dessert to the table. I thought that surely this cake would make us feel better until Tom confessed, "I'm sorry, Jenny, I'm afraid I've lost my appetite." He was obviously still concerned about the ring and the plumber's bill. I'd spent hours baking that cake and I was secretly crushed when he barely looked at it and then refused it. He hadn't even commented that I had written our names in hearts in pink icing on the top of the cake.

Trying to sound cheerful, I sidled up to Tom in front of the fire and tried to reminisce about our first date and our wedding day. "Next time," he ordered in an accusatory tone, "don't wear your ring while you cook or take a bath."

He had uttered the words that initiated a historical event…our first fight! It wouldn't be our last either but was by far our worst.

I shouted that he had ruined our first anniversary.

He retorted, "I wasn't the one that lost the ring!"

"We don't need to find the diamond," I replied angrily, "because you…you have a heart of stone!"

I covered my beautiful cake and returned it to the refrigerator. Our perfect evening was in shambles and we could hardly kiss one another good night as we turned off the lights. True to our wedding promise, we agreed not to go to bed angry, each muttering a forced, I'm sorry. I cried myself to sleep dreaming of the perfect anniversary.

The next morning, still pouting, we headed for the breakfast table. Reluctantly, we agreed to share the morning devotional. We were incredulous as Tom read the Scripture for the day, "For where your treasure is, there will your heart be also" (Matthew 6:21, KJV). Instantly, we were both convicted.

"We lost sight of our real treasure," Tom said. "It's not the heart-shaped diamond, but our hearts that really matter."

"That's the real treasure," I agreed.

Tom took me into his arms and asked, "Can you forgive me for breaking your heart?" Those words not only melted my husband's heart of stone, but mine, too. The diamond didn't seem to matter much as we walked into the kitchen to prepare breakfast.

"Say, Jenny, I have a great idea," Tom told me. "Let's do something wild and crazy to celebrate our anniversary this morning! Why don't we have a piece of that cake you made instead of fruit and cereal for breakfast," he suggested.

He *had* noticed my beautiful cake. I sliced two large pieces giggling at the wickedness of having such a gooey sugary dessert for breakfast. We even blew out the candle and uttered a prayer of forgiveness and thanksgiving.

No sooner had Tom tasted his first bite of cake, than he jumped up excitedly.

"Now that's the enthusiasm I wanted to see for my cake," I teased.

"Is this cake supposed to have nuts?" he asked.

"No," I answered curiously.

Reaching inside his mouth, Tom pulled out the heart-shaped stone! Tom had found my diamond! "If only I hadn't been so stubborn," he admonished himself, "we could've found the diamond last night and still celebrated our anniversary."

Today whenever we run into problems, God has taught us that our *real* treasure can only be found in our hearts, and not in the diamond heart on my finger. The ring is the only heart of stone that we have allowed in our marriage since that first anniversary.

AS TOLD TO SUSAN WALES

The face is the mirror of the mind,
And eyes without speaking confess
The secrets of the heart.

ST. JEROME

THE RING BEARER

And all at once a pleasant truth I learned,
For while the tender service made me weep,
I loved thee for the tear thou couldst not hide,
And pressed thy hand, and knew the press returned.

ALFRED, LORD TENNYSON

Marie and I had met our freshman year in college, and as time went on we knew that one day we would be married. I had proposed our senior year at Christmas and now that our graduation was near, we were making plans to become man and wife.

It may come as a surprise to some people, but not everyone loves weddings. I, for one, despised them. But when it came time to set a date, as a prospective groom I had to inform my bride-to-be that I wasn't prepared to endure the frills, pomp, and circumstance of a big wedding. As we began to broach the subject of our wedding day, I told Marie that I personally was in favor of eloping. The look of horror in her eyes told me that I was in for a big debate—one I was going to lose.

"But, Jeff, I've always dreamed of a wedding with all the trimmings," Marie said, doing her best to convince me.

I, on the other hand, was afflicted with a deep fear of walking down the aisle in front of all those people.

She continued, "Those people are our family and friends...they love us and want to share our special day."

Marie persuaded me to discuss my wedding phobia with our pastor.

Reverend Smith was a compassionate man who understood both sides of our dilemma.

"Perhaps you'd like to set up a private session, Jeff, to discuss your fears," he urged me when he realized that our wedding plans had reached an impasse.

The next week I spent two hours with Reverend Smith, who helped me uncover the source of my apprehension as I revealed to him my deep-rooted fears. Although I had a better understanding of my wedding phobia, I still wanted to elope.

"Why don't you discuss this with Marie, and the two of you pray about it and come back in a week. Perhaps we can reach a compromise," he suggested.

I dropped by Marie's house and told her that I had been traumatized as a child...at a wedding.

"Tell me about it," she urged.

I sat back on the sofa facing the woman I wanted to marry, while she perched hopefully on the edge of the nearby chair.

I silently prayed that Marie would understand and abandon her plans for a big wedding. So I began to pour out my heart, determined to persuade her to see it my way. I began, "When I was a kid, about eight years old, my father forced me to be the ring bearer in the wedding of one of his friends. I was determined to do my very best and make him proud of me.

"Over and over, my mother stressed the importance of my job. I had to dress in a funny looking suit and carry a pillow with the rings for the bride and the groom. A real nice lady, the wedding director, gave me all the instructions on the night of the rehearsal. It was a cinch! All I had to do was carry that pillow down the aisle. The only thing about the job that alarmed me was that I was going to have to walk back up the aisle with a girl...the flower girl. I was eight years old and I *hated* girls!

"When the night of the actual wedding arrived, I overheard the groomsmen discussing, 'Who's got the ring?' I tried to tell them that I did, but nobody would listen. I offered my pillow that held two rings to one of the men, but he told me those weren't the *real* rings; he would put the real ones in his pocket.

"When the minister asked for the rings, I remembered that my mother had told me that the rings were my responsibility so I walked over to one of the groomsmen and reached inside his pockets. No ring but everyone in the congregation began to laugh. Unfortunately for me, all the guys were dressed just alike and I couldn't remember which one put the rings in his pocket so I continued down the line reaching into every one of the groomsmen's pockets. The flower girl finally came over to me and took me back to where I had been standing and the wedding continued, but I was humiliated beyond belief."

Marie suddenly interrupted me with her laughter and tears.

"Jeff," she said. "We didn't meet in college, after all!"

She suddenly jumped up and didn't return for a long time as I sat perplexed on the sofa. When Marie finally reappeared she was carrying an old photograph. Because of her hysterics, she silently thrust the picture toward me. I could hardly believe my eyes. It was a picture of me at the wedding I had just described to her. On my arm was the little flower girl.

"That's me, Jeff," she exclaimed as she pointed to the flower girl.

Until that very moment Marie and I hadn't known we'd first met as children at the wedding of her mother's cousin and my father's friend. We decided that we were destined to marry, even as children, as we walked down the aisle together.

The picture settled it. Marie could have the wedding she wanted. It was a sign from God. And he healed the trauma of my first big wedding because our wedding day—with all the pomp and circumstance—was the happiest day of my life.

Once again I escorted the flower girl up the aisle...this time as my bride.

As told to Susan Wales

I Thee Wed

Then before all they stand, the holy vow
And ring of gold, no fond illusions now,
Bind her as his. Across the threshold led,
And every tear kissed off as soon as shed,
His house she enters, there to be a light,
Shining within, when all without is night;
A guardian angel o'er his life presiding,
Doubling his pleasures and his cares dividing.

SAMUEL ROGERS

JUST THREE WORDS.

WHEN THE THREE WORDS ARE SPOKEN, THE COURSES OF TWO INDIVIDUALS CHANGE FOREVER. THE DREAMS AND DESTINIES OF A MAN AND A WOMAN MERGE.

JUST THREE WORDS.

TWO BECOME ONE.

WHEN A GROOM RECITES THE WORDS *I THEE WED* TO HIS BRIDE HE PAYS THE HIGHEST COMPLIMENT. HE IS—WITH GOD, HIS FAMILY, AND BEST FRIENDS—LOOKING ON, SAYING TO HER, "THERE IS NO OTHER, NOR WILL THERE EVER BE. YOU ARE THE

PERSON I HAVE CHOSEN AS MY PARTNER, MY BEST FRIEND, MY LOVER, MY COMPANION...FOR LIFE."

WHEN A BRIDE SAYS *I THEE WED* TO HER GROOM, SHE IS REVEALING THE DEEPEST PLACES OF HER SOUL, GIVING HIM THE KEY TO HER OWN PERSONAL GARDEN OF EDEN. SHE IS CHOOSING HIM TO BE THE FATHER OF HER CHILDREN, HER COMFORTER, PROTECTOR, AND ALLY IN LIFE. SHE SAYS, "NEVER WILL I WANT ANOTHER. NEVER WILL I WALK AWAY. NEVER WILL I ALLOW MY LOVE FOR YOU TO DIE."

JUST THREE WORDS.

I HEARD THE VOICE
OF AN ANGEL

Her angel's face
As the great eye of heaven shined bright,
And made a sunshine in the shady place.
EDMUND SPENCER

My younger brother Tom called me one day to make an exciting announcement I didn't want to hear: He was getting married.

After my long pause, he asked, "What's wrong, Ted? Aren't you happy for me?"

A huge lump moved up from my heart to my throat and I could barely speak. Now the youngest of my five siblings was going to take the walk down the aisle before me. It was a walk that I so badly wanted to take myself.

After the long, uncomfortable silence, I managed to compose myself and offer my sincere congratulations.

"Of course," my brother continued, "we want *you* to sing at my wedding."

I had sung at almost every wedding in the area so there was no way I could refuse my little brother.

I was genuinely happy for my brother, but I dreaded his wedding day because I knew I would once again walk down the aisle alone.

Always the singer…never a groom, I thought to myself as I hung up the phone.

"But, Lord," I cried out, "what about me? Haven't I been praying for years for you to bring a wife for me? How could you let this happen…my younger brother getting married before me?"

My brother's big day finally arrived and as I drove to his wedding, I was in pretty bad shape. This was one wedding I didn't want to attend. I thought about the fact that I had no love in my life, not even a prospect. I prayed on the way to the church that God would give me the strength to get through yet another wedding.

I was going to be singing a duet with a friend of Tom's, so I arrived at the church early to rehearse. The moment I stepped inside I heard an angelic voice melodiously filling the sanctuary. It was as though the voice was calling to me. Without noticing the others who had gathered early, I walked down the aisle in the sanctuary to see the source of that beautiful voice. I looked up and gazed upon a face that was every bit as beautiful as the voice I had heard. And she was rehearsing the music for *our* duet.

I stood there, mesmerized by her voice and her face that at that moment I thought were surely sent from heaven.

"Hi, Ted," my brother welcomed me. But I didn't even hear him…I was in a world all of my own that was filled with the sight and sound of her.

All during the ceremony, I could think of nothing else but the angelic singer. When the time came for our duet, I found myself falling in love at the melodious sound of her voice while we sang "We Are One in the Bonds of Love" for my brother and his bride.

After the wedding, I didn't waste any time. I arranged to spend time with my new friend. It wasn't long before I knew she was the woman I wanted to spend my life with, and fourteen months later, I married the angel.

God had a special plan for me all along. On the day I dreaded most, the Lord turned my sorrow into joy as he brought Kim into my life.

And to this day Kim and I continue to celebrate God's bringing us together as we sing for young couples on their wedding days.

TED ENGSTROM, AS TOLD TO SUSAN WALES

A HEAVENLY HAM

☙

Small cheer and great welcome
Makes a merry feast.
WILLIAM SHAKESPEARE

Throughout history during wartime, betrothed couples have often had to sacrifice or forego the weddings of their dreams. The following is a tale of a post Civil War bride written by Cynthia Blyth Halsey in Worth, remembering to celebrate the one hundredth anniversary of the United Daughters of the Confederacy by the New York Chapter in 1963.

There should be a special dish for a wedding dinner…but heaven only knew where it was to come from when Major Charles Seldon married Miss James. Rations were thin in Northern Virginia after April of 1865. The bride and her mother combed the smoke house, ransacked the cellar…and finally rested from their search in front of the great hall fire. "Only heaven knows where we'll get anything. It looks like a choice of johnny cake with bacon…or without." But heaven did know, because as they stood there a fifteen-pound ham fell down the chimney and landed with a crash at their feet.

No, it wasn't a miracle. It seems that they'd hung the ham to cure in the old chimney because the smoke house was unsafe. This one had been forgotten…and the suspending rope had frayed through just at the right time. A merry wedding followed.

Sounds like a miracle to me!

THE MISSING
CANDELABRA

※

There are two ways of spreading light;
To be: The Candle or
The mirror that reflects it.

EDITH WHARTON

It was one of the largest weddings ever held at Wilshire. Fifteen minutes before the service was scheduled to begin, the church parking lots were overflowing with cars and scores of people were crowding into the foyer, waiting to be properly seated. It was the kind of occasion that warms the heart of a pastor.

But that was fifteen minutes before the service.

At exactly seven o'clock the mothers were seated, and the organist sounded the triumphant notes of the processional. That was my cue to enter the sanctuary through the side door at the front and begin presiding over the happy occasion. As I reached for the door a voice called from down the hall, "Not yet, Pastor. Don't open the door. I've got a message for you."

I turned and through the subdued lighting I saw the assistant florist hurrying as fast as she could toward me. Her speed didn't set any records for she was about eight months pregnant and waddled down the hall with obvious difficulty. She was nearly out of breath when she reached me. "Pastor," she panted, "we can't find the candelabra that you are supposed to use at the close of the ceremony. We've looked everywhere, and it just can't be found. What on earth can we do?"

I sensed immediately that we had a big problem on our hands. The couple to be married had specifically requested that the unity candle be a part of the wedding service. We had gone over it carefully at the rehearsal—step by step. The candelabra, designed to hold three candles, was to be placed near the altar. The mothers of the bride and groom would be ushered down the aisle, each carrying a lighted candle. Upon reaching the front of the sanctuary, they were to move to the candelabra and place their candles in the appropriate receptacles. Throughout the ceremony the mother's candles were to burn slowly while the larger middle one remained unlighted. After the vows had been spoken, the bride and groom would light the center candle. This was designed to symbolize family unity as well as the light of God's love in the new relationship.

I felt good about all this at the rehearsal. I had a special verse of Scripture that I planned to read as the couple lighted the middle candle. We had it down to perfection.

We thought.

The notes from the organ pealed louder and louder as I stalled in the hallway. I knew that the organist by now was glancing over her left shoulder wondering where in the world the minister was.

"Okay," I said to the perplexed florist, "we'll just have to 'wing it.' I'll cut that part out of the ceremony and improvise until the close."

With those words I opened the door and entered the sanctuary, muttering behind my frozen smile, "What on earth are we going to do?"

The groom and his attendants followed me in. The bride and her attendants came down the left aisle of the sanctuary. When the first bridesmaid arrived at the front, she whispered something in my direction.

The puzzled look on my face was a signal to her that I did not understand.

She whispered the message again, opening her mouth wider and emphasizing every syllable. By straining to hear above the organ and through lip-reading I made out what she was saying: "Go ahead with the unity candle part of the ceremony."

"But how?" I whispered through my teeth with a plastic smile.

"Just go ahead," she signaled back.

We made it through the first part of the ceremony without any difficulty.

Everyone was beaming in delight because of the happy occasion—except the first bridesmaid who had brought me the message. When I looked in her direction for some additional word about the candelabra, she had a stoic look on her face and her mouth was tightly clamped shut. Obviously, she was out of messages for me.

We continued with the ceremony. I read a passage from 1 Corinthians 13 and emphasized the importance of love and patience in building a marriage relationship. I asked the bride and groom to join hands, and I began to talk about the vows they would make. There wasn't a hitch. I was beginning to feel better, but I still had to figure out some way to conclude the service. Just now, however, we needed to get through the vows and rings.

"John, in taking the woman whom you hold by your hand to be your wife, do you promise to love her? . . ."

"That's the funniest thing I've ever seen," the bride interrupted with a loud whisper. I turned from the bewildered groom to look at her and noticed that she was staring toward her right, to the organ side of the front of the sanctuary. Not only was she looking in that direction, so were all the attendants, and so was the audience! One thousand eyes focused on a moving target to my left. I knew it was moving, for heads and eyes followed it, turning ever so slightly in slow motion style.

The moving target was none other than the assistant florist. She had slipped through the door by the organ and was moving on hands and knees behind the choir rail toward the center of the platform where I stood. The dear lady, "great with child," thought she was out of sight, beneath the rail. But in fact, her posterior bobbed in plain view, six inches above the choir rail. As she crawled along she carried in each hand a burning candle. To make matters worse, she didn't realize that she was silhouetted—a large moving, "pregnant" shadow—on the wall behind the choir loft.

The wedding party experienced the agony of smothered, stifled laughter. Their only release was the flow of hysterical tears while they fought to keep their composure. Two or three bride's attendants shook so hard that petals of the flowers in their bouquets fell to the floor.

It was a welcome moment for me when the vows were completed and I could say with what little piety remained, "Now let us bow our heads and close our eyes for a special prayer." This was a signal for the soloist to sing "The Lord's Prayer." It also gave me a chance to peep during the singing and to figure out what in the world was happening.

"Psst! Psst!"

I did a half turn, looked down, and saw a lighted candle being pushed through the greenery behind me.

"Take this candle," the persistent florist said.

The soloist continued to sing, "Give us this day our daily bread…"

"Psst. Now take this one," the voice behind me said as a second candle was poked through the greenery.

"…as we forgive those who trespass against us…"

I was beginning to catch on. So I was to be the human candelabra. Here I stood, with a candle in each hand and my Bible and notes tucked under my arm.

"Where's the third candle?" I whispered above the sounds of "…but deliver us from evil…"

"Between my knees," the florist answered. "Just a minute and I'll pass it through to you."

That's when the bride lost it. So did several of the attendants. The last notes of "The Lord's Prayer" were drowned out by the snickers all around me.

I couldn't afford such luxury. Somebody had to carry this thing on to its conclusion and try to rescue something from it, candelabra or no candelabra. I determined to do just that as I now tried to juggle three candles, a Bible, and wedding notes. My problem was complicated by the fact that two of the candles were burning, and the third one soon would be.

It was a challenging dilemma, one that called for creative action—in a hurry. And there was nothing in the *Pastor's Manual* that addressed this predicament. Nor had it ever been mentioned in a seminary class on pastoral responsibilities. I was on my own.

I handed one candle to the nearby hysterical bride who was laughing so hard that tears were trickling down her cheeks. I handed the other one to the groom who was beginning to question all the reassurances I had passed out freely at the rehearsal. My statements about "no problems," and "we'll breeze through the service without a hitch," and "just relax and trust me," were beginning to sound hollow.

I held the last candle in my hands. They were to light it together from the ones they were each holding. Miraculously, we made it through that part in spite of jerking hands and tears of smothered laughter. Now we had three burning candles.

In a very soft, reassuring voice, I whispered, "That's fine. Now each of you blow out your candle."

Golly, I said to myself, *we're going to get through this thing yet.*

That thought skipped through my mind just before the bride, still out of control, pulled her candle toward her mouth to blow it out, forgetting that she was wearing a nylon veil over her face.

"Poooff!"

The veil went up in smoke and disintegrated.

Fortunately, except for singed eyebrows, the bride was not injured.

Through the hole in the charred remains of her veil she gave me a bewildered look. I had no more reassurances for her, the groom, or anybody. Enough was enough.

Disregarding my notes concerning the conclusion of the ceremony, I took all the candles and blew them out myself. Then, peering through the smoke of three extinguished candles, I signaled the organist to begin the recessional…now! Just get us out of here! Quickly!

Everything else is a blur.

But I still turn pale when prospective brides tell me about "this wonderful idea of using a unity candle" in the ceremony.

BRUCE McIVER

From *Stories I Couldn't Tell While I Was a Pastor* © 1991, Word Publishing, Nashville, Tennessee. All rights reserved.

KINDNESS THROUGH MUSIC

Music has charms to soothe the savage beast,
To soften rocks,
Or bend a knotted oak.
WILLIAM CONGREVE

Our wedding was special because we were surrounded by friends and family who shared in the celebration. It was a beautiful outdoor wedding, under a bower in the rose garden at a Victorian mansion in California's wine country. The guests all assembled. Classical flute and guitar music of our choosing filled the air with a melodious tribute to our love. A processional welcomed each member of the wedding party. We stood in front of the rabbi and nervously but joyously said our vows.

We turned, now man and wife, joined with great hope and happiness. We walked down the aisle past our beaming families and friends. Suddenly, I noticed what the chamber musicians were playing: "Zippedy-Doo-Dah." I was stunned. I whispered, "'Zippedy-Doo-Dah?' Is that what you asked them to play?"

My darling bride smiled happily and said, "Want to skip down the aisle, honey?"

Skip down the aisle we did.

The light-hearted tune was Meladee's gift to me—the promise of a lifetime of humor and laughter as well as serious love.

MELADEE McCARTY AND HANOCH McCARTY

From *Acts of Kindness.*

151

THE LOOK
OF LOVE

A loving heart is the truest wisdom.

CHARLES DICKENS

For many years, the word *family* always meant pain. I grew up in an alcoholic home, and my mother died when I was sixteen. A month later, my father committed suicide. I was sent to live with my eighty-eight-year-old grandfather, who soon passed me to an all-girl school in Mississippi. At that early age, I was forced to leave behind all that was familiar and was left on my own, struggling to find my way.

At twenty-one, I thought I had finally found my way. I got married and was blessed with two beautiful children. For a while everything seemed to fall into place. But then the marriage soured and I spent ten difficult years trying to salvage the unsalvageable. We finally divorced.

Terrified and alone, I desperately tried to raise my children with a strong sense of family and comfort. But I felt helpless and exhausted. I kept asking myself where I could turn, whom I could turn to. One Sunday, a friend encouraged me to attend a church service with her.

I remember most vividly the music…the wonderful music. The people were amazingly friendly and embracing. I felt like I was being welcomed into a family for the first time in my life.

The minister spoke words that reached straight into my heart. As I listened to him preach about God's infinite love and grace, I realized that

I had never known Christ on a personal level. The minister said what I desperately needed to hear. I accepted the Lord as my Savior.

It was at that precise moment that my life began to change for the better. Immediately God's magnificent love began to heal the deep scars in my life. I could feel the effects instantly, yet the process was a long one that required dedication and complete openness.

During my eight years as a single mother, my two children and I had worked extremely hard to rebuild and reorder our lives. For the longest time, my children were all I had in my life—they were my reason for living. When I accepted God into my heart, I began to see that life was worth living for myself *and* for my children, that life was a precious gift to all of us.

During those years, my sixteen-year-old son declared that he was the man of the house. He was determined to protect both me and his sister from all harm. He informed me that we were a secure family unit, and if I ever remarried, he would leave home. But by the time I had accepted the Lord and my son was ready to leave for college, he had changed his mind. He wanted me to find someone with whom to share my heart. He wanted me to be okay; he wanted me to be happy.

I prayed very hard, asking God to send me someone. I prayed for a man who would love and accept me and my children. I wanted to have the kind of marriage and family that God designed.

A friend I hadn't heard from in ages called one night and suggested we meet for dinner and talk. On a Saturday night, we met at a restaurant and began catching up on each other's life. My friend mentioned a wonderful man she wanted me to meet. I had to laugh; this same friend had set me up on a disastrous blind date some years earlier.

I told her that she had already lost all of her matchmaking credibility. She ignored my protests and continued to talk about this man. The more she talked, the more interesting this man became. She decided to call and invite him to join us that very night. He agreed to come for coffee after dinner.

I never believed in love at first sight, but when Gene walked in—tall, slim, gray just at the temples—I was instantly convinced! Gene spoke with the polished voice of a professional speaker, but it was the gentleness in his eyes that made the biggest impression on me. I could see immediately that there was a lot to this man. Unlike his predecessor, this blind date looked promising.

The three of us laughed, talked, and laughed some more—I couldn't remember when I had laughed so hard. I enjoyed myself immensely. Gene suggested that we all go hear a jazz performer after dinner. My friend excused herself gracefully. Personally, I didn't want the evening to end.

Gene called the next day and asked me out for Valentine's Day, only two nights away. I eagerly accepted. I purchased two Valentine's cards: Card A was inscribed to a friend, Card B was more special and romantic. When Gene arrived for our date with beautiful red roses and a romantic card, I quickly produced Card B. We were off to a candlelit, extremely romantic Valentine's dinner celebration.

Gene made me feel beautiful and brilliant. He showed a great deal of interest in me and wanted to know everything about my life. At one point, he turned to me and whispered, "You're wonderful." I had never felt the way Gene made me feel: safe and secure, protected and comforted.

Our next date was two nights later and it was another fabulous evening. I knew already that I was falling in love with him. When we went back to my house, Gene blurted out, "Lynn, I believe that I'm going to end up marrying you."

"You know, I believe you're right," I heard myself saying.

As time passed, we both could see the hand of God at work in our lives. My son totally approved. Our families meshed smoothly. I realized that God had answered every detail of my prayers. Three months later we were married in the chapel at our church, attended by our children.

Since that day—for nineteen years now—*family* has meant only love.

AS TOLD TO ANN PLATZ

ROCKING CHAIR WEDDING

⟨⟩

Focus on making things better, not bigger.
Be your best, be yourself.

ANONYMOUS

One of the blessings of being a pastor is to perform weddings. On June 17, 1999, a lovely wedding was held on the front porch of our home, a log cabin in rural Georgia. This ceremony was the shortest, simplest, and most relaxed I have ever performed.

The bride was the eighty-year-old grandmother of our daughter-in-law, and her eighty-one-year-old groom was her eighth-grade sweetheart. They had fallen out of touch, but a high school reunion had reacquainted them after sixty-seven years.

The happy couple made an appointment to see me and asked me to marry them. They wanted a simple, no-fuss wedding. No flowers. No guests. No fanfare.

The day of the ceremony, they arrived in the early afternoon dressed very casually in slacks and shirts. Katie had a white baseball hat with BRIDE on the front. Dick's hat had GROOM written on it. The "nervous" couple came right up on the porch, sat in our rocking chairs, and began to rock.

While getting acquainted, I learned that they both were active outdoors people. She loved swimming, walking, and fishing and he intended to (and did, in fact) buy a van that pulled a camper for their trips after a

Callaway Gardens honeymoon. All during our conversation, Dick and Katie continued to rock.

I began the ceremony by asking, "Have you both duly considered this relationship which you are about to enter?"

"We sho have!" Dick said loudly. He took Katie's hand in his and continued to rock.

I continued with the ceremony while the bride and groom continued their rocking. Earlier they had requested not to repeat the vows and we agreed that they would simply say "I do" after I read them. Each one answered in turn—and continued to rock.

They bowed their heads as I prayed this benediction.

"Our Father, we thank you for the joy of living and especially the joys of love and marriage. You have loved us and you have made us so we can love and be loved in return.

"Thank you that we need not walk the road alone, but that you provide someone to share our dreams and comfort us in our sorrows. Bless these two as they begin their lives together. In Jesus' name, amen."

After I pronounced them man and wife, they each smiled, leaned toward each other, and sealed their union with a kiss.

Then they continued to rock!

REV. BILL LAWRENCE

THE WEDDING MARCH

Marriages are made in heaven
and consummated on earth.

MOTHER BOMBIE (1590) ACT IV, SCENE 1
JOHN LYLY

Weddings throughout the world are celebrated with the magnificent strains of the Wedding March from a Midsummer's Night Dream. The oft-played wedding tune was written by the great German composer Felix Mendelssohn in the age of romanticism. What inspired the young composer to write such an extraordinary piece? Perhaps it was the story of his grandparents' romance.

Mendelssohn's grandfather, Moses, was born with a deformed and twisted body. In fact, he was a hunchback. People would avert their stares to avoid looking upon the grotesque young man as he would walk through the streets of Hamburg, Germany. Despite his freakish appearance, the sensitive young man was the same on the inside as everyone else, with the same desires in life—purpose, happiness, contentment, and most of all love. But who would ever have him?

Early one spring, Moses accompanied his father to the tailor to have clothes made for his misshapen body. As Frumtje, the tailor's daughter, walked down the stairs into her father's shop, Moses' heart stopped as he gazed upon the most beautiful creature he had ever seen. At that very moment, Moses knew with all his heart that this lovely girl must be his future bride. But how? Like everyone else, she averted her eyes at the mere sight of him and quickly excused herself.

When her father dismissed him, Moses rushed up the stairs in search of Frumtje. When he found her he mustered up every ounce of courage inside of him and blurted out, "Do you believe that marriages are made in heaven?"

"Why, yes," the flustered young woman replied. "Do—do you?"

Moses knew he had to seize the moment or lose her forever so he began, "When a baby boy is born in heaven, the Lord shows him his future bride—and you see, he told me that you were to be my bride."

Horror clouded the face of the shocked young girl as she heard the words of the young man with the twisted body. "I?" she gasped. "I, your wife!"

Undaunted by the look of astonishment on her face, Moses continued. "When the Lord showed me that you would be my wife, I cried, 'No! A hunchback woman is a tragedy! Please let me carry the hump for her.'"

Upon hearing his words, the young woman's heart was filled with love and her mind with a deep revelation. Moses and Frumtje were later married and they lived happily ever after. They were blessed with children and, later, grandchildren, including Felix Mendelssohn, whose music delights couples everywhere as they walk up the aisle together in the first moments of their marriage, as man and wife.

RETOLD BY SUSAN WALES

THE NERVOUS GROOM

The art of being wise is the art of
knowing what to overlook.
WILLIAM JAMES

One of the greatest joys of living in a small town is that it's easy to get to know your neighbors well. Small-town people seem to connect with one another in a way that is impossible in a big city. My parents lived in such a town in South Carolina, and they genuinely loved and cared about all the local citizens. This—and the fact that my father was influential in state politics—gained them an invitation to nearly every wedding in the county.

For many years Mother and Daddy ate their evening meals at a popular local restaurant where everyone knew each other. They often chatted with the waitresses and knew all about their families...especially one in particular, who was a little older than the rest.

This woman was very anxious to get married. In fact, she was desperate. One evening, when my parents came in to dine she informed them that she was engaged. She invited them to the wedding, which was to be held in mid-August, just a few months away. They assured her that they would be there.

The wedding day arrived and it was very hot, nearly 103 degrees! The ceremony was held in a small country church that was not air-conditioned. Nevertheless, it was clear to everyone as the wedding party began their procession down the aisle that this was a very happy occasion for the bride. She had saved for many years to have the funds to make her wedding everything she dreamed of. Her dress was exquisite and had so many layers of ruffles that there was barely room for her father to stand next to her in the aisle. She had gone all out with flowers, her bouquet, and a beautiful candelabra.

The groom was very nervous standing at the front of the church. He had been in an automobile accident the week before and had been determined, despite some lingering pain, not to distract in any way from the bride, the various prewedding activities, or the importance of this day.

As the minister began to say the marriage vows, the groom's nervousness started to get the best of him, and he started swaying.

"Oh, my, I think he is going to faint," Mother whispered to Daddy. Before she could finish the sentence, the groom passed out and fell against the stand that held dozens of lighted candles. Flames went everywhere, including the organ keys. The veteran church organist, however, did not miss a note and played on calmly as the ushers gingerly picked lighted candles from around her.

The bride was in tears. Her beautiful wedding was being ruined. To the rescue came the bride's father, who jumped to his feet and caught the groom. He tried to steady the hapless man, who was still swaying. He looked dazed and disoriented, and his eyes were rolling around. He wasn't responding intelligently to anything anyone said to him.

Guessing (and hoping!) that the combination of heat, nerves, and pain medication was to blame for his future son-in-law's odd condition, the father propped him up by standing against his back, and signaled for the minister to go ahead with the ceremony. The bride smiled bravely and tried to look as if everything was normal.

"Do you think that this will be legal?" Mother whispered again to Daddy. "Poor thing, I don't think he even knows where he is."

Daddy smiled a sweet smile and whispered back, "Oh, I don't think anyone here would tell. Let's just get 'em married."

ANN PLATZ

To Have and to Hold

What greater thing is there for two human souls
than to feel that they are joined...
to strengthen each other...
to be at one with each other in silent
unspeakable memories

GEORGE ELIOT

ONE OF YOUR PRIMARY HUMAN NEEDS IS INTIMACY. NOT JUST TO HAVE, BUT TO HOLD.

THE WORD INTIMACY IS ALMOST ALWAYS AUTOMATICALLY EQUATED WITH THE ACT OF PHYSICAL UNION. IN MARRIAGE, THAT IS A BEAUTIFUL PART OF THE DEFINITION, BUT A HUSBAND AND WIFE ARE MORE THAN LOVERS IN THE SEXUAL SENSE. THEY ARE—FOR EACH OTHER—THE PRIMARY SOURCE OF EMOTIONAL, MENTAL, AND SPIRITUAL "KNOWING."

GOD'S DESIGN WAS FOR MAN AND WOMAN NOT JUST TO BE LEGALLY JOINED FOR PRACTICAL REASONS, BUT TO BE PRESENT WITH EACH OTHER IN A DEEP AND PASSIONATE WAY, JOINING SOUL TO SOUL AS BODY TO BODY. WHEN THEY STAND AT THE ALTAR AND PLEDGE TO KEEP THEMSELVES ONLY FOR ONE ANOTHER, EACH IS SAYING BEFORE GOD AND WITNESSES: "I

WILL MEET YOUR NEEDS FOR AFFECTION, COMMUNION, COMMUNICATION, AND AFFIRMATION. I WILL SEEK THOSE SAME THINGS FROM NO ONE ELSE BUT YOU."

"TO HAVE" IS THE FLOUR AND SALT OF YOUR WEDDING VOW.

"TO HOLD" IS THE SUGAR AND SPICE.

ISAAC AND REBEKAH, REVISITED

❧

You can't reason with the heart; it has its own laws,
And thinks about things which the intellect scorns.
MARK TWAIN

While I would never presume to compare my love life with that of Isaac and Rebekah, I have experienced parallels to the way they found one another. All of us had to rely upon God to present a perfect mate, and in the end our stories were ones only God could have written.

Tom was ordained in 1978 but chose to go into business instead of the ministry. Over the years his secular pursuits began to gradually chip away at his faith. A hurtful relationship deepened the damage. By summer of 1993, Tom's father died and Tom found himself struggling emotionally and spiritually. At this crossroads he realized that he had lost his simple faith. He began to pray that God would guide him as he attempted to piece together their relationship. And he asked God to bring a woman into his life who would love both God and himself.

Over time Tom reasoned that teaching children in Sunday school might help him regain the basics of his beliefs. The Sunday before he was to meet the children, he met his coteacher—me!

I was divorced, and like Tom, hoping to meet someone who would bless my life emotionally and spiritually. I felt God had assured me this would happen. About five years before I met Tom, God had directed me during prayer to Genesis 24. In this story Abraham sent his servant to find a bride for his son Isaac. The servant found Rebekah, and one of the gifts he gave her as a promise of her forthcoming marriage was a bracelet.

As I read I understood that God was telling me these details would be repeated in my life: I would marry, and my husband-to-be would come bearing a bracelet. So I watched and prayed, and cherished this promise in my heart.

The church Tom and I attended had ten thousand members, so we had never met before we were teamed for Sunday school. Initially we weren't romantically interested in each other, but over the next few months we developed a good friendship. We both loved being with, teaching, and planning activities for the ten-year-old children we taught. Even during Tom's two-month business trip out of town, we talked almost every day to plan for our class.

Slowly our friendship grew, and five months after we met, we had our first date. We got together to celebrate Tom's birthday. All was well until I gave him a casual peck on the cheek and wished him a happy birthday. You would have thought I had just dropped a rock on his toe! I was hurt and confused by his negative reaction.

As Tom drove me home, we talked. He shared his hurts and fears from that earlier relationship and his spiritual and emotional struggles from the previous summer. Then we prayed together. Tom asked God to help him see his plan for us. After the prayer, Tom said he felt God directing us to continue our relationship.

As we dated, though, our relationship became a battle between Tom's fear of a committed relationship and my frustration with his indecision. Even though he sensed God was opening a new chapter in his life, Tom repeatedly tried to pull away from our growing closeness. I tried, sometimes unsuccessfully, not to react with anger. Yet through it all we prayed, alone and together, and God spoke to each of us. God urged Tom to keep seeing me, and he encouraged me to be patient with Tom.

As time passed I saw that Tom was beginning to fall in love with the Lord. And I realized that I was falling in love with Tom.

God continued to work on both of us. I knew God had freed Tom to love again when one day he told me I was his "wondrous gift from above"—the very woman he had prayed for the previous summer. Within that week, Tom was on his knees in my living room proposing marriage. The engagement present? *A bracelet!*

We were married in a small historical country church in my hometown. Tom planned the wedding and wrote the vows, including the Genesis 24 story in a congregational responsive reading.

No, we weren't Isaac and Rebekah, but Tom and Linda were just as happy.

LINDA TERRY

*It is the man and woman united
that makes the complete human being.
Separate she lacks his force of body
and strength of reason;
he her softness, sensibility
and acute discernment.
Together they are most likely
to succeed in the world.*
BENJAMIN FRANKLIN

GUITAR LOVE

*If music be the food of love
then play on!*
SHAKESPEARE

When I went away to college, I met and fell in love with the most wonderful man in the world. But upon meeting him, my father described him as "every parent's nightmare."

Admittedly, Wayne was unemployed. And his hair was shoulder-length. And he had dropped out of college. And his only and most treasured possession was a guitar.

But I loved him!

Near the end of my senior year, I received a great job offer back in California. Now that I think about it, the job was probably arranged by my father. On graduation day, Wayne told me that he planned to follow me to California and that he wanted to marry me. I was so happy I cried tears of joy—until he told me he was going to ask my father's permission.

When my father and Wayne disappeared at my graduation dinner, I knew Father would ask Wayne all the pertinent questions like, "How do you plan to support her?" "Where are you going to live?" and maybe "What are you going to eat?"

When they reappeared, Father spoke for both of them. "We have decided," he said, "that if Wayne wants to marry you, he needs to go back to college. We'll talk about marriage after he graduates."

Wayne and I cried as we parted. We knew that both my parents were secretly hoping that I would meet someone else.

No one was more surprised than my parents when eventually Wayne graduated from college and landed a great job in California. "Are you sure you want to marry Wayne?" they grilled me.

"I want your blessing," I assured them, "but forsaking all others, I will marry Wayne!"

Eventually my father reluctantly gave us his permission. Wayne and I were officially engaged.

There was just one big problem. "I can't afford an engagement ring yet," Wayne apologized. "But I can promise that we will always make beautiful music together forever!" I assured my romantic fiancé all that mattered was that we were together. Secretly, however, I was concerned. What would my parents think if Wayne couldn't even buy me a ring?

A few weeks later when we were celebrating Valentine's Day, Wayne presented me with a box of chocolates and in it was a beautiful diamond engagement ring. "Are you sure that you can afford this?" I asked. "You've only been working a couple of weeks."

Wayne just smiled and winked as he said, "God just dropped it down from heaven!"

Later, I discovered that he sold his beloved guitar to pay for my ring. His incredible sacrifice made the ring even more special to me, and it helped my parents see what a great heart Wayne possessed.

Those first few years we were married weren't easy. We ate a lot of beans as we struggled in the music industry. Eventually, however, Wayne became a successful businessman with closely cropped hair, a three piece suit, and a mortgage. He provided me with everything I could ever want or need.

One day, as we searched a music store, Wayne lamented that he wished he still had his old guitar. Instantly I decided what I would get him for our anniversary—a new guitar. Why hadn't I thought of that earlier?

A couple of months before our anniversary, I ran into an old college friend of Wayne's. We reminisced for a while, but as we were parting, he said offhandedly, "Oh, tell Wayne that I met an old acquaintance of his last week at the gym."

"Who?" I asked, assuming I'd probably know him, too.

"Oh, you wouldn't know him. He just got to know Wayne when Wayne sold him his guitar."

Needless to say, my heart skipped a beat. But what were the odds that this guy still owned the guitar after all these years? *Lord, let it be!* I prayed.

I quickly jotted down the acquaintance's name and said good-bye and raced home to dial information, quietly breathing prayers. A few minutes later, I introduced myself to the stranger on the phone. Excitedly I told my story while he listened politely.

"Yes," he said. "I remember Wayne. And I still have that guitar."

On the night of our anniversary, I gave my husband one of the greatest surprises of his life. He was so astonished when he saw the guitar he could hardly speak. "How did you ever find this?" he asked.

"Let's just say that God dropped it down from heaven," I answered.

Wayne and I are still making beautiful music together. And my parents agree I couldn't have found a better guy had I looked the whole world over.

KITTY AND WAYNE, AS TOLD TO SUSAN WALES

DREAMING ON
THE FAIRWAY

*There can be no true love
even on your own side, without devotion;
devotion is the exercise of love, by which it grows.*

ROBERT LEWIS STEVENSON

I don't know if it was love at first sight or not, but something pulled John and me together. We met. We laughed. We started to date. And almost right away, we began dreaming about the future.

John was tall, athletic, outgoing, and he wanted to become a golf pro. I couldn't imagine anything more marvelous than being married to a golf pro. We both felt certain that God had brought us together—to share both our dreams and our lives. We met in April, got engaged in August, and were married in December.

For our honeymoon we went to Sea Island, Georgia. Even while we were on our honeymoon, John was studying for the Professional Golf Association school he would begin attending as soon as we returned.

When he scored number one in his class and in the state, it seemed to both of us that our dreams were well on their way to becoming reality.

From the beginning of our marriage, I had envisioned John coming home for lunch in the afternoons. We would have a fun life that centered around his activities at the country club.

Yet that dream was not to be. A few years into our marriage, John realized that he needed to leave his current golf job to become a consultant in the golfing industry. That way he could make more money and have more control and leverage in developing his career as a pro.

His first consulting job took him to Wisconsin—as it turned out, to stay. This wasn't the dream we had had in mind either. John wanted me to quit my own job and join him. But the request left me stunned. I loved my job. If I quit, I would miss both the work and the people. Besides, I didn't know a soul in Wisconsin. All I could imagine were cows upon cows. I hadn't realized they even golfed there.

But a decision had to be made. And the decision was based on my answer to a question: *How much was I willing to help John pursue his dreams?*

Trembling with uncertainty, I said yes, and we moved to Wisconsin with our firstborn. Starting over wasn't easy. I had made my decision out of love for my husband. But I was still uncertain whether or not we'd done the right thing. And I kept wondering where my own dreams fit in to all of this.

As time passed, we struggled to carve out a life together. Nothing seemed to come together. I'll admit, I felt vindicated—we'd followed John's half of the dream, and it seemed to have taken us nowhere. Finally we arrived at a breaking point. I prayed and prayed for God to give me guidance. After all, hadn't God given us a dream to share? Wasn't it God's dream, too?

One day we were driving through the city. For some reason, I leaned over to John and asked, "If you could do anything you wanted professionally, what would you do?"

His brow furrowed for a moment. "I'd like to run golf tournaments with Legacy Ministries—tournaments like the one I did for Crawford-Limits," he replied. "My business would be benefit fund-raisers out there on the greens."

And with barely a hesitation, I replied, "We could call it Golf for Goodness Sake."

We looked at each other and smiled. Immediately, an entire plan seemed to tumble out, and a feeling of rejuvenation stirred within us. During the next hour, it was as if a light shined down upon us—and our dreams became one again.

The company, founded in 1992, now produces over one hundred tournaments a year to raise money for nonprofit organizations and important causes. We're both convinced that this work is important. Much of the money that John has helped to raise has gone to charities for juvenile diabetes, Downs syndrome, Alzheimer's dsisease, and cancer. This has allowed John to really make a difference in the lives of others while doing what he loves most.

Today I am busy with our two small daughters. John and I love and support each other in both our work and marriage. We take the vows of our marriage very seriously—to love, to honor, to cherish. And we've added one of our own...to dream.

SUZANNE WHITE

Oh, hasten not this loving act,
Rapture where self and not-self meet;
My life has been awaiting you,
Your footfall was my own heart's beat.
PAUL VALERY

THE BIRTHDAY CARD

When I am dead my dearest,

Sing no sad songs for me;

Plant thou no roses at my head,

Nor shady cypress tree.

Be the green grass above me

With showers, and dewdrops;

And if thou wilt remember

And if thou will forget.

CHRISTINA ROSETTI

A lot of people feel disappointed, even cheated, when retailers display merchandise for upcoming holidays back-to-back, blurring the lines of distinction between Thanksgiving, Christmas, and New Year's. Greeting card stores seem especially guilty of promoting one holiday ever so early, then crashing it into the next. And so it was that spring with the usual holiday pileup. All at once Mother's Day cards and Father's Day cards were fighting for shelf space before Easter cards were even cleared away.

But in my family it's a real convenience. In one fell swoop, I can gather not only my parents' Mother's and Father's Day cards, but also my husband's, my niece's and my best friend's birthday cards.

This particular May I found myself in my usual rush-rush, hurry-hurry mode, scurrying from work to home with a pit stop at the Hallmark store just before hitting the Chinese food drive-through. My mind was racing, as is normal for most lifestyles these days, forty thoughts zipping around in the brain at once. But my number-one priority was getting my mom's Mother's Day card in the mail by tomorrow morning at the latest. I was convinced that disaster would strike if that card arrived a day or two late. Timing was everything.

The next card I needed in a hurry was my husband's birthday card. "Nothing mushy, gushy," I could hear him say. I scanned the rows for the humor section. That made me think about asking his advice about that rattle in my car engine, although I already knew all too well what I'd hear. "Sweetie," he'd say. "If God wanted your dear sweet husband to give you advice all the time, he'd have made me a psychiatrist!"

My hubby was a real tease. Probably the most important thing he taught me was to laugh…a lot. "It's the only thing that'll keep you young," he'd rib.

I paid the cashier, and just as I exited the store, it began to rain. We greatly needed the precipitation, but if you've ever been in an Atlanta rush hour in a rainstorm, you know your drive will be total torture. Pulling out onto I-75 was just as I had predicted. So I pressed the autodial on my cell phone and called the Chinese restaurant, pleading for a delay of at least forty-five minutes on the to-go order. A little frustrated, and not totally satisfied that I had communicated very well, I decided to try to get my neck and shoulders to relax.

I took deep breaths and inched up into a crowded lane. I took more deep breaths. After ten minutes, no cars in any of the four lanes had moved more than a yard. I tried stretching my fingers, ankles, and toes. Still no traffic relief.

After idling for twenty minutes, I noticed that I was just about the only one with my car still running. So I too gave up hope and turned my car key to OFF.

Then the rain started beating down so hard that I couldn't see the car's bumper directly in front of me. It was rather deafening. But I cracked my window just a hair because the smell of rain has always been one of my favorite things. That staved off the boredom for a few minutes, but soon I started looking around inside the car for something to do.

My greeting cards! Perfect! I could spend the time filling out all my greeting cards. I had my Daytimer with all the addresses I needed and even managed to dig out a pen from the bottom of my purse.

My mom's Mother's Day card was easy. I wrote lots of "I Love Yous" and such. The ooey-gooier the better. I knew if I didn't say something to bring tears to her eyes, then I'd not done my job well.

"Enough of that!" I said aloud as I reached for my husband, Stephen's, card, complete with his preference: a joke and a zinger. I giggled as I thought how terribly different my mom's and husband's personalities were. Were. But from the very first time I brought Stephen home—for the big interview, as my husband coined it—they were teasing each other unmercifully.

Were.

And then I felt my heart kind of sag. It was one of those times with all your might you try NOT to think about something. But the harder you push it away, the faster it lands in your lap. I glanced down at the "Happy Birthday, Hubby" card and sighed sadly. I couldn't believe it. After nine years of my husband's passing, I had bought him a birthday card.

You would think between the rain, the traffic jam, and the now sure-to-be-cold Chinese food, I'd be a writhing blob of Jell-O. But much to my great surprise, a comforting feeling came over me. It was kind of like a warm chill, if you can imagine, wrapped around my shoulders—like a hug.

Out of the blue, God had sent me a little gift from heaven. On a really rotten day where virtually everything had gone awry, God stepped in. For just a couple of hours, he let me forget the burden and sadness of widowhood. At the same time, he gave me a hefty kick in the pants to remind me that my Stephen was still with me. His spirit, wisdom, and even his silly humor were all right here, even nine years after God called my dear sweet husband home.

Especially on a day like that day, I thought this was a generous and awesome gift from my Lord. And right there on I-75 I told him so. I thanked him also for his unique ways of getting our attention.

Happily, I was stuck in that rainy metal logjam for another thirty minutes, all the while enveloped in happy memories of my lovable, often laughable husband and the life we shared for such a short time.

DEE ANN GRAND

Thy love is such I can no way repay,
The heavens reward thee manifold I pray.
Then while we live, in love let's so persever,
That when we live no more, we may live ever.
ANNE BRADSTREET

A PERFECT DAY

For memory has painted this perfect day
with colors that never fade.

CARRIE JACOBS BOND

When I first met David Wilson at college, I was suspicious of his impeccable manners and the respect he showered on me. I'd been accustomed to guys who were too cool to be concerned about my comfort or my feelings. He just seemed like *too* much of a gentleman. I assumed he must be a phony, since nobody could be that perfect.

How wrong I was!

As time wore on, I became accustomed to David's treating me like a lady, and I realized the value of being with such a loving and sensitive man. I realized that I had found someone very special, and as our relationship progressed I knew I wanted to spend the rest of my life with David.

I shouldn't have been surprised that David's proposal was such a special one, but even he surpassed my expectations.

My birthday was only days away when David showed up at my office with a dozen red roses. "I'm going to kidnap you for the day," he announced.

I glanced over at Stella, my boss, and she was smiling and nodding. David had planned this out, making all the arrangements for me to have the day off.

We drove along the coast down to Corona Del Mar, our favorite beach. We settled on a nice spot, and David spread out a blanket, opened the umbrella, and put the picnic basket down. We ate delicious strawberries and sipped sparkling cider. It seemed like a perfect day…but it was only the beginning.

David suggested that we go for a walk along the ocean's edge. We walked hand-in-hand for about an hour, and when we returned, I noticed roses on the sand marking the path back to our blanket. Because this was typical of David, I knew he had them placed there. *Pretty special for a birthday,* I thought. But then I remembered who I was with.

But there was more…much more.

When we got back to the spot where our blanket had been, there was a big beautiful white tent, palm trees, and a table laid with starch white linens, china, crystal, a hurricane lamp, and a buffet table with giant shell ornaments. A server welcomed us and said, "Welcome to your ocean view reservations. Your table is waiting."

The waiter handed me a personalized menu that included all my favorite dishes. After our salads were served she brought out a very special bottle of wine that David and I had purchased while wine tasting in the Santa Inez Valley on a special date he had planned for me two years before.

This is it! He's going to propose! I thought. My palms began to sweat and my heart raced. But no sooner had this thought occurred to me, the server said, "I understand you're celebrating your birthday…Happy birthday!"

Suddenly a wave of disappointment washed over me, but when I realized that this was not going to be a proposal, I was no longer nervous and relaxed to enjoy my birthday dinner with David.

Afterward, David suggested that we walk to our favorite spot on the beach. Suddenly David fell to one knee and spoke the most beautiful words I have ever heard as he asked me to be his wife, promising me that he would make every effort to see that my life with him was as close to perfect as possible. Knowing he would live up to that promise, I said yes as he slipped the most gorgeous pear-shaped diamond ring on my finger. We hugged and cried as onlookers cheered and applauded.

Reminiscing about the past when we'd first met and all the special times we'd shared, we then talked excitedly about our future and what was ahead. David then escorted me back to the tent where the candlelight was flickering and the moon was rising over the water. He took me in his arms and we danced until the last glimmer of the rays of the sun disappeared. It had been a *perfect* day and a *perfect* proposal.

David and I were married a year later. As we live out the days of our marriage, I've realized that although David is not perfect (nor am I!), his thoughtfulness fills even those imperfect days with love.

I will forever carry the memories of that *perfect* day at the ocean when it all began.

RUBRIA PORRAS WILSON

Two happy lovers make one single breath,
one single drop of moonlight in the grass.
When they walk, they leave two shadows that merge,
and they leave one single sun blazing in their bed.
PABLO NERUD

PETALS OF LOVE

❧

Love adds a precious seeing to the eye.
WILLIAM SHAKESPEARE

My mother, Margaret Williams, was nearing her seventieth birthday and we knew she was expecting a celebration. As a matter of fact, she had hinted strongly to her four children, individually of course, what lovely parties her friends' children had given them. She also declared that they had not spared any time or expense in their planning. I got the message loud and clear!

After a quick call to my sister, Mary Ashley, I soon discovered that as her gift Mother wanted cherry trees.

"Cherry trees? Why?" I asked.

It seems that when Mother was growing up in her hometown of Orangeburg, South Carolina, the most gorgeous Yoshino cherry trees grew along the river bank at the Edisto Gardens. Mother told Mary Ashley that upon her death she wanted the family to plant these trees in honor of her.

We certainly didn't have to wait until she died to plant the cherry trees. We decided to do it for her birthday. We got busy and planned a tea at the Arts Center, located out in the gardens. About five hundred people attended the birthday party and over seventeen thousand dollars was raised to purchase Yoshino cherry trees. Over a thousand trees were planted. That was nine years ago and hundreds more have been planted since to honor someone or commemorate the passing of another birthday in our family. It's become quite the tradition. This family tradition has made all of my family passionate about Yoshino cherry trees. I can spot them in the dead of winter. When I see one in full bloom, in all its glory, it thrills me to no end.

I am a true romantic and I love flowers! My husband, John, knowing of my love for flowers, filled my bed with pink rose petals on our tenth anniversary. This was his way to remind me of his love for me and also of the promise he made to me the night before we married.

Knowing that I had been hurt by a previous divorce, John took my hands and kissed my fingertips and then gently said, "I vow and declare that my love will erase from your memory every tear you ever cried. Your life with me will be a bed of roses." His expression of love was so powerful and healing to me. What did I do to ever deserve a husband like John? His love and sensitivity had opened a locked portion of my heart.

As our nineteenth anniversary approached this year, I smiled and with a twinkle in my eye inquired as to what Mr. Rose Petals was up to this year in honor of our anniversary. He laughed and taunted me. "You'll see." What could he do to ever top the bed filled with roses?

The day before our anniversary, we found a house we wanted to buy. The evening of our anniversary, John and I headed out to our favorite anniversary restaurant, The Ritz Carlton. We discovered that we were an hour early so we drove by the new house. As we drove in the circular drive, I noticed the trunks of the trees. "John look what's all around us! Yoshino cherry trees!"

"One, two, three, four, five, six, seven, eight!" John counted out loud.

They were large, mature cherry trees. They must have been at least twenty-five years old.

"Eight," I said triumphantly, "means new beginnings."

Just about that time the wind began to blow causing the trees to swing back and forth. Cherry blossoms instantly filled the air and rained down upon us, carpeting the driveway with soft pink petals. Here we were again on our anniversary blessed with a visual sign of our love. This time it was a gift for both of us and we knew right away who the messenger of this dear message was!

A 'N PLATZ

From This Day Forward

Childhood wonder upon her face
Visions of flowers, cake, and lace
White horses, picket fences, and blue skies
Long ago dreams in a little girl's eyes.
SUSAN WALES

THERE'S SOMETHING BEAUTIFUL—ALMOST MAGICAL—ABOUT THE WORDS *THIS DAY*.

THIS DAY, YOUR WEDDING DAY, IS THE FULFILLMENT OF CHILDHOOD DREAMS. YOU WEAR THE GLISTENING WHITE GOWN, DRINK IN THE FRAGRANCE OF A CHURCH FILLED WITH FLOWERS AND OF BEST FRIENDS SHEDDING JOYFUL TEARS AS YOU PLEDGE A LIFETIME OF LOVE TO THE ONE YOU HAVE CHOSEN. YOU AND HE ARE THE CENTER OF ATTENTION.

THIS DAY IS YOUR DAY!

BUT THERE IS MORE TO *THIS DAY* THAN THE MUSIC, MISTY EYES, AND CELEBRATION. *THIS DAY* IS A MILESTONE THAT MARKS A TURNING POINT. FROM *THIS DAY* AS A HUSBAND AND WIFE, YOU WILL WALK TOGETHER INTO THE GREAT UNKNOWN. YOUR VOWS ARE THE MOMENTUM, AND THE

TRIMMINGS—RIBBONS, CAKE, AND YARDS OF WHITE TULLE—
ALL PART OF THE RITUAL TO UNFURL YOUR SAILS IN THE OPEN
SEA.

THOUGH YOU MAY NEVER WANT *THIS DAY* TO END, IT WILL
END...CALLING YOU TO NEW BEGINNINGS.

THIS DAY IS A NEW DIRECTION IN GOD'S DIVINE DESIGN. IT IS
YOUR DAY. IT IS HIS DAY. AND GOD, ALONGSIDE YOU AND
YOUR BELOVED, IS LOVING EVERY MINUTE OF IT!

THE BLUE SCARF

The setting sun, and music at the close,
As the last taste of sweets, is sweetest last,
Writ in remembrance more than things long past.

WILLIAM SHAKESPEARE, *KING RICHARD*

When Meredith, Ed White's wife of twenty-five years, was killed in an auto accident, Ed was sure his life had ended too. He would have given all he owned to have just one day, even one hour, to tell his Meredith good-bye.

But life went on for Ed. In fact, he quickly learned that responsible, single, middle-aged men were in great demand. Every one of his friends seemed to have a widow or divorcée that they couldn't wait to introduce to Ed. But he ignored the avalanche of invitations that began to appear shortly after Meredith's death.

It was three years later that Ed finally accepted a social invitation to a large gathering at the home of friends. As guests crowded around the buffet, Ed still ached with a feeling of incompleteness. *Meredith should be by my side,* he thought. Somehow, he survived until the end of the evening.

But as he was leaving, he caught sight of a beautiful silk scarf across the room. The scarf brought back a flood of other memories. He studied the face of the woman who wore it. *It couldn't be her…or could it?* he wondered.

The woman was preparing to leave, too, and he followed her out.

Catching up with her, he said, "That's a beautiful scarf you're wearing."

She muttered a quick thank you and began to walk faster.

"I guess I'm not very good at this," he told her, trying to keep up. "I'm Ed. And you are…?"

"Sunny," she answered without a trace of enthusiasm.

It is her. It must be her, he thought to himself, but the woman with the scarf seemed to share no such recognition. He worked hard to persuade her to join him for a late-night coffee, and finally succeeded.

As they sat across from one another in the booth, she barely looked at him. But he tried again. "That scarf you're wearing…"

She interrupted him. "I don't mean to appear rude but I should have never worn this scarf."

"And why not?" he asked. "It matches your blue eyes perfectly."

Definitely the same eyes, he thought. But how much they had changed, hidden by what seemed to be a veil of sadness. When she began to cry, he offered her his handkerchief.

"I'm sorry, I was rude," she said appearing to soften, but still keeping her eyes looking downcast. "This scarf just reminds me of all the mistakes I've made in my life. All the bad choices. What might have been. You see, I haven't had a very happy life. Things could have been different if I had only followed my heart instead of my ambitions."

"Don't you believe in second chances?" he asked.

"Why, I…yes, I suppose I do," she said, raising her eyes to meet his for the first time. "But I've already had plenty. It's too late for me now…was it Ed, did you say?"

"Yes, Ed. Ed White." Now as she looked at him, her countenance began to change. A smile of recognition spread across her face.

"So where did you get that scarf, Sunny?" he asked gently.

"From…you!" she said, and they both burst out laughing.

You see, nearly three decades earlier, Sunny had been Ed's first love, but she had refused his proposal, choosing instead to go to California to pursue her career. At first devastated over his loss, Ed had eventually met and fallen in love with Meredith.

Life had not been as kind to Sunny. A failed marriage had found her once again living alone in a tiny apartment, struggling to make ends meet in New York. But lately Sunny had begun to talk to God about her past, praying for forgiveness and another chance. As for the scarf, she had searched it out just this evening to wear to the party as a sign of faith that—though she never expected to see Ed White again—God had graciously heard her prayer.

That very evening, he did!

When Ed and Sunny were married later that year, Ed was swept away with gratitude that his beaming bride, Sunny, was by his side—right where she belonged. And the blue scarf she wore reminded them both that God does indeed give second chances—and third and fourth ones, too.

SUNNY AND ED WHITE,
AS TOLD TO SUSAN WALES

Love gives naught but itself
and takes naught but from itself.
Love possesses not nor would it be possessed
for love is sufficient unto love.
KAHIL GIBRAN

LET THERE BE LIGHT

Lovers alone wear sunlight.

E. E. CUMMINGS

It had all the makings of a disaster. First off, I wasn't even home when my favorite niece, Paige, called to announce her engagement…and to say that she wanted to be married before she left for school. Oh, and one more thing: She wanted to be married at *my house* in three weeks.

From a pay phone at the golf camp I was attending, I gasped. Not only was I away from home then, but a long-planned visit to Ireland loomed. The trip meant I would be away from home for the crucial ten days before the wedding was to take place.

I stuttered that sure, we could pull off a formal wedding in a few weeks, even with my immediate and imminent absences. I hung up the phone wondering what I'd just done. I sorely wanted to make Paige's dreams come true, but could we really plan and present a wedding in the time, and with the distractions, we had? I determined to try my best.

Once I returned from camp, Paige and I talked and planned and then talked and planned some more. In the days before I left the country, we got the tent, tables, chairs, flowers, music, food, and everything else that goes into making the perfect wedding. She arranged for her aunt and cousin to cater the wedding breakfast at the eleven o'clock ceremony for seventy-five guests. We handled as many of the details as possible before I left for my trip.

I returned from Ireland on Thursday night. By Friday morning, the tent was erected and all of the tables were set up. Beautiful garlands draped the courtyard, fish pool, and columns. The linens were pressed and starched and the china set out with care. The silverware had been polished till it shined. I was impressed! We worked hard all day and by Friday night, we were exhausted but we went to bed thinking, with great pride, *Everything is done. Everything will be perfect.*

Then came the horrible storm. We awoke at four o'clock Saturday morning to clouds dumping so much water so quickly on the tent that it was in danger of collapsing. The electricity was out. Frantic questions filled the soggy air: "How are we going to cook the wedding breakfast?" Even worse, "How are we going to dry the bridesmaids' hair?"

By ten o'clock we had relaxed a little. The rain had stopped. The tent company reerected the tent. The power was back on. Aunt Janet and Cousin Mary Ellen had all sorts of things simmering in the kitchen and the guests were arriving.

We served coffee and punch in the rose garden. The air was still misty. *That could be a problem*, I thought. Then I noticed that Paige was nowhere to be found. "Where's the bride? Does anyone know where the bride is?" These were not the kind of questions I wanted to be asking less than an hour before the wedding was supposed to start.

Paige burst in a few minutes later. Apparently she had had traffic problems in the fifty-five-mile trip from her home to mine. And in the moments between my asking where Paige was and her arriving, the sky had darkened and the clouds hung ominously low above our heads.

Once again, our frenzied yet loving plans were threatened. With a strained smile, I invited the guests into the house a bit early and treated them to the quartet's calming music. I needed calming music myself right about then. Inside, I gave up. Discouragement consumed me. *What a complete mess,* I thought gloomily. *What a terrible day to be married.*

The ceremony was finally set to begin. We directed the guests to where the two wings of the house met in the middle of the open oval foyer. Above our heads was a large skylight. Unfortunately, there was no light that day, just shades of dark gray. It was so dark that I hoped the bride would be able to see her way down the "aisle."

Then Paige and her betrothed, Tim, appeared. Paige entered from the left, the groom from the right. When I saw their beaming faces, I smiled. They were indeed a lovely couple. I could see the love in their eyes. No exterior light could brighten the room more than their smiles did.

And as they joined hands underneath the skylight, the gray clouds parted and the sun broke through triumphantly. Bright sunlight shined directly on the couple. All of us watching uttered an audible gasp.

I finally understood that regardless of how disastrously the day began, the beauty of a wedding wasn't in the details of decor or weather. It was in the love of a man and a woman, and that illumination was matchless.

BETH JONES, AS TOLD TO ANN PLATZ

LEGACY OF LOVE

But oh, she dances such a way!
No sun upon an Easter-day
Is half so fine a sight.

My mother, the late Eleanor Powell, was starstruck almost from birth. She loved acting, dancing, and any form of showbiz. As a young teenager she spent her summers working as a dancer in Atlantic City. Gus Edwards discovered her and signed her for his revue in New York City. Billed as the World's Greatest Tap Dancer, Mother danced her way to Broadway in such hits as *Fine and Dandy*, *Hot Cha*, and *Scandals*.

Then Hollywood called and Mother went on to star in several films including Cole Porter's *Born to Dance*, *Rosalie* with Nelson Eddy, *Honolulu* with Burns and Allen, *Ship Ahoy*, and *Lady Be Good* with Red Skelton. MGM cast Mother with Fred Astaire in *Broadway Melody of 1940*. She was a smashing success and finally people were starstruck over her!

During World War II, Mother was asked to accompany the famous actor Pat O'Brien of *Boys Town* fame and the beautiful actress Merle Oberon on a warbond tour. As the congenial group traveled all over the country by train, Mr. O'Brien developed a fatherly interest in my mother.

"I'd like to introduce you to that talented young actor, Glenn Ford," Mr. O'Brien told her. "Glenn needs to meet a pretty, nice young woman like you!" Mr. O'Brien had recently worked with the young actor in the popular movie, *Flight Lieutenant*. "Mark my words," he said emphatically, "this young fellow is going to be the top leading man day soon!"

Mother listened politely, but she wasn't really interested. She already had a special someone in her life. Besides, some well-meaning friend was always trying to fix her up with a dashing new star and they were all the same. She thought she was past being starstruck and could no longer be impressed.

Since moving to California, my mother lived quietly in Beverly Hills with her mother. Grandmother made sure her daughter was properly chaperoned around Hollywood. She often accompanied Ellie to social events, movies, and church. The life of a young starlet in Hollywood could be very lonely at times, so mother and daughter grew very close. Ellie was also devoted to her faith.

It was a beautiful summer night when mother and daughter happened to see *The Adventures of Martin in Eden,* starring none other than Glenn Ford. Mother was immediately mesmerized by the movie. Like millions of other young women across America, she fell in love with the handsome young actor she was watching on the big screen.

She was starstruck!

When Mother phoned Pat O'Brien to take him up on his offer to introduce her to Glenn Ford, Mr. O'Brien was amused and honored to play the role of matchmaker. He arranged a lovely dinner party at his home to introduce the popular young couple. My father was on leave and when he showed up in his uniform, he captured my mother's heart forever! For his part, Father was attracted to mother's sweet spirit and her values. They were both dating other actors, but following that enchanted evening at the O'Brien home, they only had eyes for each other.

Eleanor Powell and Glenn Ford were a real item in Hollywood. The gossip columns buzzed with the exciting details of their wholesome romance. Mother and Father fell deeply in love. My grandmother had raised her daughter to be an old-fashioned girl, so it was only appropriate that my father popped the question over an ice-cream soda. She accepted immediately!

Eleanor Powell and Glenn Ford were married in 1943 during the war, and I was born a few years later.

Just as Pat O'Brien had predicted, my father's film career soared. Father starred as the leading man in many hit films such as *Gilda* with Rita Hayworth; *A Stolen Life* with Bette Davis; *The Blackboard Jungle; Teahouse of the August Moon; Imitation General* with Red Buttons; *Torpedo Run* with Ernest Borgnine; *The Gazebo; It Started with a Kiss* with Debbie Reynolds; and *The Rounders* with Henry Fonda.

Despite all the fame and fortune my parents enjoyed, they taught me that the most important things in life were faith and values. In the fifties, while my father's star grew brighter, my mother dedicated herself to being a wife and mother. She also created the Emmy-Award-winning television series, *Faith of Our Children,* and my father became a regular participant on her show.

Both of my parents gave me a great legacy of love by teaching me the importance of loving God and others, and I have passed this legacy to my own children. What started as a simple case of stargazing ended in a Christian family whose values endure generation after generation.

As told to Susan Wales by Peter Ford

Editor's note: Peter Ford and his wife Lynda, the proud parents of three children, recently celebrated thirty years of wedded bliss. They reside in Beverly Hills with their father, actor Glenn Ford.

IT HAPPENED ON THE
BROOKLYN SUBWAY

Great loves were almost always great tragedies.
Perhaps it was because love was never truly great
until the element of sacrifice entered into it.
MARY ROBERTS RINEHART

The car was crowded, and there seemed to be no chance of a seat. But as I entered, a man sitting by the door suddenly jumped up to leave, and I slipped into the empty seat.

I've been living in New York long enough not to start conversations with strangers. But, being a photographer, I have the peculiar habit of analyzing people's faces, and I was struck by the features of the passenger on my left. He was probably in his late thirties, and when he glanced up, his eyes seemed to have a hurt expression in them. He was reading a Hungarian-language newspaper and something prompted me to say in Hungarian, "I hope you don't mind if I glance at your paper."

The man seemed surprised to be addressed in his native language. But he only answered politely, "You may read it now. I'll have time later on."

During the half-hour ride to town, we had quite a conversation. He said his name was Bela Paskin. A law student when World War II started, he had been put into a German labor battalion and sent to the Ukraine. Later he was captured by the Russians and put to work burying the German dead. After the war, he covered hundreds of miles on foot until he reached his home in Debrecen, a large city in eastern Hungary.

I myself knew Debrecen quite well, and we talked about it for a while.

Then he told me the rest of his story. When he went to the apartment once occupied by his father, mother, brothers, and sisters, he found strangers living there. Then he went upstairs to the apartment that he and his wife once had. It was also occupied by strangers. None of them had ever heard of his family.

As he was leaving, full of sadness, a boy ran after him, calling, "Paskin bacsi! Paskin bacsi!" That means "Uncle Paskin." The child was the son of some old neighbors of his. He went to the boy's home and talked to his parents. "Your whole family is dead," they told him. "The Nazis took them and your wife to Auschwitz."

Auschwitz was one of the worst Nazi concentration camps. Paskin gave up all hope. A few days later, too heartsick to remain any longer in Hungary, he set out on foot again, stealing across border after border until he reached Paris. He managed to immigrate to the United States in October 1947, just three months before I met him.

All the time he had been talking, I kept thinking that somehow his story seemed familiar. A young woman whom I met recently at the home of friends had also been from Debrecen; she had been sent to Auschwitz; from there she had been transferred to work in a German munitions factory. Her relatives had been killed in the gas chambers. Later, she was liberated by the Americans and was brought here in the first boatload of displaced persons in 1946.

Her story had moved me so much that I had written down her address and phone number, intending to invite her to meet my family and thus help relieve the terrible emptiness in her life.

It seemed impossible that there could be any connection between these two people, but as I neared my station, I fumbled anxiously in my address book. I asked in what I hoped was a casual voice, "Was your wife's name Marya?"

He turned pale. "Yes!" he answered. "How did you know?"

He looked as if he were about to faint.

I said, "Let's get off the train." I took him by the arm at the next station and led him to a phone booth. He stood there like a man in a trance while I dialed her phone number.

It seemed hours before Marya Paskin answered. Later I learned her room was alongside the telephone, but she was in the habit of never answering it because she had so few friends and the calls were always for someone else. This time, however, there was no one else at home, and, after letting it ring for a while, she responded.

When I heard her voice at last, I told her who I was and asked her to describe her husband. She seemed surprised at the question, but gave me a description. Then I asked her where she had lived in Debrecen, and she told me the address.

Asking her to hold the line, I turned to Paskin and said, "Did you and your wife live on such-and-such a street?"

"Yes!" Bela exclaimed. He was white as a sheet and trembling.

"Try to be calm," I urged him. "Something miraculous is about to happen to you. Here, take this telephone and talk to your wife!"

He nodded his head in mute bewilderment, his eyes bright with tears. He took the receiver, listened a moment to his wife's voice, then cried suddenly. "This is Bela! This is Bela!" and he began to mumble hysterically. Seeing that the poor fellow was so excited he couldn't talk coherently, I took the receiver from his shaking hands.

"Stay where you are," I told Marya, who also sounded hysterical. "I am sending your husband to you. We will be there in a few minutes."

Bela was crying like a baby and saying over and over again, "It is my wife, I go to my wife!"

At first I thought I had better accompany Paskin, lest the man should faint from excitement, but I decided that this was a moment in which no strangers should intrude. Putting Paskin into a taxicab, I directed the driver to take him to Marya's address, paid the fare and said good-bye.

Bela Paskin's reunion with his wife was a moment so poignant, so electric with suddenly released emotion, that afterward neither he nor Marya could recall much about it.

"I remember only that when I left the phone, I walked to the mirror like in a dream to see if maybe my hair had turned gray," she said later. "The next thing I know, a taxi stops in front of the house, and it is my husband who comes toward me. Details I cannot remember; only this I know—that I was happy for the first time in many years.

"Even now it is difficult to believe that it happened. We have both suffered so much; I have almost lost the capability to not be afraid. Each time my husband goes from the house, I say to myself, 'Will anything happen to take him from me again?'"

Her husband is confident that no horrible misfortune will ever befall them. "Providence has brought us together," he says simply. "It was meant to be."

PAUL DEUTSCHMAN

TOGETHER...AT LAST!

❧

Two such as you
With such a master speed
Cannot be parted nor be swept away
From one another
Once you are agreed
That life is only life forevermore
Together wing to wing and oar to oar.
ROBERT FROST

Rosemary was the only child of a Yorba Linda rancher and an eighth-generation Castilian Spanish beauty. She had a happy childhood, her life full of love, adventure, and activities around the ranch. Their doors were always open to family and friends, who were guests of great meals and joyous fiestas hosted by Rosemary's family.

John was the son of a close-knit, civic-minded family. He was the high school football hero and track star. He was nineteen and Rosemary was fifteen. The beautiful teenager fell deeply in love with her high school idol, John Raitt. The feelings were quite mutual, and they were allowed to see one another, properly chaperoned.

Alarmed that the two youths were becoming too serious, their families convened. Aside from being too young to get so serious, the families believed there were many differences between the two. She was a Catholic and he was Presbyterian. Rosemary's mother also wondered aloud what kind of future John, who aspired to be a football coach, would have. "He can't possibly provide the life that Rosemary is accustomed to having," she said. Both families agreed it was for the best that the two separate.

Their love forbidden, Rosemary and John were forced to go their separate ways. John went to the University of Southern California, where he starred on the Trojans' track and field team. He also began what would be a wonderful singing career. His magical tenor voice propelled him up the ladder of success in the world of theater and music.

The pain of Rosemary and John's separation was, for a time, unbearable. But, in order to please their families, they eventually married others and had families of their own.

John became a great success in the theater and on Broadway. Rosemary watched him perform in *Oklahoma, Showboat, Carousel*, and *Annie Get Your Gun*. She remembered the days of their youth, when she had been his girl.

Eventually, the two lost touch and only faded memories of the other and their first love lingered.

Years later, the hometown boy came back home to perform in the local theater. Afterward, Rosemary's mother came backstage to tell him she was sorry. She had been wrong about John's success. But it was too late, for John and Rosemary were both happily married.

The years passed. John was divorced, and Rosemary widowed. One day, John's manager told him he had seen Rosemary. "I met someone at a party that knew you...said she was your first love," his manager told him.

"Who?" John begged to know.

"My neighbor, Rosemary. She's a widow now."

John had the phone in his hand, and he silently prayed that Rosemary would answer as he dialed her number. She did.

"Do you know who this is?" John's voice rang out.

"No," came Rosemary's reply.

"It's your first love!" he announced.

"John!" she squealed with delight. Suddenly there was silence at the other end of the line. It had been fifty-eight years.

"Would you like to have dinner tonight?" he asked her.

"My hair's in curlers and I have a baked potato in the oven," she told him.

"I can't take no for an answer," he told her. "We've waited too long for this moment."

When John walked through the gates of her home, he saw Rosemary waiting at the door. He remembered seeing the same vibrant blue eyes he had gazed into fifty-eight years earlier.

It was as though nothing had changed between them. They talked until four the next morning. It seemed that they knew one another on a deep spiritual level and neither of their hearts had changed after all these years.

The young lovers, who had by now grown old, took up right where they'd left off as teenagers and began courting again. It wasn't long before John proposed. They were married at Rosemary's home in the gardens under the magnolia tree surrounded by their blended families, serenaded by John's daughter, singer Bonnie Raitt. It was a magnificent family celebration of love.

Always the hopeless romantic, on their wedding day John presented Rosemary with a gift for every year they'd been apart...fifty-eight presents in all!

Today, they count each day as a gift as they celebrate their golden years together.

At last, the young lovers were reunited.

Editor's note: The great Broadway singer, John Raitt, still performs his music for all his fans. Rosemary is on the board of Regents at Pepperdine University, which she helped found. Pepperdine named their musical theater in honor of the couple, The John and Rosemary Raitt Center for the Performing Arts.

I KNOW WHO YOU ARE!

⌇⌇

Grow old with me! The best is yet to be,

The last of life, for which the first was made:

Our times are in his hand who saith,

"A whole I planned,

Youth shows but half trust God:

see all, nor be afraid!"

ROBERT BROWNING

t was a spontaneous trip home to Savannah for the Thanksgiving weekend. Charlotte decided just in time to get the last seat on the last flight from Atlanta to Savannah. It would be fun to surprise her mother, her sister, and all the nieces and nephews around the holiday table.

The next day Charlotte happened to meet her friend Betty at the supermarket. Betty, delighted to see her, invited Charlotte to attend a party she was giving that night.

Charlotte demurred, saying, "Nobody will remember me after all these years. Besides, I never go to parties unescorted." Betty persisted, though, and at last, Charlotte agreed. "Okay—I could drop in for an hour," she said.

The weather was warm and glorious, Betty's house was beautiful with candlelight and flowers, and Charlotte felt glad she had chosen a becoming red dress for the occasion. As she mingled with the other quests, enjoying herself, she nevertheless watched the time. *I'll leave before it gets late,* she told herself.

After the hour was up, Charlotte moved toward the door only to be intercepted by an attractive, smiling gentleman. "Excuse me. I'm Norris Pindar," he said, "and I understand that you write."

"I know who you are—" Charlotte began.

"No, you don't," the gentleman corrected her, sure he had never met her before in his life.

"Don't you sing in the Christ Church choir? Baritone? Don't you solo every Christmas in *The Messiah*? And at Easter, don't you sing 'Were You There When They Crucified My Lord?'" *There. He stands corrected,* she thought.

"You do know who I am!" he replied, sounding amazed.

"Do you write, also?" Charlotte asked, smiling.

"No, but my wife does. She has written several books."

"Where is your wife? Maybe I know her." Charlotte searched the room with her eyes, thinking she might spot a former newspaper colleague.

"She's dead," he said.

The wedding band on his hand...speaking of his wife in present tense...suddenly she comprehended the situation. "When did it happen?" she asked. He named the date, even the time of day—just six and a half weeks before—and she immediately understood. "This is your first time out since...?"

"Yes."

"I had a sadness also. It was not as terrible as yours, but my world seemed to fall apart. My friends brought me through it," Charlotte told him. "You are doing the right thing, coming to this party. These people have loved you all your life. Let them help you now."

He seized her hand. "Please talk to me," he begged. Leading her to a sofa, he engaged her in lively conversation as others in the room took note of the woman in the red dress who was allowing the widower to hold her hand. When he let out a big laugh, full and free, one woman looked distinctly disapproving.

The next day Charlotte flew back to Atlanta, still thinking of that honest, hurting man with the good face and gentle ways. He would telephone, she felt sure. *Tomorrow, after church, after lunch,* she surmised.

Then he'd wait because perhaps I'd want a nap. He will call at four o'clock, Charlotte concluded.

The telephone rang at exactly four. As the days went by, other long-distance calls escalated their friendship. Over long conversations they explored music, poetry, and politics—everything that mattered. They fell in love.

Two weeks after Thanksgiving, Charlotte's telephone rang and Nell, an old friend, was on the line. "I have something important to tell you," Nell began. "I had to be rushed to the hospital on Thanksgiving Day. They placed me in intensive care. I was alone, unable to talk, very sick, and I began to pray for friends. Your face came to my mind, and I prayed for you for a long time.

"Charlotte, you are going to meet someone soon who you will marry. You are to begin praying for him right now, because he needs prayers. He is recovering from a deep hurt, a terrible grief."

Charlotte felt amazed. "Nell, I think perhaps I met him," she said, slowly. "I went to Savannah for Thanksgiving and someone was there—someone wonderful."

"I prayed for you on Thanksgiving, but even more intensely the next day," Nell said. "There was no telephone in my room, so I couldn't get in touch with you. This is the first moment I've been well enough to call."

She was praying for me at the very moment that I was meeting Norris, Charlotte realized. Suddenly another memory jolted her. A couple of months before she had received two telephone calls in one hour. Both Eliza and Ann had called to give her that same message: she would soon meet a man she would marry. "Pray for him," they told her. "He needs your prayers right now." Neither woman had been aware that the other called; yet both gave the same message. Charlotte had prayed that day, of course, but only once. Since meeting Norris, she had been much too happy to think of her friends' advice.

When Charlotte checked her date book she realized, stunned, that those two earlier telephone calls had arrived on Saturday. Norris's wife had died on Monday. "He needs prayer right now," she remembered her friend saying.

Coincidence? Neither Norris nor Charlotte would call it that. Consider Charlotte's last-minute decision to visit Savannah on Thanksgiving Day; her taking the last seat on the last flight from Atlanta; the party invitation she hadn't wanted to accept; her hospitalized friend's prayer the day she and Norris met; two other friends' telephone calls in which they advised her to pray for a man she would eventually meet and marry; her own prayer for that unknown man, uttered just two days before his world was shattered.

"An unseen hand guided you," Norris later said.

"A divine appointment," Charlotte agreed.

Six months after they met, Norris and Charlotte were married. Twelve years later, they are still living happily ever after, certain they came together by divine appointment.

CHARLOTTE AND NORRIS PINDAR

And I will make thee beds of roses,
And a thousand fragrant posies.
CHRISTOPHER MARLOWE

To Love, Honor, and Cherish

How many times do I love thee, dear?
Tell me how many thoughts there be
In the atmosphere
Of a newfallen year,
Whose white and sable hours appear
The latest flake of Eternity:
So many times do I love thee, dear.

ELIZABETH BARRETT BROWNING

IN A WORLD WHERE LOVE IS TOO OFTEN DETERMINED BY HOW SOMEONE MEETS YOUR NEEDS OR MAKES YOU FEEL, WEDDING VOWS SEEM ALMOST NAIVE. YOU PROMISE TO LOVE, HONOR, AND CHERISH BECAUSE GOD HAS BROUGHT YOU TOGETHER WITH SOMEONE IN HIS PLAN. YOU ARE SEEKING TO GIVE YOURSELF WHOLEHEARTEDLY.

LOVE IS NOT MERELY AN EMOTION. LOVE IS A DECISION. YOU OPEN YOUR HEART A LITTLE. LOVE BEGINS TO FILL IT. YOU CHOOSE TO OPEN IT WIDER. YOU RISK HURT. SOMETIMES YOU LET GO. LOVE FLOWS LIKE THE TIDES. SOMETIMES FEELINGS SWELL. SOMETIMES THEY RECEDE. BUT THE POWER OF THE SEA REMAINS. THIS IS ALL IN THE DIVINE DESIGN.

To HONOR IS ALSO A CONSCIOUS CHOICE YOU ARE MAKING. IT MEANS TO OFFER ESTEEM, RESPECT, AND COURTESY. YOU PROMISE TO THINK FIRST OF YOUR BELOVED AND HIS OR HER WELFARE. HONOR GIVES GLORY TO GOD BECAUSE IT IS ENTIRELY UNSELFISH. HONOR DOES NOT GRASP. IT BOLDLY OFFERS PRESENCE, NOT PRESENTS, TO THE LOVED ONE.

To CHERISH IS AN INTIMATE CARING, AND RESOLUTELY HOLDING DEAR. IT DOTES ON ANOTHER, CARRYING DEEP IMPULSES TO GIVE AND SHARE AND PROTECT. TO CHERISH IS TO EMBRACE LIKE A SOFT, STRONG SQUEEZE. IT MAY ALSO BARELY TOUCH THE LOVED ONE LIKE A BREEZE TICKLES THE FACE OF PRAIRIE GRASS.

WHEN YOU MAKE YOUR WEDDING VOWS TO LOVE, HONOR, AND CHERISH, YOU ARE TELLING YOUR SOON-TO-BE SPOUSE, "YOU ARE GOD'S GIFT TO ME. I WILL BE THERE FOR YOU. NOTHING IN HEAVEN AND EARTH CAN CHANGE THAT."

THE GREEN DRESS

Oft in the still night
Ere Slumber's chain has bound me,
Fond Memory brings the light
Of other days around me;
The smiles, the tears,
Of boyhood's years
The words of love then spoken.

THOMAS MOORE

pring had come late that year, which may have been why it hit them both so hard. Typically Meredith and Ben had reacted to the season in opposite fashions. With fresh awakenings of a youthful nostalgia, Meredith had fallen in love with her husband all over again. Ben, on the other hand, had fended off her romantic overtures, instead spending all of his free time locked up in the sunroom of their country home. Inspired by the sights and sounds that also stirred his wife's heart, Ben was painting again.

It was well into May, with tulips and daffodils adding patches of brilliance to their yard, before Meredith finally dared to venture inside the room to peek at his completed canvases. It was loneliness that pulled her more than curiosity. She was looking only for a way to connect with the husband she missed. Ben with his stubborn artistic temperament had always insisted that she not see his work until he chose to present it. Wary of his quick temper, she had learned early to comply. As she hesitated on the threshold, she reassured herself that twenty-four years of marriage carried with it some liberties. Anyway, today he was giving a seminar in a neighboring town and would not be back until evening.

The paintings were propped against the baseboards below the windows. From the doorway she could see the soft pastels of the drifting watercolors that were his trademark. But as she walked closer, she noted with surprise that the first pastoral background also included a human figure—a novelty for Ben. As Meredith examined these recent pieces she realized instantly that the same female figure was in each canvas. Her face was always hidden from view and her hairstyle, even hair color, varied from print to print. But in every scene the pale, spring-green dress she wore caught the viewer's eye like a beacon.

It was a sleeveless sundress with wide, tie-back ribbons falling in a loose, feminine bow at the small of her back. In some poses, the wind that swept the grasses into undulating waves molded the green dress against her figure. In the forest scenes, a shaft of sunlight caught her among the shadowy evergreens and her skin seemed to glow beneath it. Although the girl was never in the foreground and was often only an ethereal suggestion amid springtime greenery, Ben had managed to make her the center of attention.

Meredith envied the slim, youthful figure and gorgeous long hair, so opposite her own short, graying brown curls and the forty-five-year-old shape that had widened with the birth of each of her three sons. When she had complained about gravity and age conspiring against her, Ben had always insisted that she was as attractive as ever. Her bedroom mirror told her otherwise.

For a few days Meredith allowed her suspicions to simmer. Was the woman someone Ben had recently met and fallen in love with? Or was she a fantasy he had conjured out of marital boredom? One was almost as bad as the other. Ben still favored her with his kisses and his brown-eyed smile each morning and curved his solid warmth around her every night, but Meredith would not be deceived. Somehow they had grown apart; they had let complacency replace passion. When was the last time they had talked about their relationship, their dreams? When was the last time they had said "I love you"?

She held it in until Saturday. The morning had dawned warm and sunny and the two of them had brought their coffee onto the patio. Meredith was flipping halfheartedly through a gardening magazine and Ben was reading the paper when they were both distracted by a familiar sound. It was the honking of geese and they stood and scanned the skies. Suddenly, there they were, streaming toward them in a trembling, black skein as they flew over the southern horizon.

A rush of joy pounded through her. There was always hope, as eternal as the cycle of the seasons and the return of the geese. Impulsively, she turned to Ben. "Let's take the day off, hon, and hike down to the river. I'll pack us a lunch. We can just relax and dangle our feet and talk. It'll be like old times. What do you say?"

Ben's unshaven face creased in a weak smile of apology. "Sorry, Mer. I planned to paint today. You know what they say...."

No, Meredith did not know what "they" said. Make hay while the sun shines? Idle hands do the devil's work? The wife's always the last to know?

Her jealousy boiled over. Unable to bite back the words, she confronted him. "Ben, I looked at your paintings this week." She watched his face sober and knew she had hit a nerve. Her bones were melting and her heart hurt, but the words kept coming. "You...you've never put people in your pictures before. Who's the girl in the green dress?"

When he turned away from her to look down over the fields, she lost her ability to breathe. He was her life. She could not bear this. Her mouth tasted like copper and her vision was blurred like the watercolors that had brought them to this moment. When he finally turned to answer her, she was stumbling across the patio to the house. His quiet response carried across the yard and stabbed her before she could close the glass door between them.

"An old girlfriend, Mer. Just an old girlfriend."

Meredith had often used housework as an outlet for frustration and anger. Today she used it to distract her from panic. She knew she should have met Ben's statement with a frontal attack, but her reeling mind had become incapable of coherent argument.

It was the closets that bore the brunt of her frenetic activity. She had finished the boys' bedrooms and was now attacking the one she shared with Ben. Lifting out their clothes and thinking that she soon might be packing one set of them into suitcases brought on a wave of nausea so great that she was forced to drop them on the floor and sit on the edge of the bed with her head between her knees. As the sickness subsided, she lay down slowly on the bed—the bed they might never share again. Thoughts of finality continued to ambush her. She rolled onto her side and stared into the open closet beside the bed.

When her eyes fell upon the stack of old photo albums, her breathing quickened. Second from the bottom was the worn brown binder that held Ben's premarriage photos. It wasn't that she wanted to know. They were past that hurdle. It was simply that she had to see—had to put a face to her rival. But as Meredith slowly turned the plastic pages, she realized she had no way of knowing which girl was being immortalized in her husband's faceless portraits. She was more than halfway through the book and had just made up her mind to stop this foolishness when she found her.

Actually, there were two prints of the same woman. Her brown hair tumbled loose in waves in one of them and trailed down her back in a thick braid in the second. But the dress was unmistakable. In reality it was more blue than green, closer to aqua in a print of cornflowers and daisies. But Meredith recognized the squared neckline that set off the smooth, tanned skin, and the ties that were looped in an old-fashioned bow at the back. There was one of the girl seated in a field on a blanket. An open picnic basket gaped invitingly beside her. In the last frame, she stood atop a sand dune, face turned to the wind that was blowing fog in across the sea, plastering her damp dress to her young figure.

In both photographs, the beautiful girl had worn the dress of Ben's paintings; the garment of his dreams and his inspiration. Meredith knew it well. During that wonderful summer it had been her favorite.

CATHY MILLER

THE SECRET OF LOVE

*The face is the mirror of the mind,
and eyes without speaking
confess the secrets of the heart.*
St. Jerome

These words are ancient jewels minced from the quarry of life. Read them only if you dare treasure them. For it would be better to never know than to know and not obey.

The hand that writes them is now old, wrinkled from the sun and labor. But the hand that guides them is wise—wise from years, wise from failures, wise from heartache.

I travel from city to city. I buy jewels from the diggers in one land and sell them to the buyers in another. I have weathered nights on stormy waters. I have walked days through desert heat. My hands have held the finest rubies and stroked the deepest furs. But I would trade it all for the one jewel I never knew.

It was not for lack of opportunity that I never held it. It was for lack of wisdom. The jewel was in my hand, but I exchanged it for an imitation.

I have never known true love.

I have known embraces. I have seen beauty. But I have never known love. If only I'd learned to recognize love as I have learned to recognize stones.

My father taught me about stones. He was a jewel cutter. He would seat me at a table before a dozen emeralds.

"One is true," he would tell me. "The others are false. Find the true jewel."

I would ponder—studying each one after the other. Finally, I would choose. I was always wrong.

"The secret," he would say, "is not on the surface of the stone; it is inside the stone. A true jewel has a glow. Deep within the gem there is a flame. The surface can always be polished to shine, but with time the sparkle fades. However, the stone that shines from within will never fade."

With years, my eyes learned to spot true stones. I am never fooled. I have learned to see the light within.

If only I'd learned the same about love.

But I've spent my life in places I shouldn't have been looking only for someone with beautiful hair, a dazzling smile, and fancy clothes. I've searched for a woman with outer beauty but no true value. And now I am left with emptiness.

Once I almost found her. Many years ago in Madrid I met the daughter of a farmer. Her ways were simple. Her love was pure. Her eyes were honest. But her looks were plain. She would have loved me. She would have held me through every season. Within her was a glow of devotion the likes of which I've never seen since.

But I continued looking for someone whose beauty would outshine the rest.

How many times since have I longed for that farm girl's kind heart? If only I'd known that true beauty is found inside, not outside. If only I'd known, how many tears would I have saved?

True love glows from within and grows stronger with the passage of time.

Heed my caution. Look for the purest gem. Look deep within the heart to find the greatest beauty of all. And when you find the gem, hold onto her and never let her go.

For in her you have been granted a treasure worth far more than rubies.

Seek beauty and miss love.

But seek love and find both.

MAX LUCADO

Tell Me The Secrets, Max Lucado, © 1993, Crossway Books, Wheaton, Illinois.

TWELVE RULES FOR A HAPPY MARRIAGE

Love seeth not itself to please,
Nor for itself hath any care,
But for another gives its ease,
And builds a Heaven in Hell's despair.

WILLIAM BLAKE

♥ Never both be angry at once.

♥ Never yell at each other unless the house is on fire.

♥ Yield to the wishes of the other as an exercise in self-discipline if you can't think of a better reason.

♥ If you have a choice between making yourself or your mate look good, choose your mate.

♥ If you must criticize, do so lovingly.

♥ Never bring up a mistake of the past. Your silence will be greatly appreciated.

♥ Neglect the whole world rather than each other.

♥ Never let the day end without saying at least one complimentary thing to your life's partner.

♥ Never meet without an affectionate greeting.

♥ When you've said or done something hurtful, acknowledge it and ask for forgiveness.

♥ Remember, it takes two to get an argument going. Invariably the one who is wrong is the one who will be doing most of the talking.

♥ Never go to bed mad.

ANN LANDERS

WHAT BECAME OF JESSIE?

Though upon life's sea you wander,

in my heart you're ne'er forgot.

I shall hope with loves allegiance

That you too forget me not?

SAYING FROM A ROMANTIC TREASURY OF LOVE

*S*he was waiting for me at the insurance office where she worked in the little Missouri town of Bolivar. It had been half a century since we'd last met—in high school—although we had never gone out. It was my abiding shyness, her looks, and chicken pox that had kept us apart.

Her name was Jessie. In the spring of '42, I had planned to ask her to the high school dance, except I got chicken pox. She went instead with a boy named Milos. I had liked him, but now I wasn't sure. After the dance, due to my limited social skills, I could find no ready reason to ask her for a date.

When school ended, my family moved to St. Louis, but I never forgot her. At the University of Missouri, I met and married a girl named Sylvia. We had a son and a good marriage that lasted forty-one years until her death.

During my marriage, I sometimes thought of Jessie. Once at Thanksgiving, her image made me feel sad about what might have been, and once on a train I thought I heard the conductor call out Bolivar, and I wondered what she was doing.

A year after my wife's death, I attended a family reunion and ran into my cousin Anna, who still lived in Bolivar. "Whatever happened to that girl named Jessie?" I asked.

"Oh, she's still there," she answered. "Been a widow for ten years." Jessie had married a boy in our class named Charles. They had two sons, then separated. He died in the mid-'80s.

Anna gave me Jessie's telephone number and I called her. The conversation lasted almost an hour. Jessie told me that she had become old, gray, and fat, but I didn't believe it for a moment. We agreed to meet.

Missouri in late summer looked somnolent, the growing season all but over, touches of autumn color appearing in the maples that stood in clumps along Interstate 44. I rolled off the interstate a few miles east of Bolivar and before I knew it, her office came into view. I parked outside and walked in.

Her hair was neither gray nor the blonde of my remembrance, and she was tall and slender. Her eyes were bluer than I remembered, and her nose still tilted prettily upward.

"Well hello," she said with a dazzling smile. "Is there someone you wanted to see?" I hadn't known about her teasing side. Her hands, I noticed, were shaking.

During lunch, we found out much about each other. The next day we went to Branson, Missouri, and stayed the night—in separate rooms. "I'll visit you in Connecticut," she promised when I left a couple of days later. Within a month, she appeared at the airport.

A whirlwind of letters and phone calls followed the next year, which culminated in my selling my house and moving back where I began, within miles of her door. One evening, as we were looking at housing tracts, I asked, "Why are we doing this?" for she had always demurred at talk of marriage.

"Just in case," she said.

Robert G. Beason

Editor's note: Robert and Jessie were married on January 26, 1995— fifty-three years, four months, and eighteen days after he first saw her in Miss Williams's English class. He's been an AARP member for ten years.

Reprinted from *Modern Maturity*, March–April 1999. By permission of Robert G. Beason.

NORMA'S RIBS

⁊

*The way to a man's heart
is through his stomach.*

FANNY FERN

When I was a young woman, I worked as a secretary for the navy in London. Occasionally I joined my friends and coworkers at a local club after work for a night of dancing and fun. Later each evening a group of American G.I.s, who were stationed nearby, drove over to London and joined us at our table.

The first night the Americans came over, William, an attractive soldier in the group, caught my eye. He had the cutest dimples I'd ever seen! As I watched him, I knew somehow that he was exactly the kind of man that I wanted to marry. I felt a special attraction to him—I just couldn't explain it.

The only problem was, no matter how hard I tried to get his attention, William hardly noticed me. It was as though I was invisible. Every time I tried to start a conversation with him, he gave me a friendly nod and then walked away. Other times he put his head down on the table and fell sound asleep.

"What do you want with a man like that?" my girlfriends chided me. "He's a bore! Get out on the dance floor and meet some *fun* guys."

I always shook my head and said, "I've found the man I want."

"You're wasting your time, girl!" they'd say in unison. "He doesn't even know you're alive."

I knew they were right, but I just couldn't tear myself away from the idea that William was the man for me. I just kept praying that he would notice me one day.

A few months later two of my friends married and I volunteered to prepare their wedding dinner. I am from Barbados, so I cooked up a batch of barbecued ribs, our island specialty, using my family's spicy recipe.

As I was putting the finishes on the table, one of my friends squealed, "Well, look who's here!"

My heart leapt when I saw William at the door.

After the wedding, when everyone was gathering around the dinner table, you can imagine my delight when William took the empty seat beside me. We exchanged pleasantries, but once more, he turned away and began talking to someone else. I told myself not to be discouraged, at least he was sitting beside me.

I noticed that William's plate was piled high with my ribs. I kept my eyes on him as he bit into them. After some thoughtful chewing, he announced, "These ribs are the best things I've ever put in my mouth!"

I swelled with pride. Nothing pleases a cook more than seeing some-one enjoy her food. As William took another bite, his face burst into a wide grin and he declared to everyone, "I'm going to marry the woman who cooked these ribs."

I almost fell out of my chair. Then one of my friends yelled out, "She's sitting right beside you!"

Suddenly he turned around and for the very first time, William really noticed me. He looked into my eyes like he'd never seen me before. "Why haven't I gotten to know you sooner?" he asked.

I told him I'd been in front of him for months but he hadn't noticed. William and I spent the evening getting to know one another and when we were throwing rice at the departing newlyweds, he asked me out. We dated for a year and really enjoyed one another's company. I fell in love with William and suspected that he loved me, too, but he never made any mention of his intentions. I kept thinking, *This man sure takes his time!*

On the one-year anniversary of our first date William saw me to my door. I decided to drop a bombshell and see what happened. I said,

"Good-bye, William. It looks like I won't be seeing you anymore!"

"Wh—what do you mean?" he stammered.

"I don't date anyone for more than a year," I told him. "That's my limit."

Immediately he proposed, and we've been happily married for thirty-six years!

Am I still cooking those ribs? I confess I haven't made that dish since that fateful night when William finally noticed me. That night should have made a believer out of me: The way to a man's heart *is* through his stomach. But oddly enough, William fell in love with *me*, not just my cooking! To prove it, William has cooked our ribs ever since.

NORMA MCKINNEY

LOVE ACROSS THE MILES

His house she enters, there to be a light,
Shining within, when all without is night;
A guardian angel o'er his life presiding,
Doubling his pleasure and his cares dividing.

SAMUEL ROGERS

My son Trevor was a confirmed bachelor. At twenty-five he was working hard at a promising career and savoring his freedom. Being a fun-loving and outgoing person, he has always been a party animal. He loves a good time as well as the next Generation Xer. And he was enjoying being single.

Girls have always been drawn to Trevor, and despite his carefree, not-interested-in-long-term-commitment demeanor, his dates often heard wedding bells after just a few evenings. He seriously considered marriage only once. The girl was a wonderful person, beautiful, and crazy about Trevor. But after a time, he realized he was not ready for marriage and did not want to lead her on. He told her he was not "good marriage material" and broke off the relationship.

Shortly after this decision, he met Rentia (pronounced Ren-sha). If the name sounds a bit exotic, it is because Rentia is a Dutch Afrikaner from South Africa. She and Trevor met when she was working as an au pair for a family in a Chicago suburb and attending college as an exchange student. Trevor and my older son, Jeffrey, had gone out for a night on the town to celebrate Jeff's visit for spring break. Though they were in a crowded restaurant, Jeff and Trevor noticed Rentia's accent right away. Our family had had the marvelous opportunity to visit South Africa several years ago and became familiar with the Afrikaners' distinctive and charming way of speaking.

Trevor and Jeff found the source of the accent and introduced themselves to her. (The fact that she was a tall, gorgeous, hazel-eyed blond gave them the incentive they needed to make the first move.) Trevor and Rentia had an immediate rapport and talked nonstop about her beautiful country.

After their first date, Trevor told his father and me that he had met a girl he really liked. After a few dates, he told us he thought he had found the girl he wanted to marry. This sounded strange indeed coming from our confirmed bachelor who, a few months before, had said he "just wasn't ready for marriage." But when we met Rentia we could see why Trevor was so smitten. She was not only attractive but warm, sophisticated, and wonderful with our grandchildren.

Weeks passed and in spite of our skepticism, Trevor spoke more and more about marriage. And with unconcealed dread, he discussed Rentia's upcoming departure. Her visa expired in June. They had met in March. After a short courtship, Rentia left this country—and the man she had come to love.

For Trevor and Rentia to be married, they learned she would have to acquire a K-1 or "intent to marry" visa. These are not easy to get. The immigration red tape is unbelievable. And it is very expensive. But Trevor and Rentia, from separate countries, persevered, and after spending a fortune on long-distance phone calls and preparing a mountain of paperwork, they had done everything they could to make the visa possible. Then they had to wait.

And wait they did—for months. It was as though the paperwork had been sucked into a black hole somewhere. Rentia and her father could get no definite answers to their inquiries. Their phone calls were not returned. They often encountered voice mail instead of a real person—it was a classic example of bureaucracy at its worst.

This was especially frustrating for Rentia and her family as they were trying to plan a wedding in South Africa for her family and friends. After that ceremony, the couple would return to the United States to be married here. But how could she plan a wedding when she could not set a date?

In October, Trevor made the long trip to visit Rentia, meet her parents, and take her an engagement ring. It was a joyous week for the couple to renew their love and commitment to each other. Rentia loved the diamond ring, her family loved Trevor, and he loved them. After the visit, they were more determined than ever to see the wedding take place. But still no visa arrived.

Toward the end of the year, Trevor and Rentia set a date late in February. They thought that surely by then she would have her visa. January passed; February came and went, but no visa. My husband and I made plans to fly with Trevor to South Africa for the wedding. Trevor and Rentia resigned themselves to the possibility that he might have to return to America without his bride until the visa department took action. They did not even buy a plane ticket for Rentia. But I kept praying for a miracle. I could not believe after all this young couple had gone through that Trevor would have to come home alone.

In desperation, just before we left the country, my husband suggested that Trevor call a senator who is an old friend of ours, and his office had been helpful in the early stages of the process. When Trevor called, the senator's staff could not believe that he and Rentia had waited more than seven months for a visa. They were appalled and even suggested they might introduce legislation to prevent these kinds of delays. They proceeded to write a letter to the South African embassy to see what the problem was.

The day before the wedding was to take place, Rentia got a call from the embassy. They said they had gotten a letter from the United States Congress and that they had to "bring this situation to a close." Though Rentia's wedding day was planned out to the minute, the officials insisted she come to Johannesburg the next morning for the final interview for her visa. This meant four hours just driving. But she knew she had to do it, and she agreed.

Bright and early the morning of her wedding day, Rentia, her father, and my husband went to Johannesburg. I stayed home with Rentia's mom and we prayed. And finally, at the very last minute, the visa was granted. We were so thankful!

Then we faced the fact that we had no plane ticket for Rentia's return to America after the honeymoon. The couple's resources were gone, and they knew a ticket bought at that late date would be terribly expensive. So we began to pray again. After we had exhausted all our ideas, Rentia's cousin found a student fare for five hundred dollars! Rentia even was able to get a reservation on the same flight as Trevor.

Two weeks later, after a fabulous honeymoon in Cape Town (a gift from the bride's aunt and uncle), the couple came home to a joyous welcome from Trevor's "old" parents and Rentia's new ones. They were married in this country soon afterward, and we gave them a beautiful reception for friends and family who had missed the first wedding.

I have often heard that anything you get for free, you don't really appreciate. But if something is gained through much adversity and hardship, it is not only appreciated, but treasured. Perhaps this is why Trevor and Rentia are so happy, even though they live the simple, frugal lives of newlyweds in a small apartment. It is a joy to see them together. They revel in each other's company.

I chuckle when I see how totally devoted my son is to Rentia—not bad for someone who was not "good marriage material."

SHIRLEY ROSE

LASTING LOVE

So we grew together,
Like to a double cherry, seeming parted,
But yet an union in parturition;
Two lovely berries molded on one stem.

WILLIAM SHAKESPEARE

The courting rituals of the young Billy Graham were not convention-ally romantic, to say the least. Instead of sending twenty-year-old Ruth Bell bouquets of roses, he brought her bottles of vitamin pills. Instead of taking her dancing under the stars, he insisted that she do jumping jacks and toe-touches. The Wheaton College Bible student, who had skipped a semester due to fatigue, was more than flattered. "When I came back from our first date," Ruth, now seventy-five, recalled, "I remember telling the Lord, 'If you let me spend my life with that man, it would be the greatest privilege I could think of.'"

Her prayers were answered. In Montreat Presbyterian Church in North Carolina, on August 13, 1943, the daughter of missionaries wed the twenty-four-year-old Baptist pastor she had met at Wheaton. The next morning, Ruth awoke to find her new husband asleep on the floor. "Daddy thought the bed was too soft or something," says their daughter Gigi Tchividjian-Graham, fifty, "but Mom was devastated." Over the next five decades, Ruth would spend many more nights alone in bed, often sleeping with her husband's tweed jacket, while Rev. Billy Graham, now seventy-seven, took his spiritual message around the world.

After the wedding, the couple started a ministry in the town of Western Springs outside Chicago. They were so poor that a piece of red satin over a lightbulb served as a fireplace. As Graham's fame and mission grew, so did his travel schedule, leaving Ruth mostly alone to raise their five children. "I'd rather have a little of Bill than a lot of any other man," she said.

Intent upon making a home for her husband, Ruth built a log house on 150 wooded acres in Montreat in 1954. Graham returned there to his wife and family after each crusade. "Every time they got back together, it was like a honeymoon," says Gigi. "They shared a lot of physical love. That was very reassuring to me." Their commitment was apparent to everyone. "He would stand up whenever she came in the room," says Graham biographer William Martin, adding that a sixty-nine-year-old Graham told him, "You know, we're still lovers." Today their intimacy has been hindered by the complications of old age. He is fighting Parkinson's disease; she, a chronic lower-back problem. They spend their time at home, in twin armchairs, in front of a real fireplace. "They don't like to be separated by a lot of miles," says Gigi. "They just like knowing the other one's right there."

"What you're looking at is one person with two heads," says their friend, singer Pat Boone, of the Grahams. "They share commitment."

LOVE STORY

Two souls with but a single thought,
Two hearts that beat as one.

FREDRICH HALM

I grew up in New Orleans, Louisiana. Jerry and his family loved New Orleans. They vacationed there often. And Jerry had almost married a girl from my church. They had dated for years, but finally Jerry realized that he just wasn't ready for marriage. He ended the relationship, much to her disappointment. His mother was also very disappointed.

People in his family were beginning to think Jerry would be a bachelor forever; there were several men in the family who had never married. And, after all, he was twenty-six. That was old to be unmarried in 1967.

Even after ending the relationship with Jackette, he remained friendly with her family and still loved New Orleans. He belonged to the U.S. Coast Guard Reserve at the time and requested his two weeks active duty in New Orleans. When he was granted this request, he immediately called the sister and brother-in-law of his old girlfriend to let them know he would be in New Orleans for two weeks. In fact, he would come in a few days early if they would fix him up with a date. This couple led the youth group in my church. So they asked me if I would like to go out with this guy.

Like everyone else, I didn't really get excited about blind dates, and I told them as much. But they assured me that this guy was different. He had almost become a part of their family. He was very nice, from a great family, a Christian, and cute. "And," they told me, "he can always relocate if anything should come of this."

I agreed to go out with him. We double-dated with our mutual friends. They drove Jerry up to my house, but he did not come to the door.

There was a Beware of Dog sign on the gate. So Jerry stood in the street yelling for me. I was not used to being treated this way, especially on a first date. I finally walked out on the porch and asked why he wasn't coming in. He said it was because of the sign. About that time, my tiny Chihuahua ran out barking. The friends in the car were in hysterics and my mom and I thought it was pretty funny, too. Jerry was the only one not laughing. That was our first meeting.

I did not think he was terribly good looking, but he did have pretty blue eyes, and I liked him from the start. He asked me out the next night. We were going to a Mardi Gras parade. When he picked me up, I was wearing a beret. It was cold for New Orleans in February. Besides, I thought I looked very chic. He asked me why I was wearing the hat. I said to keep me warm. Then he said, "Well, let's do something inside, then." I countered with, "Well, my hair looks a mess now." He said, "Take it off and let me see." I did, and he assured me I looked better without the beret. What a feisty Texan he was! I did not wear the hat, but he has often said that if he knew me then like he does now, he would never have asked. It was the first and last argument he ever won.

After those first two dates, we were both smitten. He began his Coast Guard duty and did not have leave every evening. But the evenings he was off, we were together. My church had a Valentine's banquet during that week, and I asked him to come with me. He, unfortunately, had duty that night. So I went alone. When I walked into the church, Jerry stepped from behind the door and surprised me. I couldn't have been more thrilled if it had been Harrison Ford standing there. He told the amusing story of how he was able to get leave.

He asked his CEO if he could get off. The officer asked what was so important. He sheepishly said he wanted to go to a Valentine's banquet with a girl. (This guy had guts, you must admit.) Much to his surprise, the officer grinned and said, "Well, if you are crazy enough to ask, I am just crazy enough to say Yes."

That night was very significant in our lives. Jerry shared his dreams and his calling into Christian television with me. We bared our hearts as if we had always known each other and we became forever connected. That night, Valentine's Day, 1967, we fell in love. We had only had a few dates, but we both knew we were meant to be together. We were married six months later.

That was thirty-two years ago, and today I think he is very handsome. He was much too skinny back then. And he still has those incredible blue eyes. Nowadays, I feel fortunate to be able to visit New Orleans once or twice a year. Guess who relocated!

SHIRLEY ROSE

*To get the full value of joy,
you must have someone to divide it with.*
MARK TWAIN

For Better, for Worse

Fair or foul—on land or sea—
Come the wind or weather,
Best or worst, whate'er they be,
We shall share together.

WINTHROP MACKWORTH PRAED

MARRIAGE, LIKE LIFE—EVEN A LIFE SUBMITTED TO THE WILL OF THE HEAVENLY FATHER—CARRIES NO GUARANTEES.

MARRIAGE, LIKE LIFE, BRINGS UNEXPECTED AND UNPREDICTABLE EVENTS.

WE ALL GROW AND CHANGE EVEN AFTER WE SAY, "I DO."

CHANGE USUALLY ISN'T EASY, NOR IS IT WELCOMED. CHANGE DOESN'T NECESSARILY BRING OUT THE BEST IN PEOPLE; SOMETIMES IT BRINGS OUT THE WORST, IF ONLY FOR A SEASON. BUT EVEN CHANGE FOR THE WORSE CAN MAKE YOU BETTER—IF YOU ALLOW IT.

WHEN YOU PROMISE "FOR BETTER OR FOR WORSE," YOU ARE ANTICIPATING THE FACT THAT CHANGE WILL COME. IT MAY APPEAR IN MANY DIFFERENT SHAPES AND SIZES AND TEXTURES. YOU ALLOW FOR THAT. YOU SAY TO YOUR

SPOUSE, "WHATEVER COMES, I WILL STAND BY YOU, SUPPORT YOU, AND OFFER YOU ANY ASSISTANCE I CAN TO HELP YOU THROUGH THIS JOURNEY CALLED LIFE. I WILL BE WITH YOU IN YOUR GOOD TIMES AND IN YOUR TOUGH TIMES, TOO. NO MATTER WHAT, I'LL BE THERE FOR YOU."

THERE ARE NO GUARANTEES. BUT THE MOST IMPORTANT WORD TO DESCRIBE THE JOURNEY THROUGH LIFE TOGETHER IS THE WORD THROUGH. YOU CAN'T FLOAT ABOVE CHANGES. YOU CAN'T FLY AWAY FROM DANGERS. YOU DARE NOT GO AROUND THE THINGS YOU DO NOT LIKE. JUST PREPARE TO GO THROUGH THE WORST. YOU WILL FIND THAT IS THE WAY TO DISCOVER WHAT BETTER REALLY MEANS.

WRAPPED IN FORGIVENESS

❦

Nobody has ever measured,
even the poets,
how much a heart can hold.

ZELDA FITZGERALD

The home where my brother, Bob, and I grew up was filled with all the acts of rebellion and destruction: drinking, cursing, smoking, and parties. Our father was often involved in petty thievery and our mother, who worked at the local diner as a waitress, we suspected of having a drug habit. In spite of this we managed to survive. There was always enough to eat and we had clean clothes and a warm place to sleep.

Bob chose to rise above his circumstances and got involved in a youth group at our church. Our parents teased him unmercifully and I called him several choice names myself: *Jesus Freak, Mr. Clean, Bible Thumper.* The people at Bob's church took good care of him and helped him go to a Christian college when he graduated.

I was too cool to go to church. I figured, *If you can't lick 'em…join 'em.* By high school I was a drinker, a drug user, and a drug dealer. I spent some time in jail.

It was during my senior year in high school that Bob rescued me from the gutter and took me to his church. I was so low that I was ready to find God. With the help of the church members I turned my life around. I entered a treatment program and found a good job.

I soon met a lovely Christian girl, Donna, at church and she became my wife. She didn't care about my past and neither did her family. They were very forgiving people who admired me for making something out my life. Donna loved me for who I had become. I was a blessed man.

After a couple of years of marriage, I received a promotion at my job and began to go to night school. My life with Donna was going along beautifully. We were soon able to afford a little home with a picket fence in a nice neighborhood and then had our first child. Donna was the best wife a man could have. She was very good with money, could turn hamburger into a feast, and transformed our little cottage into a castle with her creativity.

Shortly after our second child was born, our dream life slowly unraveled into a nightmare. I was laid off at my job and because of my criminal record, I was unable to find employment. Everyone at church tried to help, but our lives began to fall to pieces. Donna was forced to take a secretarial job. At home alone, I began drinking again.

Donna insisted I get help but I wouldn't listen. She finally enlisted the help of our pastor and my brother, but I refused to give up drinking and even started taking drugs again.

"I love you," Donna tearfully admitted, "but it's the drugs or me."

I was shocked but because of my pride, I walked away, leaving my beautiful wife and children behind.

Initially I enjoyed being on my own without responsibility and anyone around to make me feel guilty. When I called home occasionally, Donna always said, "I love you, Ted, and you're welcome to come home when you stop drinking."

I always laughed and hung up. My brother and several men from the church tried to talk to me but I didn't want help; I wanted to be left alone.

After six months of isolation and unemployment, and in great need of cash, I got involved in a major drug deal. Right after the buyer handed me the money, he pulled out a pair of handcuffs. He was an undercover cop.

Because of my previous record and the seriousness of the crime, I was sent to a federal penitentiary in another state. I had brought such disgrace to our little family that when Donna wrote me with news and pictures of our children, I expected that she would soon ask for a divorce.

Life in prison looked pretty hopeless. Like so many other men there I feared I was losing my family. "It won't be long until the letters will stop coming," my cellmate warned me. I cried myself to sleep that night.

Bob wrote to me and insisted that I get involved with the prison fellowship. Once again it was men of faith who helped me turn my life around. The next few years in prison, the men in prison fellowship even helped me finish my college degree.

I kept in touch with Donna to let her know about the changes I was making in my life. I wrote that I knew God had forgiven me and I prayed that she would also. Her letters came frequently and were friendly, but she never made any mention of us—she just said that she was proud of me for turning my life around. When I asked if we had any hope of putting our lives back together, she wrote that we would have to wait and see.

Because the prison was such a great distance from our home, Donna was able to bring the children to see me only one time, when our church took up a collection. I was even more depressed when they left. Donna had appeared warm and loving, but she refused to talk about our future. I also felt ashamed that my young children had seen me behind bars.

I was amazed at how Donna held our home together. As a single mother, she did it all: worked, maintained the house and yard, cooked all the meals, and attended to the children. I told her in a letter how much I appreciated her and how sorry I was to have placed such a heavy burden on her shoulders.

When I was paroled, I wrote to Donna to tell her I was coming to see the children. I desperately wanted to know if she would take me back. Remembering a famous song, I wrote, "If there is any hope for the two of us to put our lives back together again, please tie a yellow ribbon around the tree in the front yard."

Bob picked me up at the bus station to drive me over to our house. As we turned into our street, I told Bob I couldn't look. I shut my eyes and covered them with my hands. I asked Bob if would he look for me. Then the car came to a stop. Bob was silent.

"Bob," I insisted, "tell me!"

Hardly able to speak, my brother whispered, "Open your eyes, little brother. You've got to see this."

Donna had wrapped our entire house in a giant yellow ribbon with a great big bow, and she and the children were waiting with open arms at the front door.

When I walked through that door of forgiveness, all the rebellion of my past melted away. I knew that my life would never be the same—and it wasn't.

AS TOLD TO SUSAN WALES

I wish I could remember the first day,
First hour, first moment of your meeting me;
If bright or dim the season, it might be
Summer or winter for aught I can say.
So unrecorded did it slip away,
So blind was I to see and to foresee,
So dull to mark the budding of my tree
That would not blossom yet for many a May.
If only I could recollect it! Such
A day of days! I let it come and go
As traceless as a thaw of bygone snow.
It seemed to mean so little, meant so much!
If only now I could recall that touch,
First touch of hand in hand! Did one but know!

CHRISTINA ROSSETTI

AN EMPTY PLACE

Where we love is home
Home that our feet may leave
But not our hearts.
OLIVER WENDELL HOLMES

Helen always thought that when Harry left her, it would be in a pine box. Instead he departed in a late-model Porsche with a late-model product manager in his company.

For a year Helen's moods rode from happy high (when anyone told her that Harry was miserable with the new woman) to desperate low (when Harry called about speeding up the divorce so that he might be free to marry again).

It was the advice of her attorney to remain unemployed ("You get a good job, and it will affect your settlement") that left Helen so much time and so little activity.

Her married friends were busy choosing up sides, and it seemed to her that they were all on Harry's side. Well, why not? He had the social life, and she had—what did she have? She had a bitter lump where there used to be a heart. She had an empty place at the table, an empty place in her bed, and as she looked around there was no way to fill the empty places.

Her married daughter and her son, who was in law school, were not much help. "Get out, Mom," they both said when they called. What did they expect her to do? Hang out in bars? Invite men to take her out? How did they think a woman who still considered herself married could go out and look for the next man? Why wasn't it easy for women the way it was for men? Why couldn't a woman just meet a younger man and take up with him the way men did with younger women? Didn't anyone understand that men between the ages of fifty and sixty were not out looking for women the same age?

And then one day Helen picked up a magazine, and there at the back in the Personals section was a series of ads she'd always glanced at but never read. Here were ads from single white males (conveniently shortened to "SWM") looking for women. Of course, for every ad from a man there were thirteen or fourteen from women. Still...

The one that caught her eye read, "California man wants to meet sophisticated New York woman 25–34 who knows books, theater, fine dining. Object: fun. Photo a must." There was a box number for replies.

In the era of AIDS and herpes, in the world of gay men and bisexuals, in the swamp out there that awaited newly single women, could Helen afford to risk answering?

On second thought, she counseled herself, what did she have to lose? You couldn't get AIDS in the mail, and besides she wasn't 25–34. So, once he saw her, all would be lost anyway.

Helen went through her box of old pictures. Here was one from 1957 in a bathing suit. She could send that. Of course, in that picture she had long hair. Now her hair was short. Maybe she could get a fall....

For three days she looked through old pictures, and just as she was ready to call a photographer, a letter came from her daughter. Inside were four sweet pictures of Helen with her two-year-old granddaughter Mavis.

Why not? she thought.

Helen went right to her desk and answered the man in California. She wrote:

Dear California Man,

If you want a truly sophisticated New York woman, please be advised that I know theater from the plays of Shakespeare to the musicals of Sondheim. I know restaurants from Soho to Harlem, and I know books from the Bible to this week's bestsellers.

So why am I writing to you?

Because despite the fact that I'm loving, blond, and thin, despite the fact that I'm articulate and supportive, I couldn't hold on to my husband of thirty years.

There must be something wrong with me, and I want to know what it is.

You want a woman 25–34. My instincts tell me that only a man over fifty would want a woman 25–34. Well, I'm not 25–34. I am 25 plus 34. I am 59. Further, I am a grandmother.

Proof is this enclosed picture. The little girl is my granddaughter.

If all of this does not horrify you, please respond, and let's see if we can help one another.

I'll show you the New York you want to see, and you can show me where I went wrong after thirty years.

You see, I lost my husband to a woman 25–34 who doesn't know what I know. But she does know one thing I don't know. She knows how to get my husband and keep him.

The answer came back the following week.

A message was left on Helen's answering machine. "Helen," the voice said, "until I read that letter, I didn't know what a dummy I'd really been. I'm the California man from the ad. I guess you know by now it's me, Harry. I'm ready to come back home. You see, you're wrong. That woman knew how to get me, but she couldn't keep me. I'm so tired of explaining who Keats is, and I'm tired of hearing that anyone who lived through World War II must be in a retirement home. I think fifty-nine is a wonderful age to begin again. Besides, that picture really tore me apart. After all, I'm that little girl's grandfather."

THE CRUCIAL
INGREDIENT

*Life in common among people who
love each other is the ideal of happiness.*

GEORGE SAND

s a writer, a dispenser of information and opinion, if not wisdom, I could never subscribe to the "ignorance is bliss" theory. We need to know things. Knowledge is good—very good. However, as far as marriage is concerned, as good as it is, knowledge is not the crucial ingredient. Commitment trumps knowledge every time. Without commitment, the knowledge necessary to make a marriage work is unattainable. Knowledge and commitment are certainly not mutually exclusive: In the best of marriages, commitment leads to knowledge. Commitment must be the foundation, however.

When Marty and I got married, we knew *nothing*. No one told us anything. There was no premarital counseling, "Engagement Encounter," or "Marriage Encounter." Marriage seminars, books, and video series were still in the distant future. We didn't know such things existed, because they didn't. In our day, after you finished college, you got married. That was the thing to do. No one told you how to do marriage; you were expected to learn on the job.

Certainly, no one told *me*. Even if people in the know had planned to teach me about marriage, they couldn't. They were too dumbstruck. Here was a crude, academically challenged basketball player from Texas about to marry an urbane, straight-A homecoming queen from Pennsylvania. All they could do was to shake their heads in awe and roll their eyes heavenward in amazement. Knowledgeable people would have issued stern warnings against this unlikely match.

Even though Marty's father was a minister and had married many couples from his parish, he did not give her any premarital counseling. All her family and friends did was to ask her over and over again, "Are you *sure* you want to do this? Are you really sure?" Certainly, we never had counseling together.

So, we got married. We did it without a course, a video series, or even a book. We just got married. Almost all our friends and classmates did the same thing in the same way.

Well, let me tell you, ignorance did not produce bliss. Marriage was hard. Learning while doing was hard. We made it only because commitment prevailed. Commitment overcame ignorance and was the glue that helped us stick together. As we learned, often the hard way, it slowly got better and better. Now, it is so good we can hardly stand it. Knowledge *and* commitment have produced a sort of bliss better described as joy. Without the commitment, we would never have lasted long enough to learn anything. Commitment always trumps knowledge.

As far as I know, all our friends and classmates did it the same way we did—just got married and learned how to be married as they went. The strange thing is that divorce has been so uncommon among this group that it is statistically inconsequential. None of us knew what we were doing. We had not been counseled, taught, or tested. The wedding vows themselves were our basic instructions: *To have and to hold from this day forward, for better for worse, for richer, for poorer, in sickness and in health, to love, to honor and to cherish, forsaking all others until death do us part.* Marty and I have the blessing of living near many couples who went to school together and married in abject ignorance just like we did. We see them on almost a daily basis. It is a joy to report that these marriages have not only endured for forty years or more, they have triumphed. They are beautiful to see, wonderful to revel in as only friends of long standing can do.

These days it is so different. Young people have access to so much marriage information. Experts teach, tutor, and test them, yet so many of their marriages end tragically in divorce. They have the knowledge. The missing ingredient is commitment, and, in marriage, commitment trumps knowledge every time.

Thanks be to God for teaching us commitment, which led to knowledge, which produced a lifetime of joy!

BOB BRINER

Editor's note: Popular author Bob Briner wrote this to honor his bride, Marty, and their long marriage before succumbing to cancer earlier this year.

PERFECT LOVE

✍

*The supreme happiness of life
is the conviction that we are loved.*

VICTOR HUGO

I have always faced partings from loved ones with pain and fear, probably because I have experienced so many of them. My mother died when I was only thirteen months old. My father and I went to live with his mother, who raised me with a lot of love and nurturing. Twelve years later, my grandmother died and her death devastated me. That's when I started to become introverted and fearful.

Then my father remarried and I went to live with his new family. It was a difficult transition. I never felt accepted and the loneliness was chilling. I cried a lot. I remember vividly the melancholy that rose in me when I'd stare out the window at night. I felt like there was a giant piece missing from my heart. I didn't understand my emotions and neither did my father, which created distance between us. Throughout my growing-up years I missed our closeness and the feeling we'd once had as family.

Once an adult, I met Andrew quite by accident one day through a mutual business acquaintance. Our connection was immediate. I wanted to know as much as possible about Andrew, and as quickly as possible. Our first date was two weeks later and we both knew quickly that there was something special between us.

At the same time, Andrew was building his business five hundred miles away from home. He was gone eleven days out of fourteen and it was a real test for us. We both knew that our relationship, even in its fledgling days, was well worth the effort, but it was still hard. When Andrew was in town, his time was split between me, his two sons, and my young son. Some weekends were incredibly wonderful and others—well, others were harried, confused, and chaotic.

At the end of the weekend, when it was time for Andrew to return to the business world, I experienced terrible depression. I loved him so much and it hurt so deeply that he couldn't stay.

All the old pain I associated with people leaving resurfaced. Every Sunday I feared that Andrew would never return. I expected, deep down, that like my mother and grandmother, he'd eventually leave me altogether.

Even as I struggled with these feelings, I knew this was no way to begin a relationship. I was driving myself crazy fearing the future and distressing Andrew even more in the present. I desperately wanted to come to terms with my emotions. Throughout my life I had heard, "You shall know the truth, and the truth will set you free." I knew that discovering and embracing the truth would be an important key to unlocking my closet of fears.

Then a wise minister told me that I was experiencing an "orphan issue." Now I had a name for my feelings. Every time Andrew left, I felt like an orphan—like all my security and hope left with him. When I was finally able to identify what was going on inside me, I was able to do something about it. With a pastor's help, I applied the truth of God's love to my life and learned to accept the truth of Andrew's love and commitment as well. Meanwhile Andrew and I prayed for guidance and patience and asked God to bless our relationship with strength and courage.

By releasing my past, I opened my heart to my future. The change, which occurred over time and with much prayer, was miraculous. Andrew and I married and God gave us great happiness. The person I am today is the person I always wanted to be: confident, secure, and full of faith in God and in my husband.

The Bible says that "perfect love drives out fear" (1 John 4:18). God's perfect love certainly did that for me.

AS TOLD TO ANN PLATZ

A NEW LOVE

God is our refuge and strength,
a very present help in trouble.

PSALM 46:1 (KJV)

The memories of my childhood are deeply riddled with insecurities, fear, and pain. Following the death of my alcoholic father, my mother found herself in ill health with few resources to care for her children and herself. Unable to work, Mother had to rely on family members. My brother, sister, and I were shuttled from one relative's home to the next. I often felt abandoned and grew terrified of being left all alone with no one to care for me.

One day I overhead my aunts and uncles speaking quietly behind closed doors in the next room. "What shall become of the children?" one relative wondered. Someone else mentioned sending Mother away to a hospital. Another spoke up and suggested, "Perhaps an orphanage will take the children."

Fear gripped my heart. I had no one and nowhere to turn. I could not possibly burden my sick mother. Then I remembered my heavenly Father—the one we had learned about from Mother and at Sunday school. Perhaps he would help me. "Dear God," I begged, "please don't let them take my mother away!'

God miraculously touched my life at this early age. The next night I knew that God had heard my prayers when I heard my mother speaking the words of the Twenty-third Psalm. Again I prayed to God and thanked him because I knew without a doubt that he was beginning to heal my mother. And he did. We survived those difficult circumstances, and along the way, God met our every need.

By the time I became an adult, I had slowly drifted away from God. At twenty-one, I met a divorced man ten years my senior who did not share my faith. I had read the Scripture, "Do not be unequally yoked," but hardly gave it a second thought. Blindly, I just breathed a sigh of relief that I would no longer be lonely and would have someone to care for me for the rest of my life. We were married, but we divorced after only three and a half years. Yet even in our failure, God blessed the marriage with our beautiful daughter, Stephanie.

Again, I was lonely and rejected, this time with a young daughter of my own to care for. Those old childhood fears began to resurface. In the years that separated me from that scared little girl listening outside the closed door, I had forgotten the power of prayer and God's love. Remembering how God had come to my rescue, I became determined to find him again. He was closer than I thought possible.

God's healing touched my life, and six months later, I met and fell in love with Bob, who exhibited all the traits I so desired in a husband. We were married soon after. I knew that the Lord had sent this wonderful man who encouraged me in all areas of my life, from family to business. It was Bob who suggested that I enter the real estate field, where I quickly became a success. Soon we were blessed with our daughter Susan, and I felt sure God had answered all of my prayers.

A few years into our marriage, again, things became rocky. Bob and I were moving in separate directions. I had become wrapped up in my career and Bob was working ninety miles away. We were becoming emotionally as well as physically distant. I felt that old emptiness forming in my heart and I panicked. Success and money weren't the answer. I didn't want to be alone and without love. I felt like that little girl again—scared, anxious, afraid to be alone, and uncertain about which way to turn.

Even with all my successes, I hadn't managed to find the balance and stability that I had always longed for. Then it hit me. I wasn't paying attention to God's will or to his presence. I wasn't being the wife that God had called me to be. As I sat in my chair, I suddenly noticed the light shining through the bay window: streams of light—a beacon to show me which way to turn. Before I realized it I was on my knees praying, drawing close to God once again.

The first thing I asked God to do for me was to give me a new love and a new heart for my husband. I knew I still loved him and that he still loved me, but I just needed to find that love again. God did just that. I felt waves of love wash over me. I felt rejuvenated and peaceful. I began to realize what a gift my husband was and that gift had come straight from God.

Although I had grown close to God in the past, I hadn't fully surrendered. Turning over my life and heart to God's will was the greatest decision I ever made. He drew my husband to him. Together, we discovered a deeper and greater love than either of us had ever known or thought possible. Our daughters benefited from our love and faith. Today both they and their families love and serve the Lord.

In addition, Bob and I decided to become partners in business as well as marriage. With God's blessings and Bob's support and expertise, the company has grown and flourished to become one of the top real estate offices in the country.

Bob and I grew as a couple in God's grace, and that has made all the difference in the world. We face the joys and sorrows of our life together. After years of pain, God washed it all away and replaced it instead with peace, comfort, happiness, and most importantly, a newfound love for God, for life, and for my beloved husband.

JENNY AND BOB PRUITT

PRINCE CHARMING
FELL OFF HIS HORSE

Child of the pure, unclouded brow
And dreaming eyes of wonder!
Though time be fleet and I and thou
Are half a life asunder,
Thy loving smile will surely hail
The love-gift of a fairy tale.

LEWIS CARROLL

That fateful day in May, I was fifteen years old and working in the local root beer stand. It was a hangout for some of the cool kids in the area. It had everything I could want: pinball machines, a jukebox, hamburgers, friends, malts, and lots of guys to flirt with. That early summer day a guy came roaring up on a motorcycle, wearing the requisite black leather jacket and sideburns. I recognized him as Jerry Schreur, age nineteen, the most notorious guy in town, and suddenly I knew he was the guy I'd been waiting for: Prince Charming on a Triumph.

On our first real date we put the top down in his Pontiac convertible and went riding around the Ottawa Beach State Park on Lake Michigan. After that weekend, I never dated another person. I lived for Jerry Schreur. He seemed to be the answer to all my needs. Being his girlfriend gave me an enormous sense of power.

Needless to say, my mother was not thrilled that her daughter was dating the town criminal. People either loved Jerry or hated him. They felt either very safe with him or completely threatened. Jerry was easily the most exciting man in town, and I was dating him!

But that wasn't enough. In my dream the princess always married Prince Charming. In my fairy tale Jerry drove up, I jumped behind him on the bike, and we rode off into the sunset. I didn't worry about what happened after that—I would simply be with him all the time and he would never let me go. "Happily ever after" would take care of itself.

Sure enough, the prince and princess married on February 28, 1964. I was eighteen and pregnant and my groom was twenty-two, a convicted felon who had been out of work for several months. We had no money for a honeymoon and lots of debt, but I was still excited. We moved into our castle—a drafty, old, one-bedroom house in the middle of a field—and I waited for the perfect life to begin.

Two years later, I was pretty convinced I had picked the wrong leading man. I had two baby boys and a husband whose mysterious silence—which I had once found so intriguing—now drove me to distraction. I needed someone to talk to. No fairy tale had prepared me for the isolation, not to mention overtime at the factory, two crying babies, no money, and a house that was falling part. I was twenty, disillusioned, and disappointed. And I didn't see any way out.

Skip to three decades later. The prince and the princess are, surprisingly, still together, and a happy ending is actually within reach. How? In a word, God. God has washed our marriage in his grace and mercy. Without an everyday grace that enables us to forgive and love each other, I know I would have quit a long time ago.

Looking back, we never should have made it. We got married for the wrong reasons: need, anger, pain, difficulty, lust, and yes, even love. We had very little faith in God or each other. I went into marriage looking for someone to take my dead father's place, cherishing me and telling me I was valuable. I married a man who expected me to take care of myself and wasn't very good at expressing his feelings. Anyone could have predicted the problems that lay ahead.

No one could have predicted how God would save us, though. The first thing we had to do was let go of the fairy tale. You can't fix a fairy tale—it doesn't really exist. And you can't fix reality—until you face it. When I found myself questioning my marriage and my choice of mate, I finally looked at both for what they were. It was only a first step, but it was an essential one.

The next step was finding something that could hold us together, and we did. We found Jesus. A friend introduced us to God's love and revealed that he had a plan for our lives. By then I was ready to exchange my script for God's—anyone's plan had to be better than mine! Jerry and I worked on forgiveness, and when we couldn't do that, we worked on prayer.

While Jerry and I struggled to learn to commit and communicate, I found myself daily strengthening my relationship with Jesus. And inherent in that relationship was obedience, which meant I would stick to the vows I'd taken that giddy day with Jerry. In his hunger for answers, Jerry followed a similar path. In obedience we both found freedom because we were doing what God wanted us to do. And in freedom we found love.

Was it worth it? Yes, for we have discovered that God can make a glue no one can dissolve. Today Jerry and I are partners who have created a life that brings us no small measure of joy and even delight. Jerry and I left the fairy tale behind a long time ago. But we believe that it is possible to keep the "happily" in "ever after." My Prince Charming got back on his horse—his convertible—and we still drive around Ottawa Beach. Only now Jerry's sideburns are gray; proving our marriage has stood the test of time.

JUDY SCHREUR

Editor's note: Jerry Schreur, Ph.D., is a minister and counselor in Grand Rapids where he and his wife Judy, a humorist and healthcare professional, are popular writers and speakers.

FINDING PEACE
AT HOME

One word frees us all
From the weight and pain of life:
That word is love.

SOPHOCLES

One of my best gifts to Rosalynn was to resolve a recurring argument. I was very busy at the time, putting the final touches on a book. I went into my study early one morning, turned on my computer, and hit a button that automatically put the date on the screen. There it was: August 18, her birthday, and I hadn't gotten her a present! Rosalynn was still in bed. So I started wondering what I could give her that I didn't have to go down to my cousin Hugh's antiques store to buy. In desperation, I tried to analyze the things that caused trouble in our marriage—in addition to my forgetting anniversaries and birthdays.

One of the things that had created a problem for us for thirty-five years or more was punctuality. I was affected by my training in the navy and, I think, inherited the trait from my father. Whether to meet a train, to attend a baseball game, or to keep an appointment, he was always there long ahead of time. If someone kept him waiting, he had no patience. He would stalk out of a doctor's office if his appointment was delayed for more than ten minutes. Unfortunately, I, too, am uncomfortable if someone keeps me waiting and if I'm late and inconvenience someone else, I get even more uptight. To the surprise of my campaign workers and some audiences, I even kept to a strict schedule during my political campaigns, in the governor's office, and in the White House.

And so Rosalynn and I had a lot of arguments about being on time. She always claimed that she was never late, and this would be true if judged by the standards of a reasonable person. What should two or three minutes matter between a husband and wife preparing to go to a movie or a party? But I was not reasonable, holding Rosalynn to a standard of absolute precision. Even before our appointed time for departure, I would remind her of the need to leave and would often produce at least a dirty look if I had to wait at the door.

So, reflecting on all this on that morning of her birthday, I wrote a note to her: "Rosalynn, I promise you that for the rest of our marriage, I will never make an unfavorable remark about tardiness." I signed it and gave it to her for a present. So far I've pretty well kept my promise, and she still agrees that it was the best birthday present I ever gave her.

PRESIDENT JIMMY CARTER

For Richer, for Poorer

*Man's greatest riches is
to live on a little with contented mind;
for little is never lacking.*

LUCRETIUS

IT'S AN OLD SAYING, BUT TRUE: MONEY CAN'T BUY HAPPINESS.

THAT'S CERTAINLY THE CASE IN A MARRIAGE RELATIONSHIP. IT'S NOT HARD TO FIND WEALTHY PEOPLE—SOME EXTREMELY SO—WHO ARE ALSO EXTREMELY UNHAPPY IN MARRIAGE. OTHER COUPLES HAVE ALMOST NOTHING, YET ARE BLISSFULLY CONTENT WITH EACH OTHER AND THE WORLD. WHETHER YOU HAVE LITTLE OR MUCH, IT'S HOW MUCH YOU APPRECIATE THE THINGS YOU HAVE AND THE LOVE YOU SHARE, NOT HOW MANY THINGS YOU HAVE TO APPRECIATE OR LOVE, THAT MAKES THE DIFFERENCE.

THE SECRET IS GRATITUDE.

WHEN YOU TAKE TO HEART THE WORDS FOR RICHER, FOR POORER IN YOUR WEDDING VOWS, YOU ARE REALIZING THE KEY TO A SUCCESSFUL MARRIAGE IS COMMITMENT TO GOD FIRST, AND THEN TO EACH OTHER. THEN, WHATEVER COMES—

POVERTY OR WEALTH—YOU CAN HANDLE THE STRESS THAT GOES ALONG WITH IT. YOU WILL BE TIED INTO THE ATTITUDE OF GRATITUDE. PRAISE AND THANKSGIVING FLOW FROM THAT, THE MOST FERTILE SOIL FOR LOVE TO GROW.

A MAN AND A WOMAN WHO BELIEVE IN, TRUST IN, AND ARE SUPREMELY THANKFUL FOR ONE ANOTHER AND THEIR LORD ARE TRULY THE RICHEST PEOPLE ON EARTH.

THE UNMATCHED GIFT

*The fragrance always remains
in the hand that gives the rose.*

HEDA BEJAR

I remember Dad going off to speak in a tiny church and coming home ten days later. My mother greeted him warmly and asked how the revival had gone. He was always excited about that subject. Eventually, in moments like this she would get around to asking him about the offering. Women have a way of worrying about things like that.

"How much did they pay you?" she asked.

I can still see my father's face as he smiled and looked at the floor. "Aw..." he stammered. My mother stepped back and looked into his eyes.

"Oh, I get it," she said. "You gave the money away again, didn't you?"

"Myrt," he said. "The pastor there is going through a hard time. His kids are so needy. It just broke my heart. They have holes in their shoes and one of them is going to school on these cold mornings without a coat. I felt I should give the entire fifty dollars to them."

My good mother looked intently at him for a moment and then she smiled, "You know, if God told you to do it, it's okay with me."

Then a few days later the inevitable happened. The Dobsons ran completely out of money. There was no reserve to tide us over. That's when my father gathered us in the bedroom for a time of prayer. I remember that day as though it were yesterday. He prayed first.

"Oh, Lord, you promised that if we would be faithful with you and your people in our good times, then you would not forget us in our times of need. We have tried to be generous with what you have given us, and now we are calling on you for help."

A very impressionable ten-year-old boy named Jimmy was watching and listening very carefully that day. *What will happen?* he wondered. *Did God hear Dad's prayer?*

The next day an unexpected check for one thousand two hundred dollars came for us in the mail. Honestly! That's the way it happened, not just this once but many times. I saw the Lord match my Dad's giving stride for stride. No, God never made us wealthy, but my young faith grew by leaps and bounds. I learned that you cannot outgive God!

My father continued to give generously through the mid-life years and into his sixties. I used to worry about how he and Mom would fund their retirement years because they were able to save very little money. If Dad did get many dollars ahead, he'd give them away. I wondered how in the world they would live on the pittance paid to retired ministers by their denomination. (As a widow, my mother received just eighty dollars and fifty cents per month after Dad spent forty-four years in the church.) It is disgraceful how poorly we take care of our retired ministers and their widows.

One day my father was lying on the bed and Mom was getting dressed. She turned to look at him and he was crying.

"What's the matter?" she asked.

"The Lord just spoke to me," he replied.

"Do you want to tell me about it?" she prodded.

"He told me something about you," Dad said.

She then demanded that he tell her what the Lord had communicated to him.

My father said, "It was a strange experience. I was just lying here thinking about many things. I wasn't praying or even thinking about you when the Lord spoke to me and said, 'I'm going to take care of Myrtle.'"

Neither of them understood the message, but simply filed it away in the catalog of imponderables. But five days later my dad had a massive heart attack, and three months after that he was gone. At sixty-six years of age, this good man whose name I share went out to meet the Christ whom he had loved and served for all those years.

It was thrilling to witness the way God fulfilled His promise to take care of my mother. Even when she was suffering from end-stage Parkinson's disease and required constant care at an astronomical cost, God provided. The small inheritance that Dad left to his wife multiplied in the years after his departure. It was sufficient to pay for everything she needed, including marvelous and loving care. God was with her in every other way, too, tenderly cradling her in His secure arms until He took her home. In the end, my Dad never came close to out-giving God.

DR. JAMES DOBSON

From *Love for a Lifetime*. Used by permission of Multnomah Publishers.

LET'S MAKE BEAUTIFUL MUSIC TOGETHER

☙

O, my luve is like a red, red rose,
That's newly sprung in June.
O, my luve is like a melodie,
That's sweetly played in tune.

ROBERT BURNS

I had just moved from New York to Los Angeles to begin my singing career in film, television, and theater. Like many struggling young performers, I had to find a second job to support myself until I became a star. As a Christian, I believed that singing with a church choir would suit me perfectly. I was also single, and my Southern Baptist mother had often told me that the best place to meet a nice man was at church.

After I landed a theatrical role in *Camelot,* I told everyone I was looking for a soloist position in a church choir. I finally found a suitable position at a Presbyterian church near Pasadena. My first big assignment was to be the soprano soloist for the Christmas program. The church had hired an orchestra for the performance, and we began practicing early in December.

At our dress rehearsal, I personally stopped to thank each orchestra member for a practice session well done. When I stopped to thank one of the cellists, a friend who knew that I wanted to meet some eligible men played matchmaker. "I want to introduce you to the flutist, Bobby Shulgold," he said. "He looks exactly like Bruce Willis."

"Yeah, sure," I replied. "I just ran into Bruce Willis a couple of nights ago, so we'll see about that." When my friend led me over to Bobby, my first reaction was one of utter shock! There stood a very hip young man with long hair and an earring in his ear. "Definitely not my type," I whispered to my friend. "But I have to admit this guy's even cuter than Bruce Willis!" I mumbled, "So much for matchmaking."

As I turned to leave, several members of the orchestra insisted that I join them for coffee across the street. Although I was exhausted from the rehearsal, I could hardly refuse. I felt greatly obliged to show my appreciation for all their long practice sessions and hard work.

When we arrived at the restaurant, Bobby grabbed the seat beside me and began to entertain me with magic tricks. *What talent,* I thought. *He not only plays a flute; he's a magician, too!* Even though I was amused by the magic tricks, I was extremely tired and thought the night would never end.

When the evening finally came to a close, Bobby insisted on walking me to my car, and we exchanged cards. I knew this guy would never be anything but a friend—he was definitely not husband material in my book—so I tried to give him the brush-off as politely as possible.

I had to admit I was flattered the next day when Bobby called, but I was still not interested. When he invited me to his house for dinner and a movie, I began to make up all sorts of excuses. To my surprise, by the time I hung up the phone, he had convinced me to go to the movie with him. I was furious that I had let this gentle man persuade me to go out with him when I had had no intention of doing so.

When the day of our first date arrived, Bobby phoned to tell me that he had been offered a gig. This was a perfectly acceptable excuse to break a date because opportunities for musicians to work are often few and far between. Frankly, I was relieved. Then Bobby took me by surprise when he asked, "Will you come to my performance?"

I hadn't planned on this, but I was backed into a corner. "Of course," I replied weakly. *I'll show him,* I thought. *I'll take a girlfriend along so he'll clearly understand that I'm not the least bit interested in him.* Bobby just was not my type.

When my girlfriend and I arrived, I made her promise not to leave me under any circumstances. "I don't want to lead the poor guy on…he's really a nice guy."

"You have my word," my friend assured me.

As the jazz ensemble began to play, Bobby's talent and good looks began to cast their spell on me. By the end of the performance I could hardly wait for my girlfriend to leave. When Bobby asked the two of us to go to dinner, I shot her a look that could kill. Luckily she caught on.

"Gee," she said, "I'm sorry to disappoint you, but I suddenly remembered that I have a report to prepare for tomorrow." Bobby and I went on to have a great dinner.

On our next date we went to a movie. When Bobby reached for my hand, no one was more surprised than me that my stomach did flip-flops. "This must be love," I happily told myself. I was right about that…before I knew it, we were madly in love. Three years later we decided to marry.

When we counseled with the minister, we discussed with him the fact that we were both musicians without steady paychecks. We were professionals and our services were in demand; even so, as anyone in the entertainment business knows, it can be feast of famine. We considered the true meaning of the wedding vows—for richer, for poorer. We knew we had to support each other in every way and that would mean both of us would have to make significant sacrifices. Bobby had been so excited about our first date, yet he had to break it. He needed to make himself available when called and he had to have an income. We knew that more such times lay ahead of us.

The minister told us that being married changes everything—that something spiritual happens when you become man and wife. Bobby said, "It couldn't possibly change anything for me! I love Renee and couldn't possibly have any stronger feelings for her than I do this very moment!" The minister smiled knowingly.

Our wedding ceremony was beautiful. Each of us was very close to a grandmother, so we exchanged our grandmothers' wedding bands. After we were married and heading toward our honeymoon destination, Bobby held my hand and looked me in the eyes. "You know," he said, "the minister was right—there is something so incredible about marriage. I love being married to you." I cried tears of joy because we both felt such a spiritual bond after our ceremony. It's almost impossible to put into words until you experience it yourself. It was all part of God's perfect plan.

Remember the vow, "for richer, for poorer"? We were tested at the onset. On our wedding night, my talented musician husband was called to do a very important recording job. These opportunities don't occur that often, and I insisted that he take advantage of his big break. Can you believe that we spent our honeymoon night in a recording studio? My understanding and concern for my husband's career and our future really touched Bobby's heart. Although we had a wonderful time in the recording studio that night, I warned Bobby that a girl has to draw the line somewhere. I told him I expected him to be by my side when our first baby arrived. "No career break or any amount of money will tear me away," he promised.

My advice to singles is "Don't judge the book by its cover. The Lord has unexpected plans for us, and his plans are greater than any we could ever concoct for ourselves." My advice to married couples is to support each other as you make beautiful music together and apart.

RENÉE BURKETT SHULGOLD, AS TOLD TO SUSAN WALES

REAL RICHES

❧

For thy sweet love remember'd such wealth brings
That then I scorn to change my state with kings.
But if the while I think on thee, dear friend,
All losses are restor'd and sorrows end.

WILLIAM SHAKESPEARE

In A.D. 1141, the Weinberg Castle in Germany held unimaginable riches: gold, silver, jewels, and treasures of every kind. The residents of the castle lived happily and peaceably for years while enjoying their good fortune.

The day came when the kingdom was threatened. Several of the watchmen came down from the towers to confer with the king and his knights inside the castle. They reported that the castle was surrounded on all sides by a massive enemy army far outnumbering their own. The king met with the knights and they mournfully concurred that the enemy would surely take over the castle, kill its occupants, and confiscate all the riches for their own.

Inside, the men of the castle sadly admitted defeat to their subjects. They not only were aware that the life they enjoyed was about to come to an end, but they would most likely lose their lives as they fought to defend their castle.

The lead of the great army surrounding the castle sent a message to the gate announcing that all the women and children would be released before the battle began. However, the wives of Weinberg sent word back to the enemy leader with their own demand: As they fled the castle, the

opposing army must allow them to carry out their most prized possessions. Aware that the women could only carry so much, the leader agreed
to their terms.

When the drawbridge was lowered and the massive gates were
opened, the attackers were move to tears by the sight before them. Each
woman carried her greatest possession in her arms...her husband.

When the residents were safely at a distance, the army charged the
castle, taking it over and claiming all the riches for their own. The women
of Weinberg shed not one tear over the loss of their fortune because they
had carried with them the only riches that really mattered—the men they
loved.

These women knew the true meaning of riches.

RETOLD BY MEGAN CHRANE

THE GIFT

☙

Love's looking together
in the same direction.
ANTOINE DE SAINTE-EXUPÉRY

Though I haven't been married long, I have already begun to understand why Solomon wrote praises of companionship in Ecclesiastes: "Two are better than one, because they have a good return for their work: If one falls down, his friend can help him up. But pity the man who falls and has no one to help him up!" (Ecclesiastes 4:9–10, NIV) One Christmas brought home the truth of this passage to me and my wife.

Christmas had always been a special time in my family. Each year when I was growing up, my family would drive to the small Georgia town where my grandparents lived. As a young boy, I looked forward to taking baskets of ham, turkey, and pies to the less fortunate families in my grandparents' town. What I remember most about these Christmases are the looks of joy and appreciation on the faces of the families with whom we could share. I am so thankful that my family taught me the true meaning of Christmas and how much greater it is to give than receive.

When I married, I decided I wanted to continue this tradition in some way. My wife, Heather Whitestone, a former Miss America, certainly cared for others as much as I did. Heather, who is deaf, has a real sensitivity to the needs of others.

We spent our first Christmas mostly receiving blessings, though, instead of giving them. We had an opportunity to go to the Holy Land with the pastor and other members of the Fort Lauderdale Baptist Church. It was the adventure of a lifetime that we will always cherish. What better place to celebrate our Savior's birth than his birthplace?

The next Christmas, we planned to return to the Holy Land, but at the last minute a speaking engagement caused us to cancel our plans. Disappointed, we accepted an invitation from Fort Lauderdale Baptist Church to attend their Christmas pageant. While it wasn't the Holy Land, Heather and I were still able to recall the warm memories of our trip from the year before as we joined the pastor and other members of our group at the pageant. It was during the service that the Lord placed it in our hearts to give a special love offering.

We asked the pastor if he would select a couple who could not afford, but would benefit from, this inspirational tour of the Holy Land. He chose a young minister and his wife. Heather and I found ourselves blessed through the cards and letters the young couple sent from the Holy Land. We were able to see and experience our original trip through the eyes and words of the couple. It was as though we were on the trip sharing every precious moment with them. A new tradition of giving, one we would fulfill as a couple, was born.

When the next Christmas arrived, Heather and I asked, "How can we top the blessings and pleasure that we received from our gift of last Christmas?" We had a very busy few months and before we realized it, Christmas was just around the corner. I prayed that God would again reveal to us how to share our blessings. When Christmas morning arrived, I awoke feeling very disappointed with myself. I got down on my knees and prayed, "Forgive me, Lord, for my poor planning. Would you show us someone to bless this Christmas?"

Later that morning, we loaded our car with packages and headed to my grandmother's house. We had just stopped for gas when a car sputtered into the station. I saw the attendant shaking his head. The family's radiator had overheated and the car had broken hoses, but there was no mechanic on duty anywhere on Christmas Day, the station manager sadly explained.

"Is there anything I can do?" I asked the young driver. He explained that he was driving his aunt and uncle and their family to Mississippi to spend Christmas. "But it looks like we won't make it," he said sadly. I wished there was a way I could help, but I knew absolutely nothing about car mechanics.

Back in the car, Heather asked what was happening. When I explained the situation, she said without hesitation, "John, we have two cars in our garage at home! Why don't we lend the family our car?" This had never occurred to me. I was suddenly awed by the power of two—God's purpose for marriage. I had the desire to help someone, but alone I hadn't known how. God used my precious wife to show me.

The family gratefully accepted our offer and celebrated Christmas dinner with their family in Mississippi. When the young driver returned the car, he thanked me profusely for rescuing his family's Christmas.

"Don't thank me," I insisted, "thank God." I then told him about my prayer. I had asked God for someone to help. He looked at me incredulously.

"You were an answer to my prayer, too!" he exclaimed. "I woke up Christmas morning knowing there wasn't any money and that there wouldn't be any presents. When I prayed, I told the Lord that it didn't bother me about not getting any presents, but could he please provide a safe journey for my family to Mississippi. He gave us you and your generosity," he said and smiled.

God answered two prayers that Christmas Day, and I learned in a fresh way the value of marriage. Heather and I can hardly wait to see what next Christmas brings!

HEATHER WHITESTONE AND JOHN McCALLUM

MONEY CAN'T
BUY YOU LOVE

✍

He who has conquered doubt and
fear has conquered failure.
JAMES LANE ALLEN

It's hard to meet people in a big city like Atlanta. I decided to enroll in a French class both to find folks of similar interests as well as to improve my French.

I was a little late for my first class and it had already started when I arrived. When I rushed into the room, I immediately noticed a very attractive girl in a seat close to the front of the class. We traded nods and smiles as I made my way to a seat.

I was late for the next class as well. I had been Rollerblading with some friends and had ripped my clothes. I didn't have time to go back home and change, so I arrived at French class looking like I had just been in a fight. I was afraid the pretty girl wouldn't smile or look my way. Instead she moved her books from the seat next to her and motioned for me to sit down.

I immediately found Joan friendly and intimidating at the same time. In retrospect, I have to laugh. There I was, an entrepreneur, a businessman. I worked with big names and numbers in my real-estate business—I could ask a banker for five million dollars without flinching, yet I couldn't get up enough nerve to ask this lovely lady out. Months passed before I managed one day to invite her to study French with me at a nearby coffeehouse. Then finally, after three months of this "study-dating," she asked *me* out on our first official date!

From there our relationship grew and grew. I think that somewhere in the back of my mind, I knew from the beginning that I would ask Joan to marry me. I just didn't know how or when. I finally gathered my resolve to propose. I confess I hadn't really thought my plan through. I didn't even have a ring. But what I feared most was that by proposing, I would be asking this beautiful girl I loved into a difficult and unpredictable life. The real-estate market fluctuated so rapidly that I never knew from one moment to the next whether I would make my bills or collapse in bankruptcy. It seemed almost selfish to ask Joan to share such a life with me, but I had to try.

I rented a small boat and we sailed out to this little cove on an island. We decided to go for a swim. Because we were in the water, I couldn't get down on one knee. So I just blurted out, "Will you marry me?"

"Oh, Rick, you're so funny," she replied.

I nearly sank to the bottom. This wasn't the response I had expected. She thought I was joking.

"Joan, I'm serious. I'm asking you to marry me," I repeated. I could see that she believed me the second time. Her eyes clouded with tears.

In my lack of planning I hadn't organized my thoughts, but I wanted to be completely honest with her. "Joan," I stuttered, "my career is so volatile. One day the real-estate market's up, the next it might plummet. No one can ever tell. The market can either be a feast or famine. I want you to know what you'll be getting into if you marry me. There are a thousand ways we could go bankrupt. We could be destitute."

Joan just shook her head at me. "First you want me to marry you and now you're trying to talk me out of it. Make up your mind!" She laughed.

"I just want you to know what could possibly happen, that's all," I assured her.

"Listen to yourself. 'Could possibly happen'—do you think any of that matters to me?" she asked. "'For richer, for poorer'—that's in the marriage vows for a reason. Marriage isn't about how much money you make. It's about how much love we have. Don't worry over what may never happen. Worry if I'm going to say yes or no," she announced with a grin.

Fortunately for me, she said yes. We got married in a beautiful ceremony filled with friends and family. When Joan left her corporate job and joined me in real estate, she made her personal philosophy her business one as well: Don't worry about the future; just concentrate on today.

Over the last five years she's taught me to find great joy in today and trust that together, we can handle whatever comes our way. Not a day passes that I don't admire her serenity and thank my lucky stars that even though I underestimated her, she more than believed in love—and in me.

RICK SKELTON

Friendship is the union of spirits,
a marriage of hearts,
and the bond of virtue.
WILLIAM PENN

BEHIND EVERY GREAT MAN IS A GREAT WOMAN

✍

A woman reasons by telegraph,
And his (a man's) stage-coach reasoning
cannot keep pace with hers.
MARY WALKER

Thomas Wheeler, CEO of the Massachusetts Mutual Life Insurance Company, and his wife were driving along an interstate highway when he noticed that their car was low on gas. Wheeler got off the highway at the next exit and soon found a rundown gas station with just one gas pump. He asked the lone attendant to fill the tank and check the oil, then went for a little walk around the station to stretch his legs.

As he was returning to the car, he noticed the attendant and his wife were engaged in a animated conversation. The conversation stopped as he paid the attendant. But as he was getting back into the car, he saw the attendant wave and heard him say, "It was great talking to you."

As they drove out of the station, Wheeler asked his wife if she knew the man. She readily admitted she did. They had gone to high school together and had dated steadily for about a year.

"Boy, were you lucky that I came along," bragged Wheeler. "If you had married him, you'd be the wife of a gas station attendant instead of the wife of a chief executive officer."

"My dear," replied his wife, "if I had married him, he'd be the chief executive officer and you'd be the gas station attendant."

Reprinted by permission from *The Best of Bits & Pieces.* © 1994, Ragan Communications, 800-878-5331, www.ragan.com.

In Sickness and in Health

In marriage, one cannot do anything
alone—not even suffer.
MARY ADAMS

JIM WAS ANYTHING BUT A GIVING HUSBAND. IN FACT, HE WAS THE MOST NEEDY MAN THAT LOIS HAD EVER KNOWN. IT'S NOT THAT JIM DIDN'T LOVE HIS WIFE; HE LOVED HER MORE THAN LIFE ITSELF. BUT JIM WAS A BEDRIDDEN INVALID.

DESPITE ALL THAT—AND MAYBE, IN SOME WAYS, BECAUSE OF IT—LOIS'S LOVE FOR JIM BURNED HOTTER AND BRIGHTER THAN THE DAY THEY WERE FIRST MARRIED. NO ONE WHO KNEW THEM WOULD SUGGEST THAT LOIS PLACE HIM IN A NURSING HOME.

"I LOVE HIM NOW MORE THAN EVER," LOIS TOLD A FRIEND, "AND I WOULDN'T WANT HIM ANYWHERE BUT WITH ME."

WHEN YOU STAND AT THE ALTAR, GLOWING WITH VITALITY, VIGOR, AND PASSION, VOWING TO LOVE IN SICKNESS AS IN HEALTH, YOU CANNOT SEE WHAT THAT MAY MEAN. YOU MAY HAVE YEARS OR DECADES TO PRACTICE LOVE IN HEALTH BEFORE SICKNESS FALLS. YOU MAY HAVE ONLY DAYS OR HOURS. SICKNESS IS SCARY, AND NEVER CONVENIENT, BUT

LOVE AND COMMITMENT WILL CAUSE YOU TO LOOK BEYOND THE FRAILTIES OF AN EARTHLY SHELL INTO THE SOUL OF YOUR BELOVED.

WHEN YOU VOW, "IN SICKNESS OR IN HEALTH," YOU ARE TELLING YOURSELF THE TRUTH ABOUT LIFE. YOU ARE PREPARING YOUR HEART FOR THE DAY, OR MANY DAYS, OF WATCHING THE ONE YOU LOVE SUFFER. YOU ARE GIVING YOURSELF A REALITY CHECK. THIS, TOO, IS ONE OF THE GLORIES OF LOVE: YOU TAKE THE BITTER WITH THE SWEET. AND YOU WATCH GOD MAKE EVEN THAT GOOD.

THE HEALING POWER
OF LOVE

☙

We are each of us angels
With only one wing
And we can only fly
Embracing each other.

LUCIANO DE CRESCENZO

I didn't know if I would make it to my fiftieth birthday or not. Charles and I had been married for twenty-five years when I discovered a lump in my breast that was later diagnosed as malignant. This began a devastating and frightening time for the entire family. From the beginning, I decided I wasn't going to quit. I would fight my best fight—for my family and for myself.

I did everything the doctors instructed me to do. I underwent the chemotherapy and radiation treatments. I watched as my hair fell out, slowly at first, and then by the handful, until I was completely bald. My scalp wasn't the only part of my body that suffered: The illness robbed me of all energy and strength.

Through it all, Charles was so strong. He hardly left my bedside. Whenever I opened my eyes, he would be there, having fallen asleep at the foot of the hospital bed, his hand still holding tightly onto mine. He was my angel watching over me, refusing to let anything take me away from him. Charles would rub my bald head and massage my back and arms. He'd tell me how much he loved me and how beautiful I was to him.

When he said he understood my pain, I believed he truly meant it.

The cancer had ravaged my body—this was evident to everyone—but if you looked into Charles's eyes you would think he was the one battling cancer. He felt everything I felt.

After two years of chemo and radiation, I was cancer free. But damage from both the disease and its treatment still clung to my body. I felt weak and empty. It was a sense of exhaustion that went beyond the physical. It was a weariness in heart and spirit that seemed irreparable.

Yet after those two long, hard years, I did make it to my fiftieth birthday. For all of us, this was a time of celebration. Charles wanted to do something that commemorated my life and my survival. He started brainstorming. With the help of our children, he put his plan into action. Unbeknownst to me, he had the children pack some clothes for me. They then drove me to the base of Kennesaw Mountain where, long before the cancer, Charles and I used to jog together.

"Honey, we are going to climb this mountain!" Charles announced. As I looked at his huge grin, I suspected that my beloved husband had lost his senses.

"Charles, I can't climb this mountain. I'm wearing a skirt, and besides, I don't have the energy to do this. It's too much." I shook my head.

Charles took my hand and pointed to the mountain. "Maybe you can't. We can. We can do this together. Just like always," he said. I could see the love and patience in his eyes. I nodded my agreement and we left the children at the base of the mountain.

We huffed and puffed. Charles kept encouraging me, saying words to keep me going and when I couldn't anymore, he almost carried me to the top. He was right. Maybe I couldn't have made it to the top alone, but together we did and it was glorious.

Climbing down the mountain was much easier, as it always is. I felt so exhilarated by the time we reached the car. Energy and life coursed within me. I had to thank both God and Charles for their amazing gift. Charles opened the trunk of the car and pulled out the sweetest and coldest watermelon I had ever tasted. While we climbed, the watermelon had been on ice in the trunk—Charles had thought of every-thing. I think it was the best-tasting food I ever ate.

Without my knowledge, Charles had also made reservations at a bed and breakfast that served good old Southern cooking: fried chicken, but-ter beans, rice, and sweet potato casserole, just like my grandmother made. I felt like I hadn't eaten in years. I'm sure I made quite a spectacle.

The next night Charles presented tickets to see the Four Tops and the Temptations at an outdoor concert. I felt like a teenager again, like we were just starting to date. I felt the years and the cancer fall away. We even danced on the lawn to our favorite song. Charles had yet another surprise: a candlelit picnic on the grass while the music played. Everything was so romantic and there I was, alive with my dear husband, spending the per-fect weekend.

Late that night, Charles broke down and cried. He admitted that there had been a point when I was so sick and so weak that he had almost given up hope. "I thought I had lost you, but then I remembered God was in charge, not me," Charles whispered. "I had to keep faith that you would recover. I had to keep faith in him. Even if you had died I knew everything would be okay. God has a reason for all that he does. I'm just thankful he chose to keep us together."

As my husband confessed his fears and faith, I looked deep into his eyes and felt the love coming from them touch my soul. I knew that I was the one who should be thankful for this wonderful man God had given to keep me safe and to always make me feel the healing power of love. I hope I have many more birthdays with this man.

MELDA COLLINS

AMAZING GRACE

❦

Love is…born with the pleasure
of looking at each other;
It is fed with the necessity
of seeing each other;
It is concluded with the
impossibility of separation!

JOSÉ MAERTÍ

At the age of nine, young Judy Taylor found darkness closing around her. Specialists confirmed to her distraught family that nothing could be done to save her sight. As time passed and Judy's vision faded, she didn't waste time feeling sorry for herself; she made the best of a sad situation by attending a high school for the blind. She triumphed there, graduating and then moved on to a mainstream college where she earned a degree in education.

Basking in her independence, Judy moved into her own apartment, which was located over an electrical shop. Judy often sat in the yard facing the shop, and when a new radio and television engineer began working there, Judy apparently caught his eye. He never failed to greet the young woman cheerfully or to tease her gently. One day when she took out the garbage, Judy discovered the workshop "voice" sitting on her bin sunning himself. "Do you mind moving?" she scolded him with smile. "This is not a garden seat!" He obliged with easy charm and introduced himself as Ian Taylor (no relation).

Ian never seemed bothered by Judy's blindness. Their encounters became more frequent and a friendship grew. Eventually the two became inseparable. It was Ian who introduced Judy to her first oak apples, pulling the tree branches low enough for her to touch them, and Ian who guided her fingers around the beautifully formed nest of a jenny wren. Judy came to rely upon Ian's companionship and his comfort—it was his shoulder that she cried on when her beloved seeing-eye dog passed away.

Judy was falling in love with Ian, but she stubbornly denied her feelings. *After all,* she thought, *who would want to take on a blind woman?* To her, it seemed impossible for their relationship to develop into anything more than a friendship.

Still, the couple's relationship deepened. And although Ian and Judy were constant companions, six years passed before he proposed. He took his time, he said, because "I wanted to be certain that what I felt for Judy was love—not pity for her blindness or admiration for the way she coped with it."

Once Ian was sure, Judy acknowledged her feelings as well. The couple set a date. On their wedding day, as the beautiful song, "See That You Love One Another," rang out in the church, Judy felt buoyant with happiness.

Judy and Ian were eventually blessed with two healthy and active sons, and the family enjoyed busy and meaningful lives. The years passed. When Judy was fifty-two, one evening a health scare sent her to the emergency room. After tests showed Judy was fine, the doctor touched her arm and casually asked, "How long have you had that squint?"

Judy's right eye had always tended to wander, but this was the first time anyone had referred to it as a squint. On their ride home, Judy told Ian, "I'd like to have my 'squint' repaired."

Judy went to an eye specialist who explained that a simple operation would correct her squint. Then the doctor softly broached the subject of Judy's blindness; he said that since both her optic nerves appeared healthy, she might be able to regain part of her vision by simply removing her cataracts. He promised no miracles but said, "You have nothing to lose."

Stunned, Judy returned home to tell Ian the news. After more than forty years in the darkness, she was being offered a glimmer of hope—the tiniest chance of regaining some sight. The thought was so overwhelming that she burst into tears. With Ian's encouragement, Judy decided to have the operation. The family tried desperately not to get their hopes up.

The half-dreaded day after the surgery finally arrived. When the dressing was peeled away, Judy slowly lifted her head. "What can you see?" a nurse asked tentatively.

"A bright horizontal light," Judy replied. As she turned her head she said, "More bright lights." Then she realized what was happening. She shouted, "I can see! I can see!"

Judy describes what her first sight of Ian, her husband of almost twenty years, was like: "That afternoon, I heard Ian's footsteps. So many times, I had listened for those steps. Then his hand took mine. And I was looking at him—my husband—for the very first time!"

This time, Ian caught Judy's eye. "I had always thought about him with his dark hair and dark eyes, and somehow knew what he would look like," Judy says. "I wasn't surprised until suddenly I became aware I was looking straight into his eyes. I shall never forget it—the first time, as an adult, I caught someone's eye. I am glad it was the eye of someone I loved."

Condensed by Susan Wales from the book, *As I See It* by Judy Taylor. Used by permission of the author.

THE ONE WHO DIDN'T EVEN TRY TO GET AWAY

*Just as there comes a warm
sunbeam into every cottage window
so comes love born of God's Care
for every separate need.*

NATHANIEL HAWTHORNE

I was invited to a party for chefs and concierges. Tired from the week's activities, I almost didn't go. At the last minute, though, I decided I would. As a restaurant critic, I knew I would see many friends and colleagues there. It sounded like a nice way to cap a busy week.

So I went. That's where I saw him for the first time. Standing across from my table with dark brown eyes and a slight smile, he nodded at me. He worked his way around the table and we struck up a conversation. Our connection was immediate and wonderful. It seemed like all the other people in the room evaporated.

I remember that I had food in my hand and that I was trying to talk and eat at the same time. It didn't exactly work. He asked me what profession I was—chef? concierge? I told him first that I was a food critic, but also that I was a new author. I had just published my first book, *No More Bad Hair Days*, which chronicled my fight with ovarian cancer.

This is usually the point in conversation when people, especially men, grow uneasy, make an excuse, and flee. The "c word" makes people extremely uncomfortable. I had grown used to this reaction, but this man surprised me. Instead of excusing himself, he stayed. He asked, with a sincerely concerned look, if I was all right.

I smiled. I leveled with him—no use hiding the relevant facts. I used words like "few short months," "not expected to," and "doctors have done everything, but…." Not only did he not flinch, he asked to see me again. This was a man of *many* surprises.

On our first date, time flew as we talked and laughed together. When I stood to go, he asked, "When will I see you again?"

"I'll be out of town on a tour to promote the book for five days," I said, grinning. He called the night I got home. He asked me on a date for the following Sunday and I eagerly accepted.

The weather turned cold and rainy on Sunday. Lou and I agreed to meet after church for a meal and a movie. From our first date, he remembered the name of my favorite restaurant, so he made reservations for brunch. As soon as we walked in, I saw two friends waving at me. Lou graciously invited them to join us. I liked the way he wanted to get to know my friends.

After a wonderful brunch, we went to the Atlanta History Center, which turned out to be a favorite place of both of us. The more we talked, the more we discovered we had in common. It was like we were cut from the same cloth. After the Atlanta History Center, we went to see the movie *Washington Square*. It was so romantic we stayed in our seats afterward, savoring the story and watching the credits roll.

On our way home from this perfect afternoon, Lou suggested we grab some dinner. I couldn't believe that all of this was happening. I enjoyed his company so much, it was like a piece of my life had fallen into place. I happily agreed to dinner. I wasn't ready for our date to end yet either.

Afterward, we went to my house and finished that cold and rainy Sunday with a card game and conversation in front of a glowing fire. That night, we both experienced an incredible meeting of minds and souls. We absolutely hated to say good-bye.

A friend was coming to town to help me repair some things. He'd be in town for five days. Lou asked if he could call me after the visit was over. True to form, five days later Lou telephoned. "Did you miss me?" was his first question. I laughed and said yes. I invited him over for dinner that night. I wanted to cook for him and sit in front of the fireplace again. It felt so wonderful to have him around. I felt like I had been waiting for this my entire life.

Six weeks later, on the Tuesday before Thanksgiving, Lou came over for dinner. He stood up and very confidently stated that he wanted me to call my attorney. "I want this in writing," he said. "I don't want anything you have. I don't want you to be my girlfriend. I want you to be my wife."

We were both crying, and of course I said yes. There was nothing in the entire world that I wanted more than to be Lou's wife.

I didn't realize there were holes in my life until I met Lou. For a long time, I had been preparing to die. Lou reminded me that no matter what happens you have to continue to live and find all the blessings in each day. He is the biggest one of all.

SUSAN HYDE

There is nothing more nobler
or more admirable than when
two people who see eye to eye
keep house man and wife,
confounding their enemies
and delighting their friends.
HOMER

ARVELLA'S LOVE LETTERS

Thanks to the human heart by which we live,
Thanks to the tenderness, its joys, and fears,
To me the meanest flower that blows can give
Thoughts that do often lie too deep for tears.

WILLIAM WORDSWORTH

In his book, *Goliath, The Life of Robert Schuller,* Schuller's son-in-law, Jim Penner, describes the night that they received the news that Dr. Schuller was clinging to his life, and undergoing emergency brain surgery. Penner was reading Arvella's forty-year-old love letters from Dr. Schuller when she joined him in the library.

"He wrote that to me the fall after we met."

Arvella's voice startled me. I was so engrossed in the letter that I hadn't heard her come in. She stood in the doorway with a sweet smile I needed so much.

"When does your plane leave?" I asked her.

"I can't get a flight out until the afternoon," she said. "All I can do is sit and wait for any news."

She crossed over to where I was and gently took the letter from my hand. She swept the skirt of her housecoat under her legs and settled herself in the easy chair. Her eyes beckoned me to sit across from her. I was mesmerized by the mood of it all and sat near the edge of my seat. She read the letter.

My darling Arvella, she read. *The days seem longer and longer now that*

we are farther and farther apart. I watch the rain outside the classroom win-
dow and I think of you. I sit at night alone in the darkness and I think of you.

I shiver when I remember the warm and glowing times we shared
together. The gathered memories, like chimes, flood my soul with melody. It is
a tune of thrills, deeper than any symphony. Yet, like a hymn, it stills all worry,
all foolish fears, because it hums in future years. Now, it echoes a duet. The
harmony high, the melody low. And may the great Musician let it swell, some
day, in fortissimo.

She laid her hand over the letter and smiled at me. I knew she wasn't
in the library anymore. She was seventeen again, an innocent, young
schoolgirl back in that little town in northeastern Iowa, lying alone on her
bed. She read on.

Reflections on a Rainy Day
by Robert Harold Schuller
Raindrops—
Those moody little raindrops
Seem to smother my window-pane.
They haunt my mind with something;
But I search for the thought in vain.
I'm sure they rest serenely
As they snooze on the fallen leaves.
Their trip has made them lazy,
And they hang on the shingled eaves.
Perhaps they're a wee bit lonesome
For their cozy bed of sky.
And now they've made their journey
They can breathe a contented sigh.
Lonesome—
Lonesome, that's all
If she were here
I'd say, "My dear,
Let's take a moonlight walk."
I'd squeeze her hand
Its warmth is grand

And off we'd stroll and talk.
She'd smile a bit.
I love her wit.
Then reach some spot of bliss.
And there we'd stop.
Her arms would drop
Around me. (It's she I miss.)
R. H. S.

"He was so exciting when I first met him. He was so sure of himself," Arvella said. "He loved the spotlight. When we were in high school, he was a senior and I was a freshman. He was in the school play." Arvella smiled as she talked. "The other actors got so upset with him because he would improvise in the middle of a performance and steal the show."

She looked up at me and said, "You know why I fell in love with him, Jim?"

I didn't have the answer.

"Because he had bigger dreams," she said. "He had bigger dreams than anyone I had ever met in my life. He used to talk about the things he was going to do. The places he was going to see, the people he was going to meet. I remember on one date, we were driving along in his car and he started telling me about the power of radio. He was fascinated by the number of people it could reach. He talked about what a great tool it could be to help people. He was…entrancing."

She looked back down at the letters in her lap. "What was so attractive about him were his dreams. He had bigger dreams. He was the most attractive man I had ever met." She paused and then smiled to herself, "He still is."

Arvella sifted through the stack of letters. She came upon an envelope that was the smallest of all. She opened the tiny flap and removed a small card. It was about the size of a thank-you note.

"This is my favorite one," she whispered. "He said he kept it in his drawer for a year before he sent it to me. This isn't really a love letter to me. It was a prayer he wrote to God."

She took a long pause. I think she wanted to be very careful that she read the words just right. She looked the letter over and said:

You be the breeze, I'll be the cloud
You be the wave, I'll be the sand
You be the wind, I'll be the feather
You be the arm, I'll be the hand.
You be the sun, I'll be the shadow
You be the hope, I'll be the dream
You be the light, I'll be the window
You be the love and I'll be the faith.
R. H. S

I had to catch myself, because those words caught my heart. My eyes started to mist up.

Arvella's face showed the anguish she was feeling. In the forty-one years they had been married, this was the only time he hadn't called her before going to bed. Now he was lying in an operating room halfway across the world and she was waiting to hear if he was alive or not.

Editor's note: Dr. Schuller eventually recovered from his surgery and continues his ministry at The Crystal Cathedral today.

From *Goliath—The Life of Robert Schuller* by James Penner. Published by Zondervan Publishing House, a division of HarperCollins Publishers Inc.

SOMEONE TO
COUNT ON

One knows what one has lost,
but not what one may find.

GEORGE SAND

*J*ust the other day, a young lady pushing a man in a wheelchair
came to the front of the church. His body was twisted and his
face was permanently contorted into a sneer. Slumped over in his wheelchair, the man seemed oblivious to his surroundings.

I walked down the steps of our pulpit to speak with her, so that I
could ascertain what their needs were. I was sure that she was an attendant assigned to care for the poor, unfortunate soul whose condition left
him helpless and disfigured. I leaned down near her ear and whispered,
"What may I do to assist you?" I was almost sure that she wanted prayer
for her patient. I was taken aback when she introduced the man as her
husband. With a strong chin and a stiff upper lip, she said that she and
her husband wanted to join the church. She spoke with pride, as if he
were standing beside her in a three-piece suit. I stumbled for words,
embarrassed by my assumption yet sorry for their predicament. As I
searched for words to answer her, she reached down to catch a stream of
saliva that was extending from her husband's lips like single strand of
spaghetti. She wiped him lovingly and stood back up to continue her
request. She explained that her husband had been in a terrible accident
that left him almost completely incapacitated. One day he was a healthy,

284

vibrant, virile man; the next he was as he sat before me. I had to swallow to hide my tears, as I was filled first with admiration and then with awe at this woman who could love this man and treat him with great affection. I knew that she was with a man who could no longer hold her, touch her, or whisper in her ear. I knew that he had not lovingly patted her while they dressed for church or given her a sly look of promised love and fulfillment. I knew that he had not dried her neck when she slipped out of the shower with beads of moisture kissing her skin. I knew that she had the task of taking care of him while no one took care of her.

I tell this story to underscore that life does bring changes. When we stand before a congregation, a preacher, and God, we make vows in a few minutes that we may have to keep for the next fifty years or more. We make those vows and walk into the future, an abyss of unexpected adventure that can lead to peril without warning. The vows are a blank check that destiny will write as we walk through life together. It is altogether possible that we might have to keep those vows, the ones that say for better or for worse, for richer or for poorer, in sickness and in health. Will we be able to keep those promises in the face of calamity, poverty, and infirmity?

We all want someone we can count on to stand by us through thick or thin. This is the lover who matters. Most people think being a good lover is about being able to perform sexual feats with great skill and sensitivity. That would be fine if we spent all of our lives in bed. But the truth of the matter is a good lover doesn't start or end in the bedroom. A good lover is the one who stays when all others have walked away. It does not matter if he is as agile as a cat and as sensitive as a frayed nerve ending. If he does not love you with his heart, stroking your body and teasing your senses will soon become meaningless. Loving the body is not enough. Your mind and your spirit need to be cared for too. Who cares if your man is built like an Adonis if he doesn't stand by you in a storm? His twinkling eyes mean nothing if he does not prove to be reliable in a crisis. Oh, my friend, being a good lover is more than hips, lips, and fingertips. It is the ability to hold the cold wind of life in your hot hands until the wind warms under your loving touch. It is standing by the bed until the light goes out in my eyes and you kiss my face one final time. It is the ability to stay with me until the machine stops and the ventilator ceases to pump air into my lungs, and I speak one last time or squeeze your hand. If you ever have to fight a real storm, you will need a lover, but not the kind you might normally seek. This is a lover of the day, not just the night. Lovers that deal with the day are more difficult to find than the kind that grope you in the night. If a tragedy occurs economically or, worse still, physically, will he still be your lover? I know these are sobering thoughts that people seldom consider, but they are the realities of life.

T. D. JAKES

"Embracing Someone Else," from *The Lady, Her Lover, and Her Lord* by T. D. Jakes, © 1998 by Bishop T. D. Jakes. Used by permission of G. P. Putnam's Sons, a division of Penguin Putnam Inc.

BASEBALL BILL

I live with those who love me
whose hearts are kind and true.

GEORGE LINNAEUS BANKS

Bill and Marlene were married right out of college and had a brilliant baseball career ahead of them. Bill was the star third baseman for a pennant-winning team and had one of the best earned run averages in his second professional year.

The year after, Bill was in an automobile accident and suffered an injury that put him out of baseball and more. His neck was broken by the collision, and he was confined to a wheelchair for the rest of his life.

Marlene was accustomed to baseball fame and a high style of living in the fast lane of celebrity. With the injury came enormous medical bills, experimental therapies, and round-the-clock nursing care. Their insurance did not cover the extensive medical treatments needed for Bill's recovery.

Marlene and Bill always enjoyed an energetic romance, but after the injury their love burned brighter even though they had little privacy during the recovery. Their intellectual conversations became the most attractive part of the day. Marlene looked forward to getting to know her husband on a deeper level and Bill was touched and strengthened by Marlene's commitment to him during this trial. During this time of physical challenge, dwindling finances, and heartbreaking disappointment, their love soared to new heights and they understood that one's greatest need is to be loved unconditionally. A tragedy simply polished the gold in their marriage to a new brilliance.

AS TOLD TO FRAN BEAVER AND DOROTHY ALTMAN

Go seek her out all courteously,
And say I come,
Wind of species whose song is ever
Epithalamium.
O hurry over the dark lands
And run upon the sea
For seas and land shall not divide us
My love and me.
Now, wind of your good courtesy
I pray you go,
And come into her little garden
And sing at her window;
Singing: The bridal wind is blowing
For Love is at his noon;
And soon will your true love be with you,
Soon, O soon.

JAMES JOYCE

THE WALK THROUGH
THE VALLEY

There is in every true woman's heart
a spark of heavenly fire,
which lies dormant in the broad
daylight of prosperity;
but which kindles up, and beams and
blazes in the dark hour of adversity.

WASHINGTON IRVING

Lee and Doug were the perfect match—her weaknesses were his strengths, and vice versa. He was methodical and organized; she creative and daring. While she was given to strong emotions, he was calm. While he liked to plan everything, she loved spontaneous decisions and flights of fancy. One of the things they held in common was gratitude—they were thankful God had brought them together.

They were both also single working parents. Lee had a successful interior design business in Los Angeles, but marriage to Doug meant relocating with her young children to Canada.

It looked as if the pair of opposites would blend beautifully and enjoy a smooth life together—until they received shattering news only weeks before their wedding.

Doug was house-hunting in Toronto for their expanded family while Lee remained in Los Angeles to plan their wedding. One weekend Lee decided to take a break from her hectic schedule to get a little sun—then she wouldn't have to worry about sunburn when they were on their honeymoon in Hawaii. She also figured a little color would also look nice when she walked down the aisle in a few weeks. As she stretched out on her towel by the pool, Lee discovered a lump the size of a golf ball on her right side.

Fear gripped her as she ran to call Doug. One of the things Lee loved about Doug was that where she was fearful, he was unflappable. "It's probably nothing," he assured her. "Don't worry unless a doctor tells you to worry."

The doctors were less comforting. They told Lee bluntly but gently that she had advanced cancer of the colon and just a twenty percent chance of survival. Lee was stunned, but she was not afraid. As she sat in the doctor's office, she knew it just didn't make any sense that she would finally fall in love, plan to marry, and then die before her new life began. She determined to see the challenge through. Though self-pity tried to creep in, Lee replaced it with thanksgiving for Doug—someone so special to walk with her through this valley of the shadow of death. Lee felt a surge of faith, knowing God had a plan for her and Doug.

When Doug heard the news, he called his family physician for some reassurance. Instead, the doctor advised Doug not to marry Lee. "There's little chance that she will survive," he said as kindly as he could. "At least wait and see."

Doug felt a surprising well of hope. He left immediately to be with Lee during surgery. He told his wife-to-be, "We're going to beat this!"

The surgery went well, but Lee's doctor still gave a negative prognosis. Lee and Doug stayed strong: They wrote their wedding vows while Lee recovered! "Our wedding is only weeks away," they told the dubious hospital staff with determination, "and we're going to be married."

Lee had to begin chemotherapy immediately. Between wedding showers and parties, she attended her treatments. As the poison liquid dripped into her veins, she thought of Doug and their future together. And she thanked God.

Lee experienced a little queasiness and lost some weight but otherwise felt fine. Hope kept her buoyant, and the cloud she floated on carried her down the aisle into Doug's supportive and loving arms. Doug told her she was a beautiful bride: "No one would ever know you're ill," he said tenderly.

When the minister reached the words in the vow, "in sickness and in health," the wedding guests sobbed openly. Doug and Lee smiled knowingly and squeezed each other's hand.

The couple enjoyed a wonderful honeymoon. The only sad part was a bleak moment when Lee was brushing her hair and much of it came out in the brush. It reminded the couple of the reality of her illness, but it didn't dissuade them from joy. Doug reminded Lee that all that mattered was that they were together.

For the next two years Lee received the powerful chemo treatments. After seven years the doctors finally gave a new prognosis: Lee was cancer free and hopefully would remain so!

Eighteen years later, as Lee and Doug celebrated their anniversary in their California home, they looked back on their saga with—what else?—gratitude. Their greatest common bond sustained them during the fight of their lives, and it remains their source of strength and joy today.

LEE MINK AND DOUG BARR

TEAMWORK

Two are better than one
For they have good return for their work.

ECCLESIASTES 4:9

hen I was growing up, my parents imparted a great example to my sister, brother, and me about teamwork. My father was a "liberated man" who helped my mother with her duties. He was never ashamed of pitching in to help around the house. He'd mop the floor, vacuum, and even don an apron if Mother needed his help.

Mother did her part as well. She helped Daddy with the traditional "men's work." Together they would paint the house, wallpaper a bathroom, wash the cars, and plant the garden. One time the two of them even added a screened porch to the back of the house. As far as they were concerned, every duty was gender indifferent.

Duties were also age indifferent—my parents included us children in their projects at every opportunity, teaching us how to work as a team.

Just as Mother and Daddy entered their golden years, I married and sadly moved two thousand miles away from them. Fortunately they are very healthy and I have had little cause for concern. My parents are enjoying their retirement. Both have boundless energy and are always involved in some new project. Recently they built a new home—quite a task for a couple their age! Daddy supervised every nail the builders hammered into their dream home and Mother enjoyed decorating when it was finished.

It gives me great peace of mind to know that they are enjoying one another's company to the fullest, still sharing their duties. And they are still teaching me about teamwork. They gave me a most poignant lesson recently when Daddy had to have surgery.

When the doctor told my father that he would have to undergo carpel tunnel surgery, my father tried to postpone it because it was the season for some serious gardening. The doctor insisted that the surgery couldn't wait.

When Mother phoned me with the news, she insisted that it wasn't necessary for me to come. "Your father won't even stay overnight at the hospital."

So I stayed in close touch by telephone. Mother called to tell me that the surgery had gone smoothly and Daddy was resting well, although in pain. Mother herself had a cold and wasn't feeling well. I wished I had gone home.

When I awoke the next day, I immediately called to see how Daddy had fared overnight and if Mother's cold was better. To my distress, there was no answer. "Ken," I told my husband, "I'm worried. Where could they be? Do you suppose Daddy has taken a turn for the worse and they're at the hospital? Or maybe Mother's cold became worse."

I sensed that Ken was concerned too as he tried to reach them several times. There was no answer. We left several urgent messages.

After three hours had passed, we decided to call the hospital. They hadn't admitted my father or my mother. Then we tried to call my brother, aunts, uncles, and cousins. No one was home. "They're at the emergency room with my parents," I told Ken as my anxiety heightened. I canceled my plans for the morning and sat by the phone and waited and prayed.

At last I received a call in the afternoon from Mother. "Where have you been?" I demanded.

She laughed.

"I'm sorry we worried you," she said, "but you know your father. He awoke early and insisted on taking a walk in garden. He spotted some tiny black bugs on his roses and we've been spraying the bushes."

"How on earth could he be spraying roses?" I asked. "Isn't his arm in a cast up to his shoulder?"

"Don't worry," Mother said. "I sprayed, he supervised."

Relieved, I marveled at their partnership. I told Ken, "They are certainly good role models for God's plan for marriage. Mother was Daddy's arm."

"Isn't that what's marriage is all about?" Ken reminded me. "Teamwork—especially in sickness and in health." I hugged Ken and thanked God for his beautiful design.

SUSAN WALES

In true marriage lies
Nor equal, or unequal
Each fulfills
Defect in each other, and always thought in thought,
Purpose in purpose, will in will, they grow
The single pure and perfect animal,
The two-cell'd beating with one full stroke, Life.

ALFRED, LORD TENNYSON

As Long As We Both Shall Live

Thy love is such I can no way repay,
The heavens reward thee manifold I pray.
Then while we live, in love so persever,
That when we live no more, we may live ever.

ANNE BRADSTREET

THERE IS AN ABSOLUTENESS TO THE WEDDING VOWS. BEFORE YOUR FRIENDS, FAMILY, AND GOD, YOU PLEDGE THAT AS LONG AS YOU DRAW BREATH, AS LONG AS YOUR HEART BEATS WITHIN YOU, YOU WILL BE THERE, WHOLLY AND TRUE, FOR YOUR BELOVED.

GOD DOESN'T TAKE YOUR VOWS LIGHTLY. THEY ARE SACRED—HOLY—TRANSCENDING THE MORTAL EARTHLY PLANE ON WHICH YOU LIVE YOUR LIFE. THE WITNESSES AND CONGREGATION GATHERED AT YOUR WEDDING HOLD YOU ACCOUNTABLE AND FAITHFUL TO THE PROMISES YOU MAKE. WHAT GOD JOINS TOGETHER, NO ONE TEARS APART WITHOUT BEING FULLY ACCOUNTABLE TO HIM.

LIFELONG MARRIAGE WAS GOD'S PLAN FROM THE TIME OF CREATION SO HE DESIGNED YOU, BODY, SOUL, AND SPIRIT, TO

BE MOST FULFILLED WITH ONE PARTNER UNTIL DEATH. THERE IS NO SECOND-BEST OPTION IN GOD'S BOOK. SO BE BOLD AS YOU PREPARE TO LOVE UNTIL DEATH DO YOU PART. AS YOU LIVE WHAT THIS MEANS, YOU WILL FIND THE MOST SATISFYING PLACE IN GOD'S GREAT UNIVERSE. YOU WILL FIND PEACE OF HEART AND DYNAMIC LOVE THAT LASTS.

YOU FIND A STATE OF GRACE THE MOMENT YOU REPEAT, "...AS LONG AS WE BOTH SHALL LIVE."

ANNIVERSARIES

Courage is grace under pressure.
ERNEST HEMINGWAY

Paul and I loved any excuse to celebrate. We marked birthdays, anniversaries, family reunions, and all of the national holidays with good food, good company, and warm togetherness. Our life had a foundation of joy.

I met Paul, a junior in college in my hometown, when I was just eighteen. He was a returning veteran who'd never expected to go to college; I was a freshman just out of high school. Our courtship was as romantic as a storybook fairy tale. I felt proud that such a man saw something special in me.

After we became engaged, we spent a year apart. Eight hundred miles away, Paul earned a master's degree while I toiled on at the local newspaper where I'd worked summers and weekends. I wrote a twice-weekly column and postponed my dreams of finishing college. It was the first of many sacrifices Paul and I both made in our forty-three years together.

But along with the sacrifices, there was love—enduring, faithful, unselfish—on both our parts. That love, on his part, encompassed kindness—the first quality of his I fell in love with. He never went to sleep without saying, "I love you." I returned his love by establishing a happy home and supporting him in everything he did, no matter what trials we faced.

The years brought six children and many changes, but we built on our foundation of joy with family parties for every occasion. We always celebrated the Fourth of July by finding a spot where we could view for free the city's beautiful and exciting display of fireworks. We would pop several bags of popcorn, fill a gallon jug with iced tea, and make an event of the evening.

On New Year's Eve, we always had a party for our friends. Paul showed his festive spirit by starting a conga line through the house just before midnight.

For Paul's birthday I always made a white cake with peanut butter and marshmallow frosting, an invention of his Aunt Helen's. Because his birthday fell in April, near Easter, the children and I decorated his cake with jelly beans spelling *DAD*.

Eventually our family nest emptied. Paul and I continued to celebrate special days and events, and the children joined us whenever they could. Then illness numbered our days together. Bedfast, Paul asked me one July 5, over and over, what day it was.

I had hung a calendar near his bed, but I'm not sure he ever really saw it. Sadness engulfed me as I realized that he was losing his grip on time. Of course, neither of us knew he had only a week more to live.

When he anxiously and tearfully repeated the date, I asked why he was concerned. He said, "You know why. This is the first year we haven't done something for the Fourth of July."

I knew.

After I lost Paul, celebrations took on a different flavor, but I kept them. Our foundation was firm and our joy was worth maintaining. This year, our daughter and son-in-law invited me to take part in the Independence Day celebration in their hometown, Sterling-Rock Falls, Illinois. The love and consideration they showed me helped me miss Paul less.

I've started a new tradition at Christmastime. So that I can celebrate with loved ones instead of alone, I leave my hometown and head West for visits with our son in San Francisco, our daughter and her husband in Huntington Beach, and a friend in San Diego.

Paul's birthday is still an important event, but I no longer bake an elaborate cake. Nowadays I buy jelly beans to put on top of graham crackers spread with peanut butter for a little private ceremony of my own.

I often get together with our friends. When invited out with couples with whom Paul and I once shared bridge games and evenings together, I make sure I stay interested, that I add to the laughter and not remind them of my loss; they are well aware of the loss of someone whose wry and witty humor was always part of the fun.

And I remember Paul daily in a little ritual. I complete a puzzle— "find six differences between pictures"—published among the classified ads in the newspaper that he worked every day. When I succeed I say, "We did it again, honey," with a real sense of accomplishment.

The celebrations keep Paul present to me. I see him in glorious sunrises and in the phases of the moon. I talk to him among the stars. I imagine him embraced by the saving arms of Jesus and helping Jesus welcome our deceased friends as newcomers to heaven. I know he's the first to throw a party for every familiar face, and I know that one day, Paul and I will celebrate our love again, on our first anniversary in heaven.

HELEN TROISI ARNEY

A LETTER FROM MY HEART

⚰

'Tis the last rose of summer
Left blooming alone
All her lovely companions
Are faded and gone.

THOMAS MOORE

Saying that final good-bye is the hardest thing a couple ever has to do, but some partners find creative ways to ease the transition for one another. Maynard Smith is one of those. He wanted his wife, Helen, to let the joy of their lives together overwhelm the pain of their parting, so he thoughtfully wove loving words into a secret letter. After his death, his secretary told Helen of the letter tucked quietly away in a safety deposit box.

When Helen read the letter, Maynard's wish was fulfilled. His touching tribute to his wife and their marriage brought comfort, thankfulness, and release—all the ingredients of a healthy and timely good-bye. Here are the words Maynard wrote from his heart.

Dearest Helen,

I'm writing this while in good health and am happy with no real worries in this world. This seems like a strange time for the thoughts I'm about to express, but what could really be a better time? I know that at some future date I am going to depart this world and I would hate it if I did not have a chance to say to you the things I feel so strongly.

To begin with, I could not have used better judgment than when I asked you to share my life with me and let me share in yours. There has never been a minute when I felt otherwise. You have been all that anyone could expect or hope for in a mate. I have never doubted your love or loyalty. I have said to others and I want to say it to you now: You are truly the finest human being I have known in my life. God did not make many, if any, like you and I have never forgotten to be grateful for my good fortune. I love you as a wife, a mother, and as a friend with a tenderness that can't be described. You have given your very best and that was always good enough—perfect in fact. You caught all the passes, made the third-down plays, and crossed the goal line when called upon.

HM may not completely appreciate her mother now and this is natural, but some day, she will realize what a fortunate daughter she has been to have a mother like you. I really don't know how to write a farewell letter to you and I suppose there is no adequate way, but I had to try as feeble as this effort is. I know as I write this that I am not able to express what I feel so deeply. Words can't do it justice. Just know in your heart, as I know, that your role in life has been one of perfection and you should never feel any regrets about anything.

Don't be sad. God could not have been better to me. I have had a great life, good fortune…my wife, my daughter, my profession, my friends, and my associates. What more could anyone ask? I have tried to be true and honorable in my life so you would be proud of me. I'm sure I could have done better and should have, but after all I was human and thus unable to be all that I would have liked to have been.

You know that I have never doubted that there is a God and a hereafter. I firmly believe this is not the end. I believe there is a place where I am going that is better than the one I am leaving.

I look forward to seeing my mother, my father, and my friends who have preceded me. And my dearest, I will be looking forward to spending an eternity with you in another land when your life is over.

Remember, you have no reason to grieve. Make a new life. Marry if you find someone that can make you happy and you can make him happy. Life and death are as natural as any other fact of life. Accept it. Living alone is no good and I want you to be happy. Just don't be as happy with anyone as I think you were with me! I could say something cute here and you know what it would be, but this is not the time.

I love you in life and I will love you in death just as truly and tenderly as the day I married you.

Me.

HELEN SMITH

THE WAY WE WERE

*Hitch your wagon to a star;
keep your seat and there you are.*

AUTHOR UNKNOWN

he Way We Were" is more than a heartfelt ballad by Barbra
Streisand. For George and me it is a theme song for a joyful part of
our life story.

When our story began we existed in separate worlds. We had both
been involved in unhappy marriages and disappointed in love. I was
working as principal of a school for juvenile delinquents in Alabama.
George and his partner owned a successful insurance agency in Georgia.

A dear friend who was a center of influence in my life kept encouraging me to try another business. Finally, I decided to take the plunge and
became an insurance sales agent in Alabama. It was very rare in those days
for a female to work in that field.

After my first year in the business, I attended my first national business conference in Georgia. The head of my Alabama agency called our
sister agency in Georgia. He happened to speak to George and said, "Why
don't you go to the conference and meet my new female agent?"

George had already planned to welcome all of the attendees to
Georgia and to extend an invitation to visit his office. Since George and
his partner had one of the top-ten agencies in the country, all of the attendees wanted to visit them.

I will never forget our first meeting. It was break time, and I had left the conference room for some fresh air. A dashing young man in a three-piece suit came up to me, holding out his hand to shake mine. He said, "You must be the new female agent from Alabama!" He kept talking and holding my hand. I don't remember what he said because I was very uncomfortable. He was too charming, too self-assured, and too much into my personal space. I finally retrieved my hand from his grip and returned to the meeting. George returned to his office.

As it turns out, my hard work and perseverance over the last year had paid off; I had written more premium-dollar contracts than any other first-year person in the nation, so I was to be honored at this conference. Since I was also the first woman to win the award, the company had to change the title from New Man of the Year to New Agent of the Year.

After the awards were given and the conference was over, the company had hired an orchestra for dancing. It seemed that everyone except me had a partner and was heading for the dance floor. I was sitting alone at a table when George came up and asked me to dance. This time, for some reason, I did not feel crowded or put off. Both of us loved dancing and we had a wonderful, crazy evening. We danced to every song that the orchestra played. George had a great sense of humor and projected a genuine love of life. It's amazing how well we got to know each other while he was twirling me around the dance floor!

Our courtship continued and Streisand's "The Way We Were" provided the soundtrack for a love that continued to grow. We were married a year later.

We enjoyed almost twenty-two years before George died of cancer. Now when I listen to our song the words make me cry. I was blessed with the perfect husband and "cherish the memories" and the man who helped create them.

MARILYN MURDOCK

THE GUIDE

❧

Love consists of this:
To be able to find joy in another's.
MARIA RANIER RILKE

e'd been married less than a year when my husband, Jerry, and I moved to Atlanta with great anticipation. I had finally gotten my big break in publishing. And Jerry, in an enormous show of support, had quit his job just so I could reach for my brass ring.

The day the movers delivered our furniture in Atlanta couldn't have gone any smoother. They were quick and careful and also understanding of our stress. In fact, one of the men kept taking time out to throw the ball for my Shetland sheepdog, Gypsy, who was being completely ignored in all the hustle and bustle.

At the end of the day we sat on the back deck and looked up at the heavens. Somehow the stars in Atlanta seemed brighter and happier to me than anywhere else I'd ever lived. I still had a week to get our nest completely built before I started my job, and Jerry had received a good job lead. We were truly feeling blessed.

The next day was Saturday, and we got to meet some of our new neighbors. On the west side was a sweet elderly couple, Art and Maggie, who laughed a lot and spoke of world travels together over their forty-seven years of marriage. They were a warm pair, and Art had a keen sense of humor: "I only married Maggie to get her to stop begging me to marry her." Maggie simply giggled like a schoolgirl and shook her head. We also met the couple who lived behind us—coincidentally they had a dog just like ours. Moving to an unfamiliar place is always such a gamble, but this time it seemed to be turning out just right.

Again that evening, Jerry and I found ourselves on our back deck, stargazing. It was becoming our nightly routine. We began imagining our future selves. Would we be like Maggie and Art, still laughing together after nearly five decades of marriage? We wondered how many times Art had told his funny "stop the begging" line. More so, we pondered how many times Maggie had laughed and pretended it was the first time she had ever heard it. They were truly friends, a sometimes rare and wonderful element in a lifelong union.

With all our good fortune, imagine how far from cloud nine I fell when we awoke on Monday morning to the sound of our lovely dog coughing and thrashing on the floor, having some sort of seizure. We rushed her to a vet but were grieved to learn that we needed to put her to sleep right away. Unbeknownst to us, she had had a brain tumor, probably for years, that finally destroyed her life. We were heartsick.

That night I sat in my new living room unable to stop the tears. I knew it was probably childish. After all, Gypsy was just a dog, right? I tried to look through the window at those stars that seemed so brilliant the night before, but they all blurred together like snow. Then my eye caught something odd. A dark, slow-moving car was creeping into our driveway. Something was very wrong.

It was a hearse. The driver, in a black suit and cap, got out of the car and walked up to ring our bell. Jerry answered, and I could hear their voices, but I couldn't make out any words. After what seemed like hours, Jerry sat beside me and said the driver needed to park in our driveway because there was no room in our elderly neighbors' drive. I looked around and for the first time noticed that there were ten or fifteen cars parked along our street, along with a fire truck and ambulance. Jerry went on to explain that apparently Art had passed away peacefully during a nap on the couch. And by the family's request, a hearse instead of the usual ambulance had been requested to move the body.

Of course we let the driver park in our driveway. Jerry immediately went next door to see if there was anything we could do. I should have gone, too, but I just sat frozen on the couch, feeling hurt and helpless. Frustrated, I threw a dog ball hard into the next room, but it only started the tears again when Gypsy didn't bring it back.

I carried so much shame that week, knowing I'd failed my new neighbor in her time of need. Guilt consumed me when I saw Maggie over the fence, although she seemed to be doing fine and was surrounded by loved ones. She even kept her normal routine of babying her day lilies and rose beds. But I still couldn't say anything. I was still distraught over Gypsy's death, and my throat seemed paralyzed.

Not too many days later, the funeral was over and all of Maggie's relatives went home. I was flattening one of our last packing boxes and stacking it outside with the others when I saw Maggie tending her garden. She had her back to me but I could hear her humming a sad tune.

I knew I needed to apologize for not visiting her. As I worked on what to say, Maggie turned around and said, "Dee Ann, come here for a minute."

My heart jumped into my throat as I walked toward our adjoining fence. Before I could stammer out a word, Maggie grabbed my hand and looked at me with her soft brown eyes. With the most tender voice she said, "I want to give you something—something to think about."

She wants to give me something? I thought.

Maggie squeezed my hand and said, "Dee Ann, I know you've been troubled these last days. Sometimes God's plans for us don't seem to make any sense at all. And I must admit I've had some choice words with him myself, but only because I miss Arty so very much." She straightened her back and lifted her chin, trying to swallow her tears. "But, young lady, I want you to try to have an open mind about what I want to tell you."

I was confused. *Is this grieving widow trying to comfort me?*

Maggie continued, "Arty was an old man, Dee Ann. He couldn't see very well anymore and that really bothered him. He didn't mind losing part of his hearing and he rarely complained about his arthritis. But not being able to work in his summer garden and not being able to read his

Bible were things he could never adjust to."

I felt like I needed to jump in and say something reassuring, but her eyes locked with mine and I thought better of it.

After a moment of silence, Maggie patted my hand and smiled. "Did you ever think that maybe, just maybe, God needed a little dog to help guide Art into the gates of heaven?"

To this day Maggie and I remain dear friends. I will forever be grateful for the sense of closure she gave me and for how she didn't judge my pain, never thinking her sorrow should have been more of a priority than mine. But most of all, I'll always remember Maggie holding my hand, comforting me at a time when she needed it most.

DEE ANN GRAND

DELAYED DELIVERY

If I could have thought thou couldst have died
I might not weep for thee;
But I forgot, when by thy side
That thou couldst mortal be;
Yet there was round thee such a dawn
Of light never seen before,
As fancy never could have drawn,
And never can restore!

CHARLES WOLFE

Stella had known that Dave wouldn't live to see Christmas. When the doctors had diagnosed her husband's terminal cancer last January, her world had shattered. But through the ensuing months Dave had managed to put his affairs in order, to show her everything she needed to learn about managing the house, everything except how to live without him. Now the loneliness weighed upon her like lethargy, stealing her energy, her ability to find joy in life, even in Christmas.

She had turned down an invitation to spend the holiday with old friends in Florida. Somehow that had seemed worse than staying home alone. Not only would she miss her husband of forty-eight years, but she would miss the snow and the familiarity of home. They had been a childless couple and in the last decade had lost several friends and even family. But it had all been bearable with Dave by her side. Bearable until now.

A snowstorm was brewing outside the window as Stella prepared a bowl of soup. She ate slowly, moving the radio knob with one hand, stopping at the sound of a familiar Christmas carol. The sudden, joyful chorus only served to deepen her loneliness. With shaky fingers she lowered the volume to a muted background.

She was surprised by the slap of damp envelopes on the floor as the mailman dropped them through the door slot. She left her soup to retrieve them. Moving to the living room, she sat on the piano bench and opened them. They were mostly Christmas cards and her eyes smiled at the traditional scenes and the loving messages inside. Carefully, her arthritic fingers arranged them among the others clustered on the piano top. In her entire house they were the only seasonal decoration. The holiday was days away and she just didn't have the heart to put up the tree or bring out the stable that Dave had lovingly built.

Suddenly engulfed by the finality of her aloneness, Stella buried her lined face in her hands, lowering her elbows to the piano keys in an abrasive discord and let the tears come. How would she get through Christmas and the dismal winter months beyond?

The ring of the doorbell startled her. Who could be calling on such a stormy day? The doorbell rang a second time. Wiping her eyes, she pulled herself up off the bench to answer it.

On her front porch, buffeted by waves of wind and snow stood a young man, his hatless head barely visible above the large carton in his arms. She peered beyond him to the driveway, but there was nothing about the small car to give a clue to his identity.

"Mrs. Thornhope?"

Stella nodded.

"I have a package for you."

Curiosity won over caution. She pushed the door open enough for the stranger to shoulder it and stepped back into the foyer to make room. He brought with him the frozen breath of the storm. Smiling, he carefully placed his burden down, then handed her the envelope that he pulled from an inner jacket pocket. Suddenly, a muffled yelp came from the box. Stella actually jumped. The man laughed and bent to straighten up the cardboard flaps wide enough for her to peek inside.

It was a dog! A yellow Labrador puppy, to be exact. The man lifted its squirming body up into his arms and explained, "This is for you, ma'am. He's six weeks old and housebroken." The young pup wiggled in happiness at being released from captivity and lapped ecstatic kisses on the young man's chin. "We were supposed to deliver him on Christmas Eve," he continued with some difficulty, trying to raise his chin out of reach, "but the staff at the kennel wanted tomorrow off. Hope you don't mind an early present."

When Stella made no move to take the animal from him, he placed him on the floor. "But who...?" she stammered.

The young man tapped the envelope in her fingers. "The letter pretty much explains everything. The dog was purchased last July while his mother was still pregnant. It was meant to be a Christmas gift. I have some other things in the car. I'll get them."

Before she could protest, he disappeared back into the snowstorm. He returned carrying another big box with a leash, dog food, and a book entitled *Caring for Your Labrador Retriever.* All this time the puppy had sat quietly at her feet, panting happily as his brown eyes watched her.

The stranger was turning to go. "But who...who bought it?"

Pausing in the doorway, his words all but snatched away by the wind, he replied, "Your husband, ma'am." And then he was gone.

It was all in the letter. Forgetting the puppy entirely at the sight of his familiar handwriting, Stella walked to her armchair by the window. Unaware that the little dog had followed her, she forced tear-filled eyes to read her husband's words. He had written it three weeks before his death and had left it with the kennel owners to be delivered with the puppy as his last gift to her. It was full of love and admonishments to be strong. He vowed that he was waiting for the day when she would join him. Until then, this dog would keep her company.

Remembering the little creature for the first time she was surprised to find him patiently looking up at her. Stella put the pages aside and reached for the bundle of golden fur. She had thought he would be heavier, but he was only the size and weight of a sofa pillow. And so soft and warm. She cradled him in her arms and he licked her jaw, then snuggled into the hollow of her neck. Her tears began again.

Finally Stella lowered him to her lap where he regarded her solemnly. She wiped vaguely at her cheeks, then mustered a smile.

"Well, little guy, I guess it's you and me." Her gaze shifted sideways to the window. Dusk had fallen and the storm seemed to have spent the worst of its fury. Through fluffy flakes that were drifting down at a gentler pace, she saw the cheery Christmas lights that edged the roof lines of her neighbors' homes. The strains of "Joy to the World" floated in from the kitchen.

Stella's grief and loneliness subsided and a new sensation of peace came over her like a loving embrace. Rising from her chair, she spoke to the little dog whose ears perked up at the sound of her voice. "You know, fella, there's a box in the basement with a tree in it and lights I think you'd like. And I think I can find that old stable too. What d'ya say we go hunt for it?"

The puppy barked in agreement, as if he understood every word.

CATHY MILLER

THE GOOD-BYE KISS

To know of someone here and
there whom we accord with,
who is living on with us, even in silence—
this makes our earthly fall a peopled garden.
WILHELM MEISTER'S APPRENTICESHIP
(1786–1830)

I am so aware in life that God is interested in details in our lives that are important to us. My father was seventy-nine years old, he had congestive heart disease, and his life was coming to an end. He knew it and all the people who loved him knew it. As he prepared for his next life there were conditions that were important to him that God was merciful and sensitive to. It was such a testimony that God is not only interested in how we live, but in how we die.

In death, it was important to my father that he leave here from his farm, in his bedroom, surrounded by his family.

My father was a very special man, loved and respected by all that knew him. He was orphaned by age nine and it seemed that everyone that he loved and knew had died before he was twelve years old. In spite of this, he grew up with a vision to have a wife and family. He worked as a tenant farmer until he was able to purchase his own farm. God was his father; he provided and instructed him in how to prosper.

He and my mother worked hard and accomplished a marriage of fifty-two years. Near the end of his life, God moved me back to Georgia from Texas, so that I could spend time with him during the last days of his life. In the year and a half that I had with him, God prepared us to say good-bye.

During his illness, God surrounded my father with all who loved him. As he convalesced, there was a steady stream of loved ones that came to visit him and tell him how much they loved him.

In spite of his weakness, he wanted to visit with everyone—and he would get really irritated if we tried to protect him. He would wake every morning and get ready for his company, no matter how weak he was.

His final wish was that he would die at home, surrounded by his family and friends. The day came and my mother called me to say that it was time to come home. He woke when I arrived and then went into a coma later that day. As my mother stood over him, stroking his head and comforting him, he regained consciousness, puckered up, and with all the strength he had in him, pulled her to him and kissed her, with the longest and most passionate kiss ever.

It was their good-bye kiss.

KAY JONES

TRAVELIN' MAN

Paradise itself were dim
And joyless, if not shared with him!
THOMAS MOORE

Throughout our marriage, my husband, Art, has traveled. In the first twenty years of our marriage, he left early Monday morning and returned late Friday evening by car or plane. As a young bride, I would cry when Art would leave and count the hours until he returned. When he was late returning home, I would pace the floor imagining all sorts of terrible things that could have happened to him. I'm embarrassed to admit that on more than one occasion, I called the hospital or the police station to make sure he wasn't in a car accident. The very thought of living without Art was too painful to comprehend.

When Art would return home from his weekly trip, I would run into his open arms…just like the movies. Art always brought me—and later the children—a little memento from each trip. Soap from the hotel, a book of matches from a well-known restaurant, or a pen that advertised, "See Rock City." After thirty years you can imagine the collection I amassed in our attic!

After our fourth child was born, our lives were perfectly normal—until Art would leave town. It seemed that something bad always happened when he was gone. He was in Seattle when Sally broke her arm, and when Eddie was bitten by the dog he was in New York. I recall that Art was in Kansas City when Jeffery got caught smoking in the boys' bathroom at school, and when Eric flunked his math test, Art was in Miami. You tell me the name of a city and I can tell you what traumatic event occurred in our family!

Now that our children are grown and have left home and Art has been promoted several times, he doesn't travel as often. It's funny, but I almost miss his time away—at least for short periods. My eyes light up when he tells me he is scheduled to go out of town. No longer a young wife and mother, I look forward to my time alone. I stash a pile of books away that I can devour while he's away. I eat frozen dinners that I prepare in the microwave or go out with my girlfriends for pizza. Yes, now when Art travels, I cherish the time we have apart and I have a glorious time. And I don't worry about his safety. My faith and trust in God has also grown through the years.

And when Art returns from one of his infrequent trips, it's like a honeymoon all over again. It's true what they say: Absence makes the heart grow fonder! My heart beats faster as I anticipate his arrival while I drive to airport to pick up my date! I always plan a romantic dinner for two, or we go out to a favorite restaurant and share what's gone on in our lives when we are apart. It's all very exciting and keeps the romance alive in our lives. Isn't it funny how we change with age? Instead of praying for him to come home, I now pray for him to travel!

But one memorable day, I wanted Art home more desperately than at any time when we were young. Like so many times before, that Monday morning I had driven my husband to the airport, pecked his cheek, waved good-bye, and drove away. I uttered the same little prayer I've been praying for thirty years—"Please, God, bring Art safely back to me"—as I watched him disappear into a tiny speck in my rearview mirror.

I glanced at the clock and realized that I was going to be late for school! You see, when Art and I first married, we hadn't planned for me get pregnant right away, but it happened. We had promised one another that when the time came for the baby to go to first grade, I would go back to college, but that time never came...only more babies! When the kids left home, I went back to college and I would be graduating in just two weeks. Art had surprised me on our drive to the airport this morning when he told me that he had planned a trip to Hawaii for just the two of us to celebrate my graduation. "And if we love it," he'd said, "I'll retire and we might just move there—life is so short!" I nodded in agreement. I had dreams of being an interior designer and I could be a designer in Hawaii just as well as I could in Chicago.

When I returned home from school that afternoon, I was still dreaming of Hawaii as I picked up the remote and began to channel surf until I settled on my favorite talk show. As I listened intently, the program was suddenly interrupted by a news bulletin. My whole world went black and the room began to spin as the tears began flowing. Because I'd been in class, I hadn't heard the earlier news bulletins, but there had been a plane crash. It was the airline Art was flying on, near the city where his meeting was scheduled.

I immediately fell to my knees and begged God to spare Art, but then the news bulletin announced, "There are no survivors." I reached for the cordless phone—not taking my eyes off the television. I tried to get through to the 800 number that was flashing across my television screen, but the lines were busy. I called out for God to please help me and give me strength. Just minutes ago, I was dreaming about Hawaii, and now my dear husband was gone! I fell to the floor, this time face down.

The doorbell rang and there stood my precious neighbor, Ann Johnson. "Was Art on that plane?" Ann asked sympathetically. We had talked over the fence to Ann and her husband, Charlie, before we left for the airport this morning, so word had spread quickly through the neighborhood. When Ann looked at my ashen, tear-streaked face, she didn't have to ask me any more questions. She hugged me and pulled me down beside her on the sofa and then said a sweet prayer asking God to sustain us through this dark hour. The next thing I knew our pastor was at the door. Carol from across the street was at my backdoor, bringing a casserole. We were all on the sofa with our eyes glued to the television when another person walked through the back door.

"What's happening?" It was a familiar voice, the most familiar I had ever known. It was the voice of my dear husband.

"Arrrrrrt? What…are you doing…here?" called out our pastor, who looked as though he'd seen a ghost. The rest of us were speechless.

"I lived here the last time I checked," he said matter-of-factly. Suddenly concerned, Art asked, "Did someone die?"

"Yeah, you," I blurted as I embraced my puzzled husband and cried. There were tears of joy mixed with relief.

"Would someone please tell me what's going on?" he pleaded.

"Didn't I put you on that airplane this morning?" I asked, still trembling.

"Yes," he explained, "but my business partner paged me. Our meeting was canceled, so I took a cab over to our office by the airport where I've been working most of the day. I didn't phone because one of the guys agreed to drop me by the house on his way to a sales call. What on earth is going on?"

Everyone spoke at once, explaining to Art that the plane on which he had reservations had crashed leaving no survivors. He was stunned and grateful—very grateful—that his meeting had been canceled and that he had missed that flight.

As Art and I sat down to dinner later that night, we prayed for the family and friends of the plane crash victims. We were awed that his canceled meeting had saved his life.

"I was ready to meet my Maker," Art assured me. "But I'm glad it wasn't my time."

I knew without a doubt that God once again heard the same old prayer that I'd been praying for thirty years and spared my husband's life. I suddenly thought of all the other wives, mothers, husbands, and family members who had uttered a prayer for their loved ones that morning, and I was even more grateful that my husband's time had not come.

I was never more happy to have Art home as I was that night.

SYLVIA TAYLOR, AS TOLD TO SUSAN WALES

THE RED CARNATIONS

The music in my heart I bore
Long after it was heard no more.
WILLIAM WORDSWORTH

When Coretta Scott agreed to marry the charismatic Martin Luther King Jr., she knew that she would have to share the great leader with the world. The late civil rights leader was the recipient of the Nobel Peace Price in the '60s for his work in human rights. He was also considered the torchbearer in the Civil Rights movement, and organized peaceful marches and protests throughout the country. Perhaps it was because Coretta Scott King knew God had called them that she was able to bear the separation and loneliness of her husband's travels.

Coretta Scott King describes her husband's thoughtfulness and love for her in her book, *My Life with Martin Luther King Jr.*

The strain of Martin's responsibilities was growing more intense. At the suggestion of his doctor, he decided to go away for a few days' rest. Then, on March 12, just before he was to leave, he called me on the telephone from his office and asked, "Did you get the flowers?"

I told him that none had come, and Martin explained that when he was downtown shopping for some much-needed clothing for himself, he had gone next door to the florist and purchased some flowers for me. The proprietor had promised to deliver them right away. I was touched by this gesture of love. By the time he had come home to pick up his bag to leave for the airport, the flowers had arrived.

They were beautiful red carnations, but when I touched them I realized they were artificial. In all the years we had been together Martin had never sent me artificial flowers. It seemed so unlike him. I kissed him and thanked him. I said, "They are beautiful and they're artificial."

"Yes," Martin said. "I wanted to give you something that you could always keep."

They were the last flowers I ever got from Martin. Somehow in some strange way, he seemed to have known how long they would have to last here.

Less than a month later, Martin Luther King Jr. left for the sanitation workers' strike in Memphis. The couple kissed good-bye like they had so many times before. In a few weeks he was planning to lead the Poor People's March in Washington.

This trip was not without risks, however Coretta and Martin both knew that his life was always in jeopardy but they could not deny the work that God had given them to do. It was not surprising that the jet that carried Martin and his delegation to Memphis had to be thoroughly checked prior to takeoff. A death threat followed Martin wherever he went.

When he arrived in Memphis, Martin called Coretta to tell her he loved her as he always did when he was away.

The next afternoon, April 4, 1968, on the hotel balcony, a gunshot shattered the lives, the hopes, and the dreams of Martin Luther King Jr. and his wife Coretta, as well as black men, women, and children throughout the world. A few hours later she received the news of her husband's death.

Once Coretta Scott King had walked the road to freedom with her husband, and now she walked alone. With God's strength she flew to Memphis and led the march in her husband's place, giving comfort and hope to all his followers. Later this beautiful and courageous widow stood in for her husband at the Poor People's March in Washington, D.C., where three thousand marchers were expected and fifty thousand came to show their support.

Today, the red carnations are a reminder of her husband's love. You see, Martin unknowingly sent this bouquet that would have to last a lifetime. Neither he nor Coretta knew what was going to happen that day in Memphis. *God knew.*

Editor's note: Mrs. King established the Martin Luther King Jr. Center for Social Change in Atlanta in her husband's memory.

From *My Life with Martin Luther King, Jr.*, Revised Edition by Coretta Scott King. Published by Henry Holt & Company.

A NOTE FROM THE EDITORS

These books were selected by the Books and Inspirational Media Division of the company that publishes *Guideposts*, a monthly magazine filled with true stories of hope and inspiration.

Guideposts is available by subscription. All you have to do is write to Guideposts, 39 Seminary Hill Road, Carmel, New York 10512. When you subscribe, each month you can count on receiving exciting new evidence of God's presence, His guidance and His limitless love for all of us.

Guideposts Books are available on the World Wide Web at www.guidepostsbooks.com. Follow our popular book of devotionals, *Daily Guideposts*, and read excerpts from some of our best-selling books. You can also send prayer requests to our Monday morning Prayer Fellowship and read stories from recent issues of our magazines, *Guideposts*, *Angels on Earth*, and *Guideposts for Teens*.